Teaching and Learning
in the Language Classroom

Also published in
Oxford Handbooks for Language Teachers

Teaching American English Pronunciation
Peter Avery and Susan Ehrlich

Doing Second Language Research
James Dean Brown and Theodore Rodgers

Success in English Teaching
Paul Davies and Eric Pearse

Teaching Business English
Mark Ellis and Christine Johnson

Teaching English as an International Language
Sandra Lee McKay

Teaching English Overseas: An Introduction
Sandra Lee McKay

How Languages are Learned (New Edition)
Patsy Lightbown and Nina Spada

Communication in the Language Classroom
Tony Lynch

Explaining English Grammar
George Yule

Teaching and Learning in the Language Classroom

Tricia Hedge

OXFORD
UNIVERSITY PRESS

OXFORD
UNIVERSITY PRESS

Great Clarendon Street, Oxford OX2 6DP

Oxford University Press is a department of the University of Oxford.
It furthers the University's objective of excellence in research, scholarship,
and education by publishing worldwide in

Oxford New York

Auckland Bangkok Buenos Aires Cape Town Chennai
Dar es Salaam Delhi Hong Kong Istanbul Karachi Kolkata
Kuala Lumpur Madrid Melbourne Mexico City Mumbai
Nairobi São Paulo Shanghai Taipei Tokyo Toronto

OXFORD and OXFORD ENGLISH are registered trade marks of
Oxford University Press in the UK and in certain other countries

ISBN 0 19 442172 4

Printed in China

To my late father

Peace of the silent hills to you
Peace of the shining stars to you
Peace of the quiet earth to you

CONTENTS

ACKNOWLEDGEMENTS

Teaching and Learning in the Language Classroom has developed out of the courses I have taught over twenty-five years to student teachers and practising teachers on BEd, Diploma, and MA courses at Ealing College of Higher Education, Temple University Tokyo, and the Centre for English Language Teacher Education at the University of Warwick. I would like to thank those teachers and others with whom I have worked in seminars around the world for what I have learned from them and for their feedback on the substance of this book. I would also like to thank Benita Studman-Badillo for her help with Website sources, Henry Widdowson for his careful advice, and my editor Anne Conybeare for her unfailing patience and encouragement.

TRICIA HEDGE

The author and publisher are grateful to the following copyright holders who have given permission to reproduce extracts and adaptations of copyright material:

Addison Wesley Longman, Inc. for extracts from: 'Competitiveness and anxiety in adult second language learning' by K.M. Bailey in H.D. Brown and S.T. Gonzo (eds.): *Readings on Second Language Acquisition*, 1983. Copyright © 1983 Prentice Hall Regents; *Recipes for Tired Teachers* by C. Sion. Copyright © 1983; *Writing as a Personal Product* by L. Donahue Latulippe, 1992. Copyright © 1993 Prentice Hall Regents; *Writing Academic English* 2nd Edition (Intermediate-Advanced) by A. Oshima and A. Hogue. Copyright © 1991 Addison Wesley Publishing Company. Reprinted by permission of Addison Wesley Longman, Inc.

AILA for 'Vocabulary learning through reading' by C. Schouten-Van Parreren. Appeared in the *AILA Review* 1989.

Authentik Language Resources Ltd. *Learner Training for Language Learning* by L. Dickinson, 1992. Trinity College Dublin. Reproduced by permission.

BBC photolibrary for photographs of Sister Wendy Becket with painting and with caravan.

Bedford/St. Martin's Press: *Academic Writing* by I. Leki. Copyright © 1989 by St. Martin's Press, Inc. Reprinted with permission of Bedford/St. Martin's Press.

The British Council for permission for *An Occasional Paper: The Foreign Language Learning Process* by D. Pickett, ETIC Publications © The British Council, 1978.

Cambridge University Press for extracts from: 'The role of group work in classroom second language acquisition' by T. Pica and C. Doughty in *Studies in Second Language Acquisition* 7/2, 1985; *Keep Talking* by F. Klippel, 1984; *A Way with Words Resource Pack 1* by S. Redman and R. Ellis, 1996; Changes 2 Student's Book by J.C. Richards, 1995; *Activate Your English* by B. Sinclair and P. Prowse, 1996; *Getting the Message 2* Student's Book by D. Murphy and J. Cooper, 1995 © Cambridge University Press; *True to Life* Upper Intermediate Class Book by R. Gairns and S. Redman, 1998 © Cambridge University Press; *Writing Skills* by N. Coe, R. Ryecroft, and P. Ernest, 1983. © Cambridge University Press; *Meanings into Words* by A. Doff, C. Jones, and K. Mitchell, 1983. © Cambridge University Press; *Classroom-based Evaluation in Second Language Education* by F. Genesee and J. Upshur, 1996 © Cambridge University Press.

Centre for Language in Primary Education: *Guide To The Primary Learning Record* by H. Hester with S. Ellis and M. Barrs, published 1993 by Centre for Language in Primary Education, London Borough of Southwark.

Chalkface Press for extracts from "Reading Stories", 1987 reprinted with permission of the publishers Chalkface Press, PO Box 23, Cottesloe, Western Australia 6011.

Susan K. Cowles: "Teaching and Learning with Internet Based Resources" <http://www.nifl.gov/susanc/inthome.htm> Copyright 1997. Reprinted with permission from Susan K. Cowles. Courtesy of the National Institute for Literacy, Washington, D.C.

Rod Ellis: 'Second language acquisition and the relevance of language teaching' by R. Ellis, 1997 from R. Ellis (ed.) *Second Language Acquisition in Context*.

Daily Express: 'I'm sorry that Anne Turville...' appeared in *Daily Express* 8 April 1996, reproduced with their permission.

Christopher Gordon Publishers, Inc. *Portfolio Assessment in the Reading-Writing Classroom* by R. J. Tierney, M. A. Carter and L. F. Desai, 1991. Reproduced by permission of the publisher.

Peter Honey Publications for permission to adapt the original Honey and Mumford Learning Styles Model. Reprinted with permission of Peter Honey Publications, Berkshire.

Image Bank for a photograph of a neon sign.

International Reading Association: 'Strategic training for using text headings to improve students' processing of content' by R. Grant, 1993. *Journal of Reading* 36/6. Reprinted with permission of Rachel Grant and the International Reading Association. All rights reserved.

Tim Jenkins for a photo from *Tales of Real Escape*, published by Usborne Reader's library.

Language Teaching Publications: *Conversation Gambits* by E. Keller and S.T. Warner, 1998. Adapted from The Original Gambits series published by Supply of Services Canada. Reprinted with permission of Language Teaching Publications.

Lawrence Erlbaum Associates, Inc. 'The child's expressible knowledge of word concepts' by J. M. Anglin, 1985 from K.E. Nelson (ed.): *Children's Language*, Volume 5. Reprinted with permission of the publisher.

Macmillan Heinemann ELT for an extract from *Reading in the Language Classroom* by E. Williams, 1986. Reproduced by permission of Macmillan Heinemann ELT.

Macmillan Publishers Limited: *Using Readers in Language Teaching* by T. Hedge, 1988; *Vista Student's Book* by S. Deller and R. Jones, 1992; *Assessment* by M. Harris and P. McCann, 1994. Reproduced by permission of Macmillan Publishers Ltd.

Keith Morrow: *Techniques of Evaluation for a Notional Syllabus* by K. Morrow, 1977, reproduced with his permission.

NCELTR for an extract reprinted from *Assessing Achievement in the AMEP* by Geoff Brindley, with permission from the National Centre for English Language Teaching and Research, Australia. © NCELTR 1989.

Oxford Cambridge and RSA Examinations: *Certificates in Communicative Skills in English: Teacher's Guide*, reproduced by permission of OCR.

Oxford University Press. 'Vocabulary Notebooks: Theoretical Under-pinnings and Practical Suggestions' by N. Schmitt and D. Schmitt from *ELT Journal* 49/2, 1995; *New Headway* Intermediate Student's Book by John and Liz Soars, Oxford University Press © 1998.

Pearson Education Limited for extracts from: *The Pre-Intermediate Choice* Student's Book by S. Mohamed and R. Aklam, 1992 © Longman Group Limited 1992; *The Pre-Intermediate Choice* Teacher's Book by S. Mohamed and R. Aklam, 1992 © Longman Group Limited 1992; *Upper Intermediate Matters* Student's Book by J. Bell and T. Gower, published by Longman Group UK Limited 1992; *Investigating English Style* by D. Crystal and D. Davy, published by Longman 1976; *A Communicative Grammar of English* by G. Leech and J. Svartvik, published by Longman Group UK Limited 1975; *Developing Strategies* Student's Book by B. Abbs and I. Freebairn, 1980 © B. Abbs and I. Freebairn 1980; *The White Mountains* by John Christopher, abridged and simplified by A. G. Eyre in Longman Structural Readers Stage 4; *Blueprint Intermediate* Student's Book © Brian Abbs &

Ingrid Freebairn 1991; *Tuning In* by M. Spratt, 1989; *Soundtracks* by S. Axbey, 1989; *Language Issues* by G. P. Ladousse © Longman Group U.K. Limited 1994; *Classroom Testing* by J. B. Heaton, 1990. Copyright © Longman Group U.K. Limited 1989. Reproduced by permission of Pearson Education.

N. S. Prabhu for an extract from *Second Language Pedagogy* published by Oxford University Press, 1987 © N. S. Prabhu and reproduced with his permission.

Rex Features for a portrait photograph of Sister Wendy Beckett.

Richmond Publishing: *Freeform 4* Student's Book by M. Downie, D. Gray and J.M. Jiménez, 1995. Reprinted by permission of Richmond Publishing.

S.E.I. for an extract from *Of Machines and Men – A Reader in Mechanical Engineering* by Donatini/Hedge, © by S.E.I. – Societa Editrice Internazionale – Torino 1988.

Earl W. Stevick for permission to reproduce an extract from *Memory, Meaning and Method: a View of Language Teaching* (second edition), published by Heinle and Heinle 1996.

Teachers of English Speakers of Other Languages, Inc.: 'Grammar Pedagogy in Second and Foreign Language Teaching' by Marianne Celce-Murcia, 1991 in *TESOL Quarterly*, vol. 25. Copyright © 1991 b Teachers of English Speakers of Other Languages, Inc. Excerpt from p. 465 used with permission.

D. Willis and J. Willis for an extract from *The COBUILD English Course 1* Student's Book by D. Willis and J. Willis, 1988. Reproduced with their permission.

Usborne Publishing: *Tales of Real Escape*, reproduced by permission of Usborne Publishing, 83–85 Saffron Hill, London EC1N 8RT. Copyright © 1994 Usborne Publishing Ltd.

Epigrams

The Art of Educational Evaluation by E. Eisner, Falmer Press 1985. Reproduced by permission of Taylor & Francis Books Ltd.

'Three educational ideologies' by M. Skilbeck, from *Challenge and Change in the Curriculum* by Skilbeck, Horton & Raggat (eds.). Hodder & Stoughton, 1982. Reproduced by permission of Hodder & Stoughton Educational.

Although every effort has been made to trace and contact copyright holders before publication, this has not been possible in some cases. We apologize for any apparent infringement of copyright and if notified, the publisher will be pleased to rectify any errors or omissions at the earliest opportunity.

INTRODUCTION

If we were able to take wing and get a bird's eye view of English language teaching (ELT) in classrooms, study circles, workshops, lecture theatres, and open learning centres across the world, we would undoubtedly see a vast heterogeneity of activity. But behind the variation I believe we would be able to discern a number of persistent concerns in the professional practice of teachers. This is because teachers are decision-makers in managing classroom processes and, whatever our educational setting, whatever its potential and its problems, our working lives are defined by the same issues. What do I set up as aims for my next lesson with this class and what kind of activities will help to achieve those aims? How do I balance its content in relation to what I see of my students' needs for English in the world outside the classroom and in relation to the examinations for which we are preparing? How do I deal with this reading text in class? What amount of out-of-class work can I reasonably expect my learners to do? How do I make best use of a textbook I am not entirely happy with? How can I motivate my learners to be more active? What are my ultimate goals with this class? And can I usefully discuss and negotiate any of these things with my learners? These are just some examples. It is certainly my experience every year that teachers arriving on teacher development courses have these same concerns, whatever their background. In the last two decades, the ELT profession has been able to access and build on a strong and fast-developing knowledge base for effective professional practice, and to look for answers to some of the questions that confront us. It is a knowledge base that derives from research and thinking in a wide range of contributing disciplines: education, applied linguistics, sociolinguistics, pragmatics, cultural studies, second language acquisition studies, curriculum studies, and psychology, to name but a few. Many of these subject areas were in their infancy in the middle decades of the twentieth century but are now vigorous in research and intellectual activity, and able to provide insights of relevance to ELT classroom practice.

The aim of this book is to explore some of those insights, in particular those which can inform teachers on issues of current concern: for example, the design of curricula which have as primary goals the development of communicative ability in learners; the design of classroom procedures for effective development of language skills; the respective roles and responsibilities of teachers and learners; the relationship between the content of teaching and the context of learning; the development of a critical pedagogy; the successful management of interactive learning, and the development of innovative teaching materials.

The discussion is not embedded in a rationale based on the belief that teachers sit at the feet of educationists and applied linguists waiting for ideas to drop, like crumbs, to sustain them. Experienced teachers are more robust and independent than that. And it would be mistaken in any event to assume that research in the contributing disciplines produces an agreed theory on language use or language learning that we can apply in immediate and direct ways. Even classroom-based research, as we shall see, has produced varying, sometimes conflicting, findings—certainly not a base for unshakeable principles about professional practice. It is more a question of having a foundation of knowledge against which we can evaluate our own ideas about teaching and learning, to which we can apply for insights in our attempts to solve pedagogic problems, and from which we can draw ideas to experiment with in our own classrooms.

The book is organized into four parts. Part One, 'A framework for teaching and learning' (Chapters 1 to 3), deals with fundamental issues that underpin discussion in the later chapters. These chapters draw on insights gained since the 1970s into learning, learners, and language in use, and discuss how these insights have influenced methodology and materials in key ways: for example, in efforts to base curricula on communicative tasks which reflect the real world outside the classroom; in the recognition of learner strategies and possibilities for training in these; in moves towards interactive methodology; in changing views of the roles of teachers and learner, and in the acknowledgement that methodology needs to be appropriate to context.

Part Two, 'Teaching the language system', and Part Three, 'Developing the language skills', use a simple framework for looking at ELT principles and practice, taking first vocabulary and grammar as components of the language system and then the familiar and traditional four language skills of listening, speaking, reading, and writing. This framework is simply a way of organizing what in practice is a complex of interrelated aspects. It is a convenience and there is no intended suggestion that language learning or language teaching can be regarded as fitting into a tidy set of boxes, or that learners and teachers do not realize the need for integration.

Part Four, 'Planning and assessing learning', moves on to global issues. Chapter 10, on course design, draws together many of the threads in earlier chapters and considers the integration of teaching the language system and language skills. Chapter 11 deals with the relationship between teaching and assessment.

All of the chapters have a similar three-point rationale. The Introductory task serves the purpose of raising some of the issues which lie at the heart of current concern because they are those on which teachers must take professional decisions. The text then explores and synthesizes insights which are available to teachers: those which emerge from research studies; those which are the outcome of experience and reflection, and those available from the action research of teachers in their own classrooms. Implications for professional practice are then taken up with reference to the design of methodology and materials.

A feature of the book is the development of criteria for evaluating classroom activities, and readers are invited to apply these to samples of textbook materials. This is because the reality of many teaching situations is that teachers are users of other people's ideas of what constitutes good practice. Even the most enthusiastic and conscientious teacher rarely has time to produce whole courses or a substantial amount of personally created materials. It is therefore important that teachers establish criteria for choosing among the materials available to them, or for evaluating a textbook chosen for them. Only through this process can teachers maximize the strengths of materials and supplement them according to the needs of their own learners.

The book is intended primarily for practising teachers of English as a second or foreign language who work with adolescent and adult students, and who wish to discover more about ideas in ELT which influence their work and the sources of those ideas. It will also be of relevance to teachers entering the profession who wish to gain an overview of theory and practice. It can be used as a reference text or handbook for the individual teacher. Alternatively it can be used as a sourcebook or as a class text by teacher educators working on in-service courses and seminars. In this latter mode, the Introductory task and the activities in the Discussion topics and projects section at the end of each chapter can be used for group discussion. The questions raising pedagogic issues at the beginning of each chapter can similarly be discussed and extended into an agenda for the group, which can formulate further issues and explore them in the references provided.

The book tries not to take a prescriptive stance in the sense of promoting certain routines or techniques, though it is probably true to say that it reflects my own stance on such issues as learner responsibility, the communicative classroom, an interactive methodology, and a learner-centred view of curriculum. The attempt not to prescribe stems from the belief that teachers need to articulate to themselves those issues which are of greatest concern to them and to look for those insights which can inform them. To prescribe would be to disregard teacher professionalism in judging what might be best for their own learners in their own circumstances. It is the essential nature of professional development that reflection on experience and the exploration of insights from other people are the primary ways we have of refining our professional practice. The aim of the book is therefore rather to encourage reflection and the building of a critical perspective.

PART ONE

A framework for teaching and learning

1 LEARNERS AND LEARNING, CLASSROOMS AND CONTEXTS

'Another language is another soul.'
CHARLES V

1 What do we know about how languages are learned?

2 How do differences among learners affect learning processes and teaching procedures?

3 What motivations do learners have for learning English?

4 What factors of context should teachers take into account?

5 What roles can learners and teachers play in the language learning process?

6 What roles can learning materials play in the classroom?

Introductory task

Consider this account of a particular teaching situation, given by Rufino, a Spanish secondary-school teacher of English.

1 What are the factors which help Rufino in his work? Think of:
   (a) social factors
   (b) educational factors
   (c) pupil factors
   (d) teacher factors.

2 What are the specific contextual factors which affect your own work as a teacher?

> My name's Rufino and I teach English in secondary school in Spain. My students are mostly the 13 to 14 age range. English language learning begins at the age of 8 here so my classes have been studying English for six years. I work in a small town in the north of Spain. There is a strong awareness of language in this region of Spain as we have two languages in the community here, Spanish and Basque. English is the third language we learn and it's a foreign language. There is very

little exposure to English in society here. Even Sky News on the TV is dubbed.

English is an obligatory part of the school curriculum, but the fact that it is a compulsory subject for all students does not pose a problem as most pupils are highly motivated and parental attitudes are positive and supportive. In fact, learning English is part of a personal agenda for most people as it enables us to move around in the European community. It isn't difficult to see real reasons for learning English for jobs or studies, or for travelling.

There are twenty-five pupils in each of my classes, which is fine. It isn't too many to prevent me from keeping a sense of them as individuals, each with their own strengths and weaknesses and needs. Each class has a total of three hours a week of English. Teachers have a good deal of flexibility in deciding how to use these hours as long as we keep to the curriculum objectives set out by the educational authorities. The national curriculum is fairly new and in our school we have teams of teachers working on an interpretation of the objectives set out for each year of schooling. Our task is to translate the objectives into courses, using a mixture of bought-in textbooks and our own materials, especially for project work, which has become very popular. I've been glad to see project work introduced as I believe we need to focus on using English in the classroom for purposes that are as real as possible. I also like being able to set up a project and then standing back a little while my pupils organize themselves in collaborative work. It's part of learner-centred teaching for me with this age group as I believe they really need to develop skills of organization and working together. Schools work out their own guidelines for assessment and we set our own tests within the English curriculum, but if students want to go on to the university they must take a public entrance examination. My colleagues and I are learning a lot as we put our policies together and design our courses.

As for resources, well, I suppose teachers themselves are a major resource. We do a pre-service course at university, either a three- or four-year course, so we are trained and qualified teachers. There are also some opportunities for in-service training, for example, in seminars organized by local teachers' centres, or by British publishers, or sometimes by professional organizations like TESOL. However, these are all voluntary and sometimes they are expensive and travelling is involved. We are well-resourced in schools. I have a blackboard, an overhead projector, a cassette player, and a video in my classroom, and there is a self-access centre in the school. This isn't so common in schools but depends on the enthusiasm of teachers as it takes time and energy to set up a centre and to encourage pupils to use it. Personally I've put a lot of my own efforts into developing these kinds of resources because I think the age group I teach benefits tremendously from opportunities for organizing their own learning.

1.1 Introduction: issues for the language teacher

In this first chapter, the issues we look at are those which are fundamental to ELT professional practice. They are reflected in the account which Rufino gives of his teaching situation. He describes the context in which his learners study English and highlights some of the social, educational, and local factors which may advantage or disadvantage the pupils in his classes and himself as teacher: on the one hand, strong language awareness and positive attitudes to learning English in the community; on the other, lack of exposure to English.

This raises issues about the learning conditions in which his pupils study, and what is available to them and to him in terms of language input and language practice. Will there, for example, be authentic English language materials available from which listening or reading texts can be taken? In the project work he describes, will he be able to involve pupils in encounters with native speakers of English, or will they be text-based projects? Or can he set up correspondence projects with other schoolchildren in English-speaking countries?

Rufino is sensitive to his pupils as individual learners and realizes, for instance, that motivations and needs will vary as will strengths and weaknesses. In this, he reflects our professional concerns to find out how our learners differ from one another and to cater for this as much as possible.

In discussing the curriculum, Rufino comments on the role of materials in language teaching and the balance his school is trying to create between commercial materials and teacher-made materials in fulfilling curriculum objectives. And implicit in his mention of project work and self-access resources are issues concerning the relative roles of teachers and learners and where the balance of responsibility lies for a successful learning process.

In outlining these issues, he communicates a sense of awareness that language teaching is a complex endeavour, requiring a professional approach which involves decision-making at a variety of levels. The teachers in his school are not merely agents in an educational hierarchy, applying specified methods, but have the creative responsibility of building links between externally imposed curriculum objectives and their own course planning, activity design, materials development, and management of learning procedures. They are involved in a process of continuing professional self-development.

There is also implicit in what Rufino says a framework of principles upon which he bases his classroom practice. And these principles are underpinned by the views he holds of learners, learning, and language use, and are informed by his analysis of the teaching situation. If we were to abstract some of these principles from his account and present them as a teacher's credo, it might look something like this:

– In the classroom I want to focus on using English for purposes that are as real as possible.
– I need to keep a sense of pupils as individuals and to respond to the different needs they have as much as I can.
– I believe that secondary-school pupils benefit greatly from opportunities to take on more responsibility for their own learning.

The rest of this chapter will consider the insights available to teachers from the evaluation of practice, from research studies, and from theory-building in the various disciplines of applied linguistics and education which can help us to understand the issues raised by Rufino's reflections and which can inform our own decision-making.

1.2 What do we know about how languages are learned?

Any teacher seeking ideas about how languages are learned will find a surfeit of theories. However, some have proved more attractive to the ELT profession than others, probably because they concur in useful ways with ideas about the communicative classroom and can therefore be assimilated into current approaches. There are perhaps four areas of investigation and debate among second language acquisition researchers which deserve special attention from English language teachers: the nature of the input provided to learners; how learners process that input; the role of classroom interaction; and the role of error in language learning.

1.2.1 *The nature of input*

A significant idea that has emerged in recent years is that of *comprehensible input*. Krashen's (1985) input hypothesis posits that language is picked up, or *acquired*, when learners receive input from 'messages' which contain language a little above their existing understanding and from which they can infer meaning. The hypothesis makes a distinction between acquiring a language and learning it through conscious attention to language study. The acquisition process, often called a *creative construction process*, is parallel to that of a child learning its first language. A study of children's errors suggests that they use *operating strategies*, such as paying attention to the ends of words, to formulate hypotheses about rules in the language, and that these hypotheses are tested out in their own attempts to produce language and gradually revised as they receive feedback on their attempts.

The classic example of the creative construction process is the series of stages that children go through in acquiring the rules for forming the past simple tense: first, they produce accurate irregular forms such as 'held' sporadically; then they produce an incorrect form 'holded' as they perceive a rule involving the /ɪd/ sound at the end of words and overgeneralize the rule; finally they produce 'held' again as they refine the rule. Adults are thought to be capable of this same creative construction process, for which they need exposure to comprehensible input and feedback on their attempts to use newly acquired language.

Faerch and Kasper (1983) have suggested that once a language learner has formulated a hypothesis, it can be tested out in various ways. For example, one way would be to check it in a dictionary or grammar book, or with a teacher or native speaker. Another way to check it would be to wait for further examples in language input, to analyse these and compare them with the hypothesis. Alternatively, a learner could try out a language form in the classroom or in conversation and see what feedback is given about its correctness.

It is through the process of hypothesis making and testing that learners make sense of language input and impose a structure on it. They create a developing system known as *interlanguage*, which passes through a number of stages until it eventually approximates to the rules of the target language or until it stabilizes, or fossilizes, in ways that deviate from these rules.

The limitations of hypothesis testing and the creative construction process as a full explanation of second language acquisition have been much debated. There is a view, originating in Chomsky's seminal work in linguistics (1965), that there are universal language properties, i.e. a set of principles which apply to all languages, and that knowledge of these is inherent in the human mind. In other words, we are genetically pre-programmed for language learning and are constrained in the kinds of hypotheses we make.

This account tends to oversimplify a complex process. Second language researchers continue to debate the ways in which acquisition and learning relate to each other and the ways in which both might function in the language classroom. However, the notion of comprehensible input has been taken up with enthusiasm for a number of reasons.

- It confirms the need for meaningful input which will engage learners in working with language at a level which is slightly above their competence.

'Meaningful' has been variously interpreted by materials writers and teachers as 'relevant and topical to learners and their interests' or 'realistic' in terms of simulating the authentic texts and speaking situations learners may eventually have to handle. This implies a need for varied classroom materials, and many current coursebooks demonstrate a motivating range of situations and of texts, for example, newspaper articles, posters, advertisements, guides, maps, and invitations.

– It suggests the value of providing input through out-of-class resources such as readers and listening cassettes for self-access learning, or encouraging students to make use of whatever resources might be available in the community to increase input opportunities.

– It seems to confirm the usefulness of teachers adjusting their own classroom language, in line with students' proficiency, to simpler vocabulary and slower speech while retaining natural rhythm and intonation.

1.2.2 *The process of intake*

Intake refers to the ways in which learners process input and assimilate language to their interlanguage system. Learners will not process all the input available to them. Some of what they hear or read may not be understood, and some parts of input will receive more attention because, for various reasons, they seem more important or salient to the learner at a particular stage of development. The concept of intake has given us some insights into why teachers cannot control the learning process to the extent we might previously have believed. Take, for example, an initial class activity in which the teacher asks and invites questions about what students did the previous evening with the aim of practising the past simple tense. One student, thinking ahead to her turn, focuses on her need for the English word 'countryside' and uses the strategy of finding an alternative which is close to the meaning she wants to convey. She uses 'nature' and waits for the teacher's feedback. The simple past is not part of her agenda at that point and 'countryside' will probably be her intake. Hopefully, with further practice, she will eventually be able to retrieve this lexical item without hesitation.

It is clear that some kind of input is needed if language acquisition is to occur, but many questions remain about the kind of input which is most useful in facilitating the process. Does input need to be controlled in the traditional ways of the English language classroom? Why do learners notice some items more than others? Is it to do with such factors as frequency of input? Is input attended to more when it comes from the teacher as an authority figure rather than from other learners in the classroom? Does intake depend on how much work a learner has to do in comprehending or making sense of something? How do psychological factors of motivation and emotion affect the process of intake?

As yet we have an uncertain understanding of these issues. However, the answers are crucial to an effective teaching of the language system. For example, if it is the case that learners will assimilate those items on which they have to work harder to comprehend, there are implications here for the ways in which we teach new words. If learners attend to items which occur frequently in input, there are implications for the presentation of grammatical forms. If input receives more attention when it comes from the teacher, there are implications for classroom management. These issues will be revisited in later chapters.

1.2.3 *The role of interaction in the classroom*

Related to the notion of input is that of output. Learners need practice in producing *comprehensible output* (Swain 1985) using all the language resources they have already acquired. Getting feedback from the teacher and from other students in the class enables learners to test hypotheses and refine their developing knowledge of the language system. It has also been claimed that being pushed to produce output obliges learners to cope with their lack of language knowledge by struggling to make themselves understood, by speaking slowly for example, or repeating or clarifying their ideas through rephrasing. When a group of students do this while talking together, it is called *negotiation of meaning* and its aim is to make output more comprehensible. There is a principle underlying current ELT practice that interaction pushes learners to produce more accurate and appropriate language, which itself provides input for other students. This is one reason why pairwork and groupwork have become common features of contemporary classrooms.

A study by Pica and Doughty (1985) can be taken as an example of research looking at the role of groupwork in language learning. It investigated in what ways language input and output differed in a class using work in small groups and a class following a sequence of whole-class work fronted and controlled by the teacher. They studied three lower-intermediate classes of adults from a variety of language backgrounds in which students completed two communication activities involving discussion and decision-making, one about a heart transplant problem and the other about a family planning problem. One task was done in a teacher-fronted, whole-class mode with students moving together at the same pace through the activity, and the other was done in groups of four. The study gave evidence of students negotiating meaning through, for example, clarification checks such as:

S1 She is on welfare   S2 *What do you mean by welfare?*
(Pica and Doughty 1985: 236)

or:

> S1 This is very bad …   S2 *You're opposed to that? You*
> I think she never   *don't think that's a good idea?*
> estay home.
> (ibid.)

and confirmation checks such as:

> S1 The homemaker woman   S2 *The homemaker?*
> (ibid.)

It also showed the ways in which students helped each other through correction, as in:

> S1 It's *illegally* for the system   S2 It's *illegal* for the system
> (ibid.: 238)

and through completion, as in:

> S1 *Yes, I know … but the*   S2 *mentality*
> *mental—*
> (ibid.: 237)

Among the results were the following: the students produced more output in the groupwork; each student was exposed to more input in the groupwork; completions and corrections were more common in the groupwork; there was no difference in the level of accuracy in the student's output in both situations, but there was little evidence of negotiation of meaning in either situation. This last result was surprising as the tasks had been chosen as typical of those used in communicative classrooms, which aim to stimulate negotiation of meaning. However, what seemed to happen was domination of the groupwork by a few individuals. This led the researchers to pose the question of what kinds of tasks are best for obliging learners to negotiate meaning. The relative value of pairwork information-gap tasks, or, say, group discussion tasks, in terms of which need participation from all group members and which encourage negotiation of meaning, has been the focus of further studies. We will look at some of the outcomes in Chapter 8.

Claims about the value of small-group interaction in the classroom for language acquisition provide attractive support for views of educationists about the value of collaborative work and the importance of reducing dependence on teachers. They also fit well with one of the aims of communicative language teaching, which is to develop learners' ability to participate effectively in conversation.

However, an important issue in the use of work in small groups is that it implies risk-taking. Being in face-to-face encounters requires assertiveness. This may be difficult for individual personalities and may even run counter to the educational ethos which some learners have experienced previously. It is an issue which teachers will need to take into account when considering the individual needs of their learners in the educational system which they are part of.

1.2.4 *The role of error*

With a view of language learning as a creative construction process comes the view that error is an inevitable and positive part of that process. Attitudes have therefore moved on from those of the behaviourists in the 1950s and 1960s who saw error as something to be prevented as far as possible through intensive modelling and eradicated through intensive drilling. Errors are now seen as reflections of a learner's stage of interlanguage development.

There are conflicting views on the role of error correction in the classroom. For example, Krashen's interest in the possible parallels between children's acquisition of their first language and adult second language acquisition led him to suggest that error correction had dubious value in the classroom. Children, he claimed, do not generally receive explicit negative feedback on the accuracy of their language and, by analogy, adults do not require constant correction with its dangers of distraction and demotivation. However, critics were quick to point out that adult learners can be encouraged to process error correction in useful ways, and the role of the teacher is to provide feedback which learners can work on in order to refine their understanding and move to the next stage of interlanguage.

The treatment of error requires consideration of many issues. Whether or not to perform the role of diagnoser and corrector of errors is only the first. If we decide to undertake this role, we will need a careful policy for making decisions about what, when, and how to correct. Such a policy will be considered in Chapters 8 and 9.

The appropriate question to ask at the end of this section is what insights in general can we gain from the work going on in the field of second language acquisition, given the uncertain findings of studies? Perhaps the most important insight is that however much teachers and textbooks try to control what is learned in the classroom, in actual fact the learners in a class will learn different things at different rates from the input and practice. In other words, there is no easy direct relationship between the teaching objectives of our lessons and the learning outcomes for the students. Understanding this will help us to realize that our major role is to provide conditions which are conducive to learning. However, there is increasing evidence that learners progress faster with meaningful language practice in a rich linguistic environment and with an informed policy of error correction on the part of the teacher.

Certainly it can be of value to English language teachers to keep an ear open to discussions issuing from the field of second language acquisition as they can inform, confirm, challenge, and excite.

1.3 How do differences among learners affect learning processes and teaching procedures?

In the extract at the beginning of this chapter, Rufino commented on his need to keep a sense of his pupils as individuals. This comment does not only come from a humanistic concern for the welfare of the individual. It also demonstrates that he is aware, as all experienced teachers are aware, that learners differ in ways that need careful thought when making decisions about course content and methodology. What exactly are the dimensions of individual difference among learners and what insights can teachers gain from studies of these?

Unfortunately, insights are unclear and fragmentary because research has been difficult. Language aptitude, as we shall see, has been measured by tests, but other dimensions have been investigated largely by introspective methods. Three methods in particular have been used. The first is self-report, responding to interview questions and questionnaires. Here, for example, is an introspection from an American in Japan, on the issues relating to using work in small groups in multicultural training sessions:

> In particular our group work has helped me to explore more consciously the substantial cultural differences we have. I come from a society where great value is placed on the performance of the individual: here the ethos is one of consensus. How does that affect our discussions?
> (Hedge 1998: 137)

A second method is self-observation, using diaries or immediate retrospective verbal reports. In this example, a learner writes of the anxiety that comes from comparison of her progress with that of her peers and her feelings of competitiveness:

> I'm starting to find that my colleagues know more vocabulary than me. It's because they have 3 extra hours. … It irritates me that the others know more. It makes me want to join their extra lessons.
> (Ellis and Rathbone 1987: 157)

A third method is self-revelation, using think-aloud reports recorded on to cassette as learners actually perform tasks. Cohen (1987) gives a useful example, from data he collected on himself as a learner, of his attempt to deal with a new Hebrew verb through analogy:

> Now, how am I going to learn how to conjugate the verb *rigel* 'to spy' in Hebrew? Oh, I see. It is conjugated just like *diber* 'to speak'. So now I know its forms … no problem.
> (Cohen 1987: 83)

These three introspective methods all depend on learners being able to give clear, accurate, and honest accounts of what they do. There is also the issue in self-revelation of whether their attempts to report what they do will affect what they would normally do in carrying out a language learning task.

However, problems in research methodology by no means invalidate the usefulness of teachers building awareness of individual differences and the implications these might hold for the management of learning. Our awareness has been slowly developing in relation to aptitude, learning style, and learning strategies, and the affective factors of personality and motivation.

1.3.1 *Aptitude*

It is quite common to hear people say 'She has a flair for languages', or even, more specifically, 'He has a good ear for languages', and there is a body of research evidence to suggest that some people do indeed have an aptitude for language learning. The problem with the research is that it is not conclusive as to what abilities constitute aptitude or how these relate to other factors such as intelligence. Two well-known language aptitude tests, still widely used, are the Modern Language Aptitude Test (MLAT) (Carroll and Sapon 1955) and the Pimsleur Language Aptitude Battery (LAB) (Pimsleur 1966). These generally put forward a multi-componential view of aptitude as comprising four components: auditory ability, grammatical sensitivity, inductive language learning ability, and memory. Each of these components is tested in order to predict whether a student is likely to be successful in learning a foreign language. For example, the MLAT has a test of grammatical sensitivity to the first language which asks students to identify words in two sentences which have the same grammatical function. Can you decide which word underlined in the second sentence has the same function as 'London' in the first sentence?

LONDON is the capital of England.

He liked to go fishing in Maine.
A   B   C   D   E
(Carroll and Sapon 1955: 5)

(The answer is, of course, 'he' as, like 'London', it is the subject of the sentence.)

In most cases aptitude testing, if it is used at all, will already have been undertaken during a selection process for foreign language learning. It is typically done in many countries for recruitment purposes into bodies such as the army or the civil service. However, discussion in recent years has brought out implications which are of importance for teachers. Ellis (1985), for example, makes the point that the tests focus on language form rather than its communicative aspects and might therefore indicate learners who will be advantaged in more formal classroom learning. To take another example, Skehan (1989) comments that, given the composite nature of aptitude, students who achieve the same overall score on an aptitude test could well have different strengths and weaknesses among the components, and teachers working with students selected through such a test should take this into account.

1.3.2 *Learning style and learning strategies*

The components of aptitude measured by the tests described in the previous section all relate to language. More recent research has looked at other variables which seem to correlate positively with successful language learning. For example, a global learner is believed to prefer learning through global exposure while an analytic learner likes to analyse elements in detail. This might influence the learner's response to methods of presenting language. For example, in dealing with a text a global learner might predict and infer to get an overall understanding, while an analytic learner might search for small details and try to follow accurately the precise relationships between different parts of the text. Some learners can tolerate ambiguity better than others and wait for further, disambiguating information. This might well advantage beginners dealing with the presentation of simplified grammatical rules, such as:

> Use *some* in positive statements.
> Use *any* in questions and negative statements.

These learners may quickly see exceptions to the rule in language they are exposed to, as the rules are far more complex.

These characteristics are now seen as aspects of *cognitive style* or *learning style*, which can be generally defined as a characteristic and preferred way of approaching learning and processing information. The question is whether and in what ways this individual style affects language learning: the picture so far remains unclear. However, teachers of multicultural classes or expatriate teachers of monolingual classes in unfamiliar cultures will need to keep in mind that a possible cause of differences in cognitive style is the kind of teaching methodology that learners have experienced during their educational careers, and that this will have been culturally influenced.

There is evidence to suggest that culture, as learned by the child from family, community, and school, has a strong influence on learning style. At the risk of oversimplifying a complex issue, here are a few examples. Hofstede (1986) suggests that Chinese children, in learning an ideographic writing system, learn to see patterns and to learn by rote. Reid (1987) found that Korean students, in terms of sensory preference, are more visual than US or Japanese students. In other words, they like to read and receive visual input. Brown (1987) suggests that Anglo-Americans have an analytic style. On the other hand, Egyptian students (Oxford and Burry-Stock 1995) take a global approach. These and other studies are reviewed in a survey article (Oxford and Anderson 1995) which suggests the need for further research and review but which also points out the need for teachers' awareness of the issues.

The general implication of possible mismatches between learners and expatriate teachers is clear. The Anglo-American teacher of Egyptian students could well experience a cultural clash of learning styles. And with regard to the multi-cultural classroom, insights into culture and learning style highlight the teacher's need to create a variety of learning activities to cater for the range of styles.

A closely related orientation to researching language learning style has been to investigate the strategies that are used by successful language learners. These are techniques used by learners to deal with input, assimilate new language, store, retrieve, and practise using it. Oxford (1990), for example, provides a comprehensive list which can be used by teachers to prepare students for learning. Two items from her list are as follows:

Setting Goals and Objectives
Setting aims for language learning, including long-term goals (such as being able to use the language for informal conversation by the end of the year), or short-term objectives (such as finishing reading a short story by Friday).

Self-Monitoring
Identifying errors in understanding or producing the new language, determining which ones are important (those that cause serious confusion or offense), tracking the source of important errors, and trying to eliminate such errors.

(Oxford 1990: 139, 140)

The idea that there are identifiable strategies used by good learners which might be trained in the classroom has led to great interest among teachers and textbook writers, who have attempted both to find ways of improving the strategies learners already have and to raise their awareness about others they might develop. Chapter 3 takes up the topic of strategy training in more detail.

1.3.3 *Affective factors*

Most discussions have limited affective factors to personality characteristics, attitudes, and emotional responses to the language learning process. The major problem of research in this area is that data gathered by introspective methods using questionnaires and self-report often does not seem to agree with observed behaviour. Better instruments are needed. It is therefore difficult to make generalizations. However, this in itself is a useful insight for teachers given that sweeping generalizations about learners are not uncommon in these areas.

For example, there is a widely held view that extrovert learners are likely to be more successful than introverted learners, possibly because they are more assertive, more willing to experiment and take risks, and more able to make the social contacts they need to practise language. This view, however, is not conclusively supported by the findings of research. Furthermore, we need to keep the exigencies of the classroom situation clearly in mind. It may well be the case that extrovert students benefit from oral work in small groups where their assertiveness enables them to dominate and their willingness to take risks facilitates practice, but in a whole-class mode of learning, as McDonough (1983) indicates, the extroverts may be silenced by an irritated teacher. Perhaps the important implication for the teacher is to balance these personality differences by ensuring an equal share of attention and opportunity to contribute.

Ethnocentricity is an attitudinal variable which has been investigated, and it will not surprise experienced teachers that studies show a negative correlation with language learning. Perhaps the significant implication for the teacher working where English language learning is compulsory is caution in the portrayal of the related English-speaking culture, avoidance of stereotyping, and the building of positive attitudes to the study of English as a curriculum subject through motivating content and tasks.

In terms of emotional responses to learning, a variable which has received much attention is anxiety. Bailey (1995) for example, links anxiety to competitiveness and argues that if we can discover its various causes we will be in a better position to reduce it. She effected this in her own language learning by keeping a diary and then categorizing the manifestations of anxiety recorded in it, both those which facilitated learning by pushing her to perform better and those which inhibited learning.

She derived the following seven categories:

1 Overt—though private—comparison of myself with other students (e.g., self-ranking, use of comparatives and superlatives, comparison in particular skills areas, etc.).

2   Emotive responses to such comparisons (anxiety when I didn't compare favorably with the others and elation when I did), including emotional reactions to other students (e.g., the girl who'd been to France, the girl whose grammar book I bought, etc.): connotative uses of language (for instance, the foot-race imagery) in the diary entries sometimes reveal this emotion.

3   The desire to outdo the other students; here realized as the tendency to race through exams in order to finish first.

4   Emphasis on tests and grades, especially with reference to the other students.

5   The desire to gain the teacher's approval.

6   Anxiety experienced during the language class, often after making errors on material I felt I should have known (i.e., a discrepancy between an idealized self-image and a realistic assessment of myself as a language learner).

7   Withdrawal from the language-learning experience when the competition was overpowering.

(Bailey 1995: 175–6)

MacIntyre and Gardner (1991) looked in more detail at anxiety in the classroom. The greatest anxiety seems to relate to negative experiences in speaking activities. This would confirm the experience of many teachers, but the suggestion that arises from such studies, that anxiety is a response learned through early experiences and that it can increase until the whole process of learning is badly affected, emphasizes the need for 'humanistic' approaches in the widest sense of the word. It implies that teachers have both the power and the responsibility to counter the development of anxiety by building self-confidence through positive early experiences, through providing reassuring feedback, and through promoting self-perception of developing proficiency.

Krashen (1985) has suggested the notion of the *affective filter*. This is a representation of the way in which affective factors such as attitude, anxiety, competitiveness, and other emotional responses can help or hinder language learning. The filter can be imagined as a sliding barrier which moves into place when a student is, for example, tired, dispirited, tense, or angry, and which prevents the processing of input. A learner who has generally negative attitudes towards learning English will have a high affective filter and the task for the teacher will be substantial. The precise functioning of this filter is not explained, for example in relation to how it might affect the attention that students pay or do not pay to various elements of input. However, the concept of the filter highlights the role of the teacher in creating beneficial conditions for language learning.

In summary, then, although we have little conclusive evidence on the role of affective factors, some studies have proved to be of value to the teacher in challenging common assumptions and in suggesting areas for concern.

1.3.4 *Motivation for learning English*

The degree to which any of the factors discussed so far in this chapter will become significant in a particular learning and teaching situation will depend partly on the reasons why learners are learning English. Rufino's pupils were aware of how English would give them mobility in the European community. Adult learners returning to study may regard language learning as a hobby or cultural pursuit worthy of the educated person, or may have pressing reasons for wishing to communicate in English. In many state school systems now, where the pupils' future use of English is uncertain, a primary aim is to build communicative potential. Any individual may be influenced by a variety of motivations which will affect such things as anxiety, or attitude, or willingness to try new learning strategies.

A group of twenty Japanese students, at the beginning of intensive English language instruction at a UK university, were each asked to give four major motivations for learning English. The following list of statements represents in general the reasons given by members of the group and their rank-ordering:

1 To be able to communicate with people in an international
   language, both at home in Japan and while travelling in other
   countries   20

2 To be able to read a wide range of English language sources for
   study purposes in the UK and in Japan   16

3 To have a better chance of employment, status, and financial
   reward in the job market   12

4 To be able to read and listen to English language media for
   information and pleasure   9

5 To find out more about the people, places, politics etc. of English-
   speaking cultures   7

6 To take up a particular career, e.g. English language teaching,
   work in an international company   6

7 To be able to participate successfully in the country I will be
   living in for six months   5

8 To read English-language literature   3

9 Because of parental pressure   2

(Author's data)

This list suggests two kinds of motivation for learning English: needing a language as an instrument to achieve other purposes such as doing a job effectively or studying successfully at an English-speaking institution, or wishing to integrate into the activities or culture of another group of people. Indeed, Gardner and Lambert (1972) termed these two as integrative and instrumental motivation. These two kinds of motivation can be demonstrated by the statements they gave students of French in Canada against which to indicate their own reasons for learning. Of the following statements, the first two are taken as indicative of integrative motivation and the second two of instrumental motivation:

- It will enable me to gain good friends more easily among French-speaking people.
- It should enable me to begin to think and behave as the French do.
- One needs a good knowledge of at least one foreign language to merit social recognition.
- I need it in order to finish high school.

(Gardner and Lambert 1972: 148)

This integrative–instrumental distinction may be most relevant to bilingual societies such as Canada where one language spoken in the community is a minority language, or to short-stay situations in the target language community.

A decade later, Gardner and Smythe's (1981) Attitude/Motivation Test Battery (AMTB) usefully shows the complex of areas under investigation by that time. There are four main categories. The first is motivation, which involves desire to learn a language, intensity of effort to achieve this, and attitudes towards learning the language. The second is integrativeness, which involves attitudes towards the target language group and which touches on the affective factor of ethnocentricity. The third involves attitudes towards the language teacher and the language course. The fourth concerns measures of anxiety in classroom situations and in using the language. It is now clear that motivation is a highly complex phenomenon consisting of a number of variables. It is also clear that the high correlations that studies show between motivation and successful learning confirm what is already indisputable among teachers: that motivation is of crucial importance in the classroom, whether learners arrive with it or whether they acquire it through classroom experiences.

Perhaps the most useful perspective for the teacher to take is to consider what aspects of motivation can be changed and to focus on creating successful experiences which will enhance motivation. Ellis (1993b), for example, has made the point that we need to explore more fully the factors involved in motivating students to do tasks as this is something over which the teacher has some control. It would certainly be worth any teacher's time to create a checklist of ways to motivate learners in the classroom. Given the factors discussed in this chapter, it might begin like this:

– Give some time to considering group dynamics and to how to build cohesiveness within the class.
– Make sure that there is sufficient variety of input (listening, reading), of pace and intensity, of interaction, and of activity to allow learners to work in their own style and with their own strategies.
– Show awareness of differences in motivation, in emotional responses, in strategies, etc., and encourage learners to build awareness of their own preferences.
– Acknowledge that language learning is a serious endeavour requiring perseverance and involving anxiety, and be sure to give reassurance.

A recurring comment throughout this section on individual differences in learners is the uncertainty that exists in the methodology for investigating them, in the distinctions that can usefully be made in trying to classify them, and in the possible implications for the teacher. Certainly, we are not in a position to say that there are certain attitudes, personality characteristics, emotional dispositions, and learning strategies that somehow create the generically 'good language learner'.

However, there is little doubt that individual differences exist and they play a significant role in language learning. For the teacher the challenge must be how to 'enable' each learner according to his or her individual characteristics and cultural background. It may be a question of flexibility in materials design, or variety in skills work or classroom interaction. There may well be value in raising awareness in learners of their own styles and strategies and in helping them to refine and apply these in more independent resource-based learning where individualization is possible. Motivation is certainly an issue to be borne in mind when reflecting on any of the topics discussed in this book.

1.4 What factors of context should teachers take into account?

As we have seen in Rufino's account, we need to consider characteristics of the learning situation. Most of these are outside the teacher's control but they will bear heavily on decisions about choice of resources and classroom procedures. For ease of discussion they can be divided into social factors and educational factors.

Social attitudes towards English language learning will partly determine how much effort teachers have to put into motivating children, but so will social exposure to the language. The presence of English in the community will immediately facilitate practice opportunities such as writing reviews of English films and TV programmes, keeping a diary of extra-curricular activities, outside visits, or encounter projects. Its absence creates greater but not insuperable challenges for teachers, who will need to think about sources of authentic input, about manageable out-of-class practice, and about creating a balance of skills work to make the most productive use of class and out-of-class time.

The educational system in which teachers work will be influenced by cultural notions of authority which affect the potential roles of teachers and learners. Another factor will be whether the system allows for 'retaking' courses. This will determine whether or not the teacher is faced with a gradually increasing range of proficiency in classes as they move through the years. This is a real problem that many teachers face and the issues of mixed-ability teaching deserve far greater professional attention in ELT. At the very least it supports arguments for rich, varied, and flexible learning resources. But there are other factors which have more to do with the institution and all provide potential or constraint. For example:

- the extent to which the materials in use train for public examinations and the extent to which deviation from these may disadvantage students in this respect, notwithstanding the benefits of alternatives
- the hours available for teaching and the distribution of those hours
- the existence of institutional or departmental policies for such things as marking or homework and the flexibility of these
- the physical constraints of the classroom
- class size
- the resources available in the classroom and in the institution
- the cohesion that exists among English language teachers and the degree to which it fosters teamwork
- the status of teachers in the hierarchy and their involvement in book selection, policy development, etc.
- the financial/contractual status of teachers and whether they work in one institution or several
- the interest of management in continuing professional development through in-service sessions, projects in materials design, etc.
- whether classes are monolingual or multilingual.

The examination system, for example, is usually a heavily constraining factor, especially where examinations are gatekeepers to higher education or good employment prospects. It would be a matter of high risk for a teacher not to train students for these. With regard to other factors, teachers may have more flexibility. For example, to take up the last point on the list, mono-lingual classes facilitate use of the first language in the classroom and it is useful to work out a personal policy for this which can be explained and discussed in class. Many teachers feel uneasy about using the mother tongue but there are clearly advantages in doing so in some instances, for example to give a quick translation of words like 'cherry' or 'hedgehog', or to talk about learning approaches and strategies with beginners.

1.5 What roles can teachers and learners play in the learning process?

Rufino commented on his enjoyment of project work as one kind of learner-based teaching which allowed him to stand back a little and take on a less dominant role while his pupils organized themselves in collaborative work. The concept of 'role' has become very popular in ELT and is a term in common usage to denote the functions that teachers and learners perform during the course of a lesson. In the social setting of the classroom, teachers' and learners' expectations about what are appropriate functions in various learning tasks will determine the roles that each performs, and these will be culturally influenced.

1.5.1 *The teacher's roles and responsibilities*

The range of roles that teachers perform can be illustrated by analysing the sample of lesson notes from the Teacher's Book of *The Pre-intermediate Choice* shown in Materials extract 1.A. The sample is taken from the early stages of a lesson in which the aims are to revise and practise the present perfect tense and words for countries and nationalities. The corresponding section from the Student's Book is shown in Materials extract 1.B. The activities are focused on language forms and the teacher takes a dominant role in what is a largely teacher-fronted classroom. However, the final part of the sequence sees the class moving into pairwork with a corresponding change in the teacher's role.

Using a framework suggested by Harmer (1991), it is possible to identify the teacher in a number of roles in this lesson: as *controller* in eliciting nationality words; as *assessor* of accuracy as students try to pronounce the words; as *corrector* of pronunciation; as *organizer* in *giving instructions* for the pairwork, *initiating* it, *monitoring* it, and *organizing feedback*; as *prompter* while students are working together; and as *resource* if students need help with words and

Materials extract 1.A

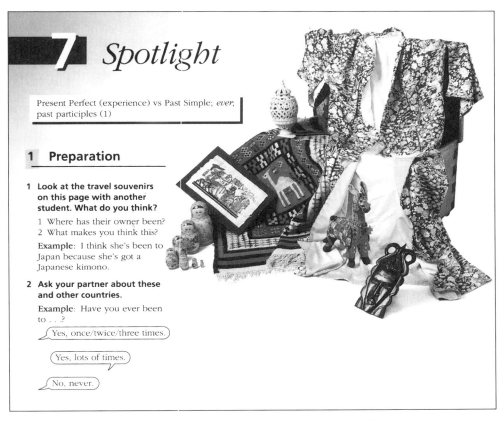

(Mohamed and Aklam: *The Pre-intermediate Choice* SB, page 40)

structures during the pairwork. Harmer's framework deals exclusively with roles that relate to classroom procedures. Other frameworks include categories which move beyond the immediate pedagogic concerns of getting the learning task done into areas much influenced by attitudes in the social and cultural environment.

A study undertaken with a multicultural group of experienced teachers (Karavas-Dukas 1995) from widely differing worldwide contexts and representing a variety of teaching approaches, asked them what roles they performed as teachers. The list below shows the role categories that emerged and the percentage of teachers who mentioned functions pertaining to a particular category. As can be seen most clearly in category 1, teachers had different labels to describe the same or similar roles. However, what is noticeable here is a general balance among the four main categories of source of expertise, management roles, source of advice, and facilitator of learning.

Materials extract 1.B

1 Preparation

AIMS

- To revise and practise the use of the Present Perfect, +/– *ever*, to talk about experiences.
- To revise a variety of country and nationality words.

1 Students say which countries they think the owner of the travel souvenirs has been to.

Possible answers

I think she has been to Russia because she has got some Russian dolls.
I think she has been to Africa because she has got an African mask.
I think she has been to Egypt because she has got an Egyptian papyrus.
I think she has been to Tunisia because she has got a Tunisian pottery lamp.
I think she has been to Libya because she has got a Libyan carpet.
I think she has been to Pakistan because she has got a Pakistani horse.

NB There is also an Ecuadorian parrot on the page.

Refer students to the travel souvenirs and ask them to name them open-class. Elicit nationality adjective with the object. If students have problems pronouncing the nationality words, this is the time to correct them. As you do so highlight shifting word-stress on country and nationality words. (Ja'pan vs Japan'ese, 'Egypt vs E'gyptian and 'Ecuador vs Ecua'dorian.)
    Elicit the example sentence from their book by asking an individual student which country they think the owner of the kimono has been to.
    Get students to repeat the example sentence, stressing the country in the first part of the sentence and the name of the object in the second part eg. I think she's been to *Russia* because she's got some Russian *dolls*.
    Put students in pairs to make similar sentences about other objects before checking open-class.

(Mohamed and Aklam: *The Pre-intermediate Choice* SB, page 58)

1 **Source of Expertise** (46.4%)
1.1 Denoting authoritarian stance?
Instructor

Presenter
Actor
Pedagogist

1.2 Denoting supportive stance?
Informant

Input provider
Information provider
Resource
Source of knowledge

2 **Management roles** (35.7%)
Manager
Organizer
Director
Administrator
Public relations officer
Arranger

3 **Source of advice** (53.5%)
Counsellor
Advisor
Personal tutor
Psychologist
Listener

4 **Facilitator of learning** (64.2%)
Learning facilitator
Helper
Guide

5 **Sharing roles** (17.8%)
Negotiator
Participant
Student

Catalyst to group discussion   Cooperator
Prompter
Mediator

6 **Caring roles** (25%)   7 **Creator of classroom**
                                         atmosphere (14.2%)
Friend   Entertainer
Sister/mother   Motivator
Caretaker   Source of inspiration
Supporter

8 **Evaluator** (10.7%)   9 **Example of behaviour and**
                                         hard work (3.5%)

(Karavas-Dukas 1995)

It seems that a large number of the teachers perceived a need to fulfil the general roles of instructor, organizer, counsellor, and helper and, indeed, these are common to a range of classroom methods. However, as well as being partly dependent on personality or particular method, the precise interpretation of these functions would also be to some extent socially and culturally dependent. In a setting where the teacher is afforded high status, is an authority figure, and remains at some distance from students, prompter might well refer to prompting the individual student with a display question to respond in a typical classroom sequence of initiation→response→feedback, for example:

Teacher What's Peter's job, Marianne?
Student He's a … [*pause*]
Teacher Yes, he's a car …
Student mechanic … he's a car mechanic.
Teacher Yes, good.

On the other hand, in a setting where the teacher is perceived as a more equal partner in the learning process, and where teacher and students participate jointly in activities, as in writing conferences, *prompter* could refer to the teacher's role in helping a student to remember and formulate a point, as in the following extract:

Teacher Do you remember how we described Mr Birling's character
             yesterday? We said he was …
Student Yes, he was a hypocrite, he was unfeeling, cold …

The potential problem for teachers, when experiencing change in methodology and in the roles they need to perform, lies in the precise circumstances in which they need to perform them. In the first example above, the teacher remains at the front of the class, in control and responsible for learner activity. In the second example, the teacher has given responsibility to groups of students for their own activity and has sat down with a group in the course of circulating to monitor and help.

It is when there is a tension between the requirements of the learning task for teacher behaviour and cultural expectations of what is appropriate teacher behaviour that problems can arise for both teachers and learners. For a teacher to move successfully from functioning traditionally as prompter in the first situation above to functioning successfully in the second situation may require far more than a simple change in methodology. It may require a change in self-perception. And for the students to accept that a teacher sits with them as they work together in class requires a corresponding change in their perceptions of authority and responsibility. This may be particularly the case with secondary-school classes where authority entails discipline.

Research in recent years has attempted to investigate the responsibilities of the teacher in terms of providing effective teaching, though the concept of effectiveness in relation to teaching is quite complex. Many teachers would list careful planning of a coherent pedagogic process as a necessary dimension of teacher competence. Indeed, research in education supports this belief by suggesting that effective teaching pays attention to creating a logical sequence of activities in a lesson, with clear aims and clear links. In terms of lesson planning, this means achieving a balance between a 'magical mystery tour' and 'It's Thursday, this must be Venice'. With regard to the latter, every teacher trainer has a version of a typical lesson extract from an over-structured lesson. Here is one of an anxious trainee doing a 'warm-up' to include revision of the past simple tense, and concerned to keep to the five minutes allocated in her plan:

> **Teacher** And what did you do in the summer, Sven?
> **Sven**   I went to my summer house in the country.
> **Teacher** Very nice. And what did you do, Gunilla?
> **Gunilla** My husband and I … we went to Rhodos for the sun.
> **Teacher** Mm, it's lovely there. And how about you, Bo?
> **Bo**   I came a Buddhist and spent the summer in a monastery in Tibet.
> **Teacher** … *be*came, Bo. Say after me … became … Good. Mai Brit, tell us what you did.

Over-precise timing can result in teaching the lesson but not necessarily the students.

The field of educational management has much to say about planning and what are considered to be the characteristics of an effective plan. For example, Everard and Morris (1985) suggest the following: it is purposeful, task specific, temporal, integrated, adaptable, and cost-effective. It is interesting to review these characteristics in terms of effective lesson planning. If we applied them to lesson planning, the following features could be derived:

– The learning activities are clearly linked to prioritized aims for the lesson.
– The types of activity are clearly identified and the learner and teacher roles associated with them.
– Times are specified but timing is monitored for its appropriateness as the lesson proceeds.
– The activities are interdependent in seeking to achieve the aims of the lesson.
– The plan allows for flexibility and contingency in adapting to the emerging needs of the students and to the unexpected event.
– The plan is economical in terms of time and energy spent on input and output.

These features can be observed in the lesson plan overleaf. This teacher has decided that it is useful to write in the interactions as a check on her planning, that she has an appropriate variety in pace, in intensity of learning load, and in the balance between input and practice. Her timings are approximate. In practice, she found the students needed less time to formulate their sentences and she was therefore able to build in more time for feedback.

Another aspect of teaching competence is the ability to manage activities and interactions successfully in the sense that learners know what they need to do and why they are doing it, are motivated to work actively, are monitored and guided when help is needed, and can work undisturbed by discipline problems. The management of interaction needs care and subtlety, as reflected in this teacher's views of groupwork:

> I think monitoring of any group activity has to be done very subtly and there are a number of points to look for. I think, when the group work starts initially, one has to allow each group to gather its own momentum. One cannot go to a group and say, for example, 'Right, you've got this, this and this to do', and then you try and push them at a rate which is faster than they are capable of going at the beginning. So, at the initial stages of group work I tend to stand back and let each group gather its own momentum. If at any time I see a group is stuck, then I go in as quietly and unobtrusively as possible and I try to encourage them by asking a few stimulating questions, what I hope are stimulating questions, which will get their minds working on the right track.
> (Cauldwell 1983: 27)

As this aspect of classroom management looms large as a concern of trainee and novice teachers, it is quite common to find suggestions for self-help composed by tutors, as in the checklist on page 33 for teachers of multilingual adult classes.

Lesson plan

The students

A group of 20 adult intermediate students, of mixed nationalities and languages, studying 8 hours part-time per week in a UK private language school. They have all studied English formally at school and need to apply their knowledge in communication. The class is 50 minutes in duration.

Aims

Functional: making deductions about the past
Structural: *might/could/must have* + past participle
                 perhaps, certainly
Phonological: weak form of *have* in the structure *might have had*
Skills: main focus on oral skills

Aids and materials

Blackboard
Magazine pictures of more and less open-ended situations, mounted on card, e.g.:
– a very happy young man reading a letter
– an elderly woman in black, weeping
– police with guns outside a shop
– children in sportswear holding a prize

Procedures	Interactions	Approx. timing
1 Show the students a picture and ask: What's the situation? What do you think has happened? Elicit suggestions, e.g.: *Perhaps he's passed his exams.* *Perhaps he's got a new job.*	T ⟷ class	5 minutes
Then ask students if they know another way of saying the same thing and elicit: *He might have/ could have …*	T ⟷ individual SS	
2 Do choral and individual practice with the class emphasizing the weak form of *have.*	T ⟷ class	5 minutes
3 Show a second picture, asking the same questions as with the first, and elicit, e.g.: *They've certainly won the match.* *They must have won the cup.*	T ⟷ class T ⟷ individual SS	5 minutes
4 Do choral and individual practice, continuing focus on pronunciation.	T ⟷ class	5 minutes

5 Ask concept questions, e.g.: Which question form is more sure? What part of the verb are *passed, won*?	T ⟷ class	1 minute
6 Ask the students to form pairs. Give each pair some more pictures and ask them to make as many deductions as they can. They should write a list for each picture. Go round the class monitoring, providing vocabulary where needed, and checking the work.	S ⟷ S T ⟷ pairs SS	10–15 minutes
7 Ask each pair to show the class their pictures in turn and to tell each other their deductions. Encourage cross-class questioning. Write any uncertain vocabulary on the board for later review.	Pairs SS ⟷ class	10–15 minutes
8 Ask the students to find similar magazine pictures, write sentences about them, and bring them to class.	T ⟷ class	3 minutes

- Try writing down your instructions for the activity in full in your lesson notes and make them clear and concise.
- When you plan your lesson, make decisions about group size and where groups can be located in the classroom.
- Plan the composition of groups according to levels of proficiency, friendship, and mix of first languages.
- Prepare how to explain the rationale for the activity to your students.
- Ask one group to demonstrate part of the activity, if this is possible, before dividing the class.
- Give students time to ask for clarification.
- Ask students to repeat your instructions in the class, and elicit from them the stages they will go through.

It is evident from the Teacher's Book for *The Pre-intermediate Choice* (Materials extract 1.A), and from the lesson plan above, and also from teachers' and tutors' concerns, that planning, managing interactions, monitoring learning, giving instructions, and giving feedback are the teacher's main responsibilities. These will be revisited in forthcoming chapters as we look in detail at the teaching of particular areas of language. What, then, we may ask, are the reciprocal roles and responsibilities of the learners?

1.5.2 *The learner's roles and responsibilities*

The lesson plan on pages 32–33 shows a set of aims and a sequence of activities designed by the teacher as a means to fulfil those aims. The teacher is clear about the purposes of various activities, but to what extent are the learners? The question of a possible mismatch between teachers and learners in their perceptions of the aims and outcomes of classroom activities has been one focus of recent research. For example, Block (1994) collected oral diary accounts from six of fourteen students and from their teacher in an EFL class which met daily for two-and-a-half hours over a period of a month. By posing a set of questions as guidelines for their accounts, for example 'What were the activities which most stood out in today's class?'; 'What do you think was the purpose of these activities?' (ibid.: 475) he collected data which suggested that teachers and learners were 'operating to different systems for describing and attributing purpose to tasks' (ibid.: 473). In particular, an activity which the teacher seemed to view as routine, as a way of surviving the first part of the lesson, was taken up seriously by learners, who perceived it as valuable and in line with their needs and who engaged with it to achieve useful outcomes. One issue arising from this study is whether teaching is more effective when teachers and learners share the same purpose in approaching an activity and, if so, how shared perceptions can be achieved.

Such issues are at the heart of recent debate about learner-centred ELT, a concept which has been defined from several different perspectives. One perspective, which applies usefully to situations in which adult learners can specify discernible needs for learning English, is that of asking learners to contribute to the overall design of course content and the selection of learning procedures. This would go some way to preventing the kind of discrepancy in goals and perceptions that Block discovered. Suitable learner groups for this approach would be adult migrants or students entering higher education in English-medium institutions.

A second perspective on learner-centredness is that of learners contributing to the design of language learning activities (Clarke 1989b), an idea which would certainly ensure that the purposes of classroom activities were well understood. The idea has been taken up by Campbell and Kryszewska who describe it as 'learner-based' teaching and state its main principle as being 'that all class activities can be done using information that the learners themselves bring to class' (1992: 5). Such information can involve, for example, texts which learners find and for which they design reading activities.

A third perspective on learner-centredness is that of encouraging learners to take on a greater degree of responsibility for their own successful learning, not only by contributing to course or activity design in the ways described above, but also by continuing their learning outside class, at home, or in self-access facilities. The teacher's reciprocal responsibility is to ensure that learners have effective strategies for planning, performing, and monitoring their independent learning.

However, the perspective which is perhaps most commonly understood and practised, is that of using a methodology which allows learners greater control over the learning process. Classroom observation suggests that motivated learners wish to do this anyway. The following transcript shows a class finding their own way through the problems with which an activity presents them and obliging the teacher to go along with them. The class are dealing with a jigsaw reading activity (see 2.4.2) in which three newspaper articles are read, each by different students, and each containing different pieces of information about an incident, as well as a common account. Students then form groups to piece the full information together. The teacher has just given careful instructions for the task.

Teacher	OK. Let's start.
Yu	Is it … necessary … to write note when we read? Can we speak … without …
Ke	Yes, we must do this.
Teacher	Well, it will … um … help … you can write notes for each heading … see … Who? Where? When? … and so on. Then you can add other information you hear later.
Ao	So we have … full facts.
Yu	But can I write later when I listen?
Teacher	Do what you think is most helpful for you. OK?
Hir	What is 'outcome'?
Teacher	Can someone explain?
Ki	What happened after.
Ta	Next.
Teacher	Yes, what happened next … the result, yes? OK everyone?
Ao	What is this 'petty'?
Hid	How much … how many words do we …

(Author's data)

The teacher here seems to accept a need to relinquish control over the discourse, to let learners take over for a while, in order to get out of the activity what is most important to them. The example begs the interesting question of the extent to which teachers make available to learners opportunities to interact throughout a class in ways which assist their comprehension. Some classrooms are noticeable for the constant buzz of speaking as learners ask for clarification from the teacher and from each other.

These four perspectives on learner-centred teaching suggest a far wider range of roles for the learner than those performed in a traditional, teacher-dominated classroom. In contributing to course design, learners can research their needs, negotiate content, and help to monitor the progress of the course. In contributing to activity design, learners can explore and experiment. In developing more independent approaches, learners can plan, initiate, and organize their own work. And in a classroom where participation is high and its nature flexible, learners can question, clarify, suggest, and comment.

However, the degree to which any of these four perspectives can be taken up and explored in classrooms will depend on those factors we have investigated: factors to do with contextual constraints, with perceived roles and responsibilities of the teacher, with learner disposition and cultural expectations of classroom behaviour, with culturally influenced learning styles, and with motivations for learning English.

1.6 What roles can learning materials play?

Closely related to the roles of teachers and learners is the role of textbook materials. Any textbook is based on assumptions about learning, and the design of its activities implies certain roles for teachers and learners and assumes certain dispositions towards learning styles. In the early 1980s Allwright (1981) and O'Neill (1982) debated the role of learning materials in articles entitled respectively 'What do you want teaching materials for?' and 'Why use textbooks?' Allwright suggests that the use of textbook materials places emphasis on the *teaching* process perhaps at the expense of emphasis on the *learning* process, and that this may lead to 'teacher overload' and 'learner underinvolvement'. The logical outcome of an emphasis on learning, he argues, would be learning guides for students. There was little evidence of these in publisher's catalogues at his time of writing but some years later there was evidence of moves in the direction he advocated. For example, the excellent book by Ellis and Sinclair (1989) discussed in Chapter 3 is a move towards filling the gap; there is increasing inclusion of material to guide learners in some current textbooks as reported in survey reviews by Sinclair and Ellis (1992) and Lake (1997), and the development of institutional resources for self-access learning provides learners with opportunities for managing the course of learning themselves.

However, the revolution in the role of resources for learning that Allwright advocated can really only be described as a gradual and partial evolution of alternative roles. Perhaps the reasons for this lie in the benefits of textbook materials as outlined by O'Neill: they can offer a grammatical and functional framework which provides for the common needs of a group of learners; they allow students to prepare in advance; they provide quality of presentation, and they do not necessarily prevent a creative spinning-off in the classroom into all kinds of other activities.

The debate inevitably continues as it is at the heart of teachers' professional concerns. The content and quality of textbooks will determine the extent to which teachers can make use of insights from research into learning and learners. A group of teachers who were asked for their views of the potential and the limitations of textbooks offered the following: their comments reflect some of the points raised by Allwright and O'Neill:

> 'I've tried in recent years to encourage my students to work more independently and one of the ways they can do this, given that we don't have self-access resources here, is to prepare and preview a unit of the coursebook before we do it in class and then to go over it again when we've finished.'

> 'I tried last year to negotiate content as much as possible, but it was very, very hard work to find the relevant materials as we went along. In the second term we chose a coursebook together and added to it. The students said they appreciated following the sequence of the book. There was a grammatical syllabus in the map of the book and I think this fitted with their expectations of learning a language. It seemed to reassure them.'

> 'We have a dynamic head who is keen on in-service training and we've been working on Friday afternoons to develop some film-related materials. I've learned a lot about two things in particular: one was how to motivate pupils by challenging them to think and the other was how difficult it is to write clear instructions.'

> 'I don't really have an option. I teach nine to four every day and I need textbooks to survive. But we do have a member of staff with responsibility for building a bank of materials from things like our home-made handouts so we can share resources. It doesn't work that well yet. It's not easy to use other people's work, but the texts and leaflets people contribute are useful. One of my colleagues has put sets of photos in and they're good for groupwork.'

(Author's data)

The practical constraints outlined by the last teacher are an undeniable fact of life in many institutions and arguments about the relative merits of using commercial materials or not are academic to many teachers. They see their responsibility as choosing the most appropriate textbooks available for their classes. It is the enlightened head of department or director of studies who tries to facilitate professional development in staff by promoting opportunities for in-house materials design in teams. In any case, teachers need to build awareness of what teaching resources provide and of the care that needs to be taken in selecting and exploiting them.

Detailed criteria for selecting and evaluating textbooks are discussed in Chapter 10, but it is worth taking up one important aspect in this introductory chapter. This is the question of cultural content in materials, and the values and attitudes inherent in this. A number of writers in recent years (Valdes 1986; Byram 1989; Phillipson 1990) have reviewed the complex relationships that exist between language learning, language teaching, and culture, and some have focused specifically on the implications of using the target language culture as the vehicle for presenting the language in textbook materials (Adaskou, Britten, and Fahsi 1990; Alptekin 1993). It is commonplace for materials published in a particular English-speaking culture to use that culture as a setting for stories and dialogues. One of the reasons often given for this is the link between language and culture, a link expressed in discussions on the nature of language. For example, Wright Mills (1972) writes:

> Language, socially built and maintained, embodies ... social evaluations. ... A vocabulary is not merely a string of words; immanent within it are societal textures—institutional and political coordinates. (Wright Mills 1972: 62)

Indeed, given this link, where the stated aim of a school curriculum is to widen cultural horizons and increase understanding of other peoples and ways of life, it might be appropriate to teach English by embedding it in its cultural base, whether this be Canada, Australia, India, South Africa, Nigeria, the USA, or Britain, to name but a few. However, it is equally important to be aware of the dangers of cultural stereotyping.

Adaskou et al. (1990), while undertaking a textbook design project for secondary English in Morocco, developed a useful framework for making decisions about the cultural content of materials. They distinguish four meanings of the word 'culture', which are as follows:

- *The aesthetic sense*: by this they mean the art, literature, music, media, etc. to be found in English-speaking cultures.
- *The sociological sense*: by this they mean what has often been called 'life and institutions', that is, the nature of family life, work, leisure, customs, etc.
- *The semantic sense*: this relates to the points made by Wright Mills (1972) about the conceptual system embodied in the language.
- *The sociolinguistic sense*: by this they mean such things as politeness conventions, the ways in which language is governed by issues of status or age in relationships, and familiarity with rhetorical conventions in formal and informal letters, reports, and other written genres.

It could be argued that the last two meanings are inevitable elements in ELT materials, but decisions could be taken as to how explicit instruction should be when conventions differ between cultures. Inclusion of the first two meanings is optional, and teachers will need to take this into account when assessing a given textbook against the aims of a course or the needs or motivations of learners. Further to this, one criterion for evaluating a book would be whether the picture it presents of the foreign language culture avoids stereotyping and gives an accurate reflection of the variety of people, lifestyles, settings, politics, and points of view that one 'culture' can encompass.

1.7 Conclusion

This chapter set out to discuss some of the fundamental issues which affect our professional practice in ELT, and which are under constant review by researchers into second language acquisition, by theory builders in the disciplines of applied linguistics, and by teams of teachers working to formulate policies and practices for their own institutions. Good teachers have always taken a positively critical approach to appraising and developing their work, using what insights are available from their own and others' experience, and from the possible implications of research, especially from studies which are based in the language classroom. It is one of the ways in which we create our own continuing professional development.

One issue which this chapter has not addressed is: What exactly is it that we learn when we learn a second or foreign language? Or, to put it another way, what do we need to learn in order to be a proficient user of another language? This has been a focus of substantial discussion in our profession especially with the increasing use of communicative approaches and interactive classroom methodologies. It is to these questions that the next chapter turns.

Discussion topics and projects

1 Review two or three English language textbooks in use in your institution and investigate the motivations they give learners for learning English, both explicitly as set out in their stated aims and implicitly, such as in the content of the material.

2 At the beginning of teaching a course with a new group of adolescent or adult students, what kinds of activity could you engage them in to:
   (a) find out their reasons for learning English?
   (b) motivate them towards their language learning task?

3 Does your institution have a policy for classroom methodology? If so, what is its source (for example, national guidelines, institutional policy document, procedures derived from in-service training of the staff)? What are the main principles of the methodology? What assumptions about language learning do you think they reflect?

4 How important are the explicit teaching of grammar, pronunciation, and vocabulary in your own classes?

5 A group of teachers on an in-service training course listed the following as the most important qualities a teacher needs to have:
   – sense of humour
   – self-confidence
   – sensitivity to learners as people
   – ability to build rapport
   – ability to be methodical.

Do you agree that all these are important? Would you add any others?

6 The text below presents a set of 'hopes' about the roles and responsibilities of teachers and learners. If you were to present a similar credo, what would you include?

What I hope for in a classroom

Students

1 I hope to find the students involved in whatever they are doing, contributing to it and getting satisfaction from it on many levels of personality.

That is to say, I hope *not* to find them concentrating on merely coming up with correct responses (even in a structure drill), or on grinding out correct sentences or free conversations just for the sake of grinding out correct sentences or free conversations.

2 I hope to find the students comfortable and relaxed, even in the midst of intense intellectual activity or vigorous argument.

2 (a) This does *not* mean that they are loafing on the job. In fact, students who are really comfortable with what they are doing are less likely to loaf. (b) This also means that the students are not apprehensive that they will be punished if they fail to live up to the teacher's expectations.

3 I hope to find that the students are listening to one another, and not just to the teacher. I also hope that they will be getting help and correction from one another, and not just from the teacher.

3 This means that the students are *not* like separate lamps plugged into a single power supply, in such a way that the power used by one diminishes the voltage available to the rest.

Teacher

4 The teacher is in general control of what is going on.

4 This does *not* mean that everything the students do comes as a direct response to a specific cue from the teacher.

5 The teacher allows/ encourages/requires originality from students, whether in individual sentences, or in larger units of activity, or in choice among a range of techniques.

5 This does *not* mean anarchy or chaos.

6 One of the first things I notice is whether the teacher seems relaxed and matter-of-fact in voice and manner, giving information about the appropriateness or correctness of what the students do rather than criticizing or praising them.

6 The teacher does *not*, either by word or by unspoken message, say to students, 'Now always remember …,' 'You shouldn't have forgotten …,' 'You are a good/poor student,' or 'Now try to do this so that I may judge you on it.'

(Stevick 1976: 159–60)

7 Look again at the dimensions of culture suggested by Adaskou et al. (1990) (see page 38). Evaluate a textbook in terms of those aspects of culture it includes.

Further reading

Lightbown, P. and **N. Spada.** 1999. *How Languages are Learned* (Second edition). Oxford: Oxford University Press.

This book is a useful introduction to second language acquisition. It presents a clear overview of various theories of acquisition and issues arising from these. The authors also consider factors of individual difference in learners such as age, personality, learning styles, and motivation. The implications of the theories, issues, and factors for classroom teachers are then taken up and discussed.

McKay, S. L. 1992. *Teaching English Overseas: An Introduction.* Oxford: Oxford University Press.

The intended audience for this book is the native-speaker teacher of English who is planning to work overseas, but its usefulness is by no means restricted to this type of reader. The author looks at how factors in the teaching and learning situation influence classroom teachers in their work. In Part One she considers in turn social, political, economic, and cultural factors. In Part Two she discusses the structure of educational systems and institutions. The book is illustrated with case studies and contains many practical suggestions for dealing with the professional issues arising from contextual factors.

Skehan, P. 1989. *Individual Differences in Second Language Learning.* London: Edward Arnold.

The book usefully reviews research up to 1989 into the ways in which learners differ from one another. It investigates the dimensions of language aptitude, motivation, language learning strategies, and affective and cognitive influences. The author draws conclusions about the possible role of these factors in the building of theories of second language acquisition.

Wright, T. 1987. *Roles of Teachers and Learners.* Oxford: Oxford University Press.

The main aim of this book is to explore the roles that teachers and learners can play in the classroom and the factors which influence teacher-learner relationships. It also comments usefully on the role of materials in the classroom. The discussion is illustrated with analysis of a wide range of learning tasks and materials. The final section provides the teacher with ideas for personal classroom investigation and interpretation.

2 THE COMMUNICATIVE CLASSROOM

*'Words are the Peoples: yet there is a choise of them to be made. ...
They are to be chose according to the persons wee make speake, or
the things wee speake of. Some are of the Campe, some of the
Councellboard, some of the Shop, some of the Sheepe-coat, some of
the Pulpit, some of the Barre, &c. And herein is seene their
Elegance, and Propriety, when wee use them fitly ...'*
BEN JONSON

1 What are the components of communicative language
  ability?

2 Is communicative language ability a realistic goal for the
  English language classroom?

3 What are the issues for the communicative curriculum?

4 What are communicative tasks and what role do they have
  in learning and teaching?

5 How can we manage a communicative classroom?

6 What does communicative language teaching imply for
  authenticity in the classroom?

7 If we teach communicatively, what does this imply for
  testing?

8 What are the issues in applying a communicative approach
  in context?

Introductory task

Consider Materials extract 2.A.

1 Do you see this as a communicative task?

2 What criteria did you use to arrive at your decision?

Materials extract 2.A

VIII-I   PICTURE DIALOGUE GAME

Unit VIII / FUN AND GAMES / Level: Low intermediate / Time: 20 minutes

Language function(s): writing dialogues
Materials: large pictures each showing two people talking
In class

1 Bring in six to ten pictures, each one showing two people talking, and put them up at the front of the class. Make sure that all the students can see them clearly.

2 Arrange the students in pairs and ask each pair to choose one of the pictures to use as the basis of a short dialogue. The rest of the group should not know which pictures have been chosen. Give the students three or four minutes to write down what they think the two people in the picture are saying. Circulate, checking that the language is correct and helping as necessary.

3 Ask the pairs to read or, better still, act out their dialogues, each partner taking one role while the rest of the class tries to guess which picture has been chosen. Whenever possible, the students should justify their guesses.

(Sion (ed.): *Recipes for Tired Teachers*, page 94)

2.1 Introduction: the concept of communicative language ability

The ability to communicate effectively in English is now a well-established goal in ELT. It is by no means the only possible goal as we saw with the survey of Japanese students' reasons for studying English in 1.3.4. However, many adults can identify personal needs to communicate in spoken and written English and many schoolchildren are aware of future needs for international communication and mobility. Even in contexts where it is harder to see future purposes for English language communication among schoolchildren, it is often nevertheless thought to be sensible to build potential for this.

A brief review of statements from syllabus specifications and introductions to coursebooks will demonstrate the extent to which communicative ability has become a goal and communicative practice has become part of classroom procedure.

> To be able to operate effectively in the real world, students need plenty of opportunity to practise language in situations which

encourage them to communicate their needs, ideas and opinions.
(Abbs and Freebairn: *Blueprint Intermediate*, page 1)

To develop an ever improving capability to use English
    to communicate with others
    to acquire, develop and apply knowledge
    to think and solve problems
    to respond and give expression to experience;
and within these contexts, to develop and apply an ever-increasing
understanding of how English is organized, used and learned.
(Clark, Scarino, and Brownell 1994: 37)

Where possible, language practice should resemble real life
communication with genuine exchange of information and opinions.
(Swan and Walter 1990: vii)

Note that reference is made here to both spoken and written English, to
producing as well as receiving language. The communicative movement in
ELT encompasses all modes of language use. It has, as one of its bases, a
concept of what it means to know a language and to be able to put that
knowledge to use in communicating with people in a variety of settings and
situations. One of the earliest terms for this concept was *communicative
competence* (Hymes 1972). In coining the term, Hymes demonstrated a shift
of emphasis among linguists, away from a narrow focus on language as a
formal system, a focus most clearly seen in the work of Chomsky (1965) who
used the term 'competence' to describe knowledge of language:

We thus make a fundamental distinction between *competence* (the
speaker–hearer's knowledge of the language), and *performance*, the
actual use of the language in concrete situations.
(Chomsky 1965: 4)

For Hymes, adding the 'communicative' element to 'competence' meant
adding:

… rules of use without which the rules of grammar would be useless.
Just as rules of syntax can control aspects of phonology, and just as
rules of semantics perhaps control aspects of syntax, so rules of speech
acts enter as a controlling factor for linguistic form as a whole.
(Hymes 1972: 278)

Hymes, as a sociolinguist, was concerned with the social and cultural
knowledge which speakers need in order to understand and use linguistic
forms. His view, therefore, encompassed not only knowledge but also ability
to put that knowledge into use in communication, and for that reason other
terms thought to be more effective in describing what it means to know and
to be able to use language knowledge have developed. One of these is

Bachman's (1990) *communicative language ability*, and this will be used in this chapter.

Hymes's work proved to be of substantial influence among English language educationists, coinciding as it did with growing dissatisfaction with the predominantly structural approaches to English language teaching in the 1960s and early 1970s. Moreover, other influences were at work in the ELT profession. As the field of English for specific purposes (ESP) developed to meet the professional or academic needs of English language users, course designers had to find ways of analysing real-world tasks in order to identify their communicative demands and to specify these as learning goals. At the same time the Council of Europe, in response to the needs of professional mobility between countries, was setting up a syllabus based on functional and situational views of language. Both movements contributed strongly to the development of 'the communicative classroom'.

As the goals for ELT became more concerned with enabling learners to interact successfully with members of other societies, so the explorations of applied linguists into the components of communicative ability assumed increasing relevance and usefulness to the work of classroom teachers and materials designers. The key components, as identified by a number of researchers (for example, Canale and Swain 1980; Faerch, Haastrup, and Phillipson 1984; Bachman 1990), can be listed as: *linguistic competence*, *pragmatic competence*, *discourse competence*, *strategic competence*, and *fluency*.

We will now explore these inasmuch as they provide insights into the goals and tasks for English language learners, and the issues which arise for teachers.

2.2 What are the components of communicative language ability?

2.2.1 *Linguistic competence*

Linguistic competence is concerned with knowledge of the language itself, its form and meaning. Stern (1983) includes these two aspects in his characterization of what it means to know a language:

> The language user knows the rules governing his native language and he can 'apply' them without paying attention to them.
> (Stern 1983: 342)

> The native speaker has an intuitive grasp of the linguistic, cognitive, affective and sociocultural meanings expressed by language forms. (ibid.: 343)

Thus linguistic competence involves a knowledge of spelling, pronunciation, vocabulary, word formation, grammatical structure, sentence structure, and linguistic semantics. We can judge, then, that a learner who is able to list orally and in writing the objects in a bowl, such as an apple, an orange, two bananas, and a bunch of grapes, is developing the ability to select specific vocabulary and knows its pronunciation and graphic forms. A learner who can add prefixes correctly to 'perfect', 'legal', 'happy', 'pleasing', and 'audible' to make the negative equivalents, is developing competence in using word-formation rules correctly. A learner who can describe recent events by using 'have/has' and the past participle of the main verb is developing grammatical competence in forming the present perfect tense. In these various ways the learner is acquiring linguistic competence in the second language.

An important point for the teacher to note is that linguistic competence is an integral part of communicative competence. As Faerch, Haastrup, and Phillipson point out: 'It is impossible to conceive of a person being communicatively competent without being linguistically competent' (1984: 168). It has perhaps been a misconception about communicative language teaching that it does not aim for a high standard of formal correctness. On the contrary, it is not incompatible to have correctness in the use of rules as an ultimate goal and, at the same time, to tolerate risk-taking and error in the classroom as part of the process of achieving communicative competence.

The role of grammar or formal accuracy has been a major concern in ELT in recent years and teachers need to address a number of issues in designing courses and classroom activities for learners. Acquisition of grammar will probably involve explicit knowledge of grammatical concepts, categories, and rules, and teachers will need to decide which description of these to choose from those available. There is also the question of which procedures for raising awareness of language form and for practising it are most effective: this will be addressed in Chapter 5.

Perhaps the most difficult question to resolve has been how to achieve a balance between 'focused' or 'form-focused' classroom activities which aim at linguistic accuracy and 'unfocused' activities which involve learners in negotiation of meaning and aim at fluency. What might the most appropriate balance of these be in one lesson and to what extent will this be determined by the age, stage of learning, and existing proficiency level of learners? How can these two types of activity be integrated in a lesson or unit of materials? What should the organizing principle be? And how can focused and unfocused activities be balanced and integrated to form a coherent language learning programme over a period of time? These are key issues in ELT and they will be addressed throughout this book.

2.2.2 *Pragmatic competence*

Pragmatic competence is generally considered to involve two kinds of ability. In part it means knowing how to use language in order to achieve certain communicative goals or intentions. This has also been called *illocutionary competence*. An example would be 'It's so hot today.' This statement could have a number of *illocutionary forces*. It might be a statement about the physical atmosphere, a request to open the window, or an attempt to elicit the offer of a cold drink.

Methodology now tries to ensure that learners are given realistic presentations of language in use and its communicative intentions, for example, the present progressive might be presented through a dialogue, such as:

Jack   Hello, Anne, it's Jack here. Can I speak to Robert, please?
Anne   Hi, Jack. Robert's working in the garage at the moment. Can I get him to call you back?
Jack   Sure. Thanks.

Here is a typical situation in which reference is made to someone's actions at the time of speaking, one possible use of the present progressive. The presentation embeds the form in a *context of use*. This is in contrast to the technique many teachers were taught, myself among them, in the days of the structural approach to ELT, that of giving a running commentary while performing actions in the classroom, for example, 'I'm opening the window'; 'I'm closing the door'; 'I'm writing on the blackboard', and so on. Certainly the latter provided the form and its meaning, but the context of use was less than natural.

The present progressive, of course, has a number of functions, as the following examples demonstrate:

He's coming up the steps.
I'm leaving in five minutes.
Sally is always complaining.

The first, if said to one burglar by another on lookout at the window of a house, observing the progress of a policeman towards the scene of their crime, could function as a warning. The second, if said by a parent to dawdling children, could be a reprimand. The third might function as criticism. Students will appreciate, through comparison with their first language, that these pragmatic conditions of use are likely to apply in any language. However, in recent years, the functional approach has attempted to show the varying functional use of language forms by using functions rather than structures as their organizing principle. Some coursebooks arrange content in units entitled, for example, 'Talking about recent events', 'Inviting', or 'Speculating about the future'. In this way, a particular structure such as the present progressive can be revisited in units entitled 'Talking about present actions' (for example, 'She's washing her hair'); 'Talking about the immediate future' (for example, 'They're moving house tomorrow'), or 'Describing current situations' (for example, 'The Prime Minister is trying to defuse the situation').

Thus, one element of pragmatic competence is knowing how to perform a particular function or express an intention clearly. In order for communication to be successful, however, spoken or written messages must also be appropriate to the social context in which they are produced. Learners need to know the appropriate social conventions.

If it is the case that one language form can express a variety of functions, the converse is also true. A function can often be expressed in a variety of ways. Take these two responses to a telephone request:

> If you'd kindly wait a moment, I'll see if he's able to talk to you.
> Hang on a minute, love, and I'll get him.

The first is highly formal and polite and might be said, for example, by a young clerk in a chamber of barristers to an elderly peer of the realm. On the other hand, the second is familiar, and might be said informally by one member of the family to another. The message is identical in both cases but the choice of vocabulary and structure depends on the setting, the relative status of the speakers, and their role-relationship. Some contemporary ELT coursebooks attempt to demonstrate this variation in style. For example, in the case of the set of requests presented in Materials extract 2.B, learners are encouraged to think about the conditions under which each phrase might occur. Through such activities learners build awareness of the relationship between language and the context of its use.

It can be seen, then, that social knowledge is necessary to select the language forms to use in different settings, and with people in different roles and with different status. This has also been called *sociolinguistic competence* (Bachman 1990). It can relate as much to non-verbal as to verbal communication. For example, a person accustomed in their own society to summon a waiter by clicking their fingers would meet with little success in many English-speaking cultures and would probably cause offence. It can also relate to knowing when to speak and when to be silent, or what to say in certain circumstances. Social small talk in some societies, but not in others, might allow guests at a party to ask what other people earn. Part of communicative

Materials extract 2.B

1 Polite formulas

Asking for permission is a type of request.
Grade the formulas below.

*	not very polite
**	polite
***	very polite
****	extremely polite

..... Could I use your phone?
..... Might I possibly use your phone?
..... Sorry to trouble you, but do you mind if
      I use your phone?
..... Would you mind if I used your phone?
..... May I use your phone?
..... I'll use your phone, OK?
..... Can I use your phone?
..... I wonder if I could use your phone.

(Viney and Viney: *Handshake* SB, page 68)

competence in a foreign language is knowing what is appropriate, what is incongruous, and what might cause offence.

In these ways, the sociolinguistic component of pragmatic competence enables a speaker to be 'contextually appropriate' or in Hymes's words, to know 'when to speak, when not, what to talk about with whom, when, where and in what manner' (1972: 277).

2.2.3 *Discourse competence*

Consider the following example. The teacher is asking her English class about the Great Storm of 1987 in Britain:

> **Teacher**   What did the hurricane do?

Of the responses, she commends Student D for a number of reasons.

> **Student A** The hurricane uprooted the trees.
> **Student B** The trees were uprooted.
> **Student C** Hundreds of trees were uprooted by the hurricane.
> **Student D** It uprooted hundreds of trees.

All of these responses are grammatically acceptable, but Students B and C put new information first, and as Widdowson (1978) points out, it is more normally the case in discourse that shared information (about the hurricane) precedes new information (about its effects). Furthermore, Student D uses a reference item, 'It', as a cohesive device to relate the answer to the question and this fits in with the normal pattern of oral discourse. In this way, a unified spoken text is achieved.

Learners of English will need to become aware of how discourse works in terms of the common cohesive devices used in English. These can be demonstrated by working backwards in a conversation (Crystal and Davy 1969) between two speakers in which the final exchanges are:

B Well, it feels healthier, doesn't it?
A Yes.
B And seems healthier …
A Yes.
B The theory is that they distract each other … but that's life, isn't it?
(adapted from Crystal and Davy 1969: 102)

It is immediately apparent that this is taken from an ongoing conversation as the pronouns 'it', 'they', and 'each other' substitute for previous noun phrases or even whole situations described earlier in the conversation. The comparative 'healthier' used in a parallel structure shows both continuity of meaning and development of an earlier suggestion. Interpretation of the topic by a listener who came in at this point would be impossible. The exchanges preceding these give more clues but still the use of 'ones' has to be interpreted.

B … it still tends to be true that most of the best ones are single
    sex …
A Mm …
B As far as I can gather … best in terms of … you know …
A Records to show …
B Yes …
    […]
A I can't see why because I'm convinced that mixed ones are the
    soundest … I mean overall … the soundest …
(adapted from Crystal and Davy 1969: 101, 102)

A culturally aware listener, coming into the conversation here, might be able to interpret that the conversation is about schools, single sex and mixed ones, but many listeners would be lost if they had not heard the conversation from the beginning, where the mention of a single school starts the discussion.

This extract of authentic conversation between native speakers shows three other aspects of competence in conversational use of language: how to perform the turns in discourse; how to maintain the conversation, and how to develop the topic. Second language learners will need to acquire useful language for strategies such as initiating, entering, interrupting, checking, and confirming in conversation. For example, they will need to learn the typical discourse markers which signal the direction of discourse such as 'By the way …' (introducing an incidental remark); 'I'd like to take up an earlier point …' (returning to consider an earlier argument), and 'That's all very well but …' (challenging an argument).

Learners will also need to develop a similar kind of competence for written texts. For example, students reading technical English will have to follow the structure of different types of expository prose such as descriptions of processes, cause–effect analyses, and comparisons of systems. They will need to understand the relationships between the propositions of adjoining sentences and to interpret these relationships through formal devices, as in this example:

> The population is ageing. That is to say, there is a higher percentage of people over the age of sixty than at any time previously this century.

Here, the second sentence is a reformulation of the proposition in the first and serves as an explanation. The connective 'That is to say' links the meaning of the two.

These various abilities needed to create coherent written texts or conversation, and to understand them, have together been termed *discourse competence* (Canale and Swain 1980; Faerch, Haastrup, and Phillipson 1984), or *textual competence* (Bachman 1990).

2.2.4 *Strategic competence*

Canale and Swain define *strategic competence* as 'how to cope in an authentic communicative situation and how to keep the communicative channel open' (1980: 25). Strategic competence consists of using *communication strategies*. These strategies come into play when learners are unable to express what they want to say because they lack the resources to do so successfully. They compensate for this either by changing their original intention or by searching for other means of expression. For example, in this conversation between a native speaker of English and a Swedish student, it is possible to see a number of strategies at work.

Student	Every summer we go for a for … , you know, erm, … *fjorton dagar*, … um … fourteen days … a for … I mean …
Native speaker	Oh, a fortnight.
Student	Yes, a fortnight. We go for a fortnight to our summer stuga.
Native speaker	What's that?

Student	It's a small house in the country. It has, you know, a garden around it … [gestures a circle to show an area of surrounding land]
Native speaker	Oh, like a cottage, a country cottage …

The Swedish student only half remembers the word 'fortnight' and doesn't know the word 'cottage'. In the first instance of 'fortnight' she uses the Swedish word and then gives a literal translation of it, 'fourteen days'. She continues with the paraphrase 'two weeks'. At the same time, she invites co-operation from her listener through the implicit appeal for help in 'you know' and 'I mean'. In the second instance, 'cottage', she code-switches to Swedish first then paraphrases, assisted by gesture, and again appeals for help with 'you know'. In summary, all of her strategies could be termed *achievement strategies*. She perseveres with what she is trying to say and finds ways of compensating for her insecure or inadequate knowledge of English.

This student's efforts can be compared with an example from the classroom. A Spanish student has been asked to make statements of probability to practise 'She might have …', 'She could have …', and 'She must have …' about a picture of a sombre, black clad woman. The student ventures:

> It's a picture of a woman. She … I think she … I think she is at a funeral. Perhaps her son has died. She is very sad.

This might be called a *reduction strategy* as she avoids the forms of which she is uncertain and selects the 'perhaps' structure which she knows.

The above examples demonstrate a number of strategies. Accounts of others can be found in Faerch, Haastrup, and Phillipson (1984) and Ellis (1985). Clearly the advantages of using achievement strategies or taking risks with the language is that they keep the conversation going and may encourage the listener to provide the necessary language. Second language acquisition research suggests that the exposure of learners to language provided at a point of need and in a meaningful context which they have created for themselves in trying to express something is a good situation for acquisition.

The question arising is whether strategic competence can be trained. Certainly teachers can help students early in a language programme by teaching them appropriate questions for requesting help, for example 'What does this mean?' and 'How do you say …?', and the language to ask for vocabulary items, for example 'What do you call a person who …?' and 'What do you call a thing that …?'. The teacher can also act as listener in classroom interaction and respond to students' appeals for help, providing language at the point of need. There is little in current ELT materials, however, to suggest that learners receive much help in how to deal with problems themselves as they try to express themselves in English. Strategy training is an issue which needs to be further addressed in ELT.

2.2.5 *Fluency*

The term 'fluency' relates to language production and it is normally reserved for speech. It is the ability to link units of speech together with facility and without strain or inappropriate slowness, or undue hesitation. Faerch, Haastrup, and Phillipson include fluency as a component of communicative competence and distinguish it from strategic competence in this way:

> Whereas strategic competence presupposes a lack of [accessible] knowledge, fluency covers speakers' ability to make use of whatever linguistic and pragmatic competence they have (Faerch, Haastrup, and Phillipson 1984: 168).

They list three types of fluency:

> *semantic fluency*: linking together propositions and speech acts
> *lexical-syntactic fluency*: linking together syntactic constituents and words
> *articulatory fluency*: linking together speech segments.
> (ibid.: 143)

These types can be appreciated in the following extract from a conversation:

> **A** When will you be taking your driving test?
> **B** The day after my birthday.
> **A** And when's your birthday? Remind me.
> **B** September 27th.

The purpose of A's question is to find out the exact date of B's driving test so that she can send a good luck card. B's answer mistakenly assumes that A knows the date of his birthday. A therefore has to listen, assess that she does not get the information she wants, and formulate another question which will elicit more precise information from which she can deduce the date of the test. This ability to respond coherently within the turns of the conversation, to link the words and phrases of the questions, to pronounce the sounds clearly with appropriate stress and intonation, and to do all of this quickly, in what Johnson (1979) calls 'real time', is what constitutes fluency.

ELT has addressed the issue of how to develop fluency in various ways. Coursebooks in the 1970s often contained fluency drills, but these were aimed solely at increasing the learner's ability to link syntactic segments with ease. For example, the teacher would set up a chain drill and provide each student with a different prompt which they would have to insert in the correct syntactic position, as in:

Students I went to the theatre last night.
Teacher My aunt's house.
Student 1 I went to my aunt's house last night.
Teacher Visited.
Student 2 I visited my aunt's house last night.
Teacher Yesterday.

More recently, teachers have debated whether it is possible to teach gambits to help learners become more fluent, particularly learners who need to use English in their community or in their profession and who need to keep the attention of their listeners. We use gambits in a meeting when we want to hold the floor, for example, 'I'd just like to make another quick point'; to interrupt, for example 'Can I just come in here', or to respond, for example 'I agree with that in part but …'.

The idea of teaching gambits fits well with insights from recent research into what Nattinger (1988) has called 'lexical phrases'. These are items of prefabricated language, learned holistically as chunks, and include not only phrases but clauses and sentences too, as in the examples above. Nattinger suggests that this kind of lexical learning plays a much stronger role in language learning than previously appreciated. The advantage of teaching lexical phrases is that, if they can be retrieved quickly from memory, they will help learners to produce the language more fluently.

Certainly, practice activities in spoken English will need to involve learners in interpreting and assessing the meaning of what they hear and constructing appropriate responses independently of language input from the teacher or textbook. This implies activities in which students will determine the content of what they say in interaction with other students.

2.3 *What are the issues for the communicative curriculum?*

Having considered those aspects of communicative language ability which have been defined and explored over recent years, the question then arises of how the ELT profession has responded to the significant implications for teaching and learning a language. A list of such implications could be formulated as in Table 2.1, though this list is by no means exhaustive and teachers might add to each category items which they feel are of especial importance for their own learners. The remaining sections of this chapter will take up the key implications from this list and others will be considered in the relevant chapters of this book.

Table 2.1: Significant implications of communicative language ability for teaching and learning

If communicative language ability consists of the following …	… what does this imply for language learners?
Linguistic competence	– to achieve accuracy in the grammatical forms of the language – to pronounce the forms accurately – to use stress, rhythm, and intonation to express meaning – to build a range of vocabulary – to learn the script and spelling rules – to achieve accuracy in syntax and word formation.
Pragmatic competence	– to learn the relationship between grammatical forms and functions – to use stress and intonation to express attitude and emotion – to learn the scale of formality – to understand and use emotive tone – to use the pragmatic rules of language – to select language forms appropriate to topic, listener, etc.
Discourse competence	– to take longer turns, use discourse markers, and open and close conversations – to appreciate and be able to produce contextualized written texts in a variety of genres – to be able to use cohesive devices in reading and writing texts – to be able to cope with authentic texts.
Strategic competence	– to be able to take risks in using both spoken and written language – to use a range of communication strategies – to learn the language needed to engage in some of these strategies, e.g. 'What do you call a thing that/person who … '.
Fluency	– to deal with the information gap of real discourse – to process language and respond appropriately with a degree of ease – to be able to respond with reasonable speed in 'real time'.

2.4 What are the implications for the communicative classroom?

2.4.1 *What are communicative tasks and what are their roles in teaching and learning?*

The communicative approach to language teaching is premised on the belief that, if the development of communicative language ability is the goal of classroom learning, then communicative practice must be part of the process. Not everyone would agree with this 'product implies process' argument. There are certainly successful language learners, not least among English language teachers, who have come through an ELT curriculum where the focus has been on a study of the formal system of English and where classroom practice has been less than interactive. However, it is the current orthodoxy demonstrated in learner materials around the world and the debate of recent years has pivoted on the issue of exactly what kind of practice will lead to the development of communicative language ability. Brumfit (1984a), for example, argues for 'natural language use' and suggests the need for what he calls 'fluency activities'. We need to avoid possible confusion here as he uses the term 'fluency' in a different sense from Faerch, Haastrup, and Phillipson (1984). In his definition, fluency activities 'develop a pattern of language interaction within the classroom which is as close as possible to that used by competent performers in the mother tongue in real life' (Brumfit 1984a: 69). He lists a set of criteria necessary for achieving fluency. These have been simultaneously developed and expanded by other writers and can be summarized as follows:

– The language should be a means to an end, i.e. the focus should be on the meaning and not on the form. Other writers have made similar distinctions, for example 'message/medium' (Krashen 1982) and 'unfocused/focused' (Ellis 1982).
– The content should be determined by the learner who is speaking or writing. The learner has to formulate and produce ideas, information, opinions, etc.
– There must be a negotiation of meaning between the speakers, i.e. students must be involved in interpreting a meaning from what they hear and constructing what to say as a response. In other words, they should not be reliant on the teacher or materials to provide the language. This criterion clearly brings into play pragmatic and discourse competences as well as fluency.
– In order for the previous criterion to function, what a learner hears should not be predictable, i.e. there should be an information or opinion gap.

– The normal processes of listening, reading, speaking, and writing will be in play, for example improvising and paraphrasing in speech; in other words, students will practise and develop strategic competence.
– Teacher intervention to correct should be minimal as this distracts from the message.

In Brumfit's view, fluency activities will give students the opportunity to produce and understand items which they have gradually acquired during activities focused on linguistic form, which he calls 'accuracy work'.

Much ELT material has taken up the concept of fluency activities and presents tasks which conform to the criteria above, for example the activity in Materials extract 2.C. The aims of this activity are that in performing this task students' attention would be on the meanings they are trying to express as they think of their list of criteria. They are able to use any language resources they have acquired and are not directed into using particular structures. Members of the group would determine their own contributions and choose appropriate language for expressing ideas and opinions. They would negotiate meaning as they structure group interaction, checking that they have understood, asking for clarification and further explanation, and as they speak they would use communication strategies such as paraphrase and restructuring.

At this point you may wish to review the Introductory task to this chapter and the criteria you developed for a communicative activity. That activity and Klippel's both demonstrate the difficult task for materials designers in providing activities for the communicative classroom. One issue of great interest has been how to create the 'gap' of information or opinion which exists between speakers in the real world, and which creates the unpredictability of normal discourse. What kind of activity requires learners to negotiate meaning? Prabhu (1987) gives a useful typology of activities which have formed the basis of much contemporary material:

1 *Information-gap activity*, which involves a transfer of given information from one person to another—or from one form to another, or from one place to another—generally calling for the decoding or encoding of information from or into language. One example is pair work in which each member of the pair has a part of the total information (for example an incomplete picture) and attempts to convey it verbally to the other. Another example is completing a tabular representation with information available in a given piece of text. The activity often involves selection of relevant information as well, and learners may have to meet criteria of completeness and correctness in making the transfer.

Materials extract 2.C

93 Rescue

Aims	*Skills* – speaking
	Language –stating an opinion, giving and asking for reasons, agreeing and disagreeing, comparisons
	Other – thinking about one's values
Level	Intermediate/advanced
Organisation	Groups of five to eight students
Preparation	None
Time	10–20 minutes
Procedure	*Step 1:* The teacher explains the situation:

'The Earth is doomed. All life is going to perish in two days due to radiation. A spaceship from another solar system lands and offers to rescue twelve people, who could start a new world on an empty planet very much like Earth. Imagine you are the selection committee and you have to decide who may be rescued. Think of a list of criteria which you would use in your decision.'

Step 2: Each group discusses the problem and tries to work out a list.

Step 3: Each group presents its list of criteria to the class. The lists are discussed.

Variations	The task can be made more specific, e.g. 'Find ten criteria. You can award up to 100 points if a candidate gets full marks on all counts, e.g. appearance 5, intelligence 30, fertility 15, physical fitness 20, etc.
Remarks	Although the basic problem is a rather depressing one, it helps students to clarify their own values as regards judging others.

(Klippel: *Keep Talking,* page 104)

2 *Reasoning-gap activity,* which involves deriving some new information from given information through processes of inference, deduction, practical reasoning, or a perception of relationships or patterns. One example is working out a teacher's timetable on the basis of given class timetables. Another is deciding what course of action is best (for example cheapest or quickest) for a given purpose and within given constraints. The activity necessarily involves comprehending and conveying information, as an information-gap activity, but the information to be conveyed is not identical with that initially comprehended. There is a piece of reasoning which connects the two.

3 *Opinion-gap activity,* which involves identifying and articulating a personal preference, feeling, or attitude in response to a given situation. One example is story completion; another is taking part in the discussion of a social issue. The activity may involve using factual information and

formulating arguments to justify one's opinion, but there is no objective procedure for demonstrating outcomes as right or wrong, and no reason to expect the same outcome from different individuals or on different occasions.
(Prabhu 1987: 46–7)

You might review the activities in this chapter, and others in coursebooks, to find examples of each type.

The introduction of such activities into ELT has generated creative materials in all four modes of language use: listening, speaking, reading, and writing. It has also generated a number of issues which are the focus of current debate. The fundamental issue is how learners actually use the activities they are provided with in order to acquire language, and whether different ways of exploiting activities provide different opportunities for learning. Skehan (1996), for example, has pointed out that in performing a task under time pressure, learners may place greater emphasis on communicating messages in order to complete the task quickly and may not therefore pay much attention to correctness and completeness of language form. They may use communication strategies or string lexical phrases together to express ideas. Negotiation of meaning in such tasks will provide for the development of greater strategic competence and fluency, as described in 2.2, but will not necessarily lead to more comprehensible output and the development of greater accuracy. There is a danger, in fact, that learners may develop what Skehan calls 'undesirable fluency' (ibid., page 49) with the use of convenient but incorrect forms which they then make use of in other tasks.

We need, then, to ask the question, what will help learners to become more accurate? For example, if we take away the time pressure in a task like the one in Materials extract 2.C and give learners a chance to prepare the content of what they are going to say, they may focus more on correct expression. Alternatively, an opportunity to focus on form may be provided after the communicative task if students are recorded and then try to compare their own language for justifying the criteria with forms the teacher gives them. Similarly, in writing classes there is the useful technique of reformulation where the teacher rewrites one student's text after the class has completed a common writing task, following the ideas closely but improving the language. The class compares the two versions, discussing reasons for the changes made. In this case, learners have a chance to notice differences between their own use of language forms and those of the teacher, and can pay attention to the correct forms. This provides opportunities for intake and the further development of the learners' interlanguage systems. It is therefore possible, in the case of using a cycle of preparatory and follow-up tasks, to create a balance between accuracy and fluency activity.

An understanding of how learners use tasks can inform our decision-making about how to incorporate them into a language teaching programme. There is an argument that a series of tasks can usefully provide the basis of a programme, in which case their selection, organization, and sequencing will need to create opportunities for a focus on accuracy and input into the interlanguage system as well as fluency. Alternatively, many teachers and textbook writers see communicative tasks as an essential ingredient in a programme but as part of a balanced diet of accuracy and fluency work. Brumfit (1984a), for example, sees these as co-existing but suggests that the balance would change over time. His suggestion is that one might expect to find a preponderance of accuracy-based work early on, for beginners, but that there would be a gradual shift in emphasis as learners acquire more language and that upper-intermediate learners might be involved for a high proportion of class time in fluency work.

The issue of exactly how we might create a link between the two is still the subject of much debate. Clearly, it raises questions about the role of grammar and other elements of the formal language system in the communicative classroom. As suggested earlier, linguistic competence is a fundamental component of communicative language ability and it has perhaps been a misconception among teachers that the communicative approach somehow excuses teachers and learners from a consideration of how to develop high levels of accuracy in the use of grammar, pronunciation, and vocabulary. On the contrary, it is rather a question of how to develop communicative language ability through classroom practice but, at the same time, to ensure an understanding of how language works as a system and to develop an ability to use the system correctly, appropriately, and creatively.

Teachers and textbook designers have been preoccupied with how to integrate input on language form, rehearsal of language form, and communicative practice. The 'Presentation, Practice, and Production' (PPP) approach was one attempt to achieve integration. At the presentation stage, the teacher presents a new language item, described functionally to help learners to appreciate its communicative purpose. This can be seen in Materials extract 5.D (page 165) where learners are presented with the future with 'going to' in the context of making holiday plans. The practice stage involves controlled work focused on conditional forms as students write questions for a quiz, and the production phase aims to set up a situation in which the structure would naturally occur, as in the discussion of future government policy. Unfortunately, it has been the experience of many teachers that it is very difficult to control the language which can occur naturally in such activities. Students will use whatever language resources they have at their command and may use reduction strategies to avoid using any forms they are uncertain of. Directing their attention to the form in efforts to persuade them to practise it while they are focused on the messages they are trying to communicate to their peers is distracting and counter-productive in terms of fluency. Various alternatives to the PPP approach have been suggested in the attempt to deal with the issue of integration and will be taken up in Chapter 10.

2.4.2 *How can we manage a communicative classroom?*

As we have seen, many communicative tasks involve learners in face-to-face encounters in the classroom. Interaction in work in small groups, as discussed in 1.2.3, provides a basis for language acquisition. It also gives students practice in communicating and negotiating meanings in establish-ing positive rapport, in maintaining a conversation with appropriate turntaking conventions and, at the same time, allows them to establish how well they can understand and make themselves understood. In lessons where reading and writing are the focus of communicative activity, work in small groups also has substantial value. For example, if students collaborate while revising drafts of writing, they can suggest improvements, correct errors, and generally act as editors while reading each other's work.

Teachers will need to consider carefully the demands made on learners by participation in this type of interaction, and to be aware of the socio-psychological factors which influence learner responses to those demands. Adults returning to English language study after experiencing traditional teacher-fronted classrooms at school can be daunted by the collaborative element of learning. There are implications here for talking about methodology, discussing its rationale, negotiating procedures, and introducing unfamiliar activities gradually.

Building cohesiveness within the group is clearly an important managerial role for the teacher. It can be at least partially achieved through attention to seating arrangements, through a progressive introduction of interaction activities from simple pairwork on a short task to more complex role-play activities, through training learners in peer feedback, and through careful management of group size.

The composition of groups is another consideration, one which assumes increasing importance as groupwork moves into the kind of teamwork required for projects or for the preparation of complex simulations. Here the teacher will need to make decisions about whether to allocate roles within the group such as chair, scribe, spokesperson, and timekeeper, or whether to let members of the group decide these among themselves. Insights are available from work in professions other than ELT where the dynamics of groupwork need careful thought. For example, it is generally acknowledged that each group will pass through a number of stages in which members discover the personalities of colleagues, organize themselves, argue about working methods and/or authority within the group, settle down into cohesiveness, and begin to perform usefully. These stages have been called 'forming', 'storming', 'norming', and 'performing' (Tuckman and Jensen 1977). One issue for the teacher is whether to keep the same groups together over a period of time on a course to allow the process of group formation to be successfully completed. Another issue is whether this process can be facilitated simply by using ice-breaking activities at the beginning of a course as groups form. An alternative would be to invite learners, after tasks have been completed, to review the procedures they have used and to improve on them.

Another perception suggests that, for a group to be effective in completing a task, it needs at least one member who is interested in keeping the group on task and achieving a useful outcome, and one member who will be interested in maintaining good relationships within the group. This will ensure that a variety of functions are catered for; those which assist the task such as suggesting ideas or asking for opinions and those which build cohesiveness such as drawing in quieter members or making compromises between different points of view (Johnson and Johnson 1987; Jacques 1991). Further issues for the teacher, then, are how to select group members and how to raise awareness of the need to perform these roles, and what kind of language might be needed. In many professional fields it is now standard practice to train for groupwork and similar ideas are being taken up in ELT.

A communicative classroom also involves the teacher in a wider range of roles beyond that of providing and presenting new language. A good deal of time will be spent on managing learning: setting up activities, organizing material resources, guiding students in groupwork, encouraging contributions, monitoring activities, and diagnosing the further needs of students. The range of roles can be demonstrated by analysing the stages of groupwork in the jigsaw reading and discussion activity in Materials extract 2.D. Notice that at stages 3 and 5 in Table 2.2, while monitoring groupwork, the teacher acts as guide to performing the task successfully; as a language resource providing words and forms at the point of need; as corrector of key errors heard as the students work together; and as diagnoser of the students' strengths and weaknesses.

Materials extract 2.D

Figure 33 Jigsaw procedure

Card for Group A

Fri. 1st Aug

Dear Mum and Dad,
We arrived this morning at a very nice camp site. It is between the railway and the road, but it is quiet. There are only two trains a day, and not much traffic! From our tent we can see the Barton rail bridge, with Barton behind it, then the mountains. It's a lovely view.
x x Sue

Mr. & Mrs. Smith
13, Belmont Drive
Reading RG9 7BD

Card for Group B

Dear Annie,   Sun 3rd Aug
We are camping next to a mountain. It's very nice but in the early morning the whole camp site is in the shade of this mountain! It's called the Grey Mountain. Yesterday we climbed to the top, and had a lovely view of Barton and the River Maddock to the north. See you soon (we're leaving tomorrow)   Sue

Annie Williams
3 Green Lane
Reading RG1 7ZF

Card for Group C

Mon 4/8

Dear Mum and Dad,
We left our camp site just outside Lugwill this morning, and have arrived in Barton, the next village north. We came by bus over the Maddock Bridge. It was a very nice journey. Last Saturday we went on a long walk, but yesterday we sun-bathed. The weather's lovely.
Hope you are well
Love
Liz

Mr. and Mrs Gunner
21 Humbledown Road
Reading RG19 2ZQ

WORKSHEET
Part One
Read your copy of the postcard and:
  1 Label as much of the map as you can.

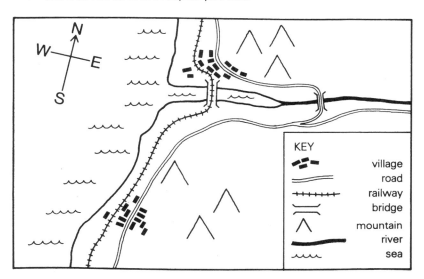

KEY

	village
	road
	railway
	bridge
	mountain
	river
	sea

2   Fill in as much of the table as you can.

Date	What did the girls do?
Friday 1st August	
Saturday 2nd August	
Sunday 3rd August	
Monday 4th August	

3   Think of a possible place for the girls' camp site, but do not mark it on your map yet.

Part Two
1   Form new groups with at least one person from groups A, B and C and exchange your information. You can then label more of your map and complete the table.
2   Discuss the possible position of the camp site and mark it on your map.

(Williams: *Reading in the Language Classroom*, pages 116, 118)

Table 2.2: Analysis of the stages of groupwork in the activity in Materials extract 2.D

Stages of the task	Learner activity	Teacher's role
1 Teacher explains task and invites questions	Students listen and ask questions to clarify	Manager of activity
2 Teacher organizes students into groups	Students move into groups	Classroom organizer
3 Students work in groups to read postcard, etc.	– Individual reading – Checking meaning with peers – Discussion of information – Decisions about map and table	Guide Language resource Corrector of errors Monitor Diagnoser
4 Teacher organizes students into triads, each of the three members having read a different postcard	Students move into new groups	Classroom organizer
5 Students exchange information	– Each student reports – Students complete maps and tables – Students discuss location of campsite	Guide Language resource Corrector of errors Monitor Diagnoser
6 Class and teacher check	Students give feedback as the teacher elicits	Corrector of errors Evaluator

It is not surprising that some teachers feel intimidated by the demands of their task within the communicative classroom. Dubin and Olshtain (1986) have likened it to that of a stage director:

> Just as the theater director plays a pivotal role in sustaining the fiction of a stage drama, so the teacher/director uses the classroom stage to simulate the real world. …

> On a human level, the director makes personal connections between the scenario and each of the players, helping each one to understand the script, and interpreting parts that are unclear. The director, too, provides strong psychological support by being an individual and a group morale booster.
> (Dubin and Olshtain 1986: 81)

Teachers need to build competence and confidence in fulfilling these various roles, and in-service training is necessary within institutions to ensure that, in any moves towards implementing communicative approaches in the classroom, teachers are properly supported.

All of this is not to suggest that current methodology, influenced by ideas about the 'learner-centred' classroom, promotes learner responsibility at the expense of teacher authority. Whatever the moves in recent years towards placing greater responsibility upon learners and encouraging their independence, adult learners who choose to work with other students in language classes place themselves within the authority of teachers, and institutions require accountability from their staff. The teacher remains the ultimate organizer of activity, the one who must ensure positive learning outcomes for students, the one accountable to any external authority involved, and the arbiter of standards. Widdowson (1987) takes this view when he writes:

> The increase in learner-centred activity and collaborative work in the classroom does not mean that the teacher becomes less authoritative. He or she still has to contrive the required enabling conditions for learning, has still to monitor and guide progress. And all this presupposes an expertise, applied perhaps with more subtlety and consideration and discretion than before, but applied none the less. (Widdowson 1987: 87)

2.4.3 *What does communicative language teaching imply for authenticity in the classroom?*

With communicative language teaching has come pressure to use authentic materials, in other words, materials which have not been designed especially for language learners and which therefore do not have contrived or simplified language. The argument is quite simply that if the goal of teaching is to equip students to deal ultimately with the authentic language of the real world, they should be given opportunities to cope with this in the classroom. It has been argued that contrived listening texts, in particular, have characteristics which in no way approximate to real spoken language. This is discussed in greater detail in 7.3.5. If students hear only unnatural language in the classroom, their first experience of hearing authentic spoken English in the real world can be demoralizing. The classroom, it is argued, can provide supported conditions of learning in which authentic texts can gradually be introduced and exploited in ways which build confidence.

Communicative methodology has displayed an increasing tendency to use authentic materials in relation to listening and reading skills. A brief review of contemporary coursebooks at the intermediate level shows the following range:

Listening   radio plays, news items, childrens' stories, travel news, weather forecasts, airport and station announcements, radio talks, debates, extracts from recorded guided tours, relaxation tapes, exercise instructions, interviews

Reading   letters, recipes, menus, newspaper articles, train timetables, horoscopes, advertisements, publicity brochures, postcards, street maps, route maps, yearbook entries, weather forecasts, curricula vitae, theatre programmes, poems, instructions for use of equipment.

Speaking and writing activities can also be referred to as authentic if they reflect the relevant criteria for task design discussed earlier (see 2.4.1) and also mirror the real-world purposes and situations in which and for which language is used. For example, writing tasks which reflect reasons for writing outside the English language classroom might include the following:

– a note to a neighbour apologizing for a noisy party
– a letter of complaint about a product to the manufacturer
– a notice to fellow students publicizing a meeting
– an invitation to a birthday party with directions for how to get there.

The use of authentic materials for work on the receptive skills of reading and listening has been surrounded by controversy. On the one hand, writers like Grellet (1981) advocate the use of texts in which nothing has been changed. On the other, many teachers would argue that the needs of learners at lower levels of proficiency demand the use of 'simulated-authentic' materials. These emulate original materials, but are contrived in some way to assist the learner. For example, the overall structure of a comparison/contrast argument can be highlighted by adding connectives such as 'whereas', 'while', 'on the contrary', 'on the other hand', and 'in comparison'. Presenting learners—for whom the building of confidence is all important—with texts which they can approach successfully is seen as the common-sense approach. It is a question of providing texts which are authentic to the needs of learners, ones with which they can interact. Widdowson (1979b), for example, argues that authenticity can only be achieved when the reader can interpret the intentions of the writer and respond appropriately to them. His argument has implications not only for the language level of the text but for the prior knowledge a learner will bring to reading or listening to it, and whether that knowledge will be sufficient for successful interpretation. For example, a learner with a passion for cars may well make sense of a book on car maintenance written at a level of English above that of his own proficiency simply because he has a good prior knowledge of the topic. On the other hand, as an English language advisor once commented to me, there is little to be gained from presenting schoolchildren in rural Mexico with a map of the London underground system and expecting them to make sense of a task to find their way from one point on it to another.

The keys to approaching a text successfully lie in the relevance of the text to the learners, its interest, the experience they can bring to making sense of it, and the appropriacy of the task required. Quite difficult texts can be made accessible through simple but appropriate tasks. For example, a weather forecast from a national newspaper might be used as part of a project with lower-intermediate students visiting the UK. They could be asked to check the forecast for the area in which they are staying and use the information to plan some weekend activities. This would approximate to the authentic purpose of reading a weather report. To give the same students a traditional set of comprehension questions about the weather forecast in order to practise weather vocabulary or structural patterns would be both inauthentic and probably above their language level.

The selection of authentic texts will, of course, depend on the particular needs of the learners in view. Pre-sessional courses for overseas students will ideally confront students with genuine texts of the type they will shortly have to deal with independently in their undergraduate studies. Preparatory courses for summer visitors to English-speaking countries can usefully present a range of authentic texts and tasks related to the role of tourist abroad. For secondary-school students of English, the scope of whose future opportunities to use the language in real-life contexts is uncertain, it is possible to argue for building 'communicative potential', but only through the judicious choice and exploitation of texts which are 'authentic' in the ways described above.

2.5 What are the issues in applying a communicative approach in context?

Particular attention has been paid in recent years to the cultural appropriacy of the communicative approach (Holliday 1994; Kramsch and Sullivan 1996) as its goals and procedures have been imported into non-western cultures. 'Cultural appropriacy' is a term which is relevant to both institutions such as schools and the wider society which forms their context. For example, a school culture of teacher-centred classrooms with a focus on the transmission of knowledge will have been influenced in part by wider cultural notions of the teacher's authority as expert and leader.

Studies of innovation suggest that it is rarely successful unless a set of factors have been carefully addressed: for example, the degree of compatibility between the existing teaching philosophy and the innovation; teachers' perceptions of its relevance to students' needs; the availability of resources for the innovation; the extent of agreement between the classroom procedures of the new approach and the existing way in which teachers conduct classroom activities, and the relative advantages of the innovation. All of these factors will influence the extent to which a communicative approach is adopted by teachers and the ways in which it is adjusted.

For example, in Rufino's account of his teaching situation at the beginning of Chapter 1, project work clearly fits with his perceptions of the value of learner-centred teaching and with his view of the needs of this age group to develop responsibility. He is able to relate project work to the real world outside the classroom and sees advantages in this as English is a useful language within the European community, which his pupils may wish to travel and work in. Project work is also manageable within the constraints of class size and the demands of the examination system. The picture might be very different in Bangladesh or Botswana, for example.

The question of teacher confidence is also relevant to the argument of appropriacy. The adoption of a communicative approach holds substantial implications for the knowledge and skills of teachers. Medgyes, for example, comments on the heavy linguistic demands made by communicative language teaching on non-native teachers whose energy is 'inevitably used up in the constant struggle with their own language deficiencies, leaving only a small fraction for attending to their students' problems' (1986: 112). His argument is essentially for restraint in introducing communicative language teaching to non-native teachers, selecting the more moderate ideas for materials and methodology and being cautious with the more far-fetched. The interpretation of what is moderate and what is far-fetched can only really be made with reference to the factors relating to innovation discussed above as they apply to a particular local context.

In many countries, the implications of the discussion so far are rather more relevant to educational authorities than to the individual teacher, who may be working with prescribed textbooks and with imposed and inspected classroom procedures. However, there is evidence to suggest that teachers who have more freedom in decision-making and who see value in a communicative approach, either because its goals coincide with their learners' needs or because they see value in the kinds of activities it offers, can adjust the approach to suit their own circumstances.

Sano, Takahashi, and Yoneyama (1984), to quote one instance, have argued that in Japanese secondary-school classrooms the need to use English is not strongly felt because it does not have an extensive role in Japanese society. For this reason, teachers have redirected their communicative goals towards self-expression and personal growth in students rather than towards authentic communicative needs in the world outside the classroom.

> By regarding the classroom as a small community and emphasizing the *subjective* side of human communication, we can provide classroom experiences which involve both learning English and general human development.
> (Sano, Takahashi, and Yoneyama 1984: 176)

Kramsch and Sullivan (1996) give a further example of how the cultural tradition in Vietnam of students forming 'family groups' with peers in their classes at university has had its own effect on the use of groupwork. Teachers and students using communicative materials such as the *Headway* course will adapt the methodology advocated in creative ways to suit their need to work collaboratively but as a whole class. These examples show how teachers and learners have found an optimal match between communicative goals and procedures, and their own context. They provide interesting argument and support for locally generated methodology.

2.6 Conclusion

Communicative language teaching sets out to involve learners in purposeful tasks which are embedded in meaningful contexts and which reflect and rehearse language as it is used authentically in the world outside the classroom. It holds many attractions, not only to those teachers and learners who are preparing for immediate needs in using English but also for a wider population of teachers and learners who are motivated by realistic language practice, by the personalization of learning, by face-to-face encounters in the classroom, and by using their prior knowledge and heuristic skills to approach a wide range of texts and tasks.

However, there are matters of concern to be addressed. One is to do with our need for better understanding of what learners do with communicative tasks and what kinds of learning are available from different types of exploitation of tasks. Another is to do with what is appropriate for different levels of learner. At what point should learners be involved in tasks which encourage them to take risks and negotiate meaning? Should the basic building blocks of the language be learned within the more 'secure' environment of a structural approach in a largely teacher-directed classroom? What is the role of form-focused instruction at different levels of the English language curriculum?

A further concern is to do with the concept of 'communicative' materials, the meaning of authenticity, and the issues involved in the choice of listening and reading texts, the choice of tasks to match texts and, indeed, the choice of language to express common functions in the English language. A brief review of coursebooks in current use would show that these issues are better understood by some writers than others, particularly in the area of matching task to text.

And, last but not least, there is the issue of whether a communicative approach is appropriate to local contexts and cultures, and how it might be adapted and used by teachers and learners in relevant ways.

These issues are at the forefront of professional debate and need to be resolved in sensible ways by teachers who wish to make their own classrooms more communicative. They will be revisited in further chapters of this book as we consider some of the prevailing classroom procedures within a communicative approach in the light of insights available from research, evaluation, and experience.

Discussion topics and projects

1 Imagine a context in which each of these utterances would be appropriate. Think about a possible setting, who is talking to whom, and what their relationship is, for example, family member, friend, or stranger.
   (a) Will you be passing the post office?
   (b) Lend us a fiver, will you?
   (c) I wonder if it would be too much trouble for you to lift my bag down for me?
   (d) 'Well, I *really* never,' said the large and growly bear to himself. 'There must be *someone* I can frighten.' And so he went growling and prowling, looking for someone to frighten.
   (e) Johnny, why are you playing with that ruler?

2 How many structures can you think of to express these functions?
   (a) suggesting a course of action
   (b) agreeing with an opinion
   (c) requesting an action
   (d) asking permission to do something

3 Look back at the characteristics of a communicative task in 2.4.1. Choose some activities in a textbook you are currently using and, against the given criteria, judge whether these are communicative.

4 Look back at Prabhu's descriptions for three types of meaning-focused activity in the classroom in 2.4.1. Check through a coursebook in current use and find examples of each one.

5 Dörnyei and Thurrell (1991) give the following suggestions for teaching two aspects of strategic competence. Would you use these with your own learners? Can you think of other ways of training strategic competence?

> *Paraphrase and circumlocution: Definitions*
> In pairs, students are given the name of an object (e.g. car) which they must define by using a relative clause (e.g. 'A car is a vehicle in which you can travel'). Each pair in turn reads out their definition, while the other pairs check whether it is precise enough. If it is not—that is, if they can find another object that the definition suits (e.g. 'bus' in this case) they get a point, and for another point they must give a more specific definition (e.g. 'A car is a small vehicle in which you can travel'). Of course, this new definition is also open to debate.
>
> *Appealing for help: Interruptions*
> Student 1 (S1) reads out a text from the course book; Student 2 (S2) interrupts S1, asking him/her to repeat a word again, for example:
> > S1 London is the capital … .
> > S2 Sorry, can you repeat this last word again …
> > *or* Sorry, I couldn't hear the word after 'the' …
> (Dörnyei and Thurrell 1991: 21, 22)

6 The following reasons are often given for using pairwork and groupwork in the communicative classroom. Do you agree with these? Would you add any from your own experience? What do you think are the disadvantages of pairwork and work in small groups. Would you place any conditions on their successful use in the classroom?

(a) It motivates students to work in face to face encounters in the classroom.
(b) It increases opportunities for practising the language.
(c) It enables students to take risks with the language and to see if they can negotiate meaning.
(d) It gives students the opportunity to monitor how well they understand and are understood.

Further reading

Clarke, D. 1989b. 'Communicative theory and its influence on materials production.' *Language Teaching* 22/2: 73–86.

This 'state of the art' article looks at how the development of a communicative approach to language teaching in the 1970s led to the production of new materials to express the new ideas of language learning. In particular, the author focuses on the authenticity debate and discusses the needs of learners, the importance of context in materials, the appropriacy of task to text, and the authenticity of task to learner.

Nunan, D. 1989a. *Designing Tasks for the Communicative Classroom.* Cambridge: Cambridge University Press.

This book gives an introduction to both theoretical and practical aspects of task design and is useful to teachers who wish to develop their own classroom materials. It covers the range of skills and considers the roles that teachers and learners can play in the performance of a classroom task. It also looks at criteria which could be used for grading tasks to form a coherent language programme.

Richards, J. C. and **T. S. Rodgers.** 1986. Chapter 5 'Communicative language teaching' in J. C. Richards and T. S. Rodgers (eds.): *Approaches and Methods in Language Teaching.* Cambridge: Cambridge University Press.

This is a clear, concise introduction to what is meant by communicative language teaching. The writers give a brief historical background to its development and investigate the theories of language and learning which underly the approach. They then consider a series of issues: the nature of a communicative syllabus; types of classroom activity; teacher and learner roles; the role of materials, and classroom management procedures.

Savignon, S. 1993. 'Communicative language teaching: state of the art' in S. Silberstein (ed.): *State of the Art TESOL Essays.* Alexandria, Va.: TESOL.

This paper reviews the development of communicative language teaching and then looks at current issues of concern, such as the place of grammar, and possible future trends. The review takes an international perspective and refers to many different sources of influence and contexts of learning.

3 LEARNER AUTONOMY AND LEARNER TRAINING

'If a teacher is indeed wise he does not bid you enter the house of his wisdom, but rather leads you to the threshold of your own mind.'
KAHLIL GIBRAN

1 What do we know about the strategies of the good language learner?

2 What insights can we gain from educational thinking on autonomous learning?

3 What are the implications for learner training in the classroom?

4 What role can self-access facilities play in language learning?

5 Are learner autonomy and learner training universally appropriate concepts?

Introductory task

The task below is intended for use at the beginning of a course. It could be undertaken in English with students from an intermediate level of language proficiency upwards, or in the first language with students at lower levels.

1 What do you think are the aims of the task?

2 What sort of learners do you think it would be suitable for?

3 What would be a sensible procedure for its classroom use?

A In your textbook find:
- the past tense of the verb 'to fly'
- what we use the past tense for
- how to ask questions about the weather
- how to ask about someone's health
- how to pronounce the word 'tomato'.

B Do you expect the textbook to:
- teach you?
- contain all the language you need?

- be a starting point?
- provide exercises?
- provide grammar?
- be a dictionary?
- be open throughout your lessons?
- be the only material you use?
- give your teacher all he/she needs?
- give you ways of assessing your progress?
- enable you to prepare new lessons in advance?
- summarize everything you learn so that you can revise at home?

3.1 Introduction: the self-directed learner

During a course in the late 1970s, I asked a group of English language teachers from around the world to define what the term 'self-directed learning' meant for them. At the time very little had been published specifically in ELT literature on aspects of learner autonomy or learner training. Their definitions ranged from the tentative: 'It means letting students choose their own topics and activities for homework', to the passionate: 'It means students' emancipation from the hands of teachers', and to the reflective: 'A self-directed learner is one who is self-motivated, one who takes the initiative, one who has a clear idea of what he wants to learn, and one who has his own plan for pursuing and achieving his goal.' In fact, from the definitions offered by this group and others in the intervening years, it is possible to build a picture of teachers' perceptions of the self-directed learner. Self-directed learners:

- 'know their needs and work productively with the teacher towards the achievement of their objectives'
- 'learn both inside and outside the classroom'
- 'can take classroom-based material and can build on it'
- 'know how to use resources independently'
- 'learn with active thinking'
- 'adjust their learning strategies when necessary to improve learning'
- 'manage and divide the time in learning properly'
- 'don't think the teacher is a god who can give them ability to master the language'.

In these definitions the teachers begin to provide some key characteristics of a learner who can take responsibility for learning: an ability to define one's own objectives; awareness of how to use language materials effectively; careful organization of time for learning, and active development of learning strategies. Many of these characteristics accord with the descriptions of the 'good language learner' which have been derived from research studies.

Since the late 1980s we have seen a proliferation of terms relating to this concept of self-directed learning: autonomous learning, self-monitoring, self-assessment, learner strategies, self-help learning strategies, strategic investment, learner training, self-study, self-access learning. The key concepts that have emerged, however, and around which others pivot, are those of *learner autonomy* (which for our purposes can be taken as synonymous with self-directed learning) as a goal for learners, and *learner training*, or the teacher's encouragement of their efforts towards that goal.

Ideas about learner autonomy and learner training have come to the ELT profession through two major sources of influence: insights from research studies into second language acquisition, and educational thinking of the last few decades.

3.2 What do we know about the strategies of the 'good language learner'?

3.2.1 *Types of learner strategy*

One set of arguments for encouraging greater independence in language learners comes from research studies into the characteristics of the 'good language learner'. It is interesting that in recent years the intuitions of experienced language teachers about what makes for a successful learner have been backed up by the findings of research into learner strategies. Rubin defines learner strategies as including:

> any set of operations, steps, plans, routines used by the learner to facilitate the obtaining, storage, retrieval and use of information, ... that is, what learners *do* to learn and *do to regulate* their learning. (Rubin 1987: 19)

A simple way of distinguishing between these is to say that what learners do to learn involves strategies that deal directly with the second language (*cognitive strategies*) and what learners do to *regulate* their learning involves strategies that manage learning (*metacognitive strategies*). For the language teacher, the issue is whether it is possible to help learners acquire and develop strategies of either kind which will enhance their ability to learn inside or outside the classroom.

Cognitive strategies

Cognitive strategies are thought processes used directly in learning which enable learners to deal with the information presented in tasks and materials by working on it in different ways. For example, this extract from a learner's diary shows her using analogy in order to distinguish the meanings of verbs in German:

> Today I learned the distinction between 'wissen' and 'kennen', i.e. 'to know'. I was pleased to discover that, because of doing French ('savoir' and 'connaître') I was able to understand the point quite well.

Analogy can be seen as part of the more general strategy of deductive reasoning (Rubin 1987), that is, looking for rules in the second language on the basis of existing knowledge about language.

Another cognitive strategy is memorization. This learner, for example, (Pickett 1978) finds that both visual and auditory memory are important:

> Visual: Shape of the word as a visual form, whether printed or hand written is memorised. I find that some words are memorised in print and some in handwriting, usually but not always my own.
>
> Auditory: The sound of the item reverberates somehow in the mind even though silently; or it may be assisted by subliminal tongue movements ...

(Pickett 1978: 110)

Examples of other cognitive strategies are repetition (i.e. imitating a model), writing things down, and inferencing (i.e. making guesses about the form or meaning of a new language item). Thus, a learner might guess the meaning of 'drawer' in the sentence 'He kept the papers safely in a locked drawer of the desk.' Several clues would help: the adjective–noun relationship between 'locked' and 'drawer'; the meaning link with 'safely', and the learner would almost certainly have knowledge about the structure of desks and the nature of drawers in them.

Metacognitive strategies

Metacognitive strategies involve planning for learning, thinking about learning and how to make it effective, self-monitoring during learning, and evaluation of how successful learning has been after working on language in some way. So, when learners preview the next unit of their coursebook, read carefully through the teacher's comments on their written work, or review the notes they have made during class, they are using metacognitive strategies.

Communication strategies

A further category sometimes included in frameworks of learner strategies is that of *communication strategies*. When learners use gesture, mime, synonyms, paraphrases, and cognate words from their first language to make themselves understood and to maintain a conversation, despite the gaps in their knowledge of the second language, they are using communication strategies. The value of these is that they keep learners involved in conversations through which they practise the language. There are examples of some of these strategies in action in 2.2.4.

Socio-affective strategies

A fourth category is that of *socio-affective strategies*, in other words those which provide learners with opportunities for practice. Examples include initiating conversations with native speakers, using other people as informants about the language, collaborating on tasks, listening to the radio or watching TV programmes in the language, or spending extra time in the language laboratory.

3.2.2 *Research into learner strategies*

Investigations into learner strategies are not without their problems. Early researchers acknowledged that observation of learners yielded insufficient information and consequently they used interviewing techniques to try to elicit retrospective descriptions of language learning experiences. More recently there has been a growing interest in using learners' introspective accounts of their learning, as in the examples quoted in 3.2.1. However, learner reports can only investigate conscious strategies and research in this field still needs an effective methodology.

There are additional problems for teachers wishing to investigate the literature on learner strategies. For example, there has been a proliferation of labels for strategies, such as 'language processing strategies', 'tactics', 'plans', and 'techniques', with no easy equivalences among them. Also, since the early studies (Naiman, Fröhlich, Stern, and Todesco 1978) into the characteristics of the good language learner, different research studies have identified different strategies and ways of categorizing strategies, so a variety of frameworks has developed, for example Ellis (1985); Oxford (1990), and O'Malley, Chamot, and Kupper (1995).

However, research into learner strategies has made an important contribution to the field of ELT by highlighting the possibility of learners becoming more self-reliant in their learning, and by generating discussion of how learners can be trained to take on more responsibility for their learning. Much of the research has tried to establish whether it is possible to facilitate learning through the use of certain strategies, or whether learners can modify their strategies and learn new, more effective ones.

An example of one such study was undertaken with seventy-five high-school students enrolled in ESL classes in the US to examine the effectiveness of strategy training (O'Malley and Chamot 1989). The students were allocated to one of three teaching groups on a random basis, each group consisting of eight to ten students. As part of the study, students were asked to present a brief oral report on a subject of personal or cultural significance. Each student prepared four reports in class and presented them on four separate occasions. Taped presentations were judged on a scale of one to five against criteria of delivery (volume and pace), appropriateness (of words and phrases), accuracy (of phonology, syntax, and meaning) and organization (coherence and cohesion).

The first group of students worked on the task as they normally would with no strategy training. A second group received training in the use of a meta-cognitive strategy termed 'functional planning' which entailed analysing the structure of an oral report and working out the language required. They also received training in the socio-affective strategy of co-operation by practising their presentations with peers who provided feedback on aspects of the reports which related to the criteria ultimately used by the judges. A third group received only this latter type of training in co-operation.

The results suggested that skills in speaking were clearly improved through strategy training and, as both the second and third groups improved relative to the untrained group, it seems that both the planning strategy and the evaluation activity in the co-operative strategy were influential.

A second example was a study undertaken by Carrell, Pharis, and Liberto (1989) with twenty-six ESL students of mixed first language backgrounds. This investigated the value of two training techniques, semantic mapping and experience–text–relationship (ETR) in pre-reading. In semantic mapping, the students usually brainstorm associations with the topic of the text they are about to read, and the teacher writes these on the board. The teacher then helps students to categorize the associations into a 'word net' on the board (see 4.4.1 for examples of this activity). The ETR method consists of three stages: discussion of student experiences that relate to the topic of the text; reading the text; and the drawing out of relationships between the students' previous experiences and the content of the text. There is no visual element in this method. The value of both activities pedagogically is that they activate the prior knowledge that students possess of the topic and bring associated vocabulary into their minds so that they begin reading with both knowledge and language to facilitate their comprehension.

In the experiment, one group of students underwent training in the semantic mapping technique and another underwent training in the ETR technique. A third group received no training. The groups were pre-tested and post-tested on their ability to answer multiple choice comprehension questions, to complete partially constructed maps of the topics of three texts, and to create their own semantic maps. The researchers also thought it useful to include a measure of learning style (see Chapter 1) in the testing as they anticipated 'a potential interaction between the students' own ... learning styles and the two training treatments' (ibid.: 661). The three research questions posed were:

> 'Does metacognitive strategy training enhance L2 [second-language] reading?' If so, 'Does one type of strategy training facilitate L2 reading better than another?' 'How is the effectiveness of metacognitive strategy training related to the learning styles of the students?'
> (ibid.: 647)

The testing procedures used in experiments of this type are difficult, but the general results suggested that the use of both techniques enhanced the second-language reading of the students involved as compared with the group that received no training. There were also interesting results concerning the relationship between individual learning styles and the two types of training which suggested, as mentioned in 1.3.2, that we need to have much more information on this aspect of learning.

It would be mistaken to suggest that small-scale studies such as these provide sufficient evidence for the efficacy of strategy training. We need many more such studies to assess the usefulness of different techniques for strategy training. Useful ideas are now available for helping students to apply direct and indirect strategies in learning English but further experimental work is needed to test out which of these applications seem to lead to improved learning.

Nevertheless, insights into learner strategies coming from such studies have contributed to ELT methodology in raising awareness about the characteristics of effective language learning. Materials extract 3.A demonstrates the way in which such information is appearing in textbooks and can be used to encourage teachers to think about their learners.

As we gradually gain possession of useful ideas about strategy training, we will hopefully be able to make more informed decisions about how to help students develop effective strategies for learning.

Materials extract 3.A

> Bear in mind at all stages of the course what the theorists tell us are the characteristics of a good learner. He/she is:
>
> – confident in his/her ability to learn
> – self-reliant
> – motivated and enthusiastic
> – aware of why he/she wants to learn
> – unafraid of making mistakes, and
> – unafraid of what he/she doesn't know
> – a good risk-taker
> – a good guesser
> – probably positive in his/her attitude to English language and culture
> – a good pattern perceiver
> – prepared to look for opportunities to come into contact with the language
> – willing to assume a certain responsibility for his/her own learning.
>
> No student will possess all these virtues! The list is given for you to encourage your students as much as possible at every stage of the course.

(Soars and Soars: *Headway Upper Intermediate* TB, page vii)

3.3 What insights can we gain from educational thinking on autonomous learning?

The other major source of ideas about learner autonomy in ELT circles has been educational thinking, where the concept of self-determination has been the focus of debate for many years. In common with other, much-quoted terms we have already listed, 'self-determination' suggests that the individual learner can reflect, make choices, and arrive at personally constructed decisions. Barrow and Woods, in their discussion of concepts in educational philosophy, describe self-determination as involving 'the notion of thinking in the sense of reflecting, calculating, memorizing, predicting, judging and deciding' (1988: 98). This implies that learners should not be passive recipients of knowledge but should use their abilities for 'judging' and 'deciding' to take on more responsibility for their own learning.

Societies which value independence of thought and action may view the self-determining person as a desirable end result of education. It has often been said that democratic societies protect their ideals through an educational process which has as its goal not only the acquisition of knowledge and skills but also the development of independent and responsible people. However, some educationists within democratic societies have questioned whether this goal has been or can be achieved through a classroom process in which the role of the teacher has traditionally been to instruct, transmit, regulate, and assess, and that of the learner has been to receive and absorb. Is there a mismatch here between the goal and what actually happens in the classroom, particularly in the formative years of primary and secondary education?

In a classroom where the learner's role is that of recipient, there is a powerful 'hidden curriculum' at work (Barnes 1976). In contrast to the overt curriculum of, for example, historical facts, scientific processes, or skills to be taught in a craft subject, the hidden curriculum refers to the learning which goes on in covert ways beneath the surface of what the teacher sets out to teach. It encompasses the shaping of learners' perceptions about learning, their own role in it, the nature of the subject they are studying, their teachers and so on, and their attitudes towards all of these. And in a teacher-directed classroom an easy perception to shape is that learners are expected to be passive. It is difficult to see, then, how directed, regulated, and passive students can convert suddenly to self-determining and responsible adults who can continue learning effectively throughout their lives.

In the 1960s and 1970s in particular there were reactions in educational writing in western cultures to this teacher-directed 'transmission' model of education (for example Holt 1969, 1979; Rogers 1969; Knowles 1975). Illich (1972) commented in this way:

> Schools are designed on the assumption that there is a secret to everything in life; that the quality of life depends on knowing that secret; that secrets can be known only in orderly successions; and that only teachers can properly reveal these secrets.
> (Illich 1972: 78)

As these comments suggest, some of the debate took radical directions in anti-establishment movements which were suspicious of institutionalized education. But even less radical thinkers called for a reorientation of teacher and student roles and more learner-centred approaches in which students could be encouraged to take on greater responsibility for their own learning. Knowles (1975), for example, claimed that:

> there is convincing evidence that people who take the initiative in learning (pro-active learners) learn more things and learn better, than do people who sit at the feet of teachers passively waiting to be taught (reactive learners).
> (Knowles 1975: 14)

These arguments have led ELT writers to reflect on how easy it is for a learner to become dependent on the teacher. If we observe what goes on in many an English language classroom, the learner might well build expectations which go something like this: 'The teacher chooses the textbook and other learning materials; the teacher decides on a programme; the teacher plans the lesson; the teacher directs the activities; the teacher corrects and assesses my work. Therefore the teacher is responsible for my successful learning. My role is to let the teacher instruct me carefully and control the steps of my learning.'

If we make no attempt to counter the possible effect of communicating this sort of message, then we may well obstruct learners from developing more active and responsible approaches. Henner-Stanchina and Riley (1978), writing about the development of an open learning centre, reflect on the tendency of the teacher-directed classroom to create passive, teacher-dependent students:

> many adults are convinced that all they have to do to learn a language is to attend a course. Simple bodily presence is all that is required from them: they will sit in the classroom, the teacher will do his job and somehow, learning will take place.

(Henner-Stanchina and Riley 1978: 78)

Recent years have seen attempts in ELT to explore what self-directed learning can mean. Holec (1979), working within the Council of Europe Modern Languages Project, gave early thought to what he called the 'autonomization' of learning and suggested that two preconditions were necessary: first, that the learner must be capable of making decisions about learning; second, that there must be a structure for learning within which a learner can take responsibility for those decisions. He regarded the learning process as a management process and included the following among the necessary techniques of management: fixing objectives for learning; deciding on the content of a learning programme; selecting method; self-monitoring of progress; and self-evaluation.

Principles about learners managing their own learning process have been put into practice in a number of countries and are well documented: for example, the autonomous learning scheme at CRAPEL, University of Nancy, France (Gremmo and Abe 1985), the self-access centres at Eurocentre, Cambridge, England (O'Dell 1992) and the British Council Institute, Barcelona, Spain (McDowell and Morris 1989). Brown (1994) reports on a similar centre at the pilot stage at the Defense Language Institute, Monterey, California. All of these provide an environment for independent learning and support systems for learners in line with Holec's preconditions.

3.4 What are the implications for learner training in the classroom?

As a result of trends in educational thinking and research into second language acquisition, ELT methodology has moved towards the view that adult and adolescent learners are capable of self-direction and able to organize and undertake language learning with the kind of self-reliance they use in other areas of their lives. Brown (1994) has usefully called this 'strategic investment' by learners in their own learning.

Some learners come to the task of learning a foreign language with the expectation of being active learners, but others come ill-equipped. For the latter group, perhaps the most useful service the teacher can perform is to encourage them in positive attitudes and prepare them in effective strategies. Dickinson (1987) and Holec (1985) make a distinction between psychological and practical preparation. The first can be described as a change in perception about what language learning involves and a change in the expectation that language can only be learned through the careful control of a specialist teacher. The second involves acquiring a range of techniques with which learners can enhance their learning. Taken together, these two kinds of preparation can be called *learner training*. This can be defined as a set of procedures or activities which raises learners' awareness of what is involved in learning a foreign language, which encourages learners to become more involved, active, and responsible in their own learning, and which helps them to develop and strengthen their strategies for language learning. The aims of learner training are presented diagrammatically in Figure 3.1.

Figure 3.1: The aims of learner training

Let us take a simple case study. Carmelita attends an English class in an adult institute two evenings a week. Her teacher spends time in class on learner training activities in which Carmelita is encouraged to think about how to preview a unit of her textbook before the lesson, how to keep a vocabulary notebook, and how to check her own progress. The teacher also introduces the students to the school's self-access centre and explains how they can use the various facilities it offers to consult reference sources and practise grammar, reading, listening, and pronunciation. The class spends one hour a week in the centre under the guidance of the teacher, but students can also go along at any time when they are free. In addition, the teacher makes suggestions for out-of-class activities, for example, borrowing readers from a class library, using cassettes, and listening to English language radio. For each of these activities she gives out worksheets and tasks to present techniques which the students can take up and use independently. Learner training, then, can lead to more effective classroom learning, self-access learning, and independent learning at home.

There are now clear guidelines for learner-training tasks and materials in ELT. Published textbooks and programmes of learner training are informed by insights from research and contain activities for strategy training. For example, the excellent materials designed by Ellis and Sinclair (1989) provide a systematic programme of activities for learners to use in order to build confidence and competence in learning English.

The following sections will present and discuss different types of learner training activity. Each type is categorized according to its primary aim.

3.4.1 *Activities which help learners to reflect on learning*

Perhaps the most difficult task for the teacher in learner training with adults accustomed to teacher-directed classrooms is to encourage the belief that a learner *can* assume more responsibility. Holec (1985) writes about psychological preparation as a gradual de-conditioning process through which a student is freed of assumptions which create teacher dependence. It is a process of 'shedding baggage' and needs to be accompanied by the development of awareness of how to exploit a range of resources and use methods of learning other than a whole-class, teacher-directed one.

The inventory 'What do you think about your writing?' in Materials extract 3.B is intended for use with a class of intermediate students who are embarking on a writing course. Its purpose is to encourage them to reflect on their needs and problems in writing and on the nature of the course they are about to follow. An inventory such as this has a number of advantages. It engages and involves the students and makes them think as they start the process of improving a particular language skill. It raises their awareness of what they come with to the course, their preconceptions and expectations of the teacher and of themselves. It suggests by implication that there are ways of being more responsible for their own learning. It suggests that the course

Materials extract 3.B

What do you think about your writing?

Tick any of the statements below which are true of you. Then join in a class discussion.

1 I think writing in English is more difficult than speaking. ☐
2 I think I don't really have any problems in writing English. ☐
3 I don't write very much in my first language. ☐
4 Writing is important to me because:
   – I may have to write English in a job. ☐
   – I have to pass examinations in English. ☐
   – I want to write letters to English friends. ☐
   – .... ☐
   – .... ☐
5 I expect to do a lot of writing in class. ☐
6 I expect to do a lot of writing by myself at home. ☐
7 I would like the teacher to look at my work and help me while I am writing in class. ☐
8 I would like my teacher to talk to me about my writing sometimes. ☐
9 I usually check through my writing before I hand it in. ☐
10 I expect the teacher to mark all of the mistakes in my work. ☐
11 I expect the teacher to mark the most important mistakes in my work. ☐
12 I want my teacher to write comments about what is good or not good in my writing. ☐
13 I make a careful note of the teacher's corrections when I get work back. ☐
14 I usually read the comments and look at the grade but I don't study the corrections in detail. ☐
15 I would like to see other students' writing sometimes. ☐

(Hedge: *Writing*, page 156)

is about learning as well as about writing in English and that they need to be actively involved in that learning. It allows the teacher to raise expectations about the methodology of the class and to justify it in a preliminary discussion. The Introductory task in this chapter is a similar device to encourage reflection about the role of the textbook, to get students to see it as a resource which they can use independently and which can best be used in combination with other sources of information and practice.

Another technique is to ask students to make personal recordings about their strengths and weaknesses. This allows the student to reflect and gives the teacher useful ideas for the class or individual guidance for the student's private practice. In the transcript below, a Chinese student reflects on his English pronunciation.

Norman! How do you do!

My name is Ke. I'm a student. I'm from China. I want to English. Sorry. I want to learn English, because English is a very useful language. I have been learning English for four years. I have learned English

Materials extract 3.C

	Learning Style	
a	You like to put new ideas into practice to see if they work.	☐
b	You are open-minded and receptive to new experiences.	☐
c	You think logically and sequentially.	☐
d	You think carefully before you act.	☐
e	You tend to live in the present.	☐
f	You like to collect and analyse information.	☐
g	You like to try an idea that appeals to you as soon as possible.	☐
h	You like information to be organised and coherent.	☐
i	You don't jump to quick conclusions.	☐
j	You act before you think.	☐
k	You are not interested in spending time discussing new ideas or data.	☐
l	You like things to be perfect.	☐
m	You like to solve problems.	☐
n	You don't participate actively in meetings and discussions.	☐
o	You are not subjective.	☐
p	You don't tend to follow things through.	☐
q	You listen carefully before you speak.	☐
r	You base your decisions on principles and theories.	☐
s	You like to be the centre of a group.	☐
t	You enjoy the challenge of problems and opportunities.	☐

from *The Manual of Learning styles*, Honey and Mumford.

pronunciation from Chinese teacher and I think I need some more practice. I found some individual sounds and a lot, and a bit different for me. And I also found some groups of sounds difficult, difficulty. Sometimes I don't know how to use English stress.

I'm afraid I don't know much about the English theory rhythm. Sorry. And my intonation is also poor. I think pronunciation and intonation are very important, but at present I feel which I need to learn vocabulary and basic sentence pattern, patterns.

Well, I'm not sure which aspects of my pronunciation English people may have difficulty in understand, understanding. However I think my poor intonation might cause some misunderstandings.

Materials extract 3. C (continued)

2 The statements refer to different kinds of learning styles. Read about four categories of learners in the box.

Look at the statements you chose in 1 again and match them with the category of learner. Put a, b, c or d in the box on the right according to the category you think the statement refers to. What kind of learner are you? (You may be a mixture of them all).

Listen to the tape and check your answers. The wording is not exactly the same.

3 Form groups with people with a similar learning style to you. Make a list of what you think are the strengths and weaknesses of your style.

4 Form new groups of at least four so that there is someone with each learning style in each group. Show each other the lists you made in 3. Make suggestions to help each other build on strengths and overcome weaknesses.

5 Listen to the tape, and focus only on the style you are weakest in. Write down the activities that strengthen this style in the chart.

6 Write one way you intend to try and improve your learning style in the future. Read it out to the people near you.

a Activitists
These are people who like to learn by being active and doing, and thrive on anything new.

b Reflectors
These are people who learn by thinking and analysing and taking their time.

c Pragmatists
These are practical realistic people who like new ideas and want to test them out in practice.

d Theorists
These are people who learn by thinking logically and rationally.

Activities to strengthen _____ Style

a ....
....

b ....
....

c ....
....

d ....
....

e ....
....

(Deller and Jones: *Vista* SB, pages 14–15)

> My English is very poor. This homework is my friend, helping me. I'm very happy to study here. I must work hard, and try to improve my English. I hope get more help. Thank you.

(data from Norman Whitney)

Teachers can use such reflections not only to assess relevant areas for instruction and guidance but also to gain an idea of how able the student is to make realistic appraisals of strengths and weaknesses, and whether there is a tendency towards under- or over-estimation of proficiency. The procedure can be followed up with further recordings of a 'journal' nature in which students reflect on how well they are progressing relative to this early diagnosis.

Some coursebooks now make explicit reference to learning styles in an introductory chapter and encourage learners to consider their own style and ways of improving it. Materials extract 3.C is an example. Here students are taken through a sequence of activities in which they progressively try to identify their own learning style, analyse its advantages and disadvantages, discuss with peers ways of working to build greater strengths, and form a personal agenda for self-development.

What all these activities have in common is involvement of the student in reflection on what they bring to the task of learning English, what they need, and what they expect. It provides the basis for discussion about how they can proceed, together with the teacher, to direct and shape the learning process.

3.4.2 *Activities which train strategies and equip learners to be active*

Training cognitive strategies

A group of learner training activities which can be introduced progressively by the teacher into a programme are those which aim to increase students' knowledge of useful ways to learn and develop the strategies they need. Some of these will be cognitive strategies and will replace the techniques which learners previously expected to come from teachers. For example, instead of expecting the teacher to explain the meanings of new words, students can be trained to go through a series of techniques such as using clues in the text to guess meaning, using knowledge of affixation, and checking in a dictionary to establish a word's meaning for themselves. The use and development of other cognitive strategies can be encouraged by getting students to use textbook materials as a resource, searching for language data and analysing them to find patterns and discover rules. Materials extract 3.D is an example. Here students are given the opportunity to search in the language data provided by one unit of materials to discover the grammatical rules governing the use of the expression 'There is/are …'. These activities encourage some of the characteristics of the 'good language learner' as suggested in the early study by Naiman et al. (1978), namely:

  – The learner must be active in his approach to learning and practice.
  – The learner must come to grips with the language as a system.
  (ibid.: 103)

Materials extract 3.D

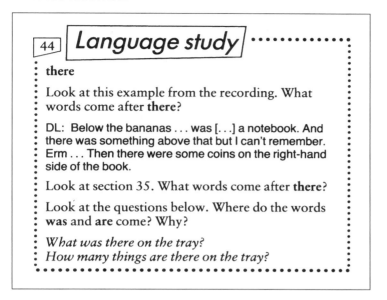

(Willis and Willis: *The COBUILD English Course* SB1, page 20)

Training metacognitive strategies

It can be productive, at the beginning of a course, to ask students to share ideas about possible metacognitive strategies or self-help strategies. Here are the responses of some students to a written activity of this kind:

'I have got a very good grammar book with some explanations about the English grammar in my own language. What I do is read the English rules and try to understand them and then I read the part which is in French.'

'I enjoy talking to myself in English every day, when I wake up, when I go to work, and any time I can do it.'

'In the mornings before I go to school I read the English newspaper. When there is an interesting article I usually cut it out and when I have the time I look up the words I did not understand.'

'I usually read all that we have done in the classroom, especially during my journey home by train. When I am at home I rewrite all notes that I have taken in a notebook.'

'I'm reading goodnight stories for the children. So now I almost know what every animal in English is called.'

'Every day I learn ten new words that I write in a small copy book with the meaning and the translation in my own language.'
(Author's data)

The discussion arising can encourage other students to adopt strategies which they find personally attractive or manageable. Some current textbook materials engage students in describing and evaluating the strategies available to them. The task in Materials extract 3.E asks students to think more generally about how to exploit resources in the world around them. Notice that it has been presented in simple language and could be used with students of relatively low language proficiency. However, many teachers teaching monolingual classes and keen to involve their learners in such self-help strategies would argue that time spent doing this kind of activity in the first language is time well spent.

Materials extract 3.E

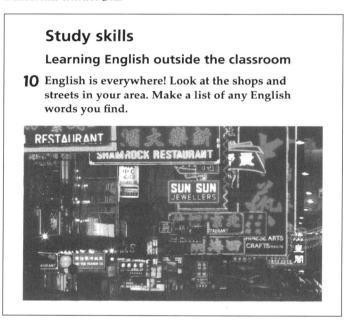

(Whitney: *Open Doors* SB2, page 23)

Metacognitive strategies are of many kinds. In her framework, Oxford (1990) includes the categories of centring learning (for example, overviewing, paying attention); arranging and planning learning (for example, setting goals and objectives, organizing, and seeking out practice opportunities); and evaluating learning (for example, self-monitoring). The activity in Materials extract 3.F would be termed 'seeking out practice opportunities'.

Materials extract 3.F

Keeping a reading journal

This is what you need to do to keep a reading journal.

1 Decide what format you want your journal to take.
It could be a spiral bound notebook or a ring binder. It needs to be the kind of paper which you can stick newspaper articles on. Start each entry on a new page and write on one side of the paper. Leave a margin if you want your teacher to write notes directly on the page.

2 Choose something every week.
One or two entries a week would be ideal. Choose a newspaper or magazine article which you find particularly interesting or it could be a text you have read in a coursebook or in the Resources Room. It could even be a brochure or leaflet you have picked up on campus or in town or an advertisement. If you can cut out the text, please stick it in your journal or put leaflets in some kind of pocket at the back. If you write about a text from a coursebook, give us the name and the page number as a reference.

3 Choose what kind of entry you want to make. Here are three ideas.
   (a) A Resuming entry
   Write a paragraph which summarizes the main points of the text.

   (b) A Responding entry
   Write a response of some kind to what you have read. If your text is a newspaper article, you could write it in the form of a letter to the editor. Here are some prompts to help you with your response.
   – What did you learn of interest from the text?
   – Did you agree or disagree with anything in the text?
   – Did you like what you read?
   – Did you like the style of the writer?
   – Was the content of some personal meaning or relevance to you?

   (c) A Reflecting entry
   Write some reflections on how you managed to deal with the text. Here are some questions to ask yourself.
   – What did you look for first in the text? A picture? A headline?
   – How long did it take you to read and understand the text?
   – Was there anything you felt was particularly difficult about the text? Did you have to look up any new words? Were you able to guess the meanings of some unfamiliar words?
   – Have you read much in your first language (or any other languages) about this topic?

In past courses, students have often chosen texts which relate to the subjects they will be studying as undergraduates. They have used them to develop their vocabulary as well. You might like to do this and make topic vocabulary lists from the text which you can try to use in your writing.

We will take in your book/file every so often to review it. If you want to ask any questions about your writing, remember to put them at the end of your entry.

(Author's materials)

This activity is intended for use at the beginning of a course and encourages students to extend both reading and writing activity. The particular guidelines were designed for a group of pre-sessional Japanese students at a UK university. The take-up was substantial, the teacher offering to review writing occasionally and linking it to oral classroom reports from students to each other on their reading.

Teachers and textbook writers can promote the use of metacognitive strategies through a range of activity types. Perhaps the most useful way to perceive the role of the teacher is as someone who can suggest a range of strategies and help students identify those which will work well for them. As students develop effective ways to learn they will be better able to organize their attempts to continue learning outside the classroom.

3.4.3 *Activities which encourage learners to monitor and check their own progress*

Materials extract 3.G is an example of a self-monitoring activity. The activity involves students in two steps. In the first, they measure the extent to which they have mastered something in the programme, and in the second they work with another student and have a chance to assess how intelligible they are. Self-assessment is an attractive alternative or addition to traditional forms of assessment for the classroom teacher. It is a particular type of meta-cognitive strategy which deserves special attention. It aims to help students develop those characteristics of the 'good language learner' which involve the ability to assess their own performance and the ability to be self-critical. A learner performing the activity can ask the questions: Did I make myself clear? Did my listener ask me to repeat anything? When these questions have been answered it is then possible to ask: Am I happy with my performance? What do I need to improve on? In this way learners can increase their awareness of their individual progress not only in knowledge of the language but also in their ability to perform it. Self-assessment personalizes the process of monitoring development, and when students have been gradually introduced to the idea of collaborative work and can respond to it productively, this too can be used in assessment activities, as in the second stage of the activity.

We can take on several roles as learners work with self-assessment. For example, we can support them as they establish criteria for evaluating themselves. This will be discussed further in Chapter 9 where ways in which teachers can help students work towards understanding the criteria for an 'effective' piece of writing will be demonstrated.

Materials extract 3.G

How much have you learned?

Imagine that you are in these situations.
What would you say in English?
How well could you express yourself?

	You			Your partner		
	Very well	Quite well	Not well	Very well	Quite well	Not well
1 Your rented TV isn't working. Ask for someone to repair it.						
2 You want to use a public pay phone but don't know how to. Ask someone nearby.						
3 You are uncertain whether some money you have been expecting has been put into the bank. Phone the bank to enquire.						
4 Request permission from your employer to leave work early. Give a reason.						
5 Ask a friend if you can borrow her car to take some friends to the seaside.						
6 Someone has opened the window in the railway carriage and it is very cold. Ask if you can close it.						

Now work with a partner. Ask the questions, listen to the answers. Assess how well your partner can express these things.

(Author's materials)

We can also provide regular opportunities for self-assessment. And we can help students establish standards for themselves by comparing their own assessment with ours. For example, in 'How much have you learned?', if the teacher elicited some responses from students after the pairwork and commented on strengths and weaknesses, students would have a basis for comparison with their self-assessment. These roles do not replace the teacher's ultimate role as arbiter of standards, but they complement it and can be especially useful when classes are large. The ability to assess one's own learning becomes particularly important for any student who wants to work independently with resources in some kind of self-access or open learning centre.

3.5 What role can self-access facilities play in language learning?

Self-access resources can vary substantially from one institution to another. However, even where funding is difficult, it is possible for a teacher or group of teachers to create simple resources. For example, a box of reading cards, each card consisting of a newspaper or magazine article with pre- and post-reading activities and with an accompanying key to answers where possible, can provide extensive reading materials for students over a long period of time.

Where funding is available, decisions need to be taken about the kind of resources to be developed, the skills that learners will need to use the resources effectively, and the kinds of preparation and practice to be done in the classroom. In Figure 3.2, the segments of the circle represent some of the facilities which a self-access centre might contain. For example, the facility 'Using written texts' could contain teacher-made tasks, magazines, authentic books, graded readers, reading cards with texts, questions and answers for checking, information books for project work, and dictionaries. If learners are to use these materials successfully, teachers will need to ensure that they can use the cataloguing system, locate items in alphabetical order, use an index, a dictionary, and so on. In the diagram these are called the 'core skills' and they are part of the training that is needed for self-access learning. Teachers might also encourage students to use the reading resources by recommending books in class, asking students to recommend books to each other by giving talks in class, or by setting projects for which students need to look up information. The ultimate aim of the self-access facility is that eventually learners will be able to use it in their own way, according to self-formulated goals, with strategies for monitoring their own progress.

As can be seen, there are many ways in which facilities can be created for reading, and for some of the other segments in the circle such as using cassettes in a listening laboratory (see 7.4.2). However, it is not so easy to think of ways to encourage speaking outside the classroom. Monologues can be prepared and practised, but dialogues require a partner. This is, perhaps, one reason for the popular procedure of setting up an English club in school, or an English common-room in a tertiary institution, for those who wish to be in a environment where only English is permitted. There are, however,

Figure 3.2: Facilities a self-access centre might contain

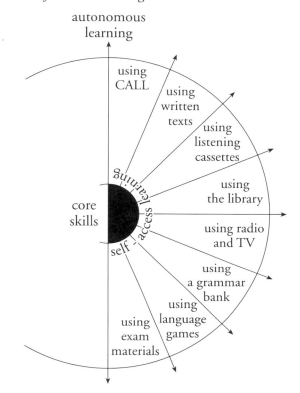

some possibilities for self-access work if students use the facilities with their friends. For example, games can be designed which students perform independently in pairs. 'Find the differences' involves two cards with almost the same picture but with a number of clear differences. For example, one picture of a living-room may have a bowl of roses on the table, three chairs, a small girl on the sofa and a standard lamp, while the other has a bowl of fruit, four chairs, a small boy in the armchair and a table lamp. Students have to discover the differences between the pictures by describing them and asking questions of each other. The pictures can relate to a topic just covered on the course so that the activity revises vocabulary recently presented.

Pronunciation is perhaps the easiest area to practise in self-access mode, with students borrowing resources to use with their own cassette recorder or in a language laboratory. Pronunciation books can be divided up and activities sorted into different boxes, for instance: consonant clusters, assimilation, weak forms, and intonation. Teachers can then direct students to those forms of practice they most need. It is useful to monitor student activity in some way. For example, the self-report form in Materials extract 3.H shows a student being over-ambitious and in need of advice about pacing himself appropriately.

Materials extract 3.H

EFL Pronunciation	Student's Name	*Tong Qu-Yi*
Self Access Diary	Teacher's Name	*Norman*
	Date	*3 Dec. 1980*

A: THE MATERIAL

Title *Stress Time*

Author *Colin Mortimer*

Chapter / Section / Part *Dialogue 1—50*

B: FOCUS

Would you say the material focussed on (please tick)

single sounds   prosodic features

consonanants - single/cluster   ✓ stress

vowels   - simple/diphthong   ✓ rhythm

                                                    intonation   *Don't listen to so much!*

other

C: TIME

Please indicate

DATE *3 Dec. 1980*

TIME   Start *14·00* Finish *14·45*

LAB No. *6*

D: PROGRESS

Which part of the material did you do (give section, page(s), exercise numbers)

Dialogue 1—50.

Interesting but I won't be able to repeat what they say on tape

E: SELF MONITORING

Would you say that your progress was

- excellent
- very good
- good
- ✓ only OK
- poor

F: FURTHER HELP

Would you say that you needed further individual practice on this point

✓ a lot
- not much
- not at all

help from the teacher

- a lot
- not much
- not at all

listen to less + repeat more

G: INDIVIDUALISED TAPES

If you made a tape or cassette of this material, and you would like the teacher to listen to it, please

1. give the name or number of your tape/cassette

2. give the name or number of the part of the tape/cassete with this material on it

---

(materials from Norman Whitney)

Developing self-access resources, then, involves both their preparation and systems for housing them, and preparation of learners for using them. Other decisions will also be needed: for example, how teachers can be prepared to exploit the resources in conjunction with their courses; whether non-teaching staff will be needed for support, and whether staff development will be needed for new forms of teacher–student interaction in the counselling duties required.

The discussion so far has focused on the kinds of self-access facility that institutions increasingly provide for their learners. However, in this high-tech age, many learners have access to personal resources for individual self-study such as electronic dictionaries. Teachers may well wish to include technical preparation for this kind of resource in learner training activities. It lends itself to useful collaborative work as learners can easily share a screen. As such dictionaries proliferate, it may also become important to help learners appreciate those which might have the greatest value for their own particular uses, such as hand-held electronic dictionaries, and their advantages and limitations.

Once students have been prepared in the necessary skills and oriented to the possibilities offered by self-access learning, they can be supported in creating their own self-study programmes, working on individual needs and interests, and monitoring their own progress. The success of self-access learning will depend on the thoroughness with which students have been prepared through a careful process of learner training.

3.6 Are learner autonomy and learner training universally appropriate concepts?

At various points throughout this chapter, qualification has been placed on the appropriacy of the concepts of learner autonomy and learner training in relation to various types of learner and various types of teaching context. The issue of how universally applicable such concepts are needs further consideration. There are a number of distinctions to be made and arguments to be disentangled.

First, a distinction can be made between perceptions of learner training for effective classroom learning, and learner training for self-directed learning in contexts other than the language classroom such as in an open learning centre or self-study at home. These can be two distinct goals. Some teachers are interested in strategy training simply because they want to improve their students' capacity to work effectively with classroom methods and materials. Materials and procedures designed with this goal in mind will engage learners in more self-reliant approaches, but in the context of working collaboratively with other students and the teacher. The point has already been made that strategy training can be beneficial where classes are large and resources are scarce. A teacher from Burkino Faso once said to me that he thought strategy training was the answer to many of the problems he faced with classes of eighty students. His learners might have few resources other than the teacher, a common textbook, and opportunities for interaction with peers, but he would make sure that they could wring the last drop of learning they could from those resources by using them strategically.

Where learner training is preparation for forms of self-reliant learning, such as self-access work or project work (see 10.3.3), or using resources in the community, it is also possible, and important, to make a distinction between those adults who are already 'active' in their approach to learning and those who are more passive. It would be a mistake to assume that all adult students need persuading to adopt independent approaches. Many come to classes with every intention of using the class as one resource among several to be exploited in learning English. The students who reported their self-help strategies in 3.4.2 had not, at that point, been involved in awareness-raising activities or in strategy training. Students with this natural positive motivation are often quick to pick up further ideas from peers or from the teacher, can respond well to strategy training, and may be keen to use any self-access resources offered. It would be patronizing to see them as in need of the psychological preparation that Holec (1979) and Dickinson (1987) refer to as part of learner training. In this sense 'training' is an unfortunate word, one that collocates rather better with 'rifle', or 'dog' than with 'learner'. For students who already have positive attitudes, the tasks for the teacher will probably be to discover the effective strategies they already possess, to build on these, to provide further ideas which might be helpful, and to facilitate activities where students can learn useful strategies from each other.

It is with students who have learned passivity from their previous educational experience that we may see most value in learner training. With these students we need to decide whether we have a legitimate role in helping them to 'shed baggage' and in breaking down their resistance, particularly when that resistance might come from cultural notions of the respective roles and responsibilities of teachers and learners which have fostered certain habitual styles of learning. It has been suggested, for example, that ideas about independent learning are not so easily applicable to Asian cultures.

However, while it is true that ELT practices in more self-directed learning have originated in western cultures, is it really the case that these do not fit with eastern philosophies? There is a Chinese saying, for example: 'Tell me and I'll forget; show me and I'll remember; involve me and I'll learn.' And the Confucian proverb, 'If you give a man a fish, you feed him for a day; if you teach a man to fish you feed him for a lifetime', has been much quoted in the ELT literature on autonomous learning. Although we are concerned as teachers not to invade or impose on the cultural values of other social groups we teach, there are strong hints here that the cultural positions are less incompatible than might be supposed. Many of the Asian teachers I have worked with, studying in the West and teaching in the East, have taken the view that their role may be to mediate between cultures to find a way forward. This will undoubtedly require careful classroom discussion and support for learners stepping into a new methodology.

For example, Kell and Newton (1997) report on the effective use of tutor groups in the preparation of mainland Chinese students for using a self-access centre. These students had hitherto had no experience of self-study and had 'a deep mistrust of anything that does not involve the teacher' (ibid.: 49). A tutor group consisted of eight to ten learners who worked on a self-access 'pathway' together with a tutor who acted as guide to the materials and their demands. The term 'pathway' refers to a route through a set of connected materials designated on a work-card. For example, these might be organized around a topic, beginning with a unit of materials related to the topic and moving on to supplementary materials which might follow up or consolidate structures, functions, and skills work introduced in the original unit. The idea of the tutor group was to form a 'self-access class' preparatory to more independent work. The authors reported that ninety per cent of students found pathways useful and seventy per cent felt that had received appropriate levels of guidance. The study provides an example of the need for support through the early stages of more self-reliant learning when the educational tradition has not provided students with experience of this.

3.7 Conclusion

One of the things this chapter has tried to do is to point to the uncertainty that exists in interpretations of the term 'learner autonomy'. Some teachers interpret it in a procedural way and associate it with resource-based learning in institutions. For others the concept relates to a capacity to carry on learning independently throughout life, when classrooms and teachers have been left far behind, a capacity that needs gradual building and development through practice in self-directed learning. For yet others it relates more narrowly to approaching classroom-based study in more aware, independent, and effective ways. The precise interpretation will depend on educational tradition.

Consequently, learner training is perceived as having a number of possible goals. One is to prepare students to work with the systems and pathways of self-access facilities. Another is to encourage learners to take cognizance of the ways in which they can find and use language learning opportunities in the community outside the classroom. A third is to develop learners who can use the learning opportunities of the classroom effectively through applying a range of strategies to the work they do with teachers and peers. In some cases, of course, all of these goals may be relevant.

Teachers concerned to take up some of the ideas in this chapter will need to find their own interpretation of autonomy, and to explore relevant meanings for learner training within their own educational setting. Only then will it be possible to move forward cautiously and usefully into the practicalities of classroom activity.

Discussion topics and projects

1 Do you have any experiences of self-directed learning or of learner training (as a learner or as a teacher) which you can describe or evaluate?

2 The text below lists six ways in which a teacher can promote greater learner independence. What implications do you think these hold for the ways in which classroom teachers organize lessons and programmes?

- legitimizing independence in learning by showing learners that we, as teachers, approve, and by encouraging them to be more independent;

- convincing learners that they are capable of greater independence in learning, probably most effectively by giving them successful experiences of independent learning;

- giving learners increasing opportunities to exercise their independence;

- helping learners to develop learning techniques (learning strategies) so that they can exercise their independence;

- helping learners to become more aware of language as a system so that they can understand many of the learning techniques available and learn sufficient grammar to understand simple reference books;

- sharing with learners something of what we know about language learning so that they have a greater awareness of what to expect from the language learning task and how they should react to problems that erect barriers to learning.

(Dickinson 1992: 2–3)

3 Take the student's book of a published coursebook which is popular in your own teaching situation and which is intended for students who might benefit from learner training. Evaluate the extent to which it includes learner training. Look for these kinds of activities:

(a) awareness-raising activities about learning and the role of the learner
(b) strategy training activities which encourage learners to be active in their learning
(c) self-assessment activities.

4 Design a short questionnaire/inventory which you could use with students at the beginning of a course to raise their awareness of their assumptions about learning a language and/or their reactions to past learning experiences.

5 Design a learner training activity with a specific age and level of learner in mind. You could design the activity as it would look 'on the page' of a textbook or as steps in a procedure for the teacher to follow. Here are some suggestions:
(a) an activity to help learners use any available reading resources outside the classroom and to organize their reading practice
(b) an activity to help learners develop a positive attitude to errors and to work out an error-correction policy for their own class
(c) an activity to make learners aware of what might be important in writing an essay, what criteria for evaluation might be applied, and what the purpose of marking might be
(d) an activity to help learners make use of local English language news broadcasts.

6 You have acquired the resourcing to set up a self-access centre in your institution. Draw up a plan for its development using these stages as a guide:
(a) Decide on the facilities the centre will contain.
(b) Prioritize the development and make a three-year plan.
(c) Choose one facility and work out the tasks needed for its detailed development.

7 If you do not have the possibility of developing a self-access centre in your institution, what other opportunities are there for a teacher or group of teachers to encourage more self-reliant forms of learning? What activities could be promoted (for example, self-study activities), or what resources could be developed (for example, reading cards)?

8 Consider the self-access activity 'Superman versus smoking' in Materials extract 3.I.

Design an activity, with a key, for a group of your own learners for listening or reading development. You could set it out under the headings in this example.

9 To what extent have the concepts of self-direction or learner training influenced your own ELT situation? Do you think the implications they hold for institutional practice are desirable or possible, and what are the practical constraints?

Materials extract 3.1

3.4 Superman versus smoking

CLASSIFICATION   R.IT/1 = Reading. Information transfer/1

LEVEL   Intermediate

AGE   Adolescent/young adult

ACTIVITY TYPE   Information transfer

AIM   To extract and recognize relevant information from a reading text.

PREPARATION   Think about the problem of children smoking. How can they be persuaded not to start? Do you think the problem is a serious one? Make a list of three ways in which children could be prevented from trying cigarettes.

INSTRUCTIONS   Read the following text and use the information to complete the questionnaire below. Write the information on a separate piece of paper. Do not write on this card.

TASK SHEET

NOW I NEED YOUR HELP KIDS. IN MY LIFE LONG CAMPAIGN AGAINST THE DREADED NICK O' TEEN. NEVER SAY YES TO A CIGARETTE.

Over 100,000 primary school children wrote supporting Superman in his fight against smoking during the first four weeks of the Health Education Council's recent £500,000 campaign.

The campaign, which began just after Christmas, uses the Superman character to persuade 7- to 11-year-olds that they should 'crush the evil Nick O'Teen' and never say yes to a cigarette.

Most of the budget has been spent on producing and showing a cartoon television commercial, which features Superman in conflict with the arch-enemy Nick O'Teen.

The campaign, which is seen as a long-term project, is based on careful research. This showed that one in three adult smokers started before they were nine and that 80 per cent of children who smoke regularly grow up to be smokers. For boys, the average age for starting to smoke was found to be 9.7 years while for girls, it was 11.2 years.

QUESTIONNAIRE

> Country __Britain__   Intended public (age, sex . . .) _____
>
> Budget _____   Media used – television ☐
>   – radio   ☐
> Opening date _____   – posters   ☐
>   – magazines/comics/
> Closing date _____   newspapers ☐
>   – other   ☐
>
>   Slogans _____
> Estimated success – high   ☐
>   – average ☐
>   – low   ☐

KEY

>   boys+girls
> Country __Britain__   Intended public (age, sex . . .) aged 7-11 __
>
> Budget £500,000 ____   Media used – television ☑
>   – radio   ☐
> Opening date December_   – posters   ☐
>   – magazines/comics/
> Closing date ?_'long term'   newspapers ☑
>   – other   ☐
>
>   Slogans 'Crush the evil Nick O Teen' ,
> Estimated success – high   ☑ 'Never say yes to a cigarette'
>   – average ☐ (over 100,000 children wrote)
>   – low   ☐

(Sheerin: *Self-access*, pages 61–2)

Further reading

Benson, P. and **P. Voller.** 1997. *Autonomy and Independence in Language Learning.* London: Longman.

This is a set of papers which provides an overview of the field. They raise issues related to the skills which learners can apply to direct their own learning and the extent to which institutions support or suppress capacity for autonomous learning. The book also explores practical ways of implementing ideas about independence in methods and materials for EFL teaching.

Dickinson, L. 1987. *Self-instruction in Language Learning.* Cambridge: Cambridge University Press.

The first part of the book contains a series of case studies of self-instruction for both adult and school learners and, through discussion of these, explores the fundamental philosophy underlying moves towards more autonomous learning and the values of various approaches to self-instruction. The second part discusses such practical issues as designing self-instruction materials, preparing learners to use them, and encouraging learners in self-assessment procedures.

Dickinson, L. 1992. *Learner Training for Language Learning.* Trinity College, Dublin: Authentik Language Learning Resources.

This is a short handbook for language teachers and, as such, offers an accessible way into the topic of learner training. It reviews the background in terms of key concepts and goes on to define learner training in terms of three areas: skills and knowledge in language awareness, language learning awareness, and learning techniques. Each of these is taken up, described, and illustrated.

Ellis, G. and **B. Sinclair.** 1989. *Learning to Learn English.* Cambridge: Cambridge University Press.

The authors provide a course in learner training for English language students at lower-intermediate and intermediate levels. The aim is to let learners discover which learning strategies suit them best so that they can learn more successfully. It can be integrated with other materials, or each unit can be used separately for systematic training. The materials cover various aspects of learning grammar, vocabulary, listening, reading, speaking, and writing, and include advice to learners in using a self-access centre.

Oxford, R. 1990. *Language Learning Strategies: What Every Teacher Should Know.* Boston, Mass.: Newbury House.

This book provides both background theory about learning strategies and examples of classroom procedures which teachers can exploit to introduce strategy training into their classrooms. The book is based on research into strategies and tries to work out the implications for classroom practice. It contains useful taxonomies of learning strategies which the teacher can work with in setting up learner training programmes.

Sheerin, S. 1989. *Self-access.* Oxford: Oxford University Press.

This is a resource book designed to help ESL and EFL teachers with the practicalities involved in establishing and managing self-access study facilities. The book is divided into five chapters which deal with the following: setting up self-access facilities; learner orientation and training; suggestions for reading and listening activities; suggestions for speaking and writing activities; and activities which focus on grammar, vocabulary, and language functions. There are useful ideas for a wide range of learning situations.

Wenden, A. 1991. *Learner Strategies for Learner Autonomy.* Englewood Cliffs, N.J.: Prentice Hall.

The writer provides a detailed discussion of the principles underlying learner autonomy and investigates related research studies. She also offers practical advice and procedures for the classroom. The book contains many activities intended to help teachers design and evaluate materials and plans for autonomous learning.

PART TWO

Teaching the language system

4 VOCABULARY

> '*When* I *use a word,*' *Humpty Dumpty said, in rather a scornful tone, 'it means just what I choose it to mean—neither more nor less.*'
>
> '*The question is,*' *said Alice, 'whether you* can *make words mean so many different things.*'
>
> LEWIS CARROLL

1 What do we know about the lexical system of English?

2 How do second language learners acquire vocabulary?

3 What factors affect vocabulary acquisition?

4 How can we develop a variety of techniques for teaching meaning?

5 Can we encourage effective strategies for vocabulary learning?

6 How can we expose learners to vocabulary?

7 What criteria can we use for evaluating the vocabulary component of a coursebook?

8 What activity types can we develop for the teaching of vocabulary?

Introductory task

The extract below is taken from the introspections of a proficient learner and user of several languages. It focuses on strategies for learning vocabulary. Read the passage and consider these questions:

1 What strategies have you used as a language learner for learning vocabulary?

2 Do you encourage learners to keep vocabulary notebooks? If so, what guidelines or training do you give them?

3 Do you encourage learners to use any other strategies for vocabulary learning?

> 'In handling vocabulary I always make my own vocabulary notebook. The order in which I note down words that I select for this book is always: first English, then if need be a phonetic transcript of the word in the foreign language, then the orthographic version in the foreign language, and finally if need be an example of its use in a phrase or very short sentence. I order it this way round because it is more difficult to remember from English into the foreign language than the other way about and the act of writing it in this order helps to bridge the gap that way round.

> 'The selection of words that I make for the vocabulary notebook is based on frequency in the first place with considerable weight being given to the functional, notional or situational relevance of the item for me. The arrangement of words tends to vary but frequently I find that I have three different vocabulary lists going on at the same time. The first one is chronologically arranged. The second one may be alphabetically arranged and drawn upon the chronological list, though not incorporating all of it. The third vocabulary list is either grammatically or situationally ordered. In the grammatical list I might for example group all adverbs together; … '
> (Pickett 1978: 70)

4.1 Introduction: the task of learning vocabulary

In the literature of English language teaching and learning a recurring theme has been the neglect of vocabulary. In the early 1970s Wilkins wrote: 'Linguists have had remarkably little to say about vocabulary and one can find very few studies which could be of any practical interest for language teachers' (1972: 109), and almost a decade later Meara commented that vocabulary acquisition had 'received short shrift' from applied linguistics (1980: 221). Ellis (1995) expressed the view that the situation had not changed significantly.

This neglect sits uncomfortably with the significance placed on vocabulary learning by learners themselves. Pickett's (1978) subjects, one of whom is quoted in the extract in the Introductory task, pointed to the role that vocabulary learning had played for them. Another introspected in this way:

> 'This brings me to the subject of vocabulary learning, which to me always seems the key to any language. I am quite happy to pronounce

badly and make grammatical mistakes but there is no escape from learning words.'
(ibid.: 71)

The neglect of vocabulary is also surprising in view of the fact that errors of vocabulary are potentially more misleading than those of grammar. Sometimes the context of the utterance would lead a listener to question their first interpretation, but a chance response such as 'Yes, my father has an affair in that village' (confusing the Swedish *affär* meaning 'shop' with the English 'affair' which can mean 'extra-marital relationship') gives the listener the wrong impression.

It is also clear that the task of vocabulary learning is a substantial one for the EFL learner. Richards (1976) suggested that a native-speaker child on entering school at the age of five or six would already have a productive vocabulary of some 2,000 to 3,000 words. Compare this with the basic lexicons of similar size used to design the higher levels of graded readers intended for EFL adults (for example, Heinemann Guided Readers Upper Level at 2,200 words or Collins English Library Level Six at 2,500 words) and the substance of the learning task becomes evident. The lexicon of adult native speakers has been variously estimated since the beginning of this century, but a more recent study (Goulden, Nation, and Read 1990) gives an estimate of 17,000 words for the average educated speaker.

Despite the traditional neglect, recent years have seen a greater awareness of the questions which need to be addressed with regard to vocabulary learning by researchers, materials designers, and teachers. An agenda of issues might well contain the following:

– What strategies do learners use to acquire new words or to retain them?
– What exactly do learners learn about a word when they acquire it?
– How is a second language learner's mental lexicon organized and how does it develop over time?
– In the initial stages of learning a foreign language, which words are the most useful to learn?
– Why are some words easier to learn than others?
– How do learners build an understanding of the relationships among words?

The answers to some of these questions clearly depend on insights obtainable from research studies: both linguistic studies which focus on *what* relationships exist among words in the lexical system of the English language and acquisition studies which focus on *how* vocabulary is learned.

4.2 What do we know about the lexical system of English?

In order to understand better the task involved in learning the vocabulary of the English language we need to look at two aspects of meaning. The first concerns the link between meaning and the world to which words refer. The second involves the sense relations that exist among words.

4.2.1 *Denotative and connotative meaning*

If a word has reference to an object, action, or event in the physical world, this can be described as its *referential* or *denotative meaning*. Novice language learners can make the mistake of believing that one language maps neatly on to another and the task of learning it means simply learning new words for sets of objects, or states, or concepts. However, even the task of learning vocabulary in relation to physical objects is complicated by the fact that languages reflect the world in different ways and use different categories to describe it. Learners are therefore faced with different labelling systems. For example, every human being has two grandmothers, but there is only one word in English for both your mother's mother and your father's mother (apart from the very formal and clumsy 'maternal grandmother' and 'paternal grandmother'). However, some languages have two different words. English has two words for a large area of water, 'sea' and 'lake', whereas Swedish has one, *sjö*, presumably because some Swedish lakes have wide channels to the sea and it is difficult to distinguish where the lake ends and the sea begins.

As well as denotative meaning, learners have to deal with the complexities of *connotative meaning*. This term relates to the attitudes and emotions of a language user in choosing a word and the influence of these on the listener or reader's interpretation of the word. A simple example of this would be to consider the following group of adjectives used to describe people and to decide which have positive associations and which negative.

obstinate	energetic	ambitious	stubborn	single-minded
arrogant	confident	opportunistic	reliable	complacent
dogmatic	wise	determined	fanatical	rebellious

Some of these will invariably be positive, for example 'wise', or negative, for example 'arrogant', but others will depend on the context of use and the impression the speaker or writer is trying to create. 'Ambitious' is a good example.

An example of how the associations of words can be used to influence the reader towards the writer's viewpoint can be seen in this extract from an article on the arrest of General Augusto Pinochet in October 1998:

It is hard to describe the impact of the glorious news. It was as though fortifications which had seemed unbreachable had suddenly collapsed, as if some imposed unnatural silence were suddenly rent by a howl. Most victims of human-rights violations in South America have seen all their desire for justice smashed against the solid walls of impunity and amnesty. They have lived recounting their experiences and met studied silences.

(from Marcela López Levy: 'Clipping the condor's claws' in *New Internationalist*, April 1999)

Notice, for example, the effect of choosing the word 'smashed', similar in meaning to the more neutral 'destroyed' but with associations of shocking personal violence. And the expression 'rent by a howl', normally associated with creatures such as dogs or wolves and again suggesting sudden shock. In this short passage there are many other ways in which connotative meaning is used to persuade the reader towards a particular viewpoint and to convey the political passion of the writer.

Connotative meaning derives from a mix of cultural, political, social, and historical sources and learners will be aware of this phenomenon in their own language. The teacher can help to develop appropriate awareness of connotative meaning in the target language while dealing with texts, for example. But there are implications here, too, for encouraging extensive exposure to authentic reading and listening material so that students will encounter and learn from a wide range of texts containing connotative meaning.

4.2.2 *Meaning relations among words*

The second aspect of meaning involves the sense relations that exist among words. These relations can be found in two dimensions which linguists have often referred to as 'axes'. The horizontal axis represents *syntagmatic relations*, those between items in sentences. For example, a learner has to understand that we can say 'My car was badly damaged in the accident' but not *'My car was badly injured in the accident'. Only one of these verbs can collocate with the noun 'car'. The vertical axis represents *paradigmatic relations*, the complex relationships that exist between items in the whole lexical system. For example, learning the meaning of a word involves knowing how that meaning is defined in relation to other similar or opposite words. Learning English therefore means gradually acquiring a knowledge of *synonyms*, *antonyms*, and other relations in its semantic structure.

Syntagmatic relations

Syntagmatic relations are relations between words as they occur in sequence. In the English language there are words which co-occur with high frequency, for example, 'a long road', 'a ripe banana', 'a savage dog'. These are collocations. As well as nouns and adjectives we can find noun + verb collocations such as 'the dog barked' (not 'roared'), the sun shone (not 'glowed'), or verb + noun collocations such as 'he's picking strawberries' or 'she's collecting stamps', or noun + present participle collocations in compounds, such as 'train-spotting' and 'bird-watching'.

There are other words which do not co-occur naturally, for example, *'a tall road', *'a mature banana', and *'a barbaric dog'. With these particular examples, it would become easier for a learner over time to realize their non-compatibility as these adjectives frequently collocate with other nouns, for example, 'a tall man', 'a mature person', and 'a barbaric practice'. A growing knowledge of acceptable collocations will build associations which give learners clues about compatibility. However, with other collocations it is not possible to predict from knowing the meaning of each word in the collocation what is and what is not acceptable. These more idiomatic expressions are normal in the speech and writing of native speakers and therefore need to be a part of language learning. Examples include binominal idioms where the sequence of words is set, for example, 'cloak and dagger' and 'kith and kin'; phrasal verb idioms, for example, 'stand down' and 'get over'; catch phrases, for example, 'keep smiling' and 'chin up'; metaphors, for example 'donkey's years' and 'a pig's ear', and similes such as 'as pleased as Punch' and 'as thick as two short planks'. Nattinger (1988) suggests that such expressions should be seen as categories of 'lexical phrase' which learners can be encouraged to store as chunks of speech and retrieve holistically as they compose. The practical advantage of including them in a language course, which Nattinger argues for, is that instruction can help learners avoid incongruity and that having such phrases ready as whole 'chunks' for language production assists fluency. However, there are issues here for the teacher. Learning to understand idioms is one thing, but learning to produce them is perhaps another. Many idioms carry quite subtle nuances in meaning and learners need to be aware of this, develop preferences, and make choices which they feel are appropriate for themselves. Idioms seem to engender great enthusiasm in some learners and the teacher may need to guide them towards the most useful ones. Collocations, both idiomatic and non-idiomatic, are a problematic area for learners. A wide variety of activities for teaching them can now be found in textbooks, but these need to be carefully assessed by teachers.

Paradigmatic relations

Words not only have sequential relationships, but exist in complex relationships with other words in the language in a network of meanings. Linguists debate the precise categorization and naming of these relationships, but some terms are frequently used by teachers and textbook designers. The most common are *synonymy, antonymy*, and *hyponymy*.

Synonymy

A simple way of defining synonymy is to say that, in a given context, one linguistic item can be exchanged for another without changing the meaning of the sentence or utterance. For example, in the sentence:

> He answered the question courteously.

'politely' would probably be regarded as synonym as it could be substituted for 'courteously' without changing the meaning. It would be a mistake to suggest that words are substitutable in all contexts. In fact synonyms are hard to find because meaning depends on context. Could we, for example, substitute 'sadly' for 'unhappily' in the context of this sentence?

> He set about the task unhappily as he was not convinced of a positive outcome.

However, with learners at early levels, similarity is a useful way of presenting word meaning, especially with adult learners returning to study who will have varying language resources to draw on and can relate a new word to words they already know. For example, this teacher summarizes several words elicited from the class:

> Depressed, … what does this mean? … yes he's unhappy, he's sad, look at the picture … he's … yes … miserable, he's depressed.

With higher level students, teaching synonymous words can assist with the problem of repetitious writing, for instance teaching 'questions', 'issues', 'matters', and 'concerns' through the reformulation procedure (see 9.3.4) is a way of building range and variety in vocabulary use.

Antonymy

The term antonymy covers a number of relationships often thought of as opposites. *Complementarity* is used for oppositions such as 'male' and 'female' and 'dead' and 'alive' as these are clear-cut; one excludes the other. *Converseness* is a relationship where one term implies the other, as with 'import' and 'export', 'parent' and 'child', and 'trainer' and 'trainee'. And a notoriously difficult area is that of *gradable antonymy* where it is possible to create a scale of items, for instance, 'boiling', 'hot', 'warm', 'lukewarm', 'tepid', 'cool', 'cold', and 'icy' (of water), which may or may not relate to a similar scale in the learners' first language. The same scale would not apply when talking about weather, though some items on it would, which points to one of the problems for learners in dealing with antonymy.

Words have different opposites in different contexts. To take just one example, the adjective 'soft' collocates with a number of nouns and takes a different antonym with each:

soft water	hard water
soft material	rough material
soft music	loud music
soft colour	bright colour

This constitutes another difficulty for learners to tackle.

Hyponomy

Hyponymy is a relationship whereby one word includes others within a hierarchy, so that we have superordinate words and subordinate words. So 'flower', 'carnation', and 'rose' are in a hyponymous relationship, 'carnation' and 'rose' being subordinate hyponyms of 'flower' and co-hyponyms of each other. Although linguists disagree about what precisely constitutes a hyponymous relationship, teachers and textbooks use a variety of classifications in grouping vocabulary for ease of learning. McCarthy (1990) usefully describes these as 'ways of doing x', 'one of a series', and 'part of x'. An example of the first would be 'to snigger', 'to titter', 'to giggle', 'to guffaw', and 'to roar', as ways of laughing; of the second would be 'breakfast', 'lunch', 'tea', and 'dinner' as meals of the day; and of the third would be 'keyboard', 'mouse', and 'monitor' as parts of a computer.

The general question that arises from a consideration of the linguistic relations between words is the extent to which they can be usefully and explicitly exploited by the teacher.

4.3 How do second language learners acquire vocabulary?

Just as we can ask the question, 'What does it mean to know a word?' we can also ask the question, 'When can we say that a word has been learned?' Teachers often make a distinction between 'active' and 'passive' vocabulary. Passive refers to vocabulary which can be recognized when encountered, in a text for example, but which the learner cannot easily produce in speech or writing as active vocabulary. However, this is too simple a characterization of language learning. There are words which learners can retrieve from memory and use automatically. There are others for which learners experience a 'tip of the tongue effect', recalling something of the word but not its precise form. Yet other words exist in the memory but prove difficult to recall.

It may therefore be most useful to see vocabulary knowledge as a scale running from recognition of a word at one end to automatic production at the other, through intermediate stages of making greater sense of the word and how it might be used in different contexts. However, knowledge of some words will remain at the recognition end of the continuum and will be called on in reading and listening but might never become part of a learner's productive ability. This characterization of vocabulary knowledge is complicated by the phenomenon of forgetting: this can happen quite rapidly if distracting activities interrupt effective storing of the word, or more slowly if the word has been stored in the memory but is rarely encountered or used.

4.3.1 *Strategies for vocabulary learning*

In order to learn words learners use a range of strategies. Some of these can be called *cognitive*: they are direct mental operations which are concerned with working on new words in order to understand, categorize, and store them in the mental lexicon. Examples are making associations, learning words in groups, and exploring range of meaning. Another cognitive strategy reported by learners is that of using keywords. A keyword is a word chosen from the first language which sounds like the new word in the second language, and where it is possible to make some kind of association between the two. For example, the first syllable of the Swedish word *träsko* ('clog') is similar to the English word 'tread', so one can imagine a clog-shod foot treading heavily across the floor.

Other cognitive strategies can be observed when learners first encounter an unfamiliar word and engage in lexical inferencing in order to try to establish its meaning. Take the word 'agreeable', for example, in the following text:

> … when the English discovered that the Gaelic speakers of the Scottish Highlands were producing a most agreeable beverage, they asked what it was called. The Scots replied with their Gaelic name for it, *uisgebeatha*, which means 'water of life' in Gaelic. This name was taken into English as *whiskybae* and quickly shortened to *whisky*.
> (Trask 1994: 12)

A learner might deduce from the syntactic structure that the word is an adjective located before a noun, might divide the word into its parts, realizing that '-able' is a common suffix for an adjective, might read on for evidence in the context of the text that the meaning is positive, and might look for a similar word in his or her first language. In this way, contextual cues which relate to the reader's knowledge of alcoholic beverages are used for inferencing meaning. So, too, are the intralingual cues provided by a knowledge of the morphology of English. And, thirdly, any interlingual cues from similarity to words in the learner's first language can be used to assist the inferencing strategy.

It has been suggested (Xialong 1988; Haastrup 1989; Mondria and Wit-de Boer 1991) that inferring the meaning of a word from its context relates to the retention of that word, in particular that if the meaning of a new word is inferenced in conditions which require more careful analysis and decision-making, the retention will be better. This idea that retention depends in some way on the amount of mental and emotional energy used in processing a word has currently been gaining ground in views of vocabulary teaching and learning, and it is certainly true that many learners have developed effective strategies to assist with this (see 'The relationship between input and storage' on page 121). Some of these strategies are called *metacognitive*. They are not direct mental operations but indirect strategies which facilitate learning by actively involving the learner in conscious efforts to remember new words. Metacognitive strategies include the following: consciously collecting words from authentic contexts; making word cards; categorizing words into lists; and reactivating vocabulary in internal dialogue. For further discussions of learner strategies see 1.3.2 and 3.2.

It is useful for the teacher to be aware of the variety of methods used by learners to cope with words, to encourage learners in effective strategies, and to introduce some of these through teaching.

4.3.2 *Factors affecting vocabulary acquisition*

Many factors appear to play a role in vocabulary development, though the exact nature of the role is not always clearly understood and the findings of some research studies seem to contradict the received wisdom of the ELT profession and what has been standard practice in the classroom. Some factors are to do with *input*, in other words the way in which vocabulary presents itself to learners, for example through teacher presentation, reading words in texts, learning words during peer exchange, or through self-access work of some kind. Other factors are to do with storing, organizing, and building vocabulary in the mental lexicon and being able to retrieve or recall it when it is needed.

Features of input

Frequency

Frequency has been accorded a high level of significance in ELT for many years as a result of the use of word-frequency counting as a procedure informing syllabus and materials design. The rationale for this is quite simply that the most frequently occurring words in the English language will be those most useful to learners. The beginner level of many series of coursebooks or the first stage of many series of graded readers will have a basic lexical syllabus formulated from the first 500 to 800 most frequently occurring words in

English. The vocabulary lists which form the basis of syllabus specifications for much material currently in use relate back to work done as early as the 1930s and 1940s, later revised and adjusted. A well-used frequency list was that of West (1953), which has some 2,000 headwords, each accompanied by its inflected forms, together with a list of common derivatives and compounds. But as computer corpora came into use, the methodology of such word counts came under increasing fire in terms of such features as the size of corpus used, the range of sources in spoken and written modes, the range of text-types, topics, and styles, and the topicality of meaning and the range of meanings covered for words. Very large computer corpora can now be exploited, and these have reduced some of the problems. Some modern textbooks, for example *The COBUILD English Course* by Jane and Dave Willis, are based on a lexical syllabus derived from such corpora. However, even with vastly improved techniques for assessing frequency, its use as a criterion for selecting and grading vocabulary should continue to be carefully evaluated against other possible criteria. For example, if a particular day of the week proves more frequent than another, this might not necessarily support its earlier appearance in a coursebook. In fact, learning the days of the week together as a set might well facilitate the use of mnemonics for retention or productive comparison with the first language set.

Another way in which the concept of frequency has influenced ELT is in the repetition of words in texts. A study by Kachru (1962), for example, who tested his Indian students to see which words they knew from their coursebook, showed that most learners knew the words that appeared more than seven times, but they did not know half of the words that appeared only once or twice.

Repetition of words in materials can aid the process of lexical inferencing and has been used as a principle for constructing graded reading material for many years. Certainly, if learners are to be exposed to a wide range of word meanings and associations then it will be important for them to encounter words in a variety of different situations through extensive reading and listening.

Pronunciation
In the initial stages of language learning it is common for teachers to insist on a fair amount of pronunciation practice of new words to help learners acquire the correct stress pattern of syllables. In later stages, this is often discontinued as the focus of learning changes to other aspects of language and as individual learners pick up vocabulary in their own way and at their own rates. And yet it has been claimed (Tarone 1974; Channell 1988) that learners use stress to select what is important as they listen to a stream of English and that they therefore need to know for each word both the stress pattern that would be found in a dictionary and patterns that might be heard in continuous speech. This would suggest that, if the purpose for learning

English is to listen and understand, then learning word stress is important. If learners process speech partly by recognizing syllable patterns and stress, knowledge of these stored in the mental lexicon will facilitate quick comprehension. And it goes almost without saying that a learner who wishes to be intelligible in English needs to be able to stress words correctly. There are implications here both for teaching techniques and for learner strategies in dealing with new words.

Contextualization

One of the most cogent criticisms of the traditional practice of presenting lists of isolated word to learners is given by Schouten-van Parreren (1989), who presents a four-point argument, as follows:

> (1) If the words are presented as isolated elements, there is no point of support, no 'cognitive hold' for them in the learners' memory, so despite sometimes considerable learning effort, they are quickly forgotten again.
>
> (2) If the words are presented in thematically or especially in alphabetically ordered word lists, pupils will often suffer from interference. This not only hampers learning, but can be decidedly harmful, since unlearning is far more difficult than learning.
>
> (3) Isolated words do not present a linguistic reality, as the meaning of a word is in most cases partly defined by the context (Beheydt 1987).
>
> (4) Isolated words or words in isolated sentences do not present a psychological reality, because they do not carry a message. For this reason they cannot evoke emotions or involvement in the learner, a factor which plays an often underestimated, but yet important part in long-term acquisition. (Leontjew 1979).
>
> (Schouten-van Parreren 1989: 76–7)

She goes on to argue that texts, in contrast, present a linguistic and psychological reality, and that presenting words in the context of a text will provide support and reduce interference. It is her contention that if learners have to perform certain activities on unfamiliar words in texts, there is a good chance of retaining the words. The activities comprise guessing meaning from context and from word form, verifying meaning by checking in a dictionary, and analysis of the word form to recognize relationships between the new word and others already known. As yet, there is little empirical evidence to support this contention but it certainly accords with much contemporary classroom practice which is, as mentioned earlier, based on the idea that remembering a word depends on depth of processing.

The relationship between input and storage

Depth of processing

Cognitive psychologists (for example Craik and Lockhart 1972; Craik and Tulvig 1975) have suggested that learners are more likely to remember a word if they have worked on its meaning actively; in other words, input becomes *intake* if there is a depth of processing. We lack language-learning research studies to confirm this, though it would certainly accord with teachers' intuitions and with self-reports from learners. It also seems to be true that emotional response to a word affects retention, as demonstrated in the case of taboo words: ' … if a word has obscene meaning … it certainly seems to stick more easily, as army instructors well know' (Pickett 1978: 71). And not just taboo words. I remember a student who collected 'words I like' as she borrowed graded readers from the class library. As she was an effective learner of vocabulary the strategy must have had advantages.

One study (Brown and Perry 1991) will serve as an example of how research can yield interesting insights for teachers. This tried to compare the effectiveness of the 'keyword' method of dealing with new vocabulary (see 4.3.1 above) with a method which involves a greater degree of semantic processing. Three groups of Arabic-speaking Egyptian students were involved. The first group was given a set of words with short phrase definitions and asked to choose keywords for each item. They were instructed that the keyword should be a concrete adjective or noun (as were the vocabulary items to be learned), should sound like at least one syllable of the English word, and should be taken from Egyptian colloquial Arabic. The second group was given the set of vocabulary items, the definitions, two examples of the word used in sentences, and a question they had to answer using the word. The third group were given the information and the tasks given to both other groups. Unannounced testing was undertaken on the day after instruction ended, the following day, and nine days later using a cued-recall test and a multiple-choice test. The researchers acknowledged the difficulty of knowing exactly how some students might have modified their strategy for abstract versus concrete words but, in general, the experiment provided 'some initial evidence' that the combined approach was more effective than the keyword method alone. Further research is clearly needed to compare a range of approaches to learning vocabulary. However, there appears to be growing evidence to support the experience of teachers and learners that active mental involvement aids retention. In other words, as Craik and Lockhart (1972) suggested, as a learner moves from surface-level activity based on the sound and visual image of a word to a deeper level of meaning, and at the same time relates the word to existing knowledge, then memory traces become more permanent. The message for teachers seems to be that we need to introduce and use techniques for vocabulary learning which encourage learners to work with words in this way.

Building word networks

The mental lexicon has been characterized variously as a storehouse, a library, an encyclopedia, and a computer. All of these are legitimate to a degree in describing its many capacities, but it is at present unclear exactly how learners store and organize words in the mental lexicon and what kinds of relationships are built among words as they are stored. Native speakers are certainly able to cross-refer to synonyms, antonyms, and hyponyms and are able to retrieve, very quickly, words with similar spelling or similar prefixes and suffixes. It also seems to be the case (as word-association games attest), that we organize words by meaning and that a particular word will gradually become part of a semantic cluster or lexical set: for example, 'eggs', 'bacon', 'cereal', 'toast', and 'jam' as the typical constituents of an English breakfast; 'apple', 'pear', 'peach', 'nectarine', and 'plum' as edible fruits, or 'father', 'mother', 'son', and 'daughter' as members of a nuclear family. In fact, a good deal of language teaching material is based on the assumption that learners categorize words systematically, building careful networks of meaning, which include the various kinds of relationships outlined in 4.2, and that teachers can facilitate this process through direct teaching.

However, in recent years, contradictory advice to teachers has been emerging from studies into the use of semantic links or networks in classroom materials and activities. For example, compare these extracts from research into vocabulary learning:

> Semantic links play an important role in production. This suggests the use of semantic field based presentation methods ...
> (Channell 1988: 94)

> ... in light of research motivated by interference theory and, more recently, the distinctiveness hypothesis, the possibility arises that the practice of presenting L2 students with their new vocabulary grouped together in sets of syntactically and semantically similar new words might actually impede rather than facilitate the learning of the words.
> (Tinkham 1993: 371)

The distinctiveness hypothesis (Hunt and Mitchell 1982) referred to here posits that items of information are more easily learned if they are not similar. Clearly, if further studies were to support this hypothesis, the findings would call into question much of standard ELT practice in which textbooks and teachers tend to make use of semantic links. In the light of these seeming contradictions, teachers will need to use techniques cautiously and judge for themselves whether a particular use of semantic links works for their students. It may be, for example, that the activity in Materials extract 4.1, involving adjectives with similar meanings, is best used at a secondary stage when the words can be recognized, some meanings have been acquired, and learners have reached a point where they will benefit from further opportunity to make connections and distinctions.

The general issue for teachers seems to be whether learners should simply be encouraged in non-specific ways to actively build their own associations for new words and thereby extend the networks of the mental lexicon, or whether vocabulary learning activities should include direct instruction which aims to shape the associations learners make.

Cultural factors in the building of meaning

As learners develop their vocabulary knowledge, they acquire not only new words but also new meanings associated with words they have already learned. These are acquired gradually as words are met in different contexts and eventually a word might have extensive and complex meaning associations. Figure 4.1 shows Anglin's (1985) representation of the way in which one adult expressed aspects of the meaning of the word 'dog'. Anglin's scheme illustrates Eco's (1979) comment that every word is potentially a text. This implies that, in order both to interpret meaning correctly and to choose vocabulary appropriately, learners need to become aware of such nuances. Furthermore, many of these will be culturally influenced and may not be easily accessible. For example, in Anglin's scheme for 'dog', those associations relating to dogs as family pets would not be familiar to learners from cultures where dogs are not domestic animals but are seen as scavengers. Teachers need to be aware that there will be gaps in learners' understanding of nuance and find ways of helping them to fill the gaps with further meaning associations.

Another culturally affected factor influencing acquisition is the phenomenon of prototypes. A simple definition of prototype is that it is the foremost example of a particular conceptual category, the one that springs most easily to mind when a learner hears a word, for example, 'tree'. If an oak tree is the kind of tree first thought of, then it is a prototype and other trees are non-prototypes. Of course, some concepts or objects will be more central to a particular learner because of personal experience, but it seems that some are shared widely across speakers from a particular culture. Rosch (1975) claimed that Americans from quite widely differing backgrounds perceived a robin as a classic example of a bird, a canary as a poorer example, and a penguin as even poorer. A study by Aitchinson (1992) seemed to suggest that the cabbage was the prototype among vegetables for German speakers. Aitchinson (ibid.) also raises the question of whether teachers need to be aware of how such rankings within categories might differ between English and the first languages of their learners, or even of whether teaching should be influenced by this knowledge. Do learners acquire the meanings of

Figure 4.1: Aspects of the meaning of the word 'dog' (Anglin 1985)

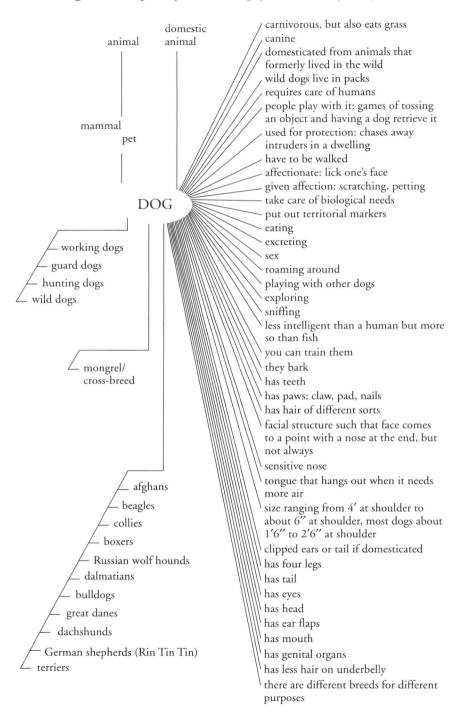

prototypes more quickly than those of non-prototypes, for example? Further research studies are needed to test such suggestions.

Prototype studies, however, have pointed out that we store certain kinds of knowledge about words. Some knowledge is basic and universal, for example, to return to Anglin's scheme for 'dog', that a dog has four legs, a sensitive nose, and barks. Other knowledge is more abstract and relates to personal or cultural experience: this is known as schematic knowledge. 'Schemata' are mental representations associated with the word which are activated in the mind when it is encountered. From the 'dog' list such associations as 'people play with it' or 'lick one's face' would be classed as cultural schematic knowledge. So the word 'dog' will evoke different associations in different cultures. The concept of schematic knowledge has taken on great significance in the field of reading in a foreign language: in 6.3.3 the ways in which classroom practice has moved to incorporate a pre-reading phase which involves activating learners' existing schematic knowledge is discussed.

This section has considered some key factors in the learning of vocabulary. The extent to which each is significant will depend partly on the purposes for learning English of any particular learner, whether mainly for reading academic texts, for example, or for appreciating literature, or for communicating in English with other non-native speakers of the language.

4.4 What are the implications for the teaching of vocabulary?

At the moment, teachers and textbook writers are in a position of trying to work out principles and procedures for teaching vocabulary on the basis of the insights we have gained about the lexical system of English and about vocabulary acquisition. These are tentative. It would be useful to have information from classroom studies as to which teaching procedures seem to enhance particular learning strategies and which strategies are effective for which aspects of vocabulary learning. In the absence of such information we need to review current methodology and materials and decide how best to exploit the ideas available with our own learners. A number of principles seem to be at work, some well-established and others more recent, and it is to these we now turn.

4.4.1 *Developing a variety of techniques for the teaching of meaning*

Learners will encounter new words in a variety of ways in the classroom, through learning materials, through the teacher's language, and through the language of other learners. Although the teacher's ultimate role may be to build independence in learners by teaching them good strategies for vocabulary learning, he or she will frequently need to explain new words. It is useful to have a repertoire of techniques for this task and to use whichever combination is appropriate to the word and to the students. Take the word 'exhausted', for example. There are a number of techniques which could be used:

— A physical demonstration, using mime and gesture, may be the most effective as it will create a visual memory for the word.
— A verbal explanation, involving a number of contexts, for example, a long journey, a hard day's work, or a strenuous physical task, will lead the learners towards meaning.
— A synonym, for example, 'very tired', has the advantage of making learners aware of paradigmatic relations in the language and that a range of words exists from which a choice can be made.

Other possible techniques are translation, pointing to objects, using visual aids such as mounted magazine pictures or blackboard drawings, using antonyms, or asking learners to check in a dictionary. Some of these require more processing from the learner and will aid retention. The teacher will need to make decisions about which words are useful to retain and choose techniques accordingly. 'Word networks', for example, can be used to establish and consolidate meaning, exploiting the natural strategy learners seem to use (see 'Building word networks' on page 122). Following an idea of Robinson (1989), the teacher can explain the meaning of a word like 'famous', give some examples, ask students to confirm by checking in their dictionaries, and then elicit some instances, drawing on students' shared knowledge of the world (see Figure 4.2(a)). It is also possible to draw on the learners' personal preferences and experiences, as in the word-network in Figure 4.2(b) for 'irritating'. A feedback session after individual work can be used to collate the examples and check them for accurate comprehension.

4.4.2 *Encouraging the development of effective strategies*

Building on what we know of the strategies used by good language learners for vocabulary acquisition, it is possible to involve students in activities which help them to develop new strategies as well as strengthen existing ones. For example, many learners can be observed writing down new words

Figure 4.2 : Word networks for 'famous' and 'irritating'

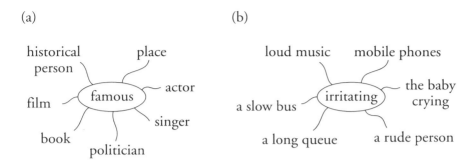

(a)   (b)

as they occur during a lesson but it is less common to find such thorough strategies for notebook keeping as those described by Pickett's subject at the beginning of this chapter. The activity in Materials extract 4.A gives students ideas for how they might design their notebooks.

It is unlikely that students would take up all of the suggestions or even that all of the students would suddenly develop into assiduous notebook keepers but, as I overheard one teacher saying, 'If, as a result of doing this activity in class, five out of my twenty-five students make effective notebooks and find them useful, it's an activity worth doing.'

Another strategy reported as useful by students is to make a word-network of vocabulary associated with a particular item as shown in Figure 4.2. This can form another section of the notebook. It is especially helpful when the coursebook in use is topic-based, but it can also be used when a text has introduced words which link to a topic.

Schmitt and Schmitt (1995) suggest a way in which keywords (see 4.3.1) and word networks can be combined with other information to create word-cards. Figure 4.3 shows an example from a Japanese student's store of word-cards.

Since students will put effort into vocabulary notebooks and word-cards it is worth ensuring that they are used repeatedly and that students review the words. A word-network can be referred to in writing about a topic, or teachers can ask students to use a certain number of words from their book in a writing task. Learners can share their books or cards with each other in pairwork, explaining a particular word and the information given. And the teacher can encourage self-testing.

Materials extract 4.A

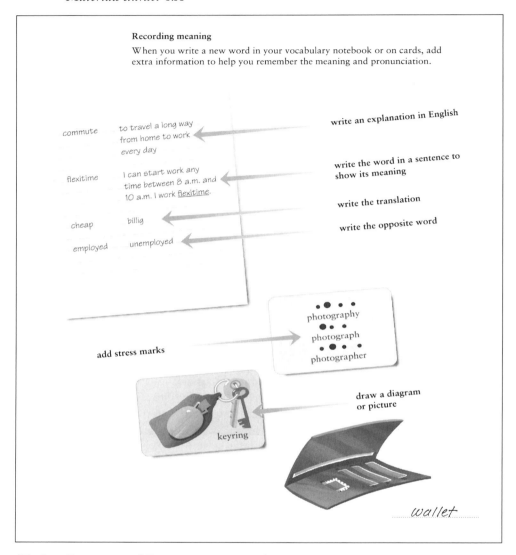

Recording meaning

When you write a new word in your vocabulary notebook or on cards, add extra information to help you remember the meaning and pronunciation.

commute — to travel a long way from home to work every day ← write an explanation in English

flexitime — I can start work any time between 8 a.m. and 10 a.m. I work flexitime. ← write the word in a sentence to show its meaning

write the translation

cheap — billig ← write the opposite word

employed — unemployed ←

add stress marks → photography / photograph / photographer

draw a diagram or picture → keyring

wallet

(Taylor: *International Express, Pre-intermediate* SB, page 7)

4.4.3 *Exposing learners to vocabulary through reading and training lexical inferencing*

The suggestion was made in 4.3.1 that if the inferencing strategy in reading unfamiliar words involves a degree of problem-solving this will help with the retention of the word. However, despite the existence of procedures for inferencing (see, for example, Nation and Coady's suggested procedure in 6.2.1), it is not easy to find good examples of activities which exploit these in

Figure 4.3: A word card for 'horror' (Schmitt and Schmitt 1995: 138)

Card 2 (front)		**Card 2** (back)	
L1 translation of *horror*	keyword illustration (*horu* =dig)	part of speech, and pronunciation	semantic map
工 た 怖 きょうふ	horu	horror (n.) [hɒrər]	emotion death horror accident war
intense fear, dread	The family watched in horror as their house burned.	-id adj. -ibly adv. -ify v.	horror movie horror-struck inspire horror
L2 information	Example sentence	Derivative information	Collocations

contemporary textbooks. In a persuasive paper, Moran (1991) analyses twenty coursebooks and finds that even where general advice is given and, in a few cases, procedures suggested, actual practice is scarce. If the textbook lacks a thorough approach, it becomes the task of the teacher to help students develop inferencing strategies, drawing attention to the guidance available and applying it through careful and repeated work. The procedure given in Materials extract 4.B, for example, might be supplemented after the third guideline, by discussion of the kinds of clues available.

Materials extract 4.B

> *Decide whether you need to understand the exact meaning of the unfamiliar word in order to understand the general sense of the sentence or the passage.*
>
> *Decide what part of speech the word is.*
> *Look in the context for clues to its general sense.*
> *Read on and confirm or revise your guess.*

Greenall and Swan: *Effective Reading*, page 16

Students can work in pairs to share their insights and build a collective picture of what they have been looking for: for example, cognate words; morphological clues such as prefixes denoting size (for example, 'mega-'); or a negative (for example, 'il-', 'dis-', 'im-'); the function of the phrase or clause in which the word occurs (for example, to give a contrasting opinion or to give a reason); and the learner's prior knowledge of the world.

It is also useful to remember the distinction between inferencing for the purpose of fluent reading and inferencing as a strategy in vocabulary acquisition. Research tends to suggest that if inferencing is easy because the text is rich in contextual clues or there is a cognate word, retention is less likely. The more active the learner needs to be, the more likely the word will be remembered. Awareness of this distinction will guide the teacher into exploiting texts both for reading strategy development and for vocabulary acquisition.

4.4.4 *Teaching the effective use of dictionaries*

With increasing interest in effective learning strategies and learner independence, the dictionary has come into focus as an important classroom and personal resource. Teachers can take on a number of useful roles with regard to dictionary use. First, if a good monolingual dictionary is kept as a class resource, the teacher can ask a student to look up an unknown word once other strategies have been tried, establishing in this way that the dictionary has a legitimate place in a sequence of strategies but is best not used automatically as a first resort. It is also a way of demonstrating that a monolingual dictionary has advantages over a small bilingual one in providing examples of contextual use and stress patterns.

Some teachers working in well-resourced circumstances introduce students to a range of monolingual dictionaries at the beginning of a course and give them a 'searching task' so that they can compare features such as accessibility and amount of information given before purchasing their own. Certainly teachers and textbook designers see it as their responsibility to train the effective use of the dictionary as a number of skills are involved in this.

The two tasks in Materials extracts 4.C and 4.D serve to demonstrate the growing interest in training learners in efficient dictionary use. Materials extract 4.C introduces learners to the format of monolingual dictionary entries and helps them to find their way around the information a dictionary offers. Question 1 gives the teacher a way into discussing the role of the dictionary. The series of questions could be usefully replicated by a teacher using whatever dictionaries are available. It can be particularly useful to take learners through sample dictionary entries like those shown in this activity to illustrate the kinds of meaning that are presented and how.

The activity in Materials extract 4.D is in line with the writers' belief that it is not practical to try to eliminate small bilingual dictionaries from the classroom. It therefore becomes the teacher's responsibility to ensure that learners are aware of the problems inherent in using these. The task teaches the importance of double-checking translations in the mother-tongue– English section.

Materials extract 4.C

Wordpower   **Work file. Dictionary skills(1)**

❶ Work in groups. List the information about words you can find in a good dictionary.

❷ Complete the exercise. Check your answers with the extracts from the *Oxford Wordpower Dictionary*.

1 In a dictionary, what do the symbols [U] and [C] mean?
2 Is the noun *pay* used with a singular or a plural verb?
3 What is the difference between *wages* and *salary*?
4 Complete the sentences below with the correct preposition.

   a. He paid £5,000 .... the painting.

   b. Can I pay .... cheque or .... credit card?

5 Is *headquarters* used with a singular or a plural verb?
6 What is the abbreviation for *headquarters*?

☆ **pay¹** /peɪ/ *noun* [U] money that you get regularly for work that you have done: *It's a dirty job but the pay is good.* ○ *a pay increase* ☛ **Pay** is the general word for money that you get regularly for work that you have done. **Wages** are paid weekly or daily in cash. A **salary** is paid monthly, directly into a bank account.
You pay a **fee** for professional services, eg to a doctor, lawyer, etc. **Payment** is money that you get for work that you do once or not regularly.

☆ **pay²** /peɪ/ *verb* (*pt, pp* **paid**) **1** [I,T] **pay (sb) (for sth)**; **pay sth (to sb) (for sth)** to give sb money for sth: *She is very well paid.* ○ *Do you want to pay by cheque or by credit card?* ○ *The work's finished but we haven't paid the builders yet.* ○ *to be paid by the hour* ○ *We paid the dealer £3000 for the car.* **2** [T] **pay sth (to sb)** to give the money that you owe for sth: *Have you paid the gas bill?* **3** [I,T] to make a profit; to be worth doing: *The factory closed down because the owners couldn't make it pay.* ○ *It would pay you to get professional advice before making a decision.*

ˌ**head ˈquarters** *noun* [plural, with sing or pl verb] (*abbr* **HQ**) the central office, etc of an organization: *Where is/are the firm's headquarters?*

(Taylor: *International Express, Intermediate* SB, page 18 and *Wordpower* Dictionary, pages 455 and 129)

Materials extract 4.D

F/8 Translation game

LEVEL	**Elementary to Advanced**
TIME	**15–20 minutes**
PREPARATION	Ensure that each member of the group possesses or has access to a good bilingual dictionary (English–mother-tongue/mother-tongue–English). Pocket dictionaries will not be adequate.
IN CLASS	1 Ask the students to work individually.
	2 Write up an English word on the blackboard: choose one which will produce a rich set of translations.
	3 Ask the students to look up in the dictionary the word on the board and to read through the translation(s) given. Then ask them to choose one mother-tongue word that translates the English word and to look that up in the mother-tongue–English section of the dictionary. They should then choose one of the English translations offered for that word and repeat the process.
	4 Ask the students to continue in this way until they have looked up, say, a dozen words. At each stage they should write down the word they look up.
EXAMPLE	Working with a German–English dictionary, one person produced this list:

BAG → *Sack* → SACK → *Laufpass* → DISMISSAL → *Entlassung* → RELEASE → *Befreiung* → DELIVERANCE → *Rettung* → SALVAGE → *Bergung* → SHELTERING → *Zuflucht* → REFUGE

(Morgan and Rinvolucri: *Vocabulary*, page 99)

4.4.5 *Evaluating the vocabulary component of coursebooks*

Contemporary coursebooks vary greatly in the degree to which they show a concern with vocabulary acquisition. Any teacher wishing to work productively with learners in this area will need to assess the vocabulary component of the book and supplement it where necessary. A first step might be to evaluate the book in terms of its professed aims in relation to vocabulary if, indeed, it states any, or to check that the claims made in the teacher's book hold good. After checking any claims, the teacher will need to evaluate the particular lexicon and methodology in relation to the needs of his or her learners. Do the semantic sets cover those of especial importance or interest to the class? Does the methodology involve teaching strategies for independent learning of vocabulary or will the teacher need to add an element of learner training to the course?

When the textbook has been produced for an international market, the teacher will need to think about the particular problems and dangers for the class in the relationship of the first language to English, especially with other Indo-European languages or with languages which have borrowed from English. Where a word has the same sound, the same form, and the same meaning, time can be saved. Where the meaning and form are similar but the sound is different, for example, 'theatre' or 'telephone', the focus of practice will be on pronunciation. Where form and sound are similar but the meaning is different we have the phenomenon of 'false friends', which needs special care.

An evaluation checklist for the teacher could include these questions:

1 Does the book explain its selection of vocabulary?
– Has the selection been made in relation to an established lexicon such as Threshold Level, COBUILD, or the Cambridge English Lexicon?
– Is the lexicon given as an appendix? For teachers in the teachers' book? For students in the coursebook?
– Is vocabulary given unit by unit? How is it listed? Active? Passive? Topic?
– Do the topic areas need to be supplemented?

2 How is vocabulary presented?
– Is vocabulary work drawn from texts?
– Are there specific activities which explicitly refer to aspects of vocabulary, for example, collocation, word formation, synonymy? If so, does the book cover those you think useful?

3 Is there a focus on how words are retained?
– Do inferencing activities encourage depth of processing?
– Are students encouraged and given guidance in strategies for learning, for example making notebooks, reviewing, testing themselves?

4 How much guidance does the teachers' book give on techniques for teaching meaning?

4.4.6 *Teaching vocabulary explicitly through a range of activity types*

It is evidently the view of many current textbook writers that, as well as indirect learning through handling the language in classroom activities, direct vocabulary instruction is useful. Teachers who wish to provide direct instruction can find many useful ideas for task types in both coursebooks and supplementary materials but they will need to formulate principles for their own classroom practice in this area. One criterion might be that vocabulary is well-contextualized, for example, through listening or reading material. A reading text can provide a springboard for a range of vocabulary-focused work, as Materials extract 4.E shows. The vocabulary work does not replace work on the learners' response to the content of the text but is part of follow-up activity. Here the authors provide information and practice on parts of speech. Students are given the opportunity to practise using words as different parts of speech and to learn how word-stress is shown in dictionaries.

Another principle might be to use the opportunities created by the students' own queries or attempts to use vocabulary, and to focus for a few moments on a word and other words related to it. This can be particularly effective as, in struggling to find the appropriate word, a learner provides a context for the meaning the teacher supplies at the point of need.

A further principle might be to allocate time in every lesson to some kind of vocabulary work and to build a checklist of the areas to be covered during a year's programme, drawn up as appropriate to the level of learners, from the various elements discussed in this chapter:

1 sense relations (for example, synonymns, antonyms, homonyms)
2 rules of word formation (for example, common prefixes and suffixes)
3 collocations and idioms
4 connotative meaning
5 strategies for learning (for example, notebooks, dictionary use).

Materials extracts 4.F, 4.G, and 4.H demonstrate the types of task which teachers can design for their own classes.

'Wordpower' in Materials extract 4.F develops knowledge of word meaning and, having presented examples, encourages students to search for others, keeping them actively analysing the language data they are exposed to in the materials. 'Collocation' in Materials extract 4.G deals with common adjective–noun collocations and provides interactive practice to assistant retention. The activity in Materials extract 4.H exploits the concept of the 'word-network' and encourages learners to activate or learn words associated with camping by suggesting a set of categories to develop.

Working to a set of principles like those just described will ensure that learners receive exposure to a rich and varied range of vocabulary which they can work on in their preferred ways for acquisition.

Materials extract 4.E

● VOCABULARY AND PRONUNCIATION

Word formation

1 Look at the entry for the word **photograph** in the
Oxford Wordpower Dictionary.

☆**photograph** /'fəʊtəgrɑːf *US*
-græf/ (also *informal* **photo**)
noun [C] a picture that is taken
with a camera: *to take a photo*
○ *a colour photograph* ○ *This
photo is a bit out of focus.* ○ *to
have a photo enlarged* ○ *That's
a lovely photograph of you.* ☛
Look at **negative** and **slide**.
photograph *verb* [T] to take a
photograph of sb/sth.

photographer /fə'tɒgrəfə(r)/
noun [C] a person who takes
photographs.
photographic /ˌfəʊtə'græfɪk/
adj connected with photographs
or photography: *photographic
equipment*.
photography /fə'tɒgrəfi/
noun [U] the skill or process
of taking photographs: *wildlife
photography*.

Notice how different parts of speech (noun and verb)
and words formed from the headword (**photographer**,
photographic, **photography**) are given in the same
entry. Is this the same in your dictionary?

Look how the stress is shown: /'fəʊtəgrɑːf/. Practise
saying the words in phonetic script.

2 Complete the charts with the different parts of speech.
The missing words are all from the article *A World
Guide to Good Manners*. Mark the stress.
Use your dictionary to help you with the
pronunciation.

3 Rewrite the sentences, using the word in italics in a
different word class.

Example
We had a long *discussion* about politics.
We ***discussed*** politics for a long time.

a She gave me some *advice* about which clothes to wear.
She _____ .

b How *high* is that wall?
What's the _____ ?

c Children should never speak to *strange* people.
Children _____ .

d I *felt* that there was someone watching me.
I had _____ .

e We had a lot of *difficulty* in finding the way here.
It was _____ .

f My son's *behaviour* at the party was very bad.
My son _____ .

g There are a lot of *foreign* people in town at the
moment.
There are _____ .

h The *shock* made my hair turn white.
I was so _____ .

Verb	Noun
	be'haviour
	ar'rangement
meet	
ad'vise	
	di'scussion
feel	
deal	
	ac'ceptance
tip	
	admi'ration

Noun	Adjective
'foreigner	
shock	
	high
	re'spectful
'difficulty	
re'serve	
	strange
of'fence	

(Soars and Soars: *New Headway Intermediate* SB, page 42)

4.4.7 *Developing resources for vocabulary teaching*

Where resourcing allows, it can be of considerable value to develop different
types of resources for vocabulary teaching. One is a set of good monolingual
dictionaries, sufficient at least for pairwork in class. Another is a bank of
word puzzles, which a group of interested teachers can design themselves.
Topic-based crosswords, for example, are popular and can be put to good use
in mixed ability classes when some learners complete tasks before others and
have time to fill.

An invaluable resource is a visual aids library for teachers to borrow from,
with pictures mounted on stiff card for durability and classified into topics

Materials extract 4.F

Wordpower

218

keep

1 make something or somebody stay in a particular position or state

to keep the food hot

2 have something and not throw it away, give it to someone else or lose it

Keep those notes. They might be useful.

3 put something in a particular place and store it there

You should either keep your Driving Licence with you, or keep it in the car.

4 repeatedly do a particular action

I kept making the same mistake.

Listen. It keeps making a funny noise!

Look at the examples here. There are three belonging to category 1, two to category 2, one to category 3, and three to category 4.

WELL, I KEPT TELLING YOU HE WAS NO GOOD!

I KEEP ON THINKING ABOUT HIM...

WHERE DO YOU KEEP THE TEA?

A: Can we keep these, please, or must we give them back?

B: No, they're for you to keep.

Close the windows. It'll keep the room warmer.

KEEP GOING! DON'T STOP!

SHH. KEEP QUIET!

SO SORRY TO KEEP YOU WAITING, COME IN!

Now look at the labels in section 216. Find six more examples of **keep**. Which categories do they belong to?

(Willis and Willis: *The COBUILD English Course 1* SB, page 91)

Materials extract 4.G

Worksheet 1

Collocation **15**

1 a We often combine words in certain ways. In English, for example, we can say:

> heavy rain   a strong wind   make a mistake   do one's homework

Other languages may use different adjectives or verbs with these nouns. It is important, therefore, to learn the different partners that words can have. This worksheet looks at some common examples.

b Which adjectives in box A can you combine with the nouns in box B?

A	
close	serious
hard	high
strong	light
big	heavy

B	
sleeper	salary
disappointment	worker
friend	accent
illness	smoker

c Complete the sentences with adjectives from **b**. Then move round the class and ask questions to complete the chart.

Find someone who ...	*Name*
… is a .... sleeper.	_____
… is a .... smoker.	_____
… is a .... worker.	_____
… has (or will have) a .... salary.	_____
… doesn't think they have a .... foreign accent when they speak English.	_____
… has had a .... illness in their life.	_____
… has recently had a .... disappointment.	_____
… has a .... friend of a different nationality.	_____

(Redman, Ellis, and Viney: *A Way with Words,* Resource Pack 1, page 57)

such as 'activities', 'food', and 'animals', and stored for easy access, for example in box files. Teachers setting up such resources will need to address a number of issues, including the following:

1 What kinds of visuals would you include (for example, magazine pictures, photographs, self-drawn flashcards)?
2 What criteria would guide your selection of the various kinds (for example, size, clarity, style, colour, appropriacy to sociocultural background)?
3 How would you gather together the resources (for example, by asking for contributions, by working with colleagues, by getting students to bring them to class)?
4 How would you classify the resources (for example, in topic areas)?
5 What would be the best format for storing the resources (for example, box files, hanging files)?
6 Who would be responsible for maintenance, security, and additions?

Materials extract 4.H

---

2 **Word power:** Travel

1 *Pair work*

Add these words to the word map.

credit card
health insurance
medicines
money belt
passport
penknife
plane tickets
rucksack
shorts
sleeping bag
swimwear
tent
traveller's cheques
vaccination
visa

Clothing
....
....
....
....
....

Camping gear
....
....
....
....

Money
....
....
....
....

Camping trip

Travel documents
....
....
....

Health
....
....
....
....

2 Now add five more words to the map.
Then compare with other students.

(Richards: *Changes 2* SB, page 40)

4.5 Conclusion

This chapter has tried to demonstrate the complexities of learning the English lexicon and, as yet, the lack of clear insights from research studies to inform teachers how they might best help their learners. Vocabulary teaching, however, is developing greater importance in the English language classroom, although it has not reached the level of consistency and systematicity that grammar teaching enjoys. Many teachers would now agree with Richards's assertion that we need 'a rich view of lexical competence' (1976: 88), and are exploring ways of providing vocabulary instruction, some of these based on what good learners tell us they do. Further research studies may help us to form insights about the most effective procedures for vocabulary teaching, but probably the most sensible approach for the contemporary classroom teacher is to experiment cautiously with the kinds of activities available in contemporary coursebooks and to gauge their usefulness in assisting learners with the very considerable task of acquiring vocabulary. Also, given that frequency, attention, practice and revision are all necessary for successful vocabulary learning, an inevitable conclusion has to be that learners need to take on a considerable measure of responsibility for their own vocabulary development. This entails active involvement with new vocabulary in class-time and strategies for acquiring vocabulary independently out of class.

Discussion topics and projects

1 Examine a textbook of your choice and answer the following:
   (a) What aims, if any, are given for the teaching of vocabulary?
   (b) Is there evidence of a lexical syllabus? How is it organized?
   (c) Do you think there is adequate provision for teaching vocabulary?

2 Review a set of three or four coursebooks used with different levels of learner in your institution. List the different types of procedure used for teaching vocabulary.

3 On the basis of discussion in this chapter and your own beliefs about vocabulary learning, formulate a set of criteria for evaluating a task designed to develop vocabulary. Use your criteria to evaluate the tasks in Materials extracts 4.I and 4.J.

4 If none exists already, would it be possible for you to set up a visual aids library for teachers in your institution? If so:
   (a) What types of materials would you collect?
   (b) What categories would you use to organize the resources?
   (c) How could you work with your colleagues to set up the library?

5 Find an authentic text you could use with a particular group of learners you teach. Decide which words you might want to introduce to students before they read the text and design pre-reading work to do this. What vocabulary-based work would you design for use while and after reading?

6 Give a group of students a text to read which contains some words which will be unknown to them. Ask them to work together to try to infer the meanings of these words together. Record the conversation. What different types of cues did they use?

7 Observe a lesson, if you can, with intermediate learners of English, and make notes on the following:
   (a) Did the teacher have any specific aims for teaching vocabulary?
   (b) Was vocabulary dealt with explicitly?
   (c) How was new vocabulary presented? Through explanation? Through demonstration? Through context?
   (d) What procedures were used to practise new vocabulary?
   (e) How much responsibility did learners take for acquiring new vocabulary?

Materials Extract 4.1

---

6 **Word power:** Adjectives

1 Pair work

Add these words to
the word map.

boring
disgusting
fascinating
odd
pointless
ridiculous
silly
terrible
terrific
unusual
weird
wonderful

awful

stupid

Reactions

exciting

strange

2   Now look at these words. Do they describe a positive (+) or a negative (−) reaction?

dreadful ......   fantastic ......   marvellous ......   pathetic ......
excellent ......   horrible ......   outstanding ......   superb ......

3 Pair work

Use some of the adjectives above to describe the most recent film you've seen.
Pay attention to word stress.

(Richards: *Changes 2* SB, page 104)

8 Decide on a topic which would be popular with a group of students you
   know and design a lesson focused on that topic. In your lesson plan, include
   some aims for vocabulary learning and procedures for helping learners
   with the topic vocabulary.

Further reading

Carter, R. 1987. *Vocabulary: Applied Linguistics Perspectives.* London: Allen
and Unwin.

This is an introductory study of modern English vocabulary and is divided
into three parts. Part One is a linguistic analysis of the English lexical system
and looks in turn at basic concepts and terms, the notion of core vocabulary,
words and patterns, and lexis in discourse. Part Two reviews three fields of
study: stylistics, lexicography, and vocabulary learning and teaching. Part
Three consists of two case studies, the first an exploration of associations in

Materials Extract 4.J

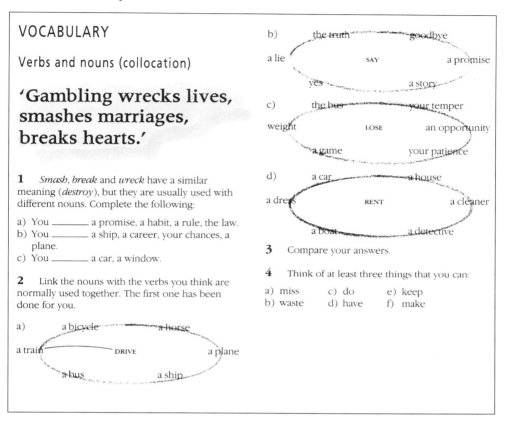

VOCABULARY

Verbs and nouns (collocation)

'Gambling wrecks lives, smashes marriages, breaks hearts.'

1 *Smash*, *break* and *wreck* have a similar meaning (*destroy*), but they are usually used with different nouns. Complete the following:

a) You _____ a promise, a habit, a rule, the law.
b) You _____ a ship, a career, your chances, a plane.
c) You _____ a car, a window.

2 Link the nouns with the verbs you think are normally used together. The first one has been done for you.

a) a bicycle · a horse · a train — DRIVE · a plane · a bus · a ship

b) the truth · goodbye · a lie · SAY · a promise · yes · a story

c) the bus · your temper · weight · LOSE · an opportunity · a game · your patience

d) a car · a house · a dress · RENT · a cleaner · a boat · a detective

3 Compare your answers.

4 Think of at least three things that you can:

a) miss   c) do   e) keep
b) waste   d) have   f) make

(Bell and Gower: *Upper Intermediate Matters* SB, page 27)

some modern literary texts and the second a discussion of style marking of lexical items in monolingual dictionaries for ESL/EFL learners. The book is a major guide to ways in which knowledge of vocabulary can be applied.

Carter, R. and **M. McCarthy.** 1988. *Vocabulary and Language Teaching.* London: Longman.

This book provides a historical overview of developments in vocabulary teaching and is divided into five parts. Part One looks at the contribution of attempts to find criteria for controlling vocabulary in pedagogic materials. Part Two provides an account of contemporary research into the structure of the lexicon. Part Three investigates recent developments in vocabulary teaching, and is followed by a set of papers in Part Four which look in more detail at issues in pedagogy. Part Five explores vocabulary in discourse and how this area has been taken up in approaches to communicative language teaching.

Gairns R. and **S. Redman.** 1986. *Working with Words: A Guide to Teaching and Learning Vocabulary.* Cambridge: Cambridge University Press.

This book provides an overview of linguistic approaches to the analysis of the English vocabulary system and uses insights from this analysis to develop principles for the learning and teaching of vocabulary. It suggests criteria for the evaluation of the vocabulary component of coursebooks, looks at traditional and contemporary approaches to presenting and practising vocabulary, and gives a range of ideas for designing practical classroom tasks.

McCarthy, M. 1990. *Vocabulary.* Oxford: Oxford University Press.

The first part of this book explains how various linguistic and psycholinguistic theories about vocabulary have contributed to our understanding of how words are organized in the language system, in the mind, and in speech and writing. Part Two looks at how these insights have influenced the design of teaching materials and reference books. Part Three provides teachers with tasks they can carry out in their own classrooms for further exploration.

Morgan, J. and **M. Rinvolucri.** 1986. *Vocabulary.* Oxford: Oxford University Press.

This book, as the authors put it, suggests 'some ways of opening up vocabulary for learners'. It is a creative resource book based on a set of assumptions about vocabulary learning which are explained in the Introduction. The rest of the book consists of activities, set out with the details of steps in classroom procedure and categorized into pre-text activities, those to be done in the course of reading, those concerned with the imagery of words, those which relate to how we categorize words internally, those which explore personal responses to words, and dictionary-based activities.

5 GRAMMAR

'Grammarians dispute and the case is still before the courts.'
HORACE

1 What is the role of grammar in the English language classroom?

2 What do we know about the learning of grammar?

3 What information can help us in the selection and presentation of grammar?

4 What principles can guide us in the teaching of grammar?

5 How can we design the grammar component of a course?

6 How do we suit approaches to the teaching of grammar to learner needs?

Introductory task

Look at Materials extract 5.A. It is designed for intermediate learners.

1 How authentically do you think the grammatical structures are contextualized? Is the link between form and communicative function made clear?

2 What do you think are the underlying assumptions about the learning of grammar?

5.1 Introduction: the role of grammar in English language teaching

Recent years have seen a resurgence of interest in the role of grammar in English language teaching. That is not to say that, for many teachers, grammar has ever taken anything other than a central role in their classroom methodology. However, the 1980s experienced an anti-grammar movement, perhaps influenced primarily by Krashen's (1982) idea that grammar can be acquired naturally from meaningful input and opportunities to interact in the classroom: in other words, that grammatical competence can develop in

Materials extract 5.A

1

What we're going to do – what the future will bring

a) Think about where you live. There are always jobs to be done: cleaning, tidying and buying new things, for example. Imagine you are going to spend all next weekend at home doing these jobs. Work with a partner and say what you're going to do.

Example
A: I'm going to sort out my clothes.
B: What else?
A: I'm going to clean the kitchen.

b) Fill in the thoughts of the second person in each cartoon, using these sentences:

a) She'll be lucky to sell a record!

b) I don't think we'll ever get there.

c) He'll probably lay an egg soon.

d) I think the sharks will be better company.

Activate your grammar

'Will' and 'going to' future

'Will' is used to forecast the future when we are fairly sure that something will happen, or to say what we want or expect to happen. It is often used after 'I think', 'I expect', 'I hope', and 'hopefully'.

Examples
Tomorrow's weather will be hot and sunny.
Hopefully in ten years' time I'll be a millionaire.

'Going to' joins the present and the future. It is used to forecast the future when there is evidence for it now, to express intentions, and to describe something that is about to happen.

Examples
It's going to rain.   (I can see the clouds.) Evidence now.

He's going to live in Italy.   (At the end of the summer.) Intention.

I'm going to be sick.   (I already feel bad.) About to happen.

➤ See Grammar Review 7 on page 82.

1   *Everything is going to work out fine!*

2   *You're going to be a STAR!*

3   *We're going to be late!*

4   *We're going to have such fun!*

c) Listen to this interview with a 19-year-old and number the statements to show the correct order.

Fly to South Africa	Visit Malawi	Live in Italy
Start university	Go to Zimbabwe	Travel to Zanzibar
Have a holiday in Malta	Get a job	

d) Listen to the interview again and read the tapescript, underlining the 'will' and 'going to' future.

(Sinclair and Prowse: *Activate Your English* SB, pages 18–19)

a fluency-oriented environment without conscious focus on language forms. The case against a methodology which presented grammatical items in a controlled sequence certainly led to some approaches which relegated grammar to a position of low priority. Disenchantment with this, and a growing concern about accuracy in learners' language, has resulted in a reassertion of the role of grammar in syllabus design and the content of lessons, and even in giving explicit attention to grammatical forms and rules (Ellis 1993c). The methodology currently suggested, however, does not necessarily replicate earlier approaches. In fact, it has become a preoccupation among applied linguists, informed teachers, and materials designers to find an approach to the teaching of grammar that fits usefully with what we know about how learners learn the grammatical system of English.

One issue for this chapter, then, is to ask what insights are available into the ways in which learners move towards accurate production of the English language and whether such insights hold implications for the usefulness of grammar-based knowledge and grammar-based practice as part of classroom methodology. Another issue is whether, and in what ways, the relative value of focused and unfocused activities might vary with such factors as the age, degree of exposure to English, and reasons for learning English of different learners (see 1.3).

If we believe that a focus on grammar is a necessary and/or a desirable part of classroom language learning, the questions that follow are how to integrate grammar teaching into a communicative methodology which pays attention to all aspects of communicative competence, and what precise form that teaching should take. And these imply further questions about the choice of grammatical structures to present, what kind of grammatical description to use, whether to use an inductive or a deductive approach, what the role of practice might be, and what forms of practice are appropriate for different types of learner.

It is important to hold in mind, as we investigate issues in the teaching of grammar, the strong relationship that exists between grammar and vocabulary. This relationship has become a key concern in current linguistic thinking and, as we shall see, has implications for the design of materials. Traditionally, grammar has been considered as being of primary importance with vocabulary in a subordinate role, but currently vocabulary is seen as of equal significance in language learning, and some teachers and methodologists would reverse their traditional roles. At various points in the discussion the link between the two will be addressed.

5.2 What do we know about the learning of grammar?

Ideas about the learning of grammar have been substantially influenced by the input hypothesis and the notion of intake, as discussed in 1.2.1 and 1.2.2. Learners receive information about language from a variety of sources in their environment and in the classroom: the teacher, the textbook, recordings, other students, reference books, and so on. This input has to be worked on for acquisition. It is generally acknowledged that acquisition involves a number of processes, which we will now look at in more detail.

5.2.1 *Noticing*

First of all, learners pick out specific features of the language and pay attention to them, that is, they *notice* items of language. For example, it is only after noticing that 'don't' seems to occur in regular ways in English to express negation that a learner can work on the relationship between meaning and form and begin to make sense of the rule involved in placing 'don't' before a main verb. In order for the learner to notice, the language feature has to be noticeable. 'Don't' will occur frequently in directives, warnings, advice, and expressions such as 'I don't think' and 'I don't know', often with the identifiable paralinguistic behaviour of head shaking. It therefore fulfils several criteria for being noticeable: it occurs frequently, it relates to the learner's common sense about basic functions of language, and its functions are those to which a learner would be likely to pay attention. Psycholinguists are still working on the task of sorting out what makes language items noticeable. After items have been noticed and the relationship between form and meaning interpreted, these items become part of *intake* into the learning process. Learners then analyse the forms in order to reason out how they fit into their existing knowledge of the language.

5.2.2 *Reasoning and hypothesizing*

Adult learners in particular tend to use their capacity to analyse new language. They are able to see the patterns in the language, create hypotheses about the rules these patterns might demonstrate, and gradually revise their hypotheses according to new information. They seem to use a set of strategies for analysing the language and reasoning about it. These have been described by Oxford (1990) as 'reasoning deductively', 'analysing contrastively', 'translating', and 'transferring', and they can be exemplified as follows.

Reasoning deductively

Learners apply rules they already know to working out the meaning of what they hear or to the formulation of what they want to say. A common error which derives from this is the inappropriate application of inverted interrogative word order, for example:

> *Can you tell me where *is the station*?
> *She doesn't know where *are they*.

Many adults report the need to have the language system laid out explicitly with rules from which they can work deductively. And the reasons for this might be various. For example, individual cognitive style may have developed from early school-based language learning experiences in which the formal system of rules was set out and deductive approaches were used. Or adult learners may need to explore the cultural link between language and thought, as this quotation shows:

> 'One of the things I seek to find out most from the syntax of a language is its basic thought system, which I often find exhibited more clearly in syntax than in any other aspect. I feel that unless I grasp this way of thinking I shall never be able to handle the language efficiently.'
> (Pickett 1978: 62)

Analysing contrastively

A learner may compare his or her first and second languages and work out their similarities and differences. Or the comparison may be between the new language and others already learned. We saw this in 3.2.1 when a learner used her knowledge of the *savoir–connaître* distinction in French to understand the *kennen–wissen* distinction in German.

Translating

Pickett (ibid.) reports a proficient English-speaking learner of several other languages telling of:

> 'the need to translate mentally in the early and consolidation stages of FL [foreign language] learning, i.e. the process is one of using English as a meta-language for getting my ideas straight on the structure and semantic range of the FL.'
> (ibid.: 61)

Used in this way, at certain stages, translation can clearly be a helpful strategy.

Transferring

Transferring is what learners do when they apply knowledge of one language to the understanding or production of another. For example, in the example given below of the stages of acquisition for negation, a Spanish learner is likely to choose 'no' rather than 'not' at the first stage because it transfers from how negation is formed in Spanish.

5.2.3 *Structuring and restructuring*

The strategies described above serve as examples of what learners do as they notice features in input and work on it in various ways to structure and restructure their knowledge of English. As learners work out new rules, these have to be integrated into the representation of English grammar they hold in their minds, and this information has to be restructured as the learner moves on to another stage of development.

Evidence of this reasoning process is seen in the errors that learners make when their reasoning is overgeneralized or influenced by the first language. The errors are systematic and are the outward sign of an internally developing system of grammar which moves through stages of interlanguage until it approximates the grammar used by proficient speakers of English.

For example, Lightbown and Spada (1999) give the stages of acquisition for negation, which may differ slightly according to the first language but which generally follow this sequence:

Stage 1
The negative element (usually 'no' or 'not') is typically placed before the verb or the element being negated:

No bicycle. No have any sand. I not like it.

'No' is preferred by some learners, perhaps due to transfer from their first language. Italian and Spanish speakers may prefer 'no' since it corresponds to the negative form in Italian and Spanish.

Stage 2
At this stage, 'no' and 'not' are alternated with 'don't'. However, 'don't' is not marked for person, number, or tense and it may even be used before modals like 'can' and 'should':

He don't like it. I don't can sing.

Stage 3
Learners begin to place the negative element after auxiliary verbs like 'are', 'is', and 'can'. But at this stage, the 'don't' form is still not fully analysed:

You can't go there. He can't eat nothing. She don't like rice.

Stage 4
'Do' performs its full function as a marker of tense and person:

It doesn't work. We didn't have supper.

For some time, however, learners may continue to mark tense on both the auxiliary and the verb:

I didn't went there. She doesn't wants to go.
(Lightbown and Spada 1999: 77–8)

5.2.4 *Automatizing*

Once a learner can achieve regular and consistent responses in conversation to a certain type of input, then it can be said that the language involved has been automatized. This can be seen in an exchange between two colleagues as they respectively move in an out of a lift:

A Did you get my message?
B Yes, I did. I'll let you know today.

Here B makes a quick and appropriate short-form response followed by a choice of a particular future form to indicate a speedy reply. How is this process of automatization achieved? In producing language a learner plans and chooses what to say and how to say it by paying attention to whether the form communicates a meaning successfully. Through repeated practice of the successful form its use will ultimately become automatic, in just the same way as it does with children acquiring their first language. This process can be observed occurring naturally as learners acquire English outside the classroom. The question for the teacher is whether classroom practice can assist. Sharwood Smith (1981) claims that explicit knowledge gained in the classroom can become implicit and form the basis of automatic production through practice:

> Let us also suppose that this type of activity is repeated again and again. In such situations, it is surely reasonable to suppose that a certain number of structures planned and performed slowly and consciously can eventually develop into automatized behavior.
> (Sharwood Smith 1981: 166)

This description of what learners do as they use grammatical information available to them is tentative and partial as it relies on uncertain insights from research. Teachers could easily be seduced into thinking that such a description provides a straightforward framework for classroom procedures and that trying to encourage the processes in sequence will lead to the successful teaching of grammar. But this notion needs to be qualified in various ways.

One qualification is that the ways in which these processes of noticing, reasoning, restructuring, and automatizing relate to one another is far from clear. For example, Batstone (1996) makes a point about the complexity of noticing:

> ... the cognitive load involved in noticing suggests that learners may
> need time to make sense of new language before they can make sense
> with it. In other words, it argues for receptive tasks to be clearly distinct
> from productive tasks, and for the former to precede the latter.
> (Batstone 1996: 173)

Others have commented on the role of practice. As we have seen, there is a
body of opinion which claims that explicit knowledge can become part of
the learner's internalized system through practice so that learned rules are
automatized and available for production. However, it has been noted (Eubank
1989; Ellis 1993a) that premature practice can actually confuse rather than
facilitate the intake of grammatical features. This relates to the idea of
readiness for learning. There is now substantial evidence for the claim that
learners follow a developmental route of acquisition in which structures are
acquired in sequence, but a natural sequence which may not be replicated by
the teacher or textbook. It is a predictable sequence and learners pass through
similar stages whether they are acquiring language naturally in a second-
language environment or learning in the classroom. The sequence appears to
be unmodifiable, and this inevitably raises questions about the role of practice.
Teachers are well aware that students might produce a form in focused
practice within a lesson but fail to take it up and produce it in later lessons or
even within the whole course. Intake and eventual automatization will only
occur as and when students are ready. This has implications for the timing
and type of practice which might aid acquisition of grammar.

Other qualifications are the extent to which any of the processes described
above occur consciously or unconsciously, and the relationship between
implicit and explicit knowledge in the learner. Second language acquisition
researchers make a distinction between these two. Implicit grammatical
knowledge is the intuitive knowledge of grammar which develops in the
same way as it does in young children acquiring their first language, through
natural processes and using input in the ways described above. It can
develop, without intervention from instruction, in the developmental
sequence just mentioned. Implicit knowledge develops naturally in the
foreign language classroom, too, as learners work on the input they are
exposed to and, in fact, the rate of this development can be increased through
exposure to frequently occurring structures. However, learners also receive
explicit knowledge of grammar from teachers and textbooks. What, then, is
the relationship between the two? If implicit knowledge is the primary source
from which learners try to produce language, as is generally believed, how
can explicit knowledge of grammatical rules play a role in the processes
described above?

It has been suggested that it can help in a number of ways. First, explicit
knowledge can help learners to appreciate the gap that exists between the
language which they and other students produce and native-speaker forms as

idealized in grammar texts. This can help them to monitor and check their language, and be aware of what they need to improve on. Second, it has been suggested (Seliger 1979) that knowing a pedagogical rule can help learners with the structuring process when they are ready to internalize a grammatical rule. Third, Pica (1985) has argued cautiously that instruction has a selective impact depending on the complexity of the grammatical structure in question. She found in a small-scale study, which compared learners acquiring English outside the classroom and those learning in a classroom setting, that the second group developed accurate production of the third person '-s' more quickly. She also found that classroom instruction had little effect on the use of the article. In other words, instruction seemed to facilitate in the case of linguistically simple rules, but for others, where the relationship between structure and function is not so clear, as with the use of the article, it did not seem to help.

There is, therefore, a degree of agreement among researchers, based on extensive studies, that a focus on grammar and the explicit learning of rules can facilitate and speed up the grammar acquisition process. It is this belief that has led to the reassertion of the value of grammar learning in the classroom.

The qualifications discussed above go some way towards demonstrating the issues which complicate attempts to devise procedures for the teaching of grammar. It might also be mistaken to assume that the learning of grammar is somehow discrete from other processes. We need to remember that learners have the capacity to memorize 'chunks' of language and access these ready-made items as they try to produce language. For example, I remember picking up the Swedish expression, *Tack ska du ha* (literally 'Thanks shall you have') from listening and perceiving it as two words, the already known *tack* ('thanks') with some kind of addition. It wasn't until I saw the written form much later that it was possible for me to analyse the structure. Holistic learning of this kind can enable later extrapolation from chunks which have been memorized.

This brief example points to current debate on just how language is processed by a learner: what the psychological reality is, and what the respective roles of grammar and vocabulary are. For example, it has been suggested (Pawley and Syder 1983) that learners improvise when they speak, especially in the early stages of learning a language, stringing together chunks of language in a process that owes more to memory and an understanding of word meaning than the selection of grammatical units. And some writers, for example Nattinger and DeCarrico (1992), have set out lists of lexical phrases which they believe are useful for learners to learn. What this debate brings into focus is the need to acknowledge that, although grammatical instruction and practice may have a role in helping learners to refine their interlanguage and achieve greater accuracy, other processes are at work in language development.

If learners also depend, in actual language use, on using lexical chunks in order to achieve fluency, then teaching in the early stages needs to take this into consideration and, more generally, teaching may need to pay greater attention to the acquisition of vocabulary and lexical phrases (see Chapter 4).

All of these issues make the teaching of grammar a complex and uncertain enterprise. Various suggestions have been made for classroom procedures which will be taken up in 5.4, but, before looking at these, it is also necessary to consider the role that grammatical description plays in ELT.

5.3 What information can help us in the selection and presentation of grammar?

A central issue in ELT is what role linguistic description can play in the design of classroom procedures and materials. Most teachers would concur with the view that it is difficult to teach a language without a knowledge of its structure and its functioning, but there exist many descriptions of these, each with its own method of analysis and metalanguage. Teachers and textbook writers turn to pedagogical grammars for information about the language system. These derive language data from scientific descriptions of language. These data are then selected and organized in terms of the learning needs of students of English. Pedagogical grammars therefore act as 'filters' or 'interpreters' between the detailed formal grammars of linguists and the classroom (Candlin 1973). This means that they are structured according to the age and level of proficiency of the learners and in terms of their objectives for learning English.

There are several points to bear in mind when reviewing the content and presentation of a pedagogical grammar, or of the grammar component of a coursebook. One is to remember that attempts to describe the formal system of English can only be idealizations as the system is less precise than most people imagine. It is actually very difficult to give rules for some aspects of grammar. Batstone (1994) comments on the notorious case of 'some' and 'any' for which a very simple formulation is often found in textbooks; that 'some' is found in affirmative sentences and 'any' is found in interrogatives and negative sentences, except in making offers or requests where 'some' can be used.

> With the help of computers, we are now able to undertake large-scale surveys of language as it is actually used, and to reformulate some (or any) ill-conceived idealizations. One such program has revealed beyond all doubt that the above regulation for *some* and *any* is incorrect, and that 'the use of *any* in an affirmative sentence is in fact

much commoner than its use in interrogatives' (Willis 1990: 49) as with 'Anything you can do I can do better' or 'Any fool knows that!' (Batstone 1994: 13)

Other considerations in the selection of materials are to do with changing approaches to the description of English. Contemporary ELT has been much influenced by developments in language description in the last twenty-five years which see language as more than a formal system. These developments view grammar from three main perspectives, which we will now examine in more detail.

5.3.1 *Grammar as meaning*

The first perspective views grammar as meaning.

> Linguistic meaning covers a great deal more than reports of events in the real world. It expresses … our attitudes … towards the person we are speaking to, how we feel about the reliability of our message, how we situate ourselves in the events we report, and many other things that make our messages not merely a recital of facts but a complex of facts and comments.
> (Bolinger 1977: 4)

Here 'linguistic meaning' covers lexis as well. An example of how we situate ourselves (in other words, how we express subtle shades of meaning) can be found in the ways we have of expressing compulsion and obligation, as in:

1 I must get in touch with my mother this week.
2 I have to complete this report by tomorrow.
3 I ought to phone John today.
4 I'd better complete this report by Friday.

Many native speakers would see differences in meaning in this set where each sentence has a first person subject. Number 1 implies a sense of responsibility or duty and relates to a speaker's personal authority to make decisions while number 2 implies compulsion from an external authority. Number 3 suggests that the implied obligation may not be fulfilled, and number 4 implies that something is advisable but as yet undecided. How would the meanings change, though, if numbers 1 and 4 were put into the third person?

> He must get in touch with his mother this week.
> He'd better finish this report by Friday.

These examples demonstrate how meaning can change when the same modal verb is used with different items in the grammatical set of 'person' and illustrate the complexity of the learning task for students if they are not to misunderstand or to be misunderstood.

A second example will highlight the role of intonation and how it links with grammar to express attitudes. Consider the following utterance and how it appears to provide objective information about the speaker's intentions:

> I would like to respond to Brian's comments with a point that I feel is important to the debate and then offer a further, relevant argument which might take us forward.

But if spoken with stress placement on *is*, *rel*evant and *for*ward, the attitude to what the previous speaker has said would be unmistakable.

As can be seen, consideration of grammar as meaning will influence the ways in which grammatical forms are presented as expressing concepts such as obligation. And teachers will need to keep in mind the link between grammar and intonation.

5.3.2 *Grammar in discourse*

The sense of the example above, of course, could only be fully appreciated if presented within the context of the debate and its developing discourse, and this is another perspective which can be taken towards grammar: how sentences can be combined in written texts and how utterances link in speech.

> ... the consideration of use requires us to go beyond the sentence and to look at larger stretches of language. Normal linguistic behaviour does not consist in the production of separate sentences but in the use of sentences for the creation of *discourse.*
> (Widdowson 1978: 22)

Rules, therefore, might be seen to operate across the boundaries of sentences as well as within them. This is the perspective taken in *A Communicative Grammar of English* (Leech and Svartvik 1975) which devotes one section to 'Meanings in connected discourse' and looks at how meanings can be put together in spoken or written discourse. They present six ways of organizing connections which can be exemplified as follows:

1 **Linking signals**
   These include familiar 'signposts' which signal what comes next, for example *incidentally* for changing the subject or *that is to say* to signal an explanation.

2 **Linking constructions**
   These include conjunctions used to co-ordinate and subordinate clauses, for example *and, or* and *if, because*, and adverbial links such as *however* for contrast.

3 'General purpose' links
   These include participle and verbless clauses, for example:

   > *Being a farmer*, he has to get up early.
   > He stared at the floor, *too nervous to reply*.

4 **Substitution and omission**
   This includes the use of pronouns to refer back to noun phrases, for example:

   > I like this *coat* better than *the one* (='the coat') you showed me before.

   and the auxiliary *do* to refer back to verb phrases, for example:

   > He can *cook* as well as she *does*. ('as she cooks')

   It also includes omission of infinitive clauses as in:

   > A Why don't you come and stay with us?
   > B I'd love to (do so).

   or omission through co-ordination, as in:

   > Peter ate the food but left the drink. (= 'Peter ate the food but *he* left the drink.')

5 **Presenting and focusing information**
   This includes the way in which we create contrastive focus in spoken language by using stress, for example:

   > *One* of the parcels has arrived. (but the other one hasn't)

   It also includes the way in which we can focus on important information in writing through placing it last in a sentence, for example:

   Arguments in favour of a new building plan, said the mayor, included suggestions that if a new shopping centre were not built, the city's traffic problems *would soon become unmanageable.*

6 **Order and emphasis**
   This includes variations in presenting information in order to create emphasis, using such devices as '*it*-clauses', for example:

   > It was by train that we reached Istanbul.

   and fronting, for example:

   > Never have I seen him so angry.

(adapted, with examples, from Leech and Svartvik 1975: 156–81)

These categories are to do with the more global aspects of grammar, how ideas are organized and ordered, and linked and developed through a piece of discourse.

One problem with looking at grammar in discourse is that spoken discourse in particular simply uses the rules of grammar as it wishes to and by no means conforms to them on all occasions to present the idealized forms of the grammar book. This can be seen in the following conversation:

> A Got any long-life milk?
> B Whole, semi skimmed, or skimmed?
> A Skimmed.
> B Tastes better, don't it?
> A Much better.
> B Want a bag?
> A Thanks.

This is a real conversation, as opposed to some of those found in textbooks which model grammatical structures for learners. It is characterized by omission of many items, but not in the way that omission is described in idealized ways in a pedagogical grammar such as *A Communicative Grammar of English*. Omission is possible because the participants, involved in a customer–shopkeeper transaction, are dealing with physical objects so they do not need to be explicit. A question that arises from this observation is how to keep a balance between presenting learners with language data containing examples of idealized grammar rules which they can process for intake and exposing them to authentic language data with which they will be confronted outside the classroom. If shared context frequently makes it unnecessary to textualize meanings explicitly, authentic language is hardly the most effective vehicle for demonstrating grammar.

Another problem with looking at grammar in discourse is that discourse does not keep to conventional meanings. This can be seen very clearly in the use if irony. Both of the following sentences:

> Kate is always so kind to me.
> Thank you so much for your help, John.

as part of discourse could mean the reverse of what they appear to say, for example, if they were used as ironic comment on Kate's unkindness or John's failure to help with the washing-up. In the second case, the listener would be able to interpret meaning from the context. The first may not be so immediately interpretable and a learner would need to be aware of the way in which language can be used ironically, with whom it might be advisedly used in this way, and the degree of offence, amusement, or resentment this might provoke.

This last point takes us beyond grammar into the area of *pragmatics* and the ways in which we interpret the meanings of spoken or written language from the words spoken, the forms used, the context of the discourse, and the situation in which it occurs. The following set of sentences, although they do not contain any of the formal links listed above, do contain an easily interpretable message when spoken by one neighbour to another at the front door at seven o'clock in the morning:

> Sorry. It's freezing. Do you have any jump leads? I've got to get to the airport.

There is a cultural element involved here as well. This message constitutes a request for help and such requests can be made in a number of ways, both indirectly as above, and directly as in:

> Please could you help me with my car?
> You couldn't give me a hand with starting my car, could you?

For some learners the indirect way may relate to what happens in their first language and will therefore be a more comfortable choice. For these learners, a direct request may be a new way of using language to learn as well as a new grammatical form.

If context is so important for interpreting meaning, there is a clear implication here for the contextualization of grammar in learning materials, and it is not surprising that current materials try to provide learners with rich sources of input in which they can notice contextualized grammatical items.

5.3.3 *Grammar and style*

> Where English gives us a choice of grammatical structures for a particular purpose, the different grammatical structures available are often not equivalent, since they belong to different 'styles' or 'varieties'. We believe that the appropriate choice is as important as it is difficult ...
> (Leech and Svartvik 1975: 11)

In *A Communicative Grammar of English*, Leech and Svartvik discuss varieties of English, using the term 'variety' to denote differences according to geography and situation, the latter covering a number of things: written and spoken language; formal and informal style; impersonal, polite, and familiar language; tactful and tentative language, and literary or rhetorical style. Using their set of labels, the same message can be conveyed in these ways:

> I suppose he's quite a nice little boy, isn't he? (tentative, polite)
> Nice kid. (informal, spoken)
> In all, he was a pleasant child. (formal, written)
> A cheerful child of pleasant disposition. (literary)

Notice that there are lexical variations as well: style is as much a matter of lexis as of grammar. One task for the teacher is to help students to become aware that English consists of many styles. Some of these may only need to be recognized and understood but others are crucial for production, such as the tactful style needed to avoid giving offence. For our learners, communicative ability involves knowing the different styles available, being able to recognize their characteristics sufficiently for comprehension, and making useful grammatical choices for effective interaction appropriate to the situation. For teachers and materials designers there are, therefore, careful choices to be made in what is to be selected and presented for awareness-raising, and what is to be selected and presented as a model for production.

One of the ways in which an understanding of the structure and use of the language system can help teachers is in providing insights for contextualizing grammar when it is offered to students in spoken or written texts. As we have seen, contemporary attempts to describe grammar do not view it as a separate formal system but link it to social use, and to its functioning within discourse. These descriptions can assist teachers in their attempts to develop learners' grammatical competence as part of their sociolinguistic and discourse competence (see 2.2). This brings us to a point where we need to look more closely at the implications for pedagogy of our knowledge of grammar and its acquisition.

5.4 What principles can guide us in the teaching of grammar?

Before looking at current approaches to teaching grammar it is worth summarizing what seems to be our state of knowledge about grammar acquisition, and the major implications of this.

First, the concept of 'readiness to learn' appears to be important. If, as research seems to show, learners pass through a developmental sequence and that sequence is determined by the complexity of processing involved in relation to a particular grammatical structure, then teachers cannot expect learners to acquire that grammatical structure until they are ready to do so. Second, the amount of time it takes to learn a new structure varies among learners as they link forms to functions and to their stylistic use. One implication of this is the need to recycle structures in a course, each recycling presenting new functions and possible uses. Third, the process is not a lockstep one, with progressive and complete mastery of structures in sequence. As the interlanguage system develops and restructuring occurs, learners may suddenly start to make errors in an item the teacher thought they had learned to produce accurately. The experienced teacher will wait for accuracy to return. And fourth, learners are able to learn inductively, drawing on the knowledge of English they have already acquired along with knowledge of their first and any other languages, to formulate hypotheses, test these out, and gradually restructure and refine their grammatical knowledge.

These insights clearly hold implications for the role of grammar instruction. There is now a strong consensus that the presentation of grammar to learners can facilitate learning in a number of ways: it can provide input for noticing language forms; it can help students see the difference between their own output and accurate forms of English; it can present high-frequency grammatical items explicitly to speed up learning; it can provide information about the communicative use of language structures by contextualizing them in spoken and written texts; it can give information implicitly through exposure to examples or explicitly through instruction on the stylistic variation of language form.

The value of providing grammar instruction may not be in question but, as implied in the earlier sections of this chapter, its effectiveness may be contingent on certain factors, and one of these may well be the careful contextualization of linguistic forms in situations of natural use.

5.4.1 *Presenting grammar*

Contextualizing grammar

In 5.3 we suggested three perspectives which need to be taken into account when presenting grammar: grammar as meaning, grammar in discourse, and grammar and style. The importance of contextualizing a grammatical structure in relation to these three perspectives can be demonstrated with some examples of the present perfect tense:

> She has attended the ante-natal classes regularly.
> You haven't forgotten my birthday again, have you?
> I haven't been to Paris for four years.
> Have you had dinner yet?
> Oh no, they've just scored another goal!
> The management has decided to make thirty staff redundant.

Which of these shows habit in a period leading up to the present time and which shows indefinite events in a period leading up to the present time? Which show attitude as part of meaning? Which functions as a complaint and which as an invitation? Which is stylistically formal and which informal? Ideally, the context will clarify who is speaking to whom, in what kind of setting, with what kind of purpose, in what style, with literal meaning or otherwise, and within what kind of discourse.

The contexts in which grammar is embedded need to be generally useful and appropriate to the needs of the learner group. In this way grammar becomes generative and students can transfer it to relevant situations. Contexts can be created through visuals, through the teacher miming or demonstrating in the classroom, through a dialogue, a text, a song or a video, or through a situation set up by the teacher. The particular context chosen will relate to the learners in view. For example, Materials extract 5.B first uses an authentic text in the genre of a certain kind of joke which usefully repeats the structure, and then a spoken dialogue which is relevant to students' personal lives, while Materials extract 5.H in section 5.4.4 uses visuals in cartoon format for younger adolescents.

Order of presentation

How to contextualize a grammatical item is one decision that must be taken in grammar teaching. Another is which forms of the item to teach and in what order, and which forms to leave for the recycling stages. For example, Discussion topic 4 (page 180) invites you to look at a set of present continuous forms and to decide on the criteria you would use for sequencing them in a teaching unit.

Use of terminology

A third decision concerns the degree to which grammatical terminology is useful in the presentation of grammar. Having a metalanguage may be useful for advanced learners, particularly in discussing errors in writing or in helping them to understand difficult semantic relations. And analytical learners may respond well to terminology. However, it is sometimes more appropriate simply to guide students into seeing the patterns.

Degree of explicitness

There is also a decision to be taken about how explicitly grammatical information is provided to the learner. For example, we can take Materials extract 5.A, which presents rules in some detail along with illustrative materials and opportunities to work with the rules. This is one way of tackling grammar with adult learners who have learned English formally in previous learning careers and can activate their grammar. This approach can be compared with Materials extract 5.B which presents learners with simulated authentic written and spoken texts. These are carefully structured to display the target tenses and to give learners the task of working out their different uses and discovering the rules. In other words, learners are engaged in raising their own awareness of how language works. Many materials now take this latter, inductive, approach.

The popularity of the inductive approach, sometimes known as 'discovery learning' has received theoretical support in the work of Rutherford (1987) and Sharwood Smith (1988) who present slightly varying models of the role that 'grammar consciousness raising' can play in foreign language acquisition. Rutherford, for example, says:

> The role of C-R [consciousness raising] … is … one in which data that are crucial for the learner's testing of hypotheses, and for his forming

Materials extract 5.B

T.32   Read and listen to the joke. <u>Underline</u> the verb forms that refer to the future. What is the difference between them?

A Penguin Joke!

One day a man and his wife were walking down the street when they came across a penguin.

'Oh!' exclaimed the man. 'What a surprise! What shall we do with it?'

'I know,' said his wife. 'We'll ask a policeman.' So they found a policeman and explained what had happened.

'Mmm,' said the policeman, 'I think the best thing is to take it to the zoo.'

'What a good idea!' said the woman. 'We'll go there straight away.'

The next morning the policeman was walking down the same street when he saw the couple again with the penguin. 'I thought I told you to take that penguin to the zoo,' the policeman said. 'Well, we did,' said the man. 'We took it to the zoo and we all had a really good time. So this afternoon we're taking it to the cinema, and this evening we're going to have a meal in a fish restaurant.'

PRESENTATION (1)

going to and *will*

1   John always writes himself a list at the beginning of every day. What's he going to do today? What's he going to buy?

Example
He's going to fill up the car with petrol.

Things to do
petrol
electricity bill
plane tickets from
  the travel agent
the library
a hair-cut
the dog for a walk

Things to buy
sugar
tea
cheese
yoghurt
2 avocados
apples
melon

2   **T.33**   Read and listen to the dialogue between John (J) and Anna (A).

J   I'm going to the shops soon. Do you want anything?

A   No, I don't think so. Oh, hang on. We haven't got any sugar left.

J   It's all right. It's on my list. I'm going to buy some.

A   What about bread? We haven't got any bread.

J   OK. I'll go to the baker's and I'll buy a loaf.

A   I'll be at work when you get back.

J   I'll see you later, then. Don't forget Jo and Andy are coming round for a drink tonight.

A   Ah, right. Bye.

J   Bye, honey.

● Grammar questions

I'm going to buy some (sugar).
I'll buy a loaf.

– Why does John use different future forms? What's the difference between *will* and *going to* to express a future intention?

– We don't usually say *going to go* or *going to come*. Find the examples in the dialogue where these form are avoided.

PRACTICE

1 Dialogues

John said, *I'll go to the baker's and I'll buy a loaf.* Look at the list of items. What would Anna ask? What would John say?

Example
– some stamps

Anna   *Could you get some stamps?*
John   *OK. I'll go to the post office and buy some.*

– a newspaper
– a bottle of wine
– a joint of beef
– a film for her camera

– some shampoo
– a tin of white paint
– a video
– some felt-tip pens

2 Listening

T.34   Listen to the conversations. Say what's going to happen.

Example
A   Have you seen the air tickets?
B   Yes. They're with the travellers' cheques.
A   And do you have the address of the hotel?

Example

A Have you seen the air tickets?
B Yes. They're with the travellers' cheques.
A And do you have the address of the hotel?
B No. I've just got the name. Do we need the address?
A No. Maybe not. The taxi driver will know.
B What about the milk? Have you cancelled the milk?
A Yes. No milk for a fortnight. Right?
B That's it. Well done.

> They're going to catch a plane.

> They're going to stay in a hotel.

> They're going to be away for two weeks.

46   Unit 5   On the move

3 *I think I'll …*

1 Use the prompts in **A** to make sentences with *I think
 … will*. Match them with a sentence in **B**.

Example
*I think Jeremy will win the match. He's been playing
really well recently.*

A

a … Jeremy/win the match
b … it/be a nice day tomorrow
c … I/pass my exams
d … you/like the film
e … we/get to the airport in time
f … you/get the job

B

☐ But we'd better get a move on.
☑ He's been playing really well recently.
☐ The forecast is warm and dry.
☐ You've got all the right qualifications.
☐ It's a lovely story, and the acting is superb.
☐ I've been revising for weeks.

2 Now make sentences with *I don't think … will* with the
words from **A** in Exercise 1. Match them with a
sentence in **C**.

Example
*I don't think Jeremy will win the match. He hasn't
practised for ages.*

C

☐ There's too much traffic.
☐ I haven't done any revision at all.
☐ The forecast said rain and wind.
☑ He hasn't practised for ages.
☐ You're too young and you've got no experience.
☐ It's not really your cup of tea.

3 Make true sentences about *you*.

Example
I/bath tonight
*I think I'll have a bath tonight/I
don't think I'll have a bath tonight.*

– it/rain tomorrow
– I/go shopping this afternoon
– I/be a millionaire one day
– I/eat out tonight
– we/have a white Christmas
– the teacher/give us a lot of
  homework

4 Grammar

Underline the correct verb form in
the sentences.

Example
'Oh, dear. I'm late for work.'
'Don't worry. *I'm going to give/
I'll give* you a lift.'

a 'I've got a headache.'
  'Have you? Wait a minute. *I'll
  get/I'm going to get* you an
  aspirin.'

b 'It's Tony's birthday next week.'
  'Is it? I didn't know. *I'll send/I'm
  going to send* him a card.'

c 'Why are you putting on your
  coat?'
  'Because *I'll take/I'm going to
  take* the dog for a walk.'

d 'Are you and Alan still going out
  together?'
  'Oh, yes. *We'll get married/We're
  going to get married* next year.'

e (a telephone conversation)
  'Would you like to go out for a
  drink tonight?'
  '*I'll watch/I'm going to watch* the
  football on television.'
  'Oh! I didn't know it was on.'
  'Come and watch it with me!'
  'OK. *I'll come/I'm going to come*
  round at about 7.30.'

f 'Did you phone Peter about
  tonight?'
  'No, I forgot. *I'll do/I'm going to
  do* it now. What's his number?'

1 Roleplay

Work in pairs. Your teacher will give you a role card.
Study the information on it carefully. Have telephone
conversations similar to the one between Alan Middleton
and Nina Kendle's secretary.

Remember the following expressions.

> Could I speak to … ?   >   < I'm afraid …

> What time will … be back?   <   At about …

> Is … free at lunch-time?   <   I'll check. No, she's
having/seeing/going …

> When's a good time
to try again?   <   She'll be …

> I'll phone back …   <   That's fine …

(Soars and Soars: *New Headway Intermediate* SB, from pages 45, 46, 47, 48)

generalizations, are made available to him in somewhat controlled and principled fashion.
(Rutherford 1987: 18)

Consciousness-raising tasks ask students to try to formulate rules about English through meaningful negotiation. The basic idea is to give students

Materials extract 5.C

These pairs of adjectives ending in *-ed* and *-ing* describe how something feels or how something makes someone feel.

surprised/surprising   interested/interesting
bored/boring   excited/exciting
tired/tiring   confused/confusing

1 Work in a pair and write down other pairs of words like this. Then show your words to another pair.

2 Look at the underlined words in these sentences. First write down those which the *-ing* words refer to.
(a)   (b)   (c)   (d)   (e)
Then write down those which the *-ed* words refer to.
(a)   (b)   (c)   (d)   (e)

(a) <u>Tom</u> is interested in sport. He thinks <u>football</u> is the most interesting.
(b) <u>My sister</u> looked frightened as the <u>film</u> we were watching became more and more frightening.
(c) <u>We</u> all felt disappointed about the dreadful and disappointing <u>news</u>.
(d) Some of my <u>classes</u> are very boring. I get most bored in <u>history lessons</u>.
(e) I felt very annoyed. The most annoying <u>thing</u> was his smile.

(Author's material)

sufficient examples so that they can work out the grammatical rule that is operating. A useful activity for introducing intermediate students to inductive learning is to give them examples of a simple grammatical distinction to work out, as in Materials extract 5.C.

Simple activities such as this can persuade students to use their cognitive abilities and give them confidence about using discovery learning.

Consciousness-raising reasserts the role of metalinguistic activity in language learning, but in a very different way from the grammatical explanation and application activity of the traditional deductive approach. It is still an issue as to whether talking and thinking about grammar in this way requires a technical metalanguage or whether it can be done in non-technical ways. There is now some evidence from classroom research, for example a study by Fotos (1994), that grammar consciousness-raising tasks can promote significant gains in acquiring the target grammatical structure, at least with the kinds of learners studied. But we still need information across a wider range of ages, levels of proficiency, backgrounds, and learning styles. However, where it seems to be appropriate, consciousness-raising provides teachers with a procedure which helps learners to develop their grammatical competence in a way which fits the culture of the communicative classroom.

Linking grammar and vocabulary

A final point we need to consider on the presentation of grammar takes us back to the link between grammar and vocabulary. There are patterns in the English language within which words typically occur. For example, there is a pattern: It + link verb + adjective + infinitive with 'to', as in 'It's difficult to make up your mind' or 'It's easy to say that', used commonly for comment. A Finnish friend of mine picked up this pattern very quickly, producing some idiosyncratic and creative examples such as 'It's combustive to express that point of view'. He found that using them kept him in the conversation and kept the conversation going. We need to consider presenting such patterns to our students as well as the time-honoured modals and tenses. They are typical of the lexical phrases used by native speakers (see 5.2.4).

5.4.2 *Practising grammar*

A widely prevailing approach to the teaching of grammar, which developed in the 1970s and 1980s and is still popular with many teachers, is to present a grammatical structure to learners, to ask them to practise it in controlled activities which focus on accurate reproduction of the structure, and then to set up freer activities in which students produce the target form. This Presentation–Practice–Production (PPP) model is the one followed in the lesson plan on pages 32–3. The latter two stages can be seen in Materials extract 5.D.

In these two activities students move from controlled practice of a conditional form in designing the questionnaire and in answering the questions to the freer group discussion of activity 2. The purposes of each stage of activity in the PPP model are summarized in Table 5.1 on page 166.

As far as the roles of the teacher at each are concerned, teacher correction is considered to be of importance during presentation and practice, though self-correction and peer correction are encouraged. During production the usual policy is non-intervention during the attempt to produce, with feedback given afterwards.

It is the production stage of this model in particular which has caused controversy, given our growing knowledge of grammar acquisition. Experienced teachers will be aware that some learners will perform the second activity in Materials extract 5.D with accurate production of the conditional in that

Materials extract 5.D

Set 2 — **Imaginary situations**

> If I found £5 in the street, I'd give it to the police.

1. Make up a personality quiz for a magazine.
In pairs or groups think of three questions for each section and write them down.
Then choose somebody else in the class to answer the questions.

WHAT WOULD YOU DO? FIND OUT WHAT SORT OF PERSON YOU ARE

ARE YOU HONEST?   If you found £5 on the street
  (a) ....
  (b) ....
  (c) ....

Your friend has bought a new coat which you don't like. If he asked you for your opinion
  (a) ....
  (b) ....
  (c) ....

ARE YOU PRACTICAL?   If you saw an accident in the street
  (a) ....
  (b) ....
  (c) ....

If you woke up in the night and saw your curtains on fire
  (a) ....
  (b) ....
  (c) ....

If you arrived at the airport to go on holiday and found that you didn't have your passport
  (a) ....
  (b) ....
  (c) ....

ARE YOU IMAGINATIVE?   If you won £1000
  (a) ....
  (b) ....
  (c) ....

If you could take a year off work
  (a) ....
  (b) ....
  (c) ....

2. In groups, discuss any measures you would take if you were Minister for:
Education   Social Services   the Environment   Finance   Foreign Affairs   **in your country.**

(Abbs and Freebairn: *Developing Strategies* SB, page 57)

lesson but will then cease to use it, or produce it inaccurately. Others, as the following extract demonstrates, will not necessarily use the conditional at all:

Ana   I think I can establish some new school ... experimental schools ... English will be the language for all lessons.
Carmen Yes, a good idea, but I prefer to change teacher training ...

Table 5.1: The purposes of each stage of activity in the PPP model

Stage	Purpose	Teacher's roles
Presentation	– to present new language in context so that meaning is clear – to present the new form in a natural spoken or written text so that students can see its use in discourse – to link the new form to what students already know – to check comprehension – to elicit the form from students where possible and exploit their existing knowledge	Instructor, corrector
Practice	– to help students memorize the form – to help students produce the word order – to give intensive practice through repetition – to provide opportunities for feedback and error correction – to give practice in pronouncing new forms – to develop confidence	Manager, evaluator, corrector
Production	– to reduce control and encourage students to find out what they can do – to encourage students to use the forms in expressing their own content – to help students see the usefulness of what they have learned – to check what has been learned and diagnose problems	Monitor, resource, diagnoser

Both speakers communicate their intentions clearly, but both avoid using the conditional. There may be reasons for this to do with their readiness to learn it, but one factor is they *can* legitimately use alternative forms, as here, if they imagine themselves into the role of Minister of Education. Ellis (1993b) expresses the problem inherent in the PPP model in this way:

> You can design an activity hoping that learners will produce a certain feature, but the reality is that, if they do treat it as a piece of genuine communication, there is a very good chance that they will not use the grammatical feature that you intended them to use. In other words, you can devise activities that make the use of a feature *natural* and *useful*, but it's extremely difficult to make the use of a feature *essential*.
> (Ellis 1993b: 6)

For this reason, it has become more usual to provide controlled practice and then to provide unfocused communicative activities within the wider syllabus (see 2.4.1). The implications of this approach for overall syllabus design are taken up in 10.2.4.

The controlled practice stage is less controversial. This usually includes a variety of activities with a conscious focus on form which address the range of purposes summarized in Table 5.1. A number of arguments can be offered for the value of such practice. One is that, as students produce a form in controlled activities, they provide further, extensive input for each other and more chances to notice the structure. This can be seen in Materials extract 5.B where practice activities 1 and 2 require extensive repetitions of the 'will' and 'going to' forms.

A further argument is that practice of this kind obliges students to pay attention to syntax. It is perfectly possible to understand meaning on the basis of lexis without paying much attention to syntax. For example, a learner hearing the three lexical items, 'earthquake', 'thousands', and 'homeless' could use knowledge of word-meaning and knowledge of the world to reconstruct the message. In controlled practice, students would be obliged to string together words in the correct order using grammatical devices to convey coherently the cause–effect relationship that links the three words. This is seen in Materials extract 5.B in the activity where students make true sentences about themselves, and is followed up in the 'Role Play' where students have to produce more of the content themselves and use the appropriate syntax. There is a case, too, for varying the practice between speech and writing since writing is a slower and more conscious process and students can monitor what they produce more carefully.

These arguments suggest that practice can contribute to implicit grammatical knowledge by providing frequent occurrence of a particular form for students to notice. Extensive exposure and opportunities for varied and intensive practice also allow learners to test out hypotheses as they become familiar with available forms and begin to work out the rules involved. At the same time, practice can also contribute to explicit knowledge about language forms and begin the process of learners gradually developing the ability to use a rule accurately and automatically in production.

Another type of practice can be seen in the dictogloss activity in Materials extract 5.E. At the preparation stage, the teacher works with learners in a 'warm-up' to the topic and to prepare relevant vocabulary. The text is then read twice and, on the second reading students note down the words they catch. Working in groups, they then pool their notes to try to reconstruct the text. In doing so, they use the grammar they know and consider the possible alternatives. This means that students must justify to each other the choices they proffer. Swain argues 'This results, at minimum ... in a context sensitive

Materials extract 5.E

1.10 Miracle plunge

TOPIC

Human interest story
Accidents
Domestic violence

LANGUAGE POINTS

Simple sentence structure
Past simple tense
Articles
Prepositions and prepositional phrases

WARM-UP

1 Tell the class that they are going to hear a story about a 'close shave' in an accident.

2 Explain what a close shave is.

3 Give an example of a close shave, e.g. a slate or tile falls off a roof just in front of some passers-by, but does not hit them; a car skids across a road into oncoming traffic, but miraculously skids back onto the correct side of the road; and so on.

4 Ask the students if they have ever experienced a close shave. List these on the blackboard.

5 If the students seem interested, they may want to discuss whose close shave was the most interesting/horrifying/terrifying/incredible.

PRE-TEXT VOCABULARY

high-rise (*adj*) very tall (building)
floor (*n*), **storey** (*n*) one level of a high-rise building
argument (*n*) a quarrel or disagreement
to throw (*v*) to send something through the air
to plunge (*v*) to fall
passer-by (*n*) a pedestrian
to survive (*v*) to manage to stay alive
bruise (*n*) a painful, discoloured mark on the skin

TEXT

1 A two-year-old girl lived with her mother in a high-rise building.   2 They lived on the fourth floor.   3 One day the father came to visit and an argument started.   4 The father got angry and threw the girl at a window.   5 It broke and the girl plunged towards the ground.   6 At the last moment she fell into the arms of a passer-by.   7 She survived with only a few bruises and doctors called it a miracle.

NOTES

S1 *two-year-old* – Note that there is no final *s* on *year*. The construction (number)+year+old is a fixed adjectival phrase qualifying the noun that follows (in this case *girl*).

S2 *on* – Note that *on* is the correct preposition in this place phrase (not *in* or *at*).

S3 *the father* – That is, *the girl's father*.

S3 *came* – That is, *came to the home*.

S5 *it* – That is, *the window*.

S5 *towards* – This is a preposition indicating motion.

S7 *it* – That is, *the girl's survival*.

(Wajnryb: *Grammar Dictation*, pages 36–7)

knowledge of a grammatical rule because form, function and meaning are so intimately linked … ' (Swain 1995: 135). The dictogloss technique is an interesting example of how learners can be encouraged to reflect on grammar. Swain comments on this metalinguistic function of output which is a kind of 'explicit hypothesizing' (ibid.: 135). The focus of this activity is language form, although the forms are contextually embedded in a situation and within a short piece of discourse. The pairwork mode necessitates reflection and decision-making. Swain gives dictogloss as an example of a technique which encourages what she terms 'negotiation of form' (ibid.: 131).

The point was made in sections 5.1 and 5.2 that grammatical knowledge does not develop separately from other types of knowledge in the acquisition process, and one of these other types is lexical knowledge. Arguments that we should pay attention to the links between grammatical and lexical knowledge have resulted in some interesting ideas for classroom practice. Batstone (1994), for example, describes the tension he perceives between learning and teaching grammar:

> the learner gradually reaches out for grammar from a secure basis in words, while the materials writer starts from a basis in target grammar and encourages the learner to reach out for different lexical items as she manipulates the grammar.
> (Batstone 1994: 104)

His own solution, motivated in part by the work of Rutherford (1987) and Widdowson (1990a), is to help learners 'grammaticize'; to apply their emerging

Materials extract 5F

---

1 Work with a partner. Sort out the following words and phrases into the categories shown below.

saved	their parents	a young woman	today
two children	rescue	the beach	this afternoon
the west coast	four o'clock	a rubber dinghy	swam
strong wind	heroine	blown out to sea	

PEOPLE
PLACE
TIME
EVENT
OUTCOME

2 Now work with your partner to prepare a newspaper report.

3 Read your report to the class.

(Author's materials)

knowledge of grammar by choosing what to add to words in order to create meaning. Following this idea, a 'grammaticization task' might look like the one in Materials extract 5.F (stages 1 and 2 could involve use of the first language).

Given the range of ideas, opinions, and controversies raised in this section, it is not surprising that many teachers and textbook writers see the most practical approach to grammar as an eclectic one, but the precise mix and match will depend on the needs of learners.

5.4.3 *How can we design the grammar component of a course?*

Two types of linguistic comparison have been useful in suggesting appropriate grammatical items to be selected and sequenced in a course. The first is between the learner's native language and the target language, and is known as *contrastive analysis*. The second is between the learner's interlanguage and the target language and is known as *error analysis*.

Contrastive analysis was popular in the 1960s and 1970s as a method of predicting difficulty for students. It assumed that areas of difference between two language systems would be sources of difficulty and that a set of difficult grammatical features could be drawn up to form a basis of a syllabus. In reality, however, the predictive power of the contrastive analysis hypothesis proved not to be very strong. Areas of substantial difference can prove relatively easy to learn while areas of little difference can be difficult. It has not been possible to formulate scales of difficulty for learners from various language backgrounds and contrastive analysis has therefore fallen into disfavour.

Error analysis has provided teachers with insights into the main problems which learners seem to have with English, and there are useful descriptions of these available. For example, Swan and Smith (1987) took eighteen language groups and itemized the frequently occurring errors in their production of English. Such descriptions form a database for the selection of items in courses for upper-intermediate and advanced learners where the aim of the grammar component is to give students further opportunities to refine the accuracy of their production.

However, for beginner and elementary students, the grammar component of a syllabus is usually selected and sequenced on the basis of received wisdom about what is simple to learn and what is complex. Hence the typical sequence of tenses to be found in many coursebooks: present simple of the verb 'to be'; present simple of main verbs; past simple; future with 'going to', and so on. It is probably true to say that grammar, selected and sequenced by using the procedures of contrastive analysis and error analysis, or chosen on the basis of what is perceived as simple, has for many years been the main basis of ELT course design. However, a number of criticisms have been levelled at the grammatical syllabus as a basis for course design.

The first criticism queries whether, in fact, the grammatical dimension should be the major organizing principle in the type of syllabus which sets out a list of items to be taught. If we are concerned with language as communication, the argument goes, then our primary focus should be on the purposes for which the language is being used and our secondary task should be to choose the forms to express those purposes. Following this argument, many current courses for students at intermediate level and above specify first a list of functions, such as 'making suggestions', and then select exponents from a range of possible grammatical forms according to the needs (for example, formal or familiar English) or proficiency level of the students.

The advantage of this re-prioritization is that it makes the language dimension subservient to, rather than dominant over, the needs of learners. It is not without its problems, however. These courses assume students have already acquired a working knowledge of English grammar. It is more problematic to make the functional dimension primary in a syllabus for elementary students for, unlike grammatical items, functions are not amenable to sequencing. In other words, it is much harder to apply a simple to a more complex order. As Wilkins (1979) points out:

> It is essential for the learner to achieve some degree of generalisation in what he has learned and one of the essential elements of generalisation, and I cannot stress this too much, is the grammar of the language itself. I am *not* suggesting *in any way* that the learner does not have to learn the grammar of the language. The learner does still have to master the grammatical structure. There is no way that one can 'know' a language without knowing its grammatical basis. What the new ideas amount to is that the grammatical foundation can possibly be presented in new ways which also take the communicative purposes of language into account ...
> (Wilkins 1979: 7)

A second criticism relates to the notions of simple and complex and the sequence of grammatical items presented to learners on the basis of this criterion. We have always been concerned to understand why learners fail to learn items which have been presented and extensively practised in the classroom. Research studies of the last twenty-five years have increasingly lent support to the idea that there is a relationship between the amount of mental processing needed to perceive and produce a new rule and its learnability; moreover that learnability will determine the order in which grammatical items are learned. A much-quoted example of this is the third person singular '-s' in the simple present which learners acquire quite late. An explanation might be that its use is decided by the person ('he/she/it', as opposed to 'I/you') and number ('he/she/it' as opposed to 'they') of the noun phrase which has just been spoken and the speaker has to hold this information in short-term memory in order to produce the accurate inflection. There is also the point that there is little to be gained from learning this rule as meaning is signalled by the chosen pronoun.

These considerations have led researchers to set up the *natural order hypothesis*, which claims that language rules are acquired according to a predictable sequence and that the sequence remains the same whether or not classroom learning is involved. The details of the natural order were suggested by a set of studies known as the 'morpheme studies'. The original studies, such as Brown (1973), investigated how children acquiring their first language learned certain grammatical morphemes, for example, inflections such as the third person singular '-s' in the simple present, the present progressive '-ing', the regular past '-ed', and grammatical words such as the articles 'a' and 'the'. The studies showed that children acquired these in similar sequence, although the process in some children was slower than in others.

Later research has shown that both children and adults acquiring a second language in natural settings acquire grammatical morphemes in a similar kind of developmental sequence, though the details of this may be affected by prior knowledge of another language through the process of transfer described in 5.2.2. Extensive work on developmental sequences has now been undertaken by Pienemann, Johnston, and Brindley (1988). They claim to be able to provide details of these for various learners.

The issue for second and foreign language teachers is whether this work yields reliable and useful insights for the design of language teaching syllabuses for classroom settings. Could a syllabus simply follow the natural order? If so, it would seem to resolve the difficulties experienced in finding criteria for ordering the presentation of grammatical structures. Unfortunately, as yet, there is no easy application of these ideas. Classroom factors complicate the situation. For example, in order to set up classroom interaction which provides input and practice, some structures, for example various question forms, will need to be taught early on. Other factors create the same kind of problems as do syllabuses based on grammatical notions of simplicity and complexity. Learners may pass through the same developmental stages but they do not proceed at the same rate, and groups of learners will be heterogeneous in terms of existing language proficiency. As yet we have insufficient information about the effects of instruction or how the classroom can influence and improve on natural processes.

This last point relates to a further criticism of the grammatical syllabus (and, indeed, of any course design which attempts to present and sequence linguistic items as a way of organizing learning). This issue is taken up and discussed in 10.2.3 and 10.2.4, but it is worth remarking on here, as it relates to the role of grammar in a course. The natural order hypothesis provided further fuel for an ongoing debate about the need to provide learner-centered teaching. If it is the case that learners will acquire the grammatical system according to their own internal syllabus, it has been argued that teachers should pay less attention to structuring learning through imposing an external syllabus and more attention to facilitating learning by creating a classroom environment which is rich in varied input and which provides learners with opportunities to acquire language by performing a range of learning tasks. This, as we shall see in 10.3.2, has been termed a *process approach* to course design as its main concern is with the process of learning.

Textbook writers have responded variously to these ideas about the selection and ordering of grammatical items and to queries about the value of teaching grammar. For example, in Materials extract 5.G Michael Swan and Catherine Walter, the authors of *The New Cambridge English Course,* draw two points out of the knowledge we have on how language is learned.

Materials extract 5.G

Most people seem to learn a foreign language more effectively if it is 'tidied up' for them. This helps them to focus on high-priority language and to see the grammatical regularities.

However, learners also need to encounter a certain amount of 'untidy' natural language (even if this seems to be difficult for them). Without some unstructured input, people's unconscious mechanisms for acquiring language may not operate effectively.

(Swan and Walter: *The New Cambridge English Course 1* TB, page vii)

Precise decisions about the grammar component of any course will depend on the needs of the particular group of learners for which it is being prepared. We now turn to these.

5.4.4 *How can we suit approach to learner needs?*

The ways in which learners respond to our choice of approach in teaching grammar will depend in part on their individual cognitive style. As we saw in 1.3.2, one dimension of this style is to do with whether a learner prefers to gain a global impression of something new or prefers to analyse its details. The latter type of student may well prefer to deal with grammar formally, in 'studial learning' (Ellis 1989), to look for rules and relationships, to work out the underlying system of language explicitly, and to try and apply the rules thus derived. This analytical learner is in contrast to the global learner, who might prefer experiential learning through classroom communication which encourages guessing and structuring.

There is evidence to suggest that a clash of styles between teacher and students can frustrate both, but in a multicultural classroom some clashes are inevitable. One solution is for the teacher to use different approaches and provide a variety of access to grammar to cater for different learning styles. This would need to be accompanied by learner training which encouraged learners to extend their styles by pointing out the advantages of different activity types.

Other factors will also determine both the extent to which grammar receives explicit attention in class and the approach chosen. Celce-Murcia (1993) provides a useful set of six variables to guide a teacher in appropriate focus on form (see Figure 5.1).

Figure 5.1: Variables relevant to focus on form (Celce-Murcia 1993: 294)

	Less Important	— Focus on Form —	More Important
Learner variables			
Age	Children	Adolescents	Adults
Proficiency level	Beginning	Intermediate	Advanced
Educational background	Preliterate, no formal education	Semiliterate, some formal education	Literate, well educated
Instructional variables			
Skill	Listening, reading	Speaking	Writing
Register	Informal	Consultative*	Formal
Need/use	Survival communication	Vocational	Professional

* Joos (1962) defines the consultative register as the language we use with people we deal with frequently—perhaps every day—but with whom we are not close on a personal level. This register is between formal (the language for public lectures or academic articles) and informal (the language used among peers who know each other well).

Celce-Murcia's 'rule' would be: 'the more factors the teacher identifies on the left side of the grid, the less important it is to focus on form; the more factors the teacher identifies on the right, the more important the grammatical focus.'

This rule can easily be appreciated with regard to the instructional variables listed. In writing, for example, not only is accuracy of form in more subtle features such as parallelism important (see 9.5.3), but also the ability to use complex grammatical devices such as fronting through negative inversion for emphasis, as in these examples:

> Not only did the company make five hundred workers redundant, but it …

> Hardly had the new government come into office when …

So formal writing of a professional kind places substantial demands for accurate use of a range of complex grammatical devices on the writer. In informal spoken English for survival communication, comprehension of the message by the listener is the main priority and this makes fewer demands on accuracy.

With regard to learner variables, it is perhaps more a question of finding a suitable approach than seeing a focus on grammar as more or less important. To illustrate this we can compare two sets of materials. Materials extract 5.H is taken from a course for beginners in the 11 to 14 age group in secondary school. The grammatical focus is on simple forms, demonstrated in concrete ways through stories and visuals and a problem-solving approach is applied. In other words, the pupils are helped to see language patterns for themselves. Exercise 2 can therefore be used in either of two ways depending on the complexity of the structure and on the growing familiarity of the pupils with this type of cognitive exercise:

– to *consolidate* knowledge of a structure that has been introduced
– to get pupils to *establish* the structure for themselves without an introduction from the teacher.

The procedure for both ways is for pupils to work in pairs or groups to copy and complete the table. One group then completes a table which the teacher has drawn on the blackboard and other groups check. Disagreements will need to be supported by examples noticed in the texts in the unit. Pupils then write down as many true sentences as they can and answer challenges to their truthfulness by describing, in the first language, an occasion when the sentence would be true. In this way, the first language is used to explore understanding of the second-language structure. Exercise 3 is for pairwork with role-play of the completed dialogue. Exercise 4 is a team game with pupil A choosing a word for pupil B, and provides substantial opportunity for correction and feedback. Exercise 5 elicits a blackboard chart from which pupils can derive sentences for part (b). Notice that 3 and 5 constitute further contextualization of the structure and provide practice of a game-like nature in small groups, which reduces anxiety and gives further input and feedback, and more opportunities to notice and take in the form in focus.

Materials extract 5.H can be contrasted with the sequence of activities in Materials extract 5.I, in a course for adult students who are literate and well-

Materials extract 5.H

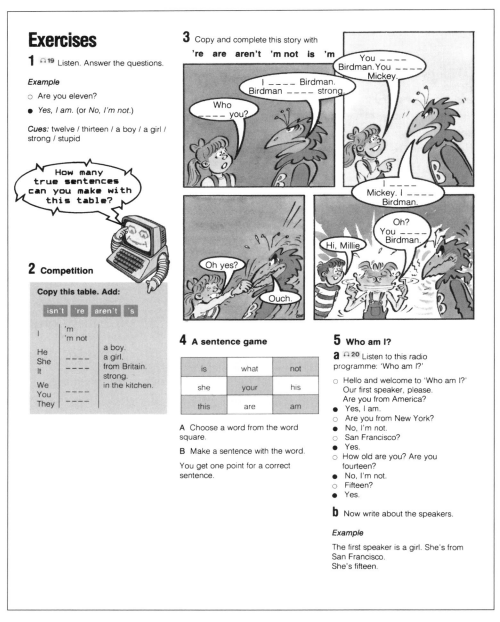

(Hutchinson: *Project English One* SB, page 11)

educated. In this course, grammar receives explicit focus in the Language Study sections. Students are introduced formally to the more complex structures of English and encouraged to reflect on how the language works.

Materials extract 5.1

LANGUAGE STUDY

1 Ways of adding emphasis

The following sentences are similar to lines found in the text on war.
Compare them with these lines and work out the ways in which the writer gives emphasis to the points she is making.

Discipline and organization made it an army.
(lines 14–15)
These men were transformed . . . into an army by drill.
(lines 25–8)
. . . pairs of individuals thrust at each other with spears.
(lines 42–3)

There are many ways of emphasizing a part of a sentence. Here are some further sentences based on the three patterns from the text.

1a

What	made it an army I like about John annoys me most	was is	discipline and organization. his honesty. people who are always late.

or

1b

What	made it an army I like about John annoys me most	was is	the way it was organized. the fact that he is so honest. the way some people are always late.

2

Drill Money John	is what is who	transformed these men into an army. makes the world go round. you should talk to.

3

It	was is	pairs of individuals John money	who that	thrust at each other. broke the vase. makes the world go round.

what = the thing which/that
who = the person who/that
where = the place which/that

Practice

1 ☐ **T.12** ☐ It is important to make such sentences *sound* emphatic when you are speaking. You will hear the first two sentences only from each of the four boxes above. Listen and mark the main stresses, then decide where the stresses are in the third sentence.

Example
What made it an army was discipline and organization.

Practise saying the sentences in pairs.

2 Restructure the following statements to make them more emphatic. Try to use patterns **1a**, **2**, and **3**.
   a. We doubt his sincerity.
   b. I admire the efficiency of the Swiss.
   c. She hates having to get up at 6 o'clock every morning.
   d. His approval of the scheme is important.
   e. Their self-righteousness is annoying.
   f. You should go to Spain for your holidays.
   g. I like London because it has beautiful parks.
   h. Nobody likes losing.

3 Join each of the following sentence-pairs using **the way** or **the fact**, and beginning with *What* . . .
   a. He never makes a fuss. I admire this.
   b. She's always on time. I appreciate this.
   c. This government has treated the Health Service so badly. This irritates everybody.
   d. The Health Service wastes less money than it used to. This is of no consequence.

4 Look at this sentence, based on lines 66–9 of the text on war. What device has the writer used to make the point more emphatically than it is made here?

The . . . anonymous mass slaughter of civilized warfare is worse than . . . taking part in a ritual 'battle' with a small . . . element of risk.

Restructure the following statements using the same device.
   a. Working until midnight occasionally is fine, but working until midnight every night isn't.
   b. Being woken by a pneumatic drill is worse than being woken by birdsong.
   c. I like living in a caravan when I'm on holiday, but I wouldn't like to live in one permanently.

5 Work in pairs.
Prepare to talk for one minute on one of the topics below, or any other topic that you feel particularly strongly about. Try to use some of these patterns for emphasis:

What really annoys me about . . .
What is most surprising . . .
It is the way some people . . . that . . .
What most people don't realize is the fact that . . .

litter	badly-behaved children
smoking	the weather
bad drivers	learning English
politics	people who wear fur coats
football	teachers who set too
exams	much homework

(Soars and Soars: *Headway Advanced* SB, pages 58–9)

Notice that, in the example given, the grammar is derived from reference to its place within a piece of discourse and the need for that discourse to move emphasis within sentences. As the last stage in the sequence of exercises, number 5 returns the student to discourse after a set of sentence-based or sentence-pair exercises. It is planned discourse with careful preparation, as appropriate to a presentation, with a conscious focus on use of the form. Notice that the practice here involves the element of sentence stress as this has a significant role in the use of this particular grammatical feature and is an essential part of a communicative approach to grammar.

Adults can be encouraged to think about the strategies they use for learning grammar. An early step would be to encourage them to reflect on the ways in which English grammar differs from that of their first language, as shown in these learners' comments:

> 'I find the relationships between time and tense particularly difficult to grasp; even the aspectual system in Russian I still find difficult to understand.'
> (Pickett 1978: 62)

> 'English and Swedish are very similar in general, but I had a lot of problems with "do", "don't", "does" and "doesn't". Somebody once told me I sounded like a character in a Jane Austen novel who says "don't" all the time.'
> (M. B. Edström: personal communication)

Part of reflecting on how grammar can be tackled is probably a realization that parts of grammar can be learned systematically, for example, the question words 'What?', 'Why?', 'Who?', 'Where?', and 'How?', or the past simple and past participle, as in 'fly–flew–flown'. Other, less obvious, parts can also be picked out and learned as paradigms, for example, the set of possible tag endings:

> It's terrible news, isn't it?
> He's new in the job, isn't he?
> They're moving house, aren't they?
> She shouldn't go to work, should she?
> I haven't got a chance, have I?

Adults can also be invited to think about self-help strategies and a useful activity would be to introduce students to appropriate grammar reference materials. In ideal circumstances this might involve taking a set of various grammars into the classroom and setting a task which invites learners to explore the different contents and layouts to see which grammar suits them best.

Adults can also be encouraged in self-correction. In writing, for example, the marking strategy of simply underlining a mistake and giving a student the chance to self-correct can make the point more memorable, particularly when the problem is something which can be easily checked in a reference book such as irregular plural forms, for example, 'woman–women'. Discerning and identifying errors is a skill which can be developed through regular practice, and it can help students to notice differences between their own production and the target form.

By considering the needs of any specific group of learners, their reasons for learning English, and factors of individual difference such as age and educational background, it should be possible for teachers to determine an appropriate approach to the teaching of grammar.

5.5 Conclusion

Unfortunately, looking at our current state of knowledge about how grammar is acquired, and at the possible roles of various classroom approaches, poses more questions than it resolves. In the face of such uncertainty, this chapter has attempted to do a number of things. First, it has tried to show that there is a complex of insights from the field of second language acquisition studies which provide description and explanation of the processes by which learners acquire English grammar. These insights suggest a framework to support the building of classroom procedures, though the framework is partial and under continual reconstruction. A number of approaches are currently in use in ELT, each of which relates to some part of the framework and which are appropriate in the context of communicative language teaching. And we are currently in the process of finding new and better ways of developing our learners' grammatical competence.

It therefore seems sensible that teachers choose eclectically from among those approaches available, in line with the needs of learners, and always remembering the need to cater for individual differences in style. There should be room for variety. Teachers can also carry out their own observations and explorations to discover what students prefer and report as useful. It is surely the case that learners will apply themselves better to the task of learning when they feel positive about the approaches used.

The main focus of discussion in this chapter has been on modes of presentation and the value of practice. However, this is only part of the picture. The other part is to provide classroom experiences which encourage interactive, realistic, message-focused output. Chapters 8 and 10 will return to this issue and provide further perspectives on it.

Discussion topics and projects

1 Review two coursebooks designed for intermediate students which have a grammatical component to the syllabus and compare them.

   (a) To what extent do you find similarities and differences in the selection and sequencing of structures?

   (b) Is an explanation given (for example, in the teacher's book) for the grammatical content and its order?

   (c) In what ways would the grammatical content of either of the books be suitable for your own intermediate learners?

2 Review this chapter and design a set of criteria for evaluating the suitability of grammar activities for a group of your own learners. Examples of possible criteria might be:

   – Is the language contextualized for meaning, social context, and within discourse?

   – What is the role of practice?

3 Consider the three grammar activities in Materials extracts 5.J, 5.K, and 5.L and evaluate each one. With what type of learner could you use each?

4 In courses which present and practise grammatical items, there is not only the issue of how to sequence these items in the overall syllabus, but also the issues of which specific forms to teach at different levels of learning and in what order to teach them. Consider this set of forms for the present continuous tense to express current actions:

> What are you doing?
> What is she doing?
> I'm writing to John.
> She's writing to John.
> Is she writing to John? Yes, she is.
> Is she writing to John? No, she isn't.
> Are you writing to John. Yes I am.
> Are you writing to John? No, I'm not.

Imagine you are going to prepare a forty-five minute lesson for a group of beginners who are unfamiliar with the present continuous.

   (a) Which of these forms would you teach?

   (b) What order would you present them in?

Design a suitable lesson plan.

5 In Materials extract 5.M, John and Liz Soars, authors of *Headway*, give a list of reasons to teachers to explain the prominence of grammar in their materials. Which of these would concur with your own views? Are there any with which you would disagree? Would you wish to add further reasons for teaching grammar explicitly in your own classes?

Materials extract 5.J

> **Focus on form 2** Tense and time

1 **Work in groups. Each group chooses an area of grammar.**
1 the present simple
2 the present continuous
3 the present perfect simple and continuous
4 the simple past and the past continuous
5 the past perfect simple and continuous
6 ways of talking about the future

2 **Draw a diagram to show the different uses of the area you chose and give an example sentence for each. Include grammar notes after your diagram.**
Example:

I'll remember to write to Auntie Jane.

I'll be really angry if you forget.

promises

threats

will

spontaneous decisions

confident predictions

There's someone at the door. – I'll answer it.

I'll be famous one day.

Positive: I will see you tomorrow.
Negative: I will not go (I won't go) to John's tomorrow.
Questions: Will you go to John's tomorrow?
Note: <u>Will</u> is followed by an infinitive without <u>to</u>

3 **Show your diagram to people from other groups. Explain the different uses of the verb forms and point out any special features.**

(Downie, Gray, and Jiménez: *Freeform 4* SB, page 91)

Materials extract 5.K

What's on in London

Dance

Anna and Steve
World Disco Champions
Tramps Mon-Fri 10.00pm

Boris Nureyev
at The Royal Ballet
Fri-Sat 8.30pm

Music

Madonna
Wembley Stadium
Wed-Thurs 8.00pm

Placido Domingo
Covent Garden
Tues only 7.30pm

Art

The paintings of David Hockney
National Gallery
Daily 10.00 to 17.00

Salvador Dali Exhibition
at The Tate Gallery
Sun-Sat (closed Mon) 10.00 to 17.30

GRAMMAR

Adverbs of manner

wonderful is an adjective. It gives information about the noun or pronoun.

● EXAMPLE
*She's a **wonderful** singer.*

beautifully, well and *badly* are adverbs. They give information about the verb.

● EXAMPLE
*They dance **beautifully**.*

Most adverbs of manner are formed by adding *-ly* to the adjective.
See page 107.

2D Practice

Work in pairs. Use these verbs and adverbs to talk about the people and the events in the programme in 2C.

VERBS	ADVERBS
act	beautifully
sing	well
dance	wonderfully
paint	

● EXAMPLES
  A *There's a Hockney exhibition at the National Gallery.*
  B *He paints really well.*

(Nolasco: *WOW 2* SB, page 57)

Materials extract 5.L

> ## 3   Every picture tells a story
> Past progressive and past simple
>
> 1   Work in pairs or groups. Look at the drawings below. For each of the four pictures write two 'background' sentences on a piece of paper using the past progressive. Leave plenty of space underneath the sentences for each picture. Examples: *The sun was shining. Geraldine and Mike were coming home from work.*
>
> 2   Under the two background sentences, write the beginning of each of the four stories (two or three sentences each) using the past simple. Example: *Geraldine heard a loud noise.*
>
> 3   Number the stories 1 to 4, then pass your work to another pair or group to continue the stories. Pass the paper on after you have written two or three sentences each time.
>
> 4   When all the stories are complete, read them to the whole class. Correct any mistakes.
>
>

(Dean: *English Grammar Lessons, Upper-intermediate*, page 22)

Materials extract 5.M

> – It is the mechanism that generates the infinite number of sentences that we produce and receive.
> – It is a tangible system, and can provide one element of a systematic approach to teaching a language.
> – It develops students' cognitive awareness of the language. Language is rule-based, and conscious or sub-conscious knowledge of the rules is the key to 'generalizability' and creativity.
> – It conforms to students' expectations of language learning, and meets an often-heard request for 'more grammar'.
> – It will be of assistance to teachers in the planning of their lessons.

(Soars and Soars: *Headway Upper Intermediate* TB, page iv)

Further reading

Batstone, R. 1994. *Grammar*. Oxford: Oxford University Press.

This book has been written for the practising English language teacher. It begins by exploring the nature of grammar, looking at both issues in the description and use of grammar and issues in grammar acquisition. The second part of the book discusses three approaches to the teaching of grammar: grammar as product, grammar as process, and grammar as skill. The discussion is illustrated by analyses of examples from a variety of coursebooks. The third part suggests small-scale research projects which teachers can use to explore the teaching and learning of grammar in their own classrooms.

Bygate, M., A. Tonkyn and **E. Williams** (eds.). 1994. *Grammar and the Language Teacher*. Hemel Hempstead: Prentice Hall International.

In the introduction to this book, Tonkyn characterizes Sections One and Two as focusing on grammar as an *object* for teachers and learners. These sections look at the nature of pedagogical grammar and at teachers' knowledge of grammar. Sections Three and Four are described as focusing on grammar as a *process*. They look at the acquisition of grammar and the ways in which teachers can assist this process. This collection of sixteen papers reflects the recent debate about the role of grammar in language teaching.

Celce-Murcia, M. 1993. 'Grammar pedagogy in second and foreign language teaching' in S. Silberstein (ed.): *State of the Art TESOL Essays*. Alexandria, Va.: TESOL. pp. 288–309

This can be described as a state-of-the-art paper which provides a perspective on the role of grammar as language teaching moved into the 1990s. It gives an historical overview of grammar teaching, looks at current challenges, and suggests pedagogical strategies.

Ur, P. 1992. *Grammar Practice Activities: A Practical Guide for Teachers*. Cambridge: Cambridge University Press.

This is a useful resource book for teachers who wish to use interesting grammar practice activities in a communicative approach. The first part of the book presents principles and practice for grammar teaching and the second part contains nearly 200 activities for practising aspects of grammar. These include detailed classroom procedures and photocopiable texts and visuals.

PART THREE

Developing the language skills

6 READING

'Reade not to contradict, nor to believe, but to waigh and consider.'
FRANCIS BACON

1 What do we know about the process of second language reading?

2 In what ways is reading an interactive process?

3 In what ways is reading a purposeful process?

4 In what ways is reading a critical process?

5 What is the role of extensive reading?

6 How do we establish goals for the reading classroom?

7 What criteria do we use to select reading texts?

8 What kinds of tasks help to develop reading ability?

9 Can we help students to read critically?

10 How can we encourage extensive reading?

Introductory task

Read the text in Materials extract 6.A. It is taken from a simplified version of the science fantasy novel *The White Mountains* by John Christopher. The words which have been replaced by nonsense words were those judged as likely to be new to intermediate readers of English, making the text as presented here approximate to what a text might look like to a learner at that level. The original words were introduced carefully by the adaptor, who provided clues in the surrounding text as to their meaning.

1 Try to guess the missing words and identify the clues that are available in the text.
2 Consider what kinds of knowledge you used to work out the meanings.

Materials extract 6.A

My Father's Watch

In our village, there were only six good clocks. The biggest clock was in the church <u>stram</u> where everybody could see it. My father owned one of the others. It stood in our kitchen. He wound it every night before he went to bed.

Once a year, the clock<u>marret</u> came from Winchester. He came on his horse. He cleaned the clock in the church <u>stram</u> first. Then he cleaned ours, and he set its hands to the correct time.

My mother always gave him something to drink, and they talked together. He told her about his life in Winchester. This was our nearest town. It was very old. Some people say that English kings once lived there, in a <u>jurrip</u>. That was a long time ago; but parts of the <u>jurrip</u> still remain.

My father was a <u>barlim</u> and he was a busy man. When the clock had been cleaned, he always left the room. 'Women can <u>taddle</u> their time with stories,' he said, 'but men have work to do.' And he went back to his <u>barl</u>.

But my father's greatest <u>fastam</u> was not the clock. It was a watch. It was fixed to a <u>wol</u> so that you could wear it on your <u>prad</u>.

My father kept it in a locked <u>dimp</u> in his desk. He only brought it out on special days. Then he fixed the <u>wol</u> round his <u>prad</u> and he wore the watch for a few hours. After that, he locked it in its <u>dimp</u> again.

(adapted from *The White Mountains* by John Christopher (abridged and simplified for 'Longman Structural Readers' by A. G. Eyre))

6.1 Introduction: making sense of a text

In recent years the term 'interactive' (Carrell, Devine, and Eskey 1988; Eskey 1988; Grabe 1993) has been used to describe the second language reading process. The term can be interpreted in two ways. First, it describes a dynamic relationship with a text as the reader 'struggles' to make sense of it. This is the struggle you became involved in as you read the extract in the Introductory task. In trying to create meaning from the text, you were undoubtedly involved in an active process, a process which Goodman (1967) called a 'psycholinguistic guessing game'. In playing the game and engaging in the struggle, you combined information from the text and knowledge you brought with you to reading it. From this perspective, reading can be seen as a kind of dialogue between the reader and the text, or even between the reader and the author (Widdowson 1979a). There is an interesting distinction to be made here: the reader may be interested in constructing a personal interpretation of a text or, on the other hand, may be more interested in trying to get at the author's original intentions. 'Making sense of a text' can imply either approach.

It is likely that you used at least six types of knowledge to help you make sense of the text:

– *Syntactic knowledge*: e.g. 'barlim' follows the indefinite article 'a' and is therefore likely to be a noun. Similarly 'taddle' follows the modal 'can' and is likely to be a main verb.
– *Morphological knowledge*: e.g. there seems to be a relationship between 'barl' and 'barlim'. The latter is derived by affixing the morpheme '-im' at the end. So possibly it could be 'farm'–'farmer', 'mill'–'miller', or 'baker'–'bakery', or some similarly related item.
– *General world knowledge*: e.g. a knowledge of the structure of desks and of what can be locked that would be suitable for keeping treasures in might suggest 'box' or 'drawer'.
– *Sociocultural knowledge*: e.g. a knowledge of the architecture of churches might suggest 'tower' or 'steeple'.
– *Topic knowledge*: e.g. a knowledge of rural life might suggest the possibilities for the father's employment.
– *Genre knowledge*: e.g. the information given that the text is from a science fantasy novel might help a reader to realize that the setting is the future and to deal with the seeming anachronism of the watch.

It can be seen, then, that a second interpretation of the term 'interaction' refers to the interplay among various kinds of knowledge that a reader employs in moving through a text. Two of these, syntactic and morphological knowledge, are to do with the language itself. As we have seen, these kinds of knowledge help a reader to decode the language of a text and can together be called linguistic, or *systemic*, knowledge. At the same time, general world knowledge, sociocultural, topic, and genre knowledge, together often referred to as *schematic* knowledge, enable a reader to work with the language of the text in order to interpret its meaning. The Introductory task is not meant to suggest that all readers would necessarily tackle a text in this way, that is, as an intensive problem-solving activity. Fluent readers reach automaticity in their reading and do not consciously control the process in the way demanded by the text above. However, the task serves to illustrate reading as an interactive process.

In recent literature on reading, the term *top-down processing* has been used to describe the application of prior knowledge to working on the meaning of a text. The term *bottom-up processing* has been used to describe the decoding of the letters, words, and other language features in the text. These terms might be useful in reflecting different processes in reading, but we need to keep in mind that the processes are in constant interplay. A reader will be involved, as you were in reading 'My father's watch', in a continual shift of focus between them, interpreting the language in terms of its schematic implications. For example, when dealing with word meaning, both types of knowledge will come into play. Cultural knowledge would provide the meaning 'the tall structure on a Christian church' for 'stram' ('tower' in the original text), and this language knowledge would inform further reading.

However, while it is true that researchers continue to investigate the precise ways in which schematic and systemic knowledge interact in processing a text, second language pedagogy now generally works on the assumption that second language readers will need help with both, and that classroom methodology needs to pay attention to both.

6.2 What do we know about the process of second language reading?

6.2.1 *In what ways is reading an interactive process?*

Schematic knowledge

The Introductory task demonstrated the importance of schematic knowledge in reading. This term has been usefully defined by Cook (1989) as follows:

> ... mental representations of typical situations ... used in discourse processing to predict the contents of the particular situation which the discourse describes.
> (Cook 1989: 69)

Certain words or phrases in the text or in the materials surrounding the text will activate prior knowledge of some kind in the mind of the reader. This is demonstrated by current research into the reading process which has uncovered what happens in silent reading by asking subjects to 'think aloud', periodically reporting on how they are tackling and responding to the text, and by recording their thoughts. These records are known as 'protocols'. The procedure requires some training as more fluent readers have automatized the strategies they use in reading, but it has provided useful insights into reading strategies. For example, in Figure 6.1, notice how the place name in the headline immediately enables the reader to predict possible content using knowledge of the world and topic knowledge of politics in the last

Figure 6.1: Excerpt from a transcript of a 'think aloud' report (text from Tales of Real Escape *by P. Dowswell in 'Usborne Readers Library')*

Text

Breakout at Pretoria Prison

By December 1979 Tim Jenkin, Stephen Lee and Alex Moumbaris were finally ready to tackle the ten locked doors that lay between them and the streets outside Pretoria Prison, South Africa.

Jenkin and Lee, who had been friends since university, had been plotting this escape since their arrival here in June 1978. Neither was prepared to sit out the 12 and eight year sentences imposed on them for being active members of the African National Congress (ANC), a political party that had been banned in South Africa.

Hatching a plot

They soon discovered that most of their fellow prisoners had reconciled themselves to long sentences and abandoned any hope of escape from this top security prison. But not Alex Moumbaris, a fellow ANC member, who had been given a 12 year sentence in 1973. When Jenkin mentioned that they were planning a breakout, Moumbaris replied that if any escape plans were being hatched then "he would definitely like to be one of the chickens".

Reader

I'm looking at the picture. These men are friends, I think. They are pleased ...

Pretoria ... this is in South Africa ... the article is about a breakout from a prison in South Africa. Are these men the prisoners ...

tackle–I don't know ... yes, okay

There are ten doors ... it's a secure ... a high secure ... a high security prison

Yes, they are political prisoners.

twenty years. And the clue 'ten locked doors' draws on general knowledge to suggest a high-security prison.

Similarly, this simile, used in a story for language learners:

> Susan George: pretty as a picture at fourteen, lovely as a prize rose at fifteen …

could be generally understood by most readers, but the full meaning could only be appreciated by a reader with the cultural knowledge to conjure up the essentially English image of the flower show and its prize exhibits. There is now a considerable body of research (for example Alderson and Urquhart

1984; Steffenson and Joag-Dev 1984) which suggests that reading methodology needs to pay attention to activating schematic knowledge before reading.

Other studies have used a recall procedure. Here, subjects are asked to write down what they can remember about the text, in complete sentences. They are encouraged to link ideas in the same way as the original text, using both their own words and words from the text. Carrell (1984) suggested that reading can also be facilitated by knowing the types of rhetorical organization used in English texts, often referred to as the *formal schemata* of texts. In her study, eighty students of English from a variety of first language backgrounds (mainly Spanish, Arabic, and Oriental) were asked to read and recall four versions of a text, each of which contained the same content information but within a different organization (description, cause–effect, problem–solution, and comparison). The recall protocols were assessed in terms of the number of ideas recalled from the original text and the organizational structure used in writing the protocol. One of the findings suggested by the study is that:

> if ESL readers possess the appropriate formal schema against which to process the discourse type of the text and if they utilize that formal schema to organize their recall protocols, more information is retrieved.
> (Carrell 1984: 460)

If this is the case, there are clearly implications here for reading instruction, particularly when students are learning English to facilitate academic study.

One of the major responses to increasing insights about the role of schematic knowledge in reading has been the focus in current reading methodology on a pre-reading stage, and in materials design on tasks to activate different types of prior knowledge. Examples of this practice will be taken up in 6.3.3.

Language knowledge

Language knowledge enables readers to work on the text. Good readers recognize, and decode quickly and accurately, words, grammatical structures, and other linguistic features, and are unaware of the process as they engage in this. In other words, a fluent reader has a good knowledge of language structure and can recognize a wide range of vocabulary automatically.

Clearly second language readers are going to have difficulties in processing texts which contain unfamiliar aspects of the English language. For example, inability to understand the cohesive devices in a text will impede understanding of the functional relationships of sentences. Cohesive devices include such things as reference items (for example, 'they', 'these matters', 'the latter'); lexical cohesion through a chain of synonyms (for example, 'funding … financing … resourcing'), or deletion of items such as relative pronouns (for example, 'which' and 'that'). Berman (1984) has suggested that deletion, another cohesive device, can make a text 'opaque' to the reader. An example would be:

> Hyperactivity in children is a common problem … many parents have to confront. They must learn to understand the symptoms … typical of this medical condition.

Here 'which' has been deleted between 'problem' and 'many', and 'which are' between 'symptoms' and 'typical'. Berman describes an experiment with twenty Hebrew-speaking students in which one group was given an original text of approximately 300 words containing a degree of opacity and a second group answered the same questions on a more 'transparent' version of the text, i.e. reworked to eliminate syntactic difficulty. The second group did consistently better, especially on questions requiring specific information. This seems to confirm the hypothesis that foreign language readers are partly dependent on processing syntactic structures successfully in order to get access to meaning. Berman's study came at a time of great interest in the role of schematic knowledge and served as a timely reminder that the role of language knowledge should not be forgotten. Understanding of the complementarity of these two kinds of knowledge should form the basis of any classroom instruction on reading.

A reader may also use discourse signals of various kinds to get through a text. These may be connectives such as 'moreover', which signals addition, or 'whereas', which signals contrast. Or they may be words that organize discourse as in 'There are two ways of dealing with this problem'. Here 'problem' refers to a situation previously described and 'ways' signals that the writer is going to discuss alternative modes of treatment. A number of such words in English work in the same way, as signposts in the text: for example, 'incident', 'event', 'episode', 'situation', 'method', 'issue', 'question', and 'matter'.

Vocabulary is another major component of reading ability with which language learners will experience difficulty, but the degree of difficulty will vary with the demands of the text, the prior knowledge of the reader, the degree of automaticity a learner has achieved in general word recognition, any specialist lexical knowledge a student might have, and the learner's first language. A major strategy in helping students to build vocabulary for reading is to encourage them to develop strategies for guessing word meanings from contextual clues and background knowledge. Students are capable of guessing 60–80 per cent of unknown words in a text if the density of new words is not too high. Nation and Coady (1988) suggest a five-step sequence to help learners when they are dealing with a text which they can follow with reasonable comprehension and to which they bring some background knowledge:

1 Finding the part of speech of the unknown word.
2 Looking at the immediate context of the unknown word and simplifying this context if necessary.
3 Looking at the wider context of the unknown word. This means looking at the relationship between the clause containing the unknown word and surrounding clauses and sentences.
4 Guessing the meaning of the unknown word.
5 Checking that the guess is correct.
(Nation and Coady 1988: 104–5)

This describes the sequence you probably followed when dealing with the unknown words in 'My father's watch'.

A concern that students should exploit their knowledge of language effectively implies a number of points for the methodology of the reading class. First, encouraging extensive reading may help some students to build a knowledge of vocabulary and an awareness of the features of written texts. Second, texts need to be chosen and tasks designed to provide support for what the learner already knows. Third, there might be value in regular use of analytical activities which draw students' attention explicitly to some linguistic features of texts. And finally, when students deal with a particular reading text in class, the teacher will need to prepare them for any specific language difficulties they might encounter in it.

In general, studies seem to show that readers who can use schematic knowledge are greatly facilitated in reading comprehension. This has substantially influenced current approaches to task design. At the same time, however, it may be the case that a certain level of language competence is necessary before any training in the use of schematic knowledge can be effective. And it is certainly the case that each reader will use an individual mix of processing strategies in relation to a particular text and topic. Teachers will need to combine their awareness of what happens in the reading process with knowledge of their students in order to decide appropriate goals and procedures for the reading lesson.

6.2.2 *In what ways is reading a purposeful process?*

Pugh (1978) and Lunzer and Gardner (1979) described various styles of reading, and their terminology for these has been taken into ELT methodology:

- *Receptive reading* is undertaken, for example, when a reader wants to enjoy a short story, follow a line of argument in a newspaper editorial, or understand the main stages in a textbook description of a manufacturing process.
- *Reflective reading* involves episodes of reading the text and then pausing to reflect and backtrack, for example, when a reader wants to check whether a new line of argument in a political text is consistent with opinions expressed earlier in the same article.
- *Skim reading* is used to get a global impression of the content of a text. An example would be previewing a long magazine article by reading rapidly, skipping large chunks of information, and focusing on headings and first lines of paragraphs.
- *Scanning* involves searching rapidly through a text to find a specific point of information, for example, the relevant times on a timetable, items in a directory, or key points in a academic text.
- *Intensive reading* involves looking carefully at a text, as a student of literature would look at a poem to appreciate the choice of words, or as a solicitor would study the precise wording of a legal document.

The point of making these distinctions is that different purposes for reading determine different strategies in approaching texts and also different rates of reading. They imply different uses of top-down (schematic) and bottom-up (linguistic) processes. Skimming, for example, uses largely top-down processes to get at the general dimensions of a text.

It is now standard practice in ELT methodology to consider real purposes for reading outside the classroom and to build these into reading activities. Rivers and Temperley, for example, in an early discussion of reading pedagogy, make the point that: 'reading activities, from the beginning, should have some purpose and we should concentrate on the normal purposes of reading' (1978: 187). They list the following purposes: to get information; to respond to curiosity about a topic; to follow instructions to perform a task; for pleasure, amusement, and personal enjoyment; to keep in touch with friends and colleagues; to know what is happening in the world; and to find out when and where things are.

Some, or all, of these purposes may be real-life ones for many language learners because English is part of their environment, or because they have immediate needs such as studying in English or using it in professional life. Even where it is difficult to identify any needs, there may be strong motivational reasons for giving students a range of purposes for reading and, consequently, for presenting them with a variety of texts, for example, brochures, articles, schedules, poems, short stories, maps, and diagrams. Traditionally, many textbook materials have limited classroom activities to slow, intensive study of texts rather than encouraging the flexibility of style that learners would use when reading in their first language. Now it is common to find activities which encourage different speeds of reading, and different degrees of pre-reading and re-reading, and searching through the text.

More importantly, however, it is now recognized that one text may be read in a variety of styles, and that readers will have different purposes at each stage of the reading process and will apply the appropriate strategies. A student of economics, for example, on seeing a news feature entitled 'Cuba: an economic profile', might skim initially to get the general schematic gist and see whether or not it is interesting or useful. He or she might then read it reflectively, with pauses to consider the opinions expressed, the political viewpoint they reflect, and whether he or she agrees with it. Parts might then be read intensively in order to take notes for an essay. The same text, then, can be tackled in a number of ways and current reading pedagogy takes this into account. A good example of a procedure designed to help students with the different stages of approaching a text is the SCROL procedure (Grant 1993):

Summary of the SCROL procedure

Here are the steps to be included in the SCROL procedure for using text headings to help understand, remember, and locate information. Conduct steps 3–5 for one heading segment (the heading and the text that follows it) at a time. Then move to the next heading segment.

1 *Survey the headings:*
In the assigned text selection, read each heading and its subheadings. For each heading and subheading, try to answer the following questions: 'What do I already know about this topic? What information might the writer present?'

2 *Connect:*
After reading all of the headings and subheadings in the selection, ask yourself 'How do the headings relate to one another?' Write down key words from the headings that might provide connections between the headings.

3 *Read the text:*
Now go back to the first heading segment and begin reading the text. Remember that headings may provide clues to important information in the text. As you read each segment, look for words and phrases that express important information about the heading. As you read, feel free to mark the text (underline, highlight, make notes in the margin) to point out important ideas and details. Before moving to the next heading segment, *stop* to *make sure* that you

understand the major ideas and supporting details. If you do not understand, reread.

4 *Outline:*

Using indentations to reflect structure, outline the major ideas and supporting details in the heading segment. Write the heading and then try to outline each heading segment without looking back to the text.

5 *Look back:*

Now, look back to the text and check the accuracy of the major ideas and details you wrote. Correct any inaccurate information in your outline. If you marked the text as you read, use this information to help you to verify the accuracy of your outline.

(Grant 1993: 483)

The first two stages aim at developing skimming in order to preview content and are as relevant to second language readers as they are to the first language college students for whom the procedure was originally designed.

These concepts of reading purpose and reading style, and their implications for the design of reading activities, will be taken up later in this chapter.

6.2.3 *In what ways is reading a critical process?*

Critical reading views reading as a social process (Kress 1985). From this perspective, texts are constructed in certain ways by writers in order to shape the perceptions of readers towards acceptance of the underlying ideology of the text. To take a simple example, a political writer using the pronoun 'we' attempts to create a bond with the reader by assuming a shared view of the topic under discussion. The implication is of 'we, the politically astute'. In this way the use of the pronoun positions the reader.

Recent years have seen much debate on the role of critical reading in ELT. For example, Spolsky (1989) argues a case for teaching 'resisting reading' with reference to the use of literary texts in Israeli high schools. One example she discusses is 'Eveline' from James Joyce's *Dubliners*. Eveline's essential characteristic is passivity, an inability to break free from a dominant father. One of the purposes of using a text like this, she suggests, is to widen students' horizons, to introduce them to unfamiliar cultural values. In doing so, however, teachers need to recognize the dangers inherent in presenting culturally alien and provocative texts which try to persuade readers to identify with the writer's own moral vision. Drawing on feminist literary theory, she stresses the importance of teaching school students to assert their own cultural values and resist the morality of the text.

Writing about a different educational context, Clark (1993) discusses the problems her overseas students face when studying international relations through the medium of English at a UK university, where their textbooks express largely western viewpoints. They need to be able to recognize the ideology of a text and decide whether they will be submissive or resistant to it. This means a careful analysis of the ways in which language choices are made by the writer: for example, the ways in which adjectival choice or choice of reporting phrase denote attitude. The following text, from a British national newspaper, contains examples of such language choices. It comments on an incident in which an assistant to a town clerk resigned from her post after finding a pornographic magazine in her office.

I AM sorry that Anne Turville was upset to find a girlie magazine in the desk drawer of her boss. She is not the only female to have been disgusted and appalled by such magazines. The daughters of a friend of mine once came across his pile of pornographic magazines and were similarly revolted. The girls successfully pressured my friend into burning them. But that did not really change anything. Men cannot alter their sexuality. They did not choose it. In some cases, such as Sophocles, they have found it a confounded tyranny. Whether we like it or not, male sexuality exists and is extraordinarily urgent.

The error of British society lies in not telling girls the truth about it. They read stories about romantic love which completely by-pass the true nature of men. So it then comes as a belated and brutal shock when they realise that some of the men in their lives—especially young men—have sex on the brain. They draw the conclusion that these individuals are particularly dirty or depraved. They are not. They are normal.

Other societies, such as those of Japan, France and even America, are more realistic. Some Japanese mothers even tell their daughters about love-making techniques. They pass on, as a matter of course, the fact that men are powerfully driven in their sexuality. It is important to tell girls about this reality of life as well as the mere 'facts'.

Daily Express April 8, 1996

What is particularly noticeable here is the way in which the modality of a series of linked statements presents them as 'truth', i.e. 'Men cannot alter their sexuality … some have sex on the brain' … 'They are normal', and leads to the implicit conclusion that reading pornography is normal. Thus the writer presents his version of reality and tries to move the reader to that same version. Attempts to position the reader are perhaps more obvious in a genre such as journalism, but persuasion is present in almost all writing.

Many readers are aware of how language is manipulated in certain kinds of texts. Wallace (1992) gives the more subtle example of the educational text in Materials extract 6.B. Here, perhaps, the reader's awareness is not so high as it would be when reading a newspaper article, and it might arguably be the teacher's responsibility, with learners uncertain of language, to heighten that

Materials Extract 6.B

THE NOANAMÁ

¹The picture shows a man rowing. What physical characteristic of the Noanamá results from rowing?

The Noanamá are a handsome people; tallish and well-built with the heavy chest and shoulders of men accustomed to rowing;¹ their dark hair in a bowl-like fringe around the head; light-skinned, narrow-nosed and high-cheekboned, mongoloid in appearance with penetrating dark eyes. The women are often beautiful, with long flowing black hair and wearing no more than a cloth about their waist. Sometimes they put 'bija', a red dye, on their faces, and flowers in their hair. For ceremonies they cover their bodies with blue 'jagua' dye in a series of designs.²

(*Reading and Thinking in English*, pages 46–7)

awareness. She points out the text's focus on physical characteristics and the ways in which men and women are described, and makes these comments:

> One kind of activity which might highlight the arguably racist and sexist discourse here, would be to consider the effect of replacing 'the Noanamá' with a European group, such as 'the British' or 'the Germans'. Clearly specific lexis would change, so we might have something like: 'The British are a fair-skinned people; tallish and slightly built with the rounded shoulders of men accustomed to working long hours in the city …'.
> (Wallace 1992: 120)

Those who advocate the development of critical reading skills as part of the reading curriculum argue that the ability to read critically depends on an awareness of how elements of language can be manipulated by writers, and that language learners need to build this awareness. Critical reading pedagogy requires close scrutiny of the language in order to see what the writer means by the text. There is a particular concern in the case of younger learners, that such 'language awareness' should be an important educational goal, and as legitimate to second language as to first language education. This is perhaps because we feel such learners are more vulnerable as the result of their inexperience and therefore more likely to accommodate to the writer's view of things than to resist it.

In the context of teaching younger learners, there has been useful discussion about the considerable methodological responsibilities of bringing together students and provocative texts. For example, the Humanities Project of the 1970s in the UK introduced themes such as employment and immigration into the curriculum for 12- to 16-year-olds. It set up the aim, following the ideas of Stenhouse, of 'developing an understanding of social situations and human acts and the controversial value issues which they raise' (Elliot 1991: 15). The project developed pedagogic principles appropriate to that aim, and some of these would be pertinent as guidelines for teachers aiming to develop critical reading skills, for example:

- that teachers should not use their authority as teachers as a platform for promoting their own views
- that the mode of enquiry in controversial areas should have discussion rather than instruction at its core
- that the discussion should protect divergence of views among participants.

(ibid.: 16)

A procedure for critical reading which was consistent with these principles might reassure those teachers who want to encourage learners to challenge a writer's assumptions but do not want to prescribe the alternatives. However, it is extremely difficult to envisage such a procedure. Even in selecting texts for a critical approach, the teacher can hardly avoid implying value judgements which go some way towards promoting their own views. Some examples of critical reading procedures are discussed in 6.3.4.

6.2.4 *What is the role of extensive reading?*

As long ago as 1955, Michael West described the purpose of his 'New Method Supplementary Readers' as 'to confer greater facility in the use of the vocabulary already gained, to give the child a sense of achievement and a taste of the pleasure to be derived from his accomplishment' (1955: 45). Recent years have seen a resurgence of interest in extensive reading, perhaps as a result of insights from second language acquisition studies into the role and nature of input in the learning process. There are a number of current trends in ELT which demonstrate this renewed interest.

Some current trends

One observable trend is that many institutions now offer their students materials for independent reading through class libraries or through self-access centres, and teachers provide accompanying activities so that students are motivated to use the resources provided. In fact, this is reflected at a national level where educational systems have acknowledged the potential of extensive reading. For example, Malaysia launched an English Language Reading Programme in 1976 with a number of aims: to expose students to written English; to motivate students to read and inculcate in them the reading habit; to help students develop their language proficiency through materials that can enrich learning; and to introduce elements of literature into language teaching (Raj and Hunt 1990). In Singapore, between 1985 and 1990, forty schools benefited from grants given by the Ministry of Education to buy fiction and non-fiction readers to be used in whole-school silent reading periods of twenty minutes every day and a weekly extensive reading period. The books could also be borrowed for reading at home (Davis 1995).

A second trend has been the development of a research interest in the value of extensive reading. As yet, very little data-based work has been done and a research agenda is needed. Those studies undertaken so far have tended to look at the general effect on language proficiency, and two of them will serve as examples.

Hafiz and Tudor (1989) set up a three-month extra-curricular extensive reading programme using graded readers with an experimental group of Pakistani ESL learners in a UK school and compared their results with two other groups of learners in the same city. The pupils read after school for twelve weeks. Although the researchers point out the difficulty of isolating extensive reading from other factors which might affect the development of learners' language in a second language environment, the results showed a significant improvement in the performance of the experimental group, especially in their writing skills. The extensive reading programme may well have been a contributory factor.

Robb and Susser (1989) describe an experiment comparing the improvement of reading comprehension by Japanese college freshmen taught by either a skills-based or an extensive reading procedure. They hypothesized that the extensive reading procedure would be superior to, or at least remain equal to, the skills-based method and their results appeared to confirm this. They concluded:

> If the extensive reading procedure is as effective as the skills procedure in terms of test scores, the implications for the teaching of FL/EFL reading are profound. By reading what they choose and (more or less) enjoying their homework, students' motivation to learn will increase, which will in turn benefit their eventual acquisition of the target language.
> (Robb and Susser 1989: 248)

A research agenda for the future could usefully include not only further comparative studies of the effects of intensive and extensive reading but also studies of the relative merits of a range of pedagogical procedures to promote extensive reading, and possibly varying approaches to be used with different types of learner such as adult and child.

Defining extensive reading

A key issue emerging from research studies has been that of defining exactly what is meant by the term 'extensive reading'. There is a lack of consensus among writers on the subject. Some use the term confusingly to describe skimming and scanning activities on longer texts read during class time. Others relate it to quantity of material, for example, 'fifty [books] per year' (Bright and McGregor 1977: 62). Yet others specify time, for example 'an hour per evening' (Krashen 1982: 183) or 'individual silent reading periods in class' (Hedge 1985: 94). Clearly the precise nature of extensive reading will vary with student motivation and institutional resources, but an ideal characterization might include the following:

– reading large quantities of material, whether short stories and novels, newspaper and magazine articles, or professional reading
– reading consistently over time on a frequent and regular basis
– reading longer texts (more than a few paragraphs in length) of the types listed in the first point above
– reading for general meaning, primarily for pleasure, curiosity, or professional interest
– reading longer texts during class time but also engaging in individual, independent reading at home, ideally of self-selected material.

Another way of characterizing extensive reading is to contrast it with intensive reading. Intensive reading activities in the classroom, on texts which are usually not more than a page or so in length, are intended to train students in the strategies needed for successful reading, such as using connectives for predicting content or guessing the meanings of unfamiliar words using clues in the surrounding text. They involve close study of texts and familiarize students with the features of written English. Teachers can train reading strategies in this way but it is only through more extensive reading that learners can gain substantial practice in operating these strategies more independently on a range of material. This is demonstrated in Figure 6.2.

The aim of extensive reading is usefully described by Hafiz and Tudor (1989) as:

> ... to 'flood' learners with large quantities of L2 input with few or possibly no specific tasks to perform on this material. The pedagogical value attributed to extensive reading is based on the assumption that exposing learners to large quantities of meaningful and interesting L2 material will, in the long run, produce a beneficial effect on the learners' command of the L2.
> (Hafiz and Tudor 1989: 5)

Figure 6.2: The relationship between intensive reading lessons and extensive reading programmes (adapted from Hedge 1985: 70)

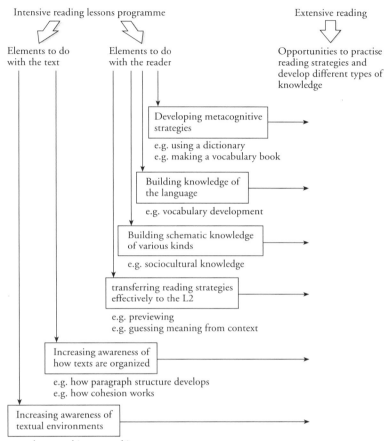

Intensive reading lessons programme   Extensive reading

Elements to do   Elements to do   Opportunities to practise
with the text   with the reader   reading strategies and
                                                develop different types of
                                                knowledge

Developing metacognitive
strategies

e.g. using a dictionary
e.g. making a vocabulary book

Building knowledge of
the language

e.g. vocabulary development

Building schematic knowledge
of various kinds

e.g. sociocultural knowledge

transferring reading strategies
effectively to the L2

e.g. previewing
e.g. guessing meaning from context

Increasing awareness of
how texts are organized

e.g. how paragraph structure develops
e.g. how cohesion works

Increasing awareness of
textual environments

e.g. how graphics are used in newspaper texts

Building a rationale for extensive reading

Despite the present dearth of research data, it is possible to build a firm rationale for the introduction of extensive reading into an ELT programme. Perhaps the strongest argument is the role it plays in developing reading ability, as discussed above. Clearly authentic reading texts will provide an authentic reading challenge but graded material can also be useful. For example, a series of graded readers provides unfamiliar vocabulary at each level to practise inferencing strategies and dictionary skills, but not in such quantity as to cause demotivation. And adapted readers can provide some of the material to be continued with in authentic texts such as chapter titles or headings and subheadings in non-fiction, accompanying visuals, and cultural and topic-specific information, which will involve learners in practising the range of reading strategies and in building their schematic knowledge.

Further arguments can be added to this. Involving learners in programmes of extensive reading can be a highly productive step towards autonomous learning (as discussed in Chapter 3). If students have a chance to read at home or to read silently in school, they are engaging in an activity which will yield substantial possibilities for them to go on learning by themselves. Extensive reading offers the learner many ways of working independently.

It would be unwise to make strong claims about the role of extensive reading in second language acquisition at this stage in our understanding of the latter. If we are persuaded by Krashen's view (see 1.2.1) that learners need to be exposed to large amounts of comprehensible input which is meaningful, relevant, and interesting, in a stress-free environment, then clearly individual extensive reading outside class time has value. It can be seen as an input-enabling activity. Whether extensive reading facilitates intake is another matter (see 1.2.2). It is difficult to know exactly how any learner will actually use the input available. One of my own students, Stephanie, reported this strategy:

> I try to read without stopping. Then I go back after each chapter and find some words I like.

Stephanie clearly responded emotionally to words and provided herself with opportunities for depth of processing (see Chapter 4) which might result in intake of new words. Other students, who try to read quickly and do not go back to check words, will not have this opportunity, but they may be working in a way which will increase their reading speed.

Extensive reading certainly has the benefit of greatly increasing a student's exposure to English and can be particularly important where class contact time is limited. This particular rationale can be appreciated immediately in relation to vocabulary learning. Wilkins (1972) makes the point that learners can effectively come to understand, through reading, which words are appropriate in which contexts:

> Through reading, the learner … is exposed to the lexical items embedded in natural linguistic contexts, and as a result they begin slowly to have the same meaningfulness … that they have for the native speaker.
> (Wilkins 1972: 132)

The opportunities that extensive reading affords learners of all ages and levels of language proficiency makes it a useful resource. Learners can build their language competence, progress in their reading ability, become more independent in their studies, acquire cultural knowledge, and develop confidence and motivation to carry on learning. With young learners there is a further value. Introducing children to books, whether in their first or a second language, contributes to the curriculum objective of encouraging critical thinking and positive attitudes towards imaginative experience.

6.3 What are the implications for the teaching of reading?

6.3.1 *How do we establish goals for the reading classroom?*

In the light of insights into the reading process and into how successful readers interact with texts, a set of general learning goals for the reading component of an English language course could include:

– to be able to read a range of texts in English
– to adapt reading style according to range of purposes and apply different strategies (e.g. skimming, scanning) as appropriate
– to build a knowledge of language (e.g. vocabulary, structure), which will facilitate development of greater reading ability
– to build schematic knowledge in order to interpret texts meaningfully
– to develop awareness of the structure of written texts in English and to be able to make use of, e.g., rhetorical structure, discourse features, and cohesive devices in comprehending texts
– to take a critical stance to the content of texts.

The teacher's responsibilities in helping learners achieve these goals will be to motivate reading by selecting or creating appropriate texts, to design useful reading tasks, to set up effective classroom procedures, to encourage critical reading, and to create a supportive environment for practising reading. Each learner will have different strengths to build on and different weaknesses to overcome. Therefore there can be no single, set, rigid methodology for reading. The teacher will need to focus on different goals at different times and to use a range of materials and tasks.

6.3.2 *What criteria do we use to select reading texts?*

R. Williams makes a key point relating to principles for the reading lesson: 'in the absence of interesting texts, very little is possible' (1986: 42). Unfortunately, access to an abundance of interesting texts is an ideal which not all teachers will be able to meet. Some will be in the favourable position of being able to select texts which meet the specific needs of their learners. This will be true of many situations where students are reading in English for academic study, for professional purposes, or to function as visitors to or immigrants in an English-speaking society. Other teachers will be dealing with prescribed texts or those available in a prescribed coursebook. Yet others will have facilities for choosing and preparing texts for classroom use but will need to formulate criteria for making that choice as students will not necessarily have any clear needs for learning to read in English. With regard to the two questions 'What kind of texts do we use in the classroom?' and 'How do we create reading purposes for those texts?' teachers may have little flexibility in addressing the first, but every teacher will need to consider the second carefully, as this might be the key to motivating students to read texts which they would not normally find interesting. Purposes can be contrived to create interest.

Where there is some freedom of choice, interest will be a key criterion in selecting texts for learners. Many teachers, in situations where there is English language material in the learners' community, have experimented successfully in asking learners to find texts themselves which they think will interest the class. This idea is developed further in 6.3.3. It is also possible to discover the reading interests of learners through a 'Reading interest questionnaire' which asks learners about the genre they like to read in their first language, for example, non-fiction, thrillers, or romance.

Another factor to be considered is variety: of topic, of length of text, of rhetorical organization (for example, description, review, comparison), and of reading purpose. If the list of purposes for reading given by Rivers and Temperley (1978) in 6.2.2 were developed into a framework for text selection with intermediate high-school or adult students, a course might well include the following:

– to get information	travel brochures, train timetables, bus schedules, notices, public signs, directories, catalogues, information leaflets, regulations, weather forecasts
– to respond to curiosity about a topic	magazine articles, newspaper editorials, advertisements, guidelines, specialist brochures
– to follow instructions	maps, route planners, recipes, assembly instructions, instructions for use, guides, manuals
– for pleasure and enjoyment	poems, short stories, plays, reviews, lampoons, skits, cartoons
– to keep in touch	postcards, notes, invitations, letters, condolences, memos, messages

– to know what is happening in the world	news articles, news in brief, TV Ceefax, faxes, news reviews
– to find out when and where	announcements, programmes, tour guides.

This is essentially a list of authentic texts, and would certainly be appropriate for intermediate students as their existing language competence would enable them to tackle such texts. For students at lower levels it is more difficult to find suitable authentic texts, though sometimes a brochure will yield a useful scanning activity, for example for the opening times of a museum and the nearest train station to it. And asking students to tackle such a text through a simple activity can build confidence. Many textbook writers accept Widdowson's (1978) argument that teaching involves contrivance and will use 'simulated authentic' texts instead, as discussed in Chapter 2.

If teachers use a framework such as the above as a guide to the selection of texts during a course, they can be sure that learners will be provided with a range of reading purposes and will be able to practise different ways of approaching a text. This is particularly important with students who are gradually developing the confidence to approach a text without expecting to understand every word. It will be necessary to create an authentic reason for reading a particular text. A simple procedure for the teacher could be to ask him or herself the following questions:

1   What is the text about? Is it a story, a biography, a report of an event, a description of a place? Why would we read this text in real life?

2   Are there different ways in which a reader would approach this text? For example, do we skim through a recipe to decide whether we would like the dish? Do we read it carefully to work out ingredients, timing, etc.? Which purpose will we choose and what strategies will learners need to fulfil that purpose?

3   What kinds of activity will help students to apply appropriate strategies? What can we set as pre-reading tasks?

The texts in Materials extracts 6.C and 6.D show a variety of reasons for reading. The tasks in Materials extract 6.C bring feelings and attitudes into play and ask the reader to agree or disagree with the writer. The tasks in Materials extract 6.D draw on the reader's existing knowledge of the topic and ask students to create a set of expectations for the content. The reason for reading is to confirm or deny those expectations. If reasons for reading are missing from textbook tasks, one of the most useful things a teacher can do for learners is to create purposes which will motivate them to read.

Materials extract 6.C

Competitive Women

The competitive woman must pay plenty of attention to her image.

Management Consultant Rennie Fritch says:

'I don't agree with people who say you have to be tougher than the toughest man in order to succeed in business.'

'Instead of trying to be macho, tough and ruthless, women should aim to be strong, resilient and fair. By doing this they can be very competitive.'

Women who try to copy their male colleagues pay a high price, claims Rennie. 'These macho women who try to be copies of men end up sacrificing everything for the company.'

She believes one of the main reasons why women fail to reach the top is their low self-image, a syndrome that starts from an early age. 'Ask a boy, who is expected by his teacher to get sixty per cent in an exam, how he himself expects to do and he will answer confidently that he expects to get seventy or seventy-five per cent,' she says. 'Ask a girl the same question and she will say that she doesn't really expect to pass but she might get fifty per cent.'

Women should be more realistic and objective about themselves. 'Let's face it,' says Rennie, 'if you don't rate yourself highly, how can you expect anyone else to?'

'Women who do make it to the top are always outstanding,' claims Rennie, 'which is not always true of men.'

'When I start meeting women who are not as brilliant as they think they are, I'll know that women have really made it,' she says.

Never underrate yourself. Men rarely do!

Believe in yourself, even if others don't.

Don't worry about making mistakes. You are entitled to make wrong decisions.

Before you read

1 Do you think there are fewer women than men in top jobs? If so, why?

Read the extract above about women in business. Do you agree with Ms Fritch? What does she think is the main reason why women fail to reach the top?

THINK ABOUT IT

1 What do you think Rennie Fritch means by 'macho women' and 'women end up sacrificing everything for the company.'?
2 Does Rennie Fritch have a high opinion of all the men who make it to the top?

🔊 LISTENING

Andrew is talking about business people and their image. Note how he describes the difference between the 'traditional' and the 'modern' image of a businessman

Discuss if you agree with what he says.

VOCABULARY

Match the words below with their dictionary definitions and underline the meaning which is used in the article.

competitive   ruthless   resilient

1   ████ **1** (of a substance) able to spring back to the former shape or position when pressure is removed: *Rubber is more* ████ *than wood.* **2** *apprec* able to return quickly to usual health or good spirits after going through difficulty, disease, change, etc.: *It's been a terrible shock, but she's very* ████ *and will get over it soon.* — ~ly *adv* —ence, -ency *n* [U]:

2   ████ **1** of, based on, or decided by competition: *the* ████ *nature of private industry*| ████ *sports* **2** liking to compete: *Jane's got a very* ████ *nature.* **3** (of a price, product, or producer) able to compete because it is at least as good, cheap, etc. as the competitors: *I always shop at that supermarket; its prices are very* ████. — ~ly *adv* — ~ness *n* [U]

3   ████ **1** (of a person or their behaviour) showing no human feelings; without pity or forgiveness: *The enemy killed women and children with* ████ *cruelty.* **2** *not always derog* firm in taking unpleasant decisions: *We'll have to be* ████ *if we want to eliminate unnecessary waste.* — ~ly *adv* — ~ness *n* [U]

(Abbs and Freebairn: *Blueprint Intermediate* SB, page 82)

Materials extract 6.D

Reading

1   Look at the pictures of Sister Wendy.
–   What does she look like?
–   What is she doing in the pictures?

2   Now read the text. Which of the things in the box above does she mention?

Sister Wendy,
TV Star!

Sister Wendy Beckett has been a nun for nearly 50 years, since she was 16. Most of the time she lives in solitary confinement in a caravan in the grounds of a Carmelite monastery in Norfolk, often not speaking to anyone for 22 hours a day. But every few months she leaves her caravan and travels round Europe, staying in international hotels and eating in famous restaurants. Why is she leading this double life? How does a nun who has devoted her life to solitude and prayer become a visitor to the Ritz?

'I think God has been very good to me.'

Sister Wendy has a remarkable other life. She writes and presents an arts programme for BBC television called 'Sister Wendy's Grand Tour'. In it, she visits European art capitals and gives her personal opinions on some of the world's most famous works of art. She begins each programme with these words: 'For over 20 years I lived in solitude. Now I'm seeing Europe for the first time. I'm visiting the world's most famous art treasures.'

She speaks clearly and plainly, with none of the academic verbosity of art historians. TV viewers love her common-sense wisdom, and are fascinated to watch a kind, elderly, bespectacled, nun who is so obviously delighted by all she sees. They are infected by her enthusiasm. Sister Wendy believes that although God wants her to have a life of prayer and solitary contemplation, He has also given her a mission to explain art in a simple manner to ordinary people. She says: 'I think God has been very good to me. Really I am a disaster as a person. Solitude is right for me because I'm not good at being with other people. But of course I enjoy going on tour. I have a comfortable bed, a luxurious bath and good meals, but the joy is mild compared with the joy of solitude and silent prayer. I always rush back to my caravan. People find this hard to understand. I have never wanted anything else; I am a blissfully happy woman.'

Sister Wendy's love of God and art is matched only by her love of good food and wine. She takes delight in poring over menus, choosing a good wine and wondering whether the steak is tender enough for her to eat because she has no back teeth. However, she is not delighted by her performance on television.

'I can't bear to watch myself on television. I feel that I look so silly — a ridiculous black-clothed figure. Thank God we don't have a television at the monastery. I suppose I am famous in a way, but as 95% of my time is spent alone in my caravan, it really doesn't affect me. I'm unimportant.'

Sister Wendy earned £1,200 for the first series. The success of this resulted in an increase for the second series. The money is being used to provide new shower rooms for the Carmelite monastery. ■

(Soars and Soars: *New Headway Intermediate* SB, page 20–1)

6.3.3   *What kinds of tasks help to develop reading ability?*

It is now standard practice in the design of reading tasks to use a three-phase procedure involving pre-, while-, and post-reading stages (Williams 1984). The intention is to ensure that reading is 'taught' in the sense of helping readers develop increasing ability to tackle texts. This is in contrast to more traditional materials in which reading would be 'tested' through a procedure in which learners would read a text with or without an introduction, possibly with some pre-teaching of vocabulary, and then would be required to answer comprehension questions. Many contemporary materials reflect this three-phase procedure.

During the pre-reading phase, learners can be encouraged to do a number of things: become oriented to the context of the text, for example for what purpose was it originally produced?; tune in to the content of the text; establish a reason for reading; express an attitude about the topic; review their own experiences in relation to the topic; activate existing cultural knowledge; and become familiar with some of the language in the text. In this way the teacher can prepare them in terms of both schematic and language knowledge, and ensure purposeful reading. A range of activity types are possible at this stage and teachers can select or combine from a repertoire, for example: talking about pictures accompanying the text; predicting from the title; agreeing or disagreeing with a set of proposals about the topic; answering a set of questions or a quiz; listing items of information they already know about the topic; or discussing the topic. The pre-reading activity in Materials extract 6.C uses a discussion question to raise interest in the topic, to create attitudes towards it, and to give teachers and students the opportunity to rehearse some key language. In eliciting opinions the teacher can provide words in the text such as 'macho', 'resilient', 'low self-image', and 'underrate'. The pre-reading task in Materials extract 6.D, which is accompanied in the textbook by several photographs, helps students to anticipate content in drawing up their own lists. This activates their prior knowledge of the topic and any relevant language they might already know.

But notice that these two examples of pre-reading work are essentially schematic preparation. Traditionally, English language learners have been prepared for reading through a focus on language knowledge, vocabulary usually, but sometimes structure. More recently, since the adoption of the idea of reading as an interactive process, while-reading activities have been used: these generally aim to encourage learners to be active as they read. Students can be given activities which require them to do any of the following: follow the order of ideas in a text; react to the opinions expressed; understand the information it contains; ask themselves questions; make notes; confirm expectations or prior knowledge; or predict the next part of the text from various clues. To encourage these activities, teachers can use a range of exercise types, for example: ask students to tick a list of expectations or find answers to their own questions; suggest they tick and cross in the margin in reaction to the writer's opinions; give them questions to stop and think about; or provide a chart for them to fill in with points of information. These are just some of the activities now used by teachers and textbook writers who believe that it might be useful to intervene in the reading process in some way. As yet, there are few research studies to show the effects of intervention, and their outcomes are contradictory. However, many students report positively on the usefulness of while-reading activities and many teachers therefore try to encourage activity, reflection, and response while reading.

Post-reading activities can be as varied as the texts they follow, but ideally will tie up with the reading purpose set, so that students check and discuss activities done while reading and make use of what they have read in a meaningful way, for example, by discussing their response to the writer's opinions or by using notes for a writing activity. After that, a wide range of activities focusing either on the content of the text can be undertaken, for example, debate, role-play, reading of contrasting texts, or focusing on its language. At this stage many teachers will want to build their students' language competence by concentrating on some linguistic features: vocabulary for example, as in Materials extract 6.C. In this way it is possible to introduce useful techniques for future bottom-up processing. It is also possible to use a text to demonstrate language features which have been studied separately as part of a language-awareness course. For example if, through an activity such as the one in Materials extract 6.E the class has been introduced to the idea of back reference in a text, they could be asked to find examples of this in the text they have just read. Similarly, a text can be studied for examples of correctives, also demonstrated in Materials extract 6.E. There will need to be careful linking between those elements of a course which focus directly on language and the kind of post-reading activity used in order to ensure that students receive useful training in 'word-attack' or 'text-attack' skills, as shown in Materials extract 6.E.

Clarke (1989b) suggests a useful way of involving students in the design of post-reading questions. After doing a pre-reading activity prepared by the teacher and individual reading of the text, students work in small groups to check their understanding and to construct key questions. The teacher elicits questions from the groups, corrects them, and then the class selects a set of questions which students answer in their groups. A class plenary ensues to discuss the answers. After training in this procedure it can be extended to texts which students have brought into class, and eventually students might prepare questions on self-chosen texts individually for other students to evaluate and answer. Clarke's procedure suggests collaborative classroom work. This can be very useful in helping students to become aware of their own thinking processes as they work on texts. And this kind of peer interaction can be highly motivating. It is worth building different kinds of classroom interaction into reading activities as well as ensuring that students have individual practice in applying the strategies they are learning. This implies a variety in the teacher's roles. During language-focused activities the teacher might well assume the more traditional role of instructor, but when it comes to the reading itself, the teacher's role will be to provide materials, design activities, and then step back. In this way the teacher acts as organizer, guide, and evaluator of how successfully students have tackled a text and of what further work might be needed.

Materials extract 6.E

After you read   **5** LOOKING AT LANGUAGE

Work in pairs.

a) **Find all the uses of *this* and *these* in the text. What does each use refer back to? For example, in the sentence *This leaflet will help you to answer these questions* on page 46, *these questions* refers to the four preceding questions.**

b) **A writer shows the connections between ideas in a text. Certain words are used to do this; e.g. *and* adds one idea to another.**

> *It is the commonest type **and** is called coronary heart disease.*

Other connecting words used in this text include:

> *because   but   consequently   however   so*
> *so . . . that*

Look back at the uses.

> Which of these words shows that one thing is the cause of another?
> Which of these words shows that one thing is the result of another?
> Which of these words contrasts two ideas?

(Murphy and Cooper: *Getting the Message 2* SB, page 50)

It is worth giving special mention to activities which develop reading speed, which is particularly important if learners face the pressures of reading English quickly for academic or professional purposes, but also important for the general learner if reading is to be enjoyable rather than a painful process of 'getting through' a text. Good readers read fast and accurately, which means that they read in groups of words rather than plodding through a text word by word. They can identify phrases and develop the skill of 'chunking' stretches of text in this way. For teachers concerned to assist learners in bottom-up processing, activities such as that in Materials extract 6.F may be useful in raising awareness of how reading speed is achieved and in practising the text-attack skill of reading in meaningful phrases. This will enable learners to approach texts appropriately in terms of matching purpose and speed of reading.

6.3.4 *Can we help students to read critically?*

A number of suggestions have been made over recent years for procedures which will help students to develop a critical perspective on texts. Clarke and Silberstein (1979) suggest the kind of critical questions which can be built into reading materials:

> 'For what purpose and for what audience is this intended?' 'What knowledge and attitudes does the author presume of the audience?' 'Are you convinced by the evidence presented by the author to support the claims made?' 'Does your own experience support the conclusions reached by the author?' and 'Do you share the author's point of view?'
> (Clarke and Silberstein 1979: 56)

Materials extract 6.F

Rate-buildup reading In this activity students have 60 seconds to read as much material as they can. They are then given an additional 60 seconds to read again from the beginning of the text. They must read more material during the second 60-second period than in the first. The drill is repeated a third and fourth time.

The purpose of this activity is to reread 'old' material quickly, gliding into the 'new'. As their eyes move quickly over the old material, students actually learn how to process the material more quickly. The exercise does not really emphasize moving the eyes quickly; instead, the material should be processed and comprehended more efficiently. As students participate in this rate building activity, they learn that indeed they can increase their reading rates.

(Anderson: 'Improving reading speed: activities for the classroom', *English Teaching Forum* 37/2, page 3)

More recently, Wallace (1992) has suggested a framework of questions for critical reading based on Kress (1985), which will enable readers to identify and resist the values underlying a text:

1 Why is this topic being written about?
2 How is the topic being written about?
3 What other ways of writing about the topic are there?
4 Who is the text's model reader?
(Wallace 1992: 114)

These questions would certainly help readers to challenge the ideology of the text in Materials extract 6.B.

Clark (1993), too, suggests a detailed set of questions for the pre-reading phase with students tackling academic texts.

> BEFORE READING THE TEXT
> ask yourself the following questions:
> - why am I reading this? What is my purpose? Why is it on my reading list?
> - what do I know about the author, the publisher, the circumstances of publication and the type of text? How do these affect my attitude towards and expectations of what I am about to read? Why?
> - what are my own views of the event(s) or topic before I start reading this particular text?
> - what other texts (written and spoken) on this or similar topics am I familiar with? What are my views about them?
>
> (Clark 1993: 120)

Teaching resisting reading is regarded as particularly important when learners are more vulnerable, for example, schoolchildren reading literature who may have insufficient experience to challenge the views of the writer and the way in which the language of the text tries to position the reader. In Materials extract 6.G pupils are asked to reflect on specific questions.

The tasks in Materials extract 6.H accompany the reading of *The Whole Town's Sleeping* by Ray Bradbury, in which a woman, Lavinia Nebbs, goes out at night alone, ignoring the fact that a murderer is on the loose. They are designed to demonstrate ' ... the assumptions the story expects readers to share. These assumptions about women and violence have become visible to readers who no longer share them. To readers whose assumptions match those of the text they are invisible' (Mellor, O'Neil, and Patterson 1987: 69).

Materials extract 6.G

- How do the ways in which stories are read change over time?

- Can it become impossible for readers to read some texts in the way the stories ask?

- Is it relevant for a reader to question how and why a story asks to be read in a particular way?

- Do certain kinds of readings support particular beliefs or assumptions?

(Mellor, O'Neil, and Patterson: *Reading Stories*, page 64)

The materials in *Reading Stories* were designed for first language students but would be of interest to teachers using literary texts in the second language classroom. Teachers who wish to explore critical procedures can use text-comparison as a basis for critical reading. For example, they can use articles on the same news item from the broadsheet and tabloid press, or from newspapers with different political leanings, to help students to appreciate how the use of language creates a different impression of the same event. A classroom debate can be set up by dividing the class in half, asking each half to read a different account and summarize the information for other students. As significant points of difference arise in the summaries, these can be listed and questioned. Why have the discrepancies occurred? What is the true version likely to be? Why has each writer presented a particular version? How has a particular impression been created through language choices?

One interesting recent development relates to the problems increasingly noticed by teachers as students access information on the Internet. There are no gatekeepers here and users may need to evaluate information carefully against what is known about its sources and sponsorship. The task in Materials extract 6.I was brought to my attention by a colleague.

The topics, smoking and abortion, are clearly those where students would benefit from being able to link the source and the likely degree of objectivity. There are now useful discussions (see, for example, Wilkinson, Bennet, and Oliver 1997) which analyse indicators of quality for Internet resources: these can give us productive ideas with regard to learner training for independent reading.

6.3.5 *How can we encourage extensive reading?*

There are two major vehicles available for extensive reading. One is the use of class readers where the teacher chooses a book and each student has a copy. The teacher formulates a programme over a specified period to involve preparatory activity, intensive reading of extracts in class for strategy training, individual silent reading in class, and private reading at home with exercises set by the teacher and follow-up work. There are useful discussions of this approach in various ELT sources (for example, Hedge 1985; Nuttall 1982; Greenwood 1988). It is often favoured by teachers who wish to retain a degree of control in checking reading, who need to keep up incentives for reading, or who see it as a structured phase before promoting more individualized reading. Many teachers, however, prefer the class library method, arguing that a box of thirty different readers for a class of thirty students provides so much more potential than a class set of the same reader. Hicks (1984) provides a typical argument:

Materials extract 6.H

During reading

1 Think about the arguments put forward by different readers of this story and to what extent you agree or disagree with their readings.
The arguments are summarised below. It may be possible to begin recording your agreement or disagreement as you read.

Two readings: a comparison		
Reading 1: 'a clever, entertaining suspense story'	Agree	Disagree
1 Has an engrossing plot.		
2 Is a cleverly constructed story.		
3 Has deft and amusing characterisation.		
4 Skilfully evokes the heroine's fear.		
5 Encourages a reading of violence as entertaining.		
Reading 2: 'unacceptable, offensive'		
1 Accepts and confirms as 'natural' that most violent attacks on women are by men.		
2 Accepts and confirms that women may be victims of violence because of what they are – women.		
3 Implies women are silly to go out alone.		
4 Implies women who are victims of violence are to blame in some way.		
5 Encourages a reading of violence as entertaining.		

2 The second area to play special attention to as you read is the way in which the character of the protagonist-victim, Lavinia Nebbs, is presented. You could jot down adjectives and phrases that refer to her. Alternatively you could take a note of relevant page numbers to refer to after you have read the story.

Reflection

Individually:
1 Complete your Two readings chart.
2 Complete the notes on Lavinia you began while reading the story.

In your groups:
1 Compare and discuss your completed charts.
2 (a) Prepare a brief statement on how Lavinia Nebbs is presented and how readers are encouraged to see her, and
    (b) consider how your reading of the story would be affected if Lavinia Nebbs were • a child   • a doctor called out to a patient?   • a young mother?
In a whole class discussion:
1 Share your conclusions.
2 Finally, try to decide: • how you think the story asks to be read   • why it invites such a reading   • how you read it.

(Mellor, O'Neil, and Patterson: *Reading Stories*, pages 70, 80)

Materials extract 6.1

Activity 2:
Is it Fools' Gold or the Real Thing?

Compare the Pairs: Practice in Evaluating Web Sites

Here are sets of web sites. Using what you know about evaluation techniques, look at the information found at each site. As you do this,
keep these basic criteria in mind: authorship, publishing body/type of web page, currency, and purpose.

A. *The White House: <http://www.whitehouse.gov>
   *The Alternative White House: < http://www.whitehouse.net>

1 Who is the author of the information? Who is sponsoring each site?
2 For what purpose is the information provided? (Information, entertainment, business, public service, advocacy?)
3 Have the sites included information, photos, or pages that have been altered?
4 How current is the information? Are there dates on the page?
5 Are there links to other sites? If so, where do these links take you?
6 Are there clear distinctions between entertainment, opinion, and factual information?

B. *The Selfhelp A-Z Index: <http://www.xs4all.nl/~kyjoshi/>
   *Clini Web: <http://www.ohsu.edu/cliniweb/>

1 Who is the author of each site, and what are the author's qualifications for establishing a health index?
2 How current is the information at each site?
3 Are there links to other sites? If so, where do these links take you?

C. *Onco Link: <http://oncolink.upenn.edu/causeprevent/smoking/>
   *Smoker's Home Page: <http://www.tezcat.com/~smokers/>

1 What does each URL tell you about each web site and its publisher?
2 Who is the author of the information? Is there a way of verifying the qualifications of that author?
3 What combinations of facts and opinions can be found at these sites?
4 How accurate and current is the information found at these sites?
5 What is the purpose of each web site? (Information, entertainment, advocacy, business, public service?)
6 Are there links to other pages? If so, where do these links take you?

(Susan Cowles: http://www.nifl.gov/susanc/inthome.htm)

> The last thing I wanted was to give the same book to the whole class
> and expect the same enjoyment. The students browsed freely amongst
> the shelves of their level and picked out what they fancied. If they didn't
> like it after a page or two, they could put it back, no questions asked,
> and select another.
> (Hicks 1984: 22)

The class library does not need to be as grand as the term suggests. It can
simply be a box, or a trolley, or a bookshelf with a selection of readers
appropriate to the age and language proficiency of the class. In well-
resourced institutions a greater number of readers can be made available in a
self-access centre, but they will then need to be graded and coded for learners
at different levels of learning. Two important issues arise if teachers wish to
organize a class library: how to select readers appropriate to learners, and
how to organize the library; and how to support learners in their extensive
reading.

Selecting material for extensive reading

Simenson (1987) usefully classifies materials for extensive reading into three
types: 'authentic' (not written for language learners and published in the
original language); 'pedagogic' (specially written for language learners with
various types of control placed on the language); and 'adapted' (adapted for
language learners from authentic texts according to various principles of
control set out by editors and publishers in guidelines for adaptors).

For teachers of students with more advanced levels of language proficiency,
especially those working with ESL learners in an English language
environment, there may well be authentic material to hand. Many teachers,
for example, have commented that students cope well with the simple
English of John Steinbeck's *Of Mice and Men* or with some contemporary
short stories such as Roald Dahl's *Kiss Kiss* collection. However, for EFL
teachers with learners at lower levels of language proficiency, the choice
seems limited to pedagogic or adapted readers. In choosing such material,
the teacher is following the same principle as when choosing a textbook of
appropriate language level. Widdowson (1979b), for example, makes this
analogy:

> Simplification is the pedagogic analogue of the linguist's idealization of
> data. The teacher simplifies by selecting and ordering the linguistic
> phenomenon he is to deal with so as to ease the task of learning.
> (Widdowson 1979b: 192)

The issue for most EFL teachers, then, is how to choose readers from the
many series available, so as to ensure an acceptable quality of material for
their learners. It is possible to find readers for beginners in which stories are

told in the present simple or present continuous, hardly a natural use of these tenses. Another criticism which has been levelled, especially at lower levels of series, is that stories read more like lists than stories, with simple sentences following one another disjointedly, for example:

He was very tired. He couldn't sleep. The hotel was too noisy.

The student has to follow the meaning by understanding how the information content of one sentence links in meaning with the content of the next. Such juxtaposition can be a useful device but needs care. The absence of connecting devices can sometimes create ambiguity and two simple sentences may be more difficult to follow than a two-clause sentence linked by 'so'. We need to decide how careful an adaptor has been and whether quality has been acceptably maintained.

However, there is an increasing number of good quality readers available (see Hill and Thomas 1988; Day and Bamford 1998) with carefully designed accessibility to the language. With judicious appraisal, a teacher can find a useful collection.

Supporting extensive reading

One way of supporting extensive reading is to provide time for short interviews with individuals about their reading. The teacher can use this time to recommend books, advise on reading problems, suggest activities, and encourage learners to reflect on their reading by discussing the books they have read. Book conferences can be carried out in the first language, but with students who have sufficient language resources, it is a chance to interact meaningfully in English.

Ideally, the book conference should be seen as supportive rather than regulatory; not so much a time for checking comprehension but a time for helping the student to respond to the text and use English in a real communicative situation. Teachers can elicit responses through a range of careful questions, sufficiently open-ended to provoke attempts at putting ideas together, for example: Where does the story take place? Who are the main characters? Did you like the story? What did you enjoy about the way the writer describes particular characters? Which characters did you sympathize with? How did the story make you feel? Do you think it was true to life?

Another useful procedure is the reading syndicate, in which members of a group read different books and share their experiences. The outcome is often a peer conference in which students can take on the roles of asking questions as well as answering them. The following transcript is part of a peer conference:

Susanna	Why did you choose this one?
Prema	When I looked at this picture … here … on the front side … I saw it was about India. Also that a film had …
Hassan	But it's old … I mean … an old story … the picture. Her clothes are old …
Susanna	… fashion. Yes, it's old-fashion. But this woman is not …
Prema	Yes, really, you know. There are two stories, one modern, one is old-fashioned.
Susanna	History. Is it a love story? Who is this? [*pointing to character on front cover*]
Prema	Yes, it is history romance. This girl is … young relative to this woman, Olivia. But I like Olivia's story …
Susanna	What happens in the story?
Prema	She is a woman who defies convention …
Hassan	What?
Prema	She is falling in love with an Indian prince.

Prema has read an adapted version of the novel *Heat and Dust* by Ruth Prawer Jhablava. Notice the kinds of questions the students ask. The teacher can make suggestions for these in preparatory training, but ideally the students will develop the confidence over time to generate their own questions. These students know each other well and the conference develops naturally into a real negotiation of meaning. Notice, too, the way in which Prema provides both vocabulary ('romance') and correction ('old-fashioned'). She is able to do this partly because she has had a meeting with the teacher who has provided these words, and also the expression 'defies convention'.

A reading syndicate can follow a five-step procedure (Parrott 1987), demonstrated here with a multicultural EFL group of fifteen intermediate part-time students, studying six hours a week in the UK.

1   The teacher divides the class into small groups or 'syndicates'.

2   The class discusses a range of books to be chosen, browsing among the books and selecting those to be distributed among the syndicates. The teacher can facilitate the process by having a list of genres and titles within each genre which are available.

3   Students each read their choice of book to a two-week deadline, using periods of class-time and reading at home.

Syndicate 1	**Syndicate 2**	**Syndicate 3**
Philippe: *Cry Freedom*	Stephanie: *Heat and Dust*	Li: *Quiet as a Nun*
Hassan: *Landslide*	Trudie: *Cry Freedom*	Karin: *Cry Freedom*
Eva: *On The Beach*	Demetra: *Landslide*	Arne: *Landslide*

Prema: *Heat and Dust*   Etsuko: *Quiet as a Nun*   Michael: *On The Beach*
Susanne: *Quiet as a Nun* Feng: *On The Beach*   Mayumi: *Heat and Dust*

4 The teacher organizes tutorials on each book with the group of three readers who have read it.

5 The syndicates meet and members recount their reading experiences to others in the group.

(adapted from Parrott 1987: 412–14)

It is possible to make a recording of the syndicate meeting and a sixth step could then be to ask students to listen to their conference, list the questions they asked, and consider what other questions they might have asked. This will prepare them for future conferences.

Clearly the logistics of this procedure require careful management, but reading syndicates usefully combine the motivation of self-chosen books, genuine classroom interaction among changing groups of learners, and potential student recommendation of books to their peers.

6.4 Conclusion

In summary, the reading lesson should aim to build learners' ability to engage in purposeful reading, to adopt a range of reading styles necessary for interacting successfully with authentic texts, and to develop critical awareness. This implies developing competence in the foreign language, awareness of the structure of written texts, and knowledge about the world. It also implies developing confidence in using these to create meaning from a text. Both competence and confidence involve preparation and practice in the supportive environment of the classroom and persuasion to carry on reading in English outside the classroom.

Discussion topics and projects

1 With other teachers, discuss your reactions to the statements on reading below:

(a) Provided the teacher has the necessary access, and time to select and prepare, an authentic text can be found for most situations. Indeed it is possible to construct a teaching programme based entirely on authentic texts.
(Williams 1984: 25)

(b) More opportunities are provided for learning through pair work rather than individual work ... by having students verbally express the decision

making processes they employed in arriving at the answer to a question or the meaning of a word.
(Richards 1990: 96)

(c) The point of the reading class must be reading ... not the reinforcement of oral skills, nor grammatical or discourse analysis and not the acquisition of new vocabulary. Improvement in any of these areas can make reading easier but none of them is reading and none contributes directly to the one legitimate goal of such a class ... the development of genuine reading habit in the language.
(Dubin, Eskey, and Grabe: 1986: 22)

(d) Learners can be productively engaged in adaptation tasks which result in the creation of actual teaching materials which can be used in the same or another class.
(Clarke 1989b: 135)

(e) It is important ... that students learn not only to understand the values of others, but, as well, to summon up their own experiences and values for comparison and, where necessary, to resist the imposition of values.
(Spolsky 1989: 173)

2 Consider these examples of things students say they do when they meet difficulty in reading comprehension, particularly when they meet a new word or phrase. Would you encourage or discourage any of these, or suggest a sequence of strategies?

(a) 'I think about whether the word is important for understanding the whole text.'
(b) 'I read on to see if the word is repeated.'
(c) 'I go to my dictionary for a translation.'
(d) 'I think if there is a Spanish word like it.'
(e) 'I ask my teacher to explain.'
(f) 'I look to see if the word has some part I know.'
(g) 'I say the word out loud.'
(h) 'I start again from the beginning of the sentence.'
(i) 'I ask the other students in my group.'
(j) 'I write it in my notebook.'
(k) 'I study the words around it.'

3 A quick survey of English language teachers in one institution demonstrated a range of procedures for 'reading' texts being used in one day. What rationale might teachers give for each procedure? Which procedures do you normally use and why?

(a) The teacher reads while the students follow in their books.

(b) The teacher reads followed by the students in turn reading a sentence at a time.

(c) The students read the passage silently while listening to a recording of the text.

(d) The students read out loud along with the teacher.

(e) The students chorus after the teacher who reads out loud phrase by phrase.

(f) The teacher reads paragraph by paragraph and asks the students to mark unknown words as they follow silently.

(g) The students, in turn, read paragraphs of the text while other students listen.

(h) The students read silently by themselves.

4 Choose or write a text for a specific level of learner. Design a lesson plan for using the text in class and provide reasons for the methodological choices that you make.

5 Review the textbook that you are currently using. What principles for the teaching of reading do you see at work in the book? What are the main ways in which you would like to improve the book?

6 Many textbooks which state the aim of improving learners' reading ability claim that they develop certain strategies through the activities they offer. Here are some of them:

(a) find a specific item of information quickly

(b) make use of accompanying information, e.g. headings, pictures, to predict the content of the text

(c) distinguish between fact and opinion

(d) guess the meanings of unfamiliar words by using contextual clues

(e) read at different speeds for different purposes

(f) recognize larger rhetorical patterns such as classification, cause–effect, problem–solution, etc.

(g) recognize coherence relations such as main idea, supporting details, examples

(h) use prior knowledge to work out meanings within the text

(i) predict the connections between parts of the text from the use of connectives

(j) use the dictionary well and understand its limitations

(k) realize that a writer does not express everything explicitly and in detail and make appropriate inferences

(l) respond appropriately to the text.

Would you add anything to the list that you feel is important? Choose a reading textbook and survey it to see if any or all of these strategies are trained.

7 If none exists, draw up a plan to set up extensive reading resources in your own institution.

(a) What rationale could you present to those who hold the purse-strings?
(b) How could you organize the resources?
(c) What kind of borrowing system would you use? How would you keep a record of what students have borrowed?

Further reading

Aebersold, J. A. and **M. L. Field.** 1997. *From Reader to Reading Teacher: Issues and Strategies for Second Language Classrooms.* Cambridge: Cambridge University Press.

This book is a study of the factors that influence both first and second language reading, and looks at strategies in reading. It then makes a link between theory and practice and deals with pedagogical issues such as the selection of appropriate texts and the planning of lessons. With ample examples and activities, this book is a good introduction to the teaching of reading.

Barnett, M. 1989. *More than Meets the Eye: Foreign Language Reading Theory in Practice.* Englewood Cliffs, N.J.: Prentice Hall Regents.

Part One of this book reviews reading research and summarizes a good many research studies undertaken up to the date of publication. Part Two considers insights from these for the foreign language classroom and deals with such practicalities as choosing texts, designing lesson plans, and testing reading. The wide coverage of topics makes this a useful reference book.

Carrell, P. L., J. Devine, and **D. E. Eskey (eds.).** 1988. *Interactive Approaches to Second Language Reading.* New York: Cambridge University Press.

This is a collection of seventeen papers which present a picture of the research from which models of interactive reading have been derived. Many aspects of reading are considered and classroom applications are explored.

Day, R. R. and **J. Bamford.** 1998. *Extensive Reading in the Second Language Classroom.* Cambridge: Cambridge University Press.

This comprehensive account of extensive reading is divided into three parts. The first part looks at the cognitive and affective dimensions of extensive reading and some of the insights that have been gained from research studies. The second part investigates issues such as authenticity and simplification, and choice of content in the development of materials for extensive reading. The third part provides useful advice for implementing a programme of extensive reading and designing activities to accompany it.

Hedge, T. 1985. *Using Readers in Language Teaching.* London and Basingstoke: Macmillan.

Intended for EFL or ESL teachers of adults and children, this book gives general principles and detailed, practical suggestions about the setting up of extensive reading programmes. It offers advice on the selection and most effective use of readers in the classroom and at home, and features extracts from a selection of readers with examples of supplementary activities for individual or class work.

Wallace, C. 1992. *Reading.* Oxford: Oxford University Press.

The book begins with a discussion of many elements in reading, for example, reading purposes, reading communities, and reading strategies. The second section contains ideas on how to help learners deal with texts and the final section suggests small-scale research activities for teachers.

Williams, E. and **C. Moran.** 1989. 'Reading in a foreign language at intermediate and advanced levels with particular reference to English.' *Language Teaching* 22/4: 217–27.

This review article looks in turn at the text, the reader, the interaction between reader and text, and the teaching of reading. It considers major issues for the teacher and how light is thrown on these by insights from research. It also contains a full and useful bibliography.

7 LISTENING

' Thought is not a trick, or an exercise, or a set of dodges.
Thought is a man in his wholeness wholly attending.'
D. H. LAWRENCE

1 What is the role of listening in the English language curriculum?

2 What do we know about the listening process?

3 What uncertainties exist for foreign language listeners?

4 How can we create reasons for listening?

5 What criteria do we use in selecting texts for listening?

6 What options are there for designing listening activities?

7 How do we build confidence in learners?

Introductory task

This listening task in Materials extract 7.A is taken from a coursebook for adults and teenagers at intermediate level. The text is taken from a radio programme.

1 What do you think is the general purpose of pre-listening work for learners?

2 What are the specific purposes of activities 1, 2, and 3?

3 Why are students given a task to do during the listening?

4 What roles must the teacher perform during this listening work?

7.1 Introduction: the role of listening in the ELT curriculum

It has been popular in ELT literature to describe listening as the 'neglected', 'overlooked', or 'taken for granted' skill. Certainly some ELT methods have assumed that listening ability will develop automatically through exposure

Materials extract 7.A

Listening

Pre-listening task

Discuss the following questions in groups.

1 Have you got a pet?
  Did you have a pet when you were younger?
  What is/was it?
  What is/was it like?
  What habits does/did it have?

2 What can animals do better than people?
  Think of birds, cats and dogs.

3 You will hear a talk by Johnny Morris, a popular expert on animals and their behaviour, who has made many television and radio programmes.

He talks about the following subjects.
  – animals compared to people
  – the benefits of having animals in our lives
  – pets in Ancient Rome and Egypt
  – a difficult animal he has known

Make guesses about the content before you listen.

Listening and note taking

> **T.28**   Listen to the talk and make notes under the headings above. When you have finished, compare your notes with another student's.

What do you think

1 Do you agree with Johnny Morris when he says that in many respects human beings are inferior to animals?

2 How many ways can you think of in which we use animals?
  How are the animals suited to this particular task?
  Example
  Eskimos use huskies to pull their sledges. Huskies are very strong, have a thick coat, and seem to enjoy working together.

3 Which animals make good pets? Why?
  Which animals don't make good pets? Why?

4 What animals are popular in your country?

(Soars and Soars: *Headway Upper Intermediate* SB, page 86)

to the language and through practice of grammar, vocabulary, and pronunciation. The audiolingual approach, for example, while perceiving listening as the 'primary' skill in the sequence listening, speaking, reading, and writing, at the same time provided only restricted practice of scripted dialogues, which had the main aim of presenting and practising language forms.

Given the role of listening in everyday life, such neglect was surprising. The point has frequently been made (Rivers and Temperley 1978; Oxford 1993; Celce-Murcia 1995) that of the time an individual is engaged in communication, approximately 9 per cent is devoted to writing, 16 per cent to reading, 30 per cent to speaking, and 45 per cent to listening. It is also undoubtedly the case that contemporary society exhibits a shift away from printed media and towards sound, and its members therefore need to develop a high level of proficiency in listening.

Current interest in oracy, the ability to understand and participate in spoken communication, is one of several more recent concerns in education which have generated a stronger focus on listening in the classroom. Even in first language education, oracy projects have aimed at encouraging schoolchildren to pay attention and to develop good listening habits and strategies. A second impulse for interest in listening has come from those involved in training students for English-medium education, particularly at the tertiary level, given the very high proportion of time students spend attempting comprehension in classrooms and lecture halls. A third impulse has come from second language acquisition research into the role of input (see 1.2.1). Input gained from listening can have a key role in language acquisition, so the development of effective strategies for listening becomes important not only for oracy but also for the process of acquiring language. Part of the debate ensuing from these ideas has focused on the nature of listening input, for example whether or not it should be made comprehensible for learners through simplification. Another part of the debate has focused on the role of listening in the early ELT curriculum, for example whether teachers should stress the importance of learners having a 'silent period' in the early stages of learning and wait for 'readiness' to produce the language (Krashen 1982; Krashen and Terrell 1983).

In terms of listening for comprehension and the development of oracy, other issues arise. How can classroom practice rehearse the kinds of listening purposes and situations that learners will experience outside the classroom? How can we help learners build confidence in dealing with authentic spoken English? What kinds of classroom procedures will develop listening ability?

In order to answer these questions, we need information about what happens during the process of listening. No one is in doubt that both participatory listening (as in face-to-face conversations, seminars, and meetings) and non-participatory listening (as in listening to lectures, radio programmes, or public announcements) are complex processes. But recent research provides useful insights and suggests ways in which teachers can help learners to become good listeners through the design of classroom procedures.

7.2 What do we know about the listening process?

7.2.1 *Bottom-up processes in listening*

As with the reading process, the terms 'top-down' and 'bottom-up' have been used to describe different aspects of listening. The knowledge we have of bottom-up strategies comes from the work of three groups of researchers: psycholinguists interested in speech perception (for example Bever 1970; Clark and Clark 1977; Conrad 1985; Marslen-Wilson and Tyler 1980); the work of communications researchers (for example Cherry 1957), and of those interested in memory (for example Neisser 1982).

In the bottom-up part of the listening process, we use our knowledge of language and our ability to process acoustic signals to make sense of the sounds that speech presents to us. In other words, we use information in the speech itself to try to comprehend the meaning. We segment speech into identifiable sounds and impose a structure on these in terms of words, phrases, clauses, sentences, and intonation patterns. At the same time, we use whatever clues are available to infer meaning from the developing speech. These clues are of several kinds:

– In the English language, the placement of stress on the meaningful words, the use of pauses which mark the edge of 'sense' groups, and the relationship of stressed to unstressed syllables, plus increased tempo, clipped enunciation, and accompanying non-verbal behaviour such as head shaking and frowning, all provide us with information as to the meaning, function, and implicit emotion of a message, for example:

  I really *don't* think/you know/that it's his responsibility.

– We employ our lexical knowledge to assign meanings to words and use logical reasoning to infer relationships between them. For example, on picking out a sequence of known words from a news broadcast:

  hurricane ... coast ... Florida ... damaged property ...
  families homeless

 we would assign the role of agent to the hurricane, perceive the coast of Florida to be the location, the damage to the property as the action, and homelessness the outcome. These are logical categories and relations which derive from our experience of the world and which enable us to impose meaning on what we hear (Bever 1970).

– The hurricane example also shows how we use a knowledge of syntactic structure to infer meaning. In the English language we tend to expect a typical structure of noun phrase as agent (the hurricane), verb phrase as action (damaged), followed by a noun phrase as object (property). This expectation helps us to impose a structure on what we hear. Native-speaker children, for example, tend not to have difficulty with active constructions such as 'The truck damaged the car' but might interpret the equivalent passive form, 'The truck was damaged by the car', as meaning the same, simply by inferring agent and object from the word order.

As listeners infer meaning from what is heard, using these strategies, this will determine expectations about what might come next. For example, switching on in the middle of a radio story and hearing the words:

The jumper lay on the ground ...

we might assign a meaning to the lexical reference 'jumper' of something red and woollen, but would quickly adjust the inference as the story continued:

... clutching his ankle and moaning softly.

Various clues enable us to work out the links in the discourse and to anticipate. For example, in this extract from the news:

It seems, then, that a number of issues arise for the British government from the latest round of talks about the beef crisis.

the discourse-organizing word 'issues' leads us to anticipate some listing or outlining of the issues in question. Or the use of a particular connective in a lecture, as in:

In contrast to the formal and teacher-directed ethos of the early twentieth-century school classroom, the contemporary classroom ...

indicates a contrastive link with the next part of the discourse.

During these processes of identifying sounds, imposing structure, inferring meaning, and anticipating what comes next, memory clearly plays a crucial role. The limitations of *echoic memory* enable us to hold word sequences for only a few seconds and only initial analysis of the language is possible, concentrating on key words or pauses or other significant features. The load on the *short-term memory* is heavy as listeners try to hold various parts of the message in mind while inferring meaning and deciding what is necessary to retain. In fact, overload can occur if there is too much unfamiliar information and the greater part of a message can be lost. Ultimately, too, it is the gist of the spoken message rather than its detailed structure that is retained and stored in the *long-term memory*. Memory, as an 'active' and 'constructive' process (Neisser 1982), is still not fully understood, but the points outlined briefly above begin to suggest that its functioning can be facilitated through choice of texts and tasks.

7.2.2 *Top-down processes in listening*

Top-down comprehension strategies involve knowledge that a listener brings to a text, sometimes called 'inside the head' information, as opposed to the information that is available within the text itself. Consider the text in Materials extract 7.B.

Materials extract 7.B

Margaret	And what other subjects did you take?
John	I got Maths, Physics and Engineering Drawing. And English too. But I only just passed that. I took French but I failed it. I'm not much good at languages. But you can take the National Certificate if you've got four O levels so I was all right.
Margaret	And where are you working?
John	In a local firm. They make parts for the motor industry, you know, … crankshafts, crankrods, connecting rods and so on … Reynolds Supply Company. They're very good. They started me off in the model shop …

(Donatini and Hedge: *Of Machines and Men: A Reader in Mechanical Engineering*, page 320)

Most of the individual words and sentences of this text would not be problematic for a British speaker of English. A second language listener might well falter at the mention of the National Certificate as sociocultural knowledge would be needed to understand the significance of this. It would be clearer if the context of the speakers was known: a young engineer is talking about his training and his first job. The listener with some knowledge of car engines might well know the terms 'crankshaft', 'crankrod', and 'connecting rod', but it would need more specialized knowledge of the organization of motor manufacturing processes to understand 'model shop' and to know why a young engineer might start work in that part of the factory.

Top-down listening, then, infers meaning from *contextual clues* and from making links between the spoken message and various types of *prior knowledge* which listeners hold inside their heads. Contextual clues to meaning come from knowledge of the particular situation, i.e. the speaker or speakers, the setting, the topic, and the purpose of the spoken text, and from knowledge of what has been said earlier. Prior knowledge, as we have seen with the reading process, has been termed *schematic knowledge* (de Beaugrande and Dressler 1981; Carrell and Eisterhold 1983). This consists of the mental frameworks we hold in our memories for various topics. Misunderstandings can arise, even between speakers of the same language, when schematic knowledge differs, perhaps because of cultural differences. For example, I remember an occasion when, having made arrangements for a gardener to call round the next 'evening', I made efforts to be at home from five o'clock and was annoyed that no one appeared. The gardener, equally annoyed, explained that he had called several times from three-thirty onwards. To him, and his rural community of origin in the west of Ireland, 'evening' signified mid-afternoon onwards. To me it signified after office hours.

One category of schemata used by listeners are *formal schemata*. These consist of the knowledge we have of the overall structure of some speech events. For example, we know that 'Once upon a time' heralds a certain kind of story which is likely to have a description of characters, an event, an outcome, and possibly a moral comment. Similarly, we might expect a formal lecture of a traditional kind to have an introduction and overview, a series of sections, possibly with a summary at the end of each, and a rounding up. Some speech events, for example a church funeral service, have a highly ritualized sequence.

A second category of schemata is that of *content schemata*, which include general world knowledge, sociocultural knowledge, and topic knowledge. Local knowledge might also be necessary to infer meaning. For example, arriving by rail at a Midlands station one morning, I joined a queue at an empty taxi rank. The man next to me turned, smiled, looked at his watch, and said 'It's the show, isn't it?' Each word was comprehensible but local information was needed in order to understand the comment: that the rank was usually full of taxis at that time but they were all occupied ferrying people to the Agricultural Show, a celebrated annual event in the neighbourhood.

In contrast to this example, many listening situations are predictable to quite some extent as they follow certain routines. Schank uses the term *script* to describe how the routines are stored in memory and defines it as 'an elaborate causal chain which provides world knowledge about an often experienced situation' (1975: 264). For example, a typical script at an airport check-in desk would involve a passenger responding to a ground steward performing these language functions: greeting, request for tickets, query about number of pieces of baggage, security query as to packing of baggage, information about when the flight will be called, and leave-taking. Examples of other scripts would be buying a train ticket, going to the doctor, asking a bank by telephone for a statement of account, or going to a restaurant. Knowledge of such scripts enables top-down processing using our understanding of how things function in the world around us.

What this section has set out to demonstrate is that the prior knowledge which listeners bring to the process of listening will greatly affect what they are able to get out of it. A study by O'Malley, Chamot, and Kupper (1995) which used 'think aloud' protocols to attempt to identify the kinds of strategies used by listeners, suggests that more effective listeners used prior knowledge to infer meaning. For example:

> 'I was thinking about what "chewing betel nut" means. And as each time that she [voice on the tape] repeated it, I tried to see what it was that she was saying, [and] how it was pronounced. I don't think that it could be chewing gum … perhaps some kind of plant. Something like that. Like here some people chew tobacco.'
> (ibid.: 155)

This student showed a positive strategy of inferencing using prior knowledge. This was in contrast to ineffective listeners who 'became embedded in determining the meanings of individual words' (ibid.: 156).

If we take into account the role of schematic and contextual knowledge, then we can add top-down strategies to those bottom-up strategies already described in 7.2.1:

– Listeners will work out the purpose of the message by considering contextual clues, the content, and the setting. It would, for example, be clear that a speaker was making a complaint from the situation, from facial expressions, from the raised volume of the voice, and from the choice of grammar and vocabulary. The first three would probably be sufficient to infer purpose correctly.
– Listeners will activate schematic knowledge and bring knowledge of scripts into play in order to make sense of content.
– Listeners will try to match their perception of meaning with the speaker's intended meaning, and this will depend on the many different factors involved in listening, both top-down and bottom-up. For example, in the following exchange:

> **Teacher**   Why are you looking out of the window, William?
> **William**   'Cos there's a police car coming up the drive, Mrs Palmer.

William has mistaken the function of the teacher's reprimand as a request for information. Or in this exchange between an English visitor and a local shopkeeper in West Cork, Ireland:

> **Shopkeeper**   How long are you here?
> **Visitor**   'Til Tuesday.
> **Shopkeeper**   No, what time did you arrive?

it is dialectal differences of grammar that has caused the misinterpretation.

It would be mistaken to see top-down and bottom-up strategies as somehow in opposition. It is now generally accepted that both function simultaneously and are mutually dependent. The current model of listening is therefore an interactive one in which linguistic information, contextual clues, and prior knowledge interact to enable comprehension. However, it is important to note that comprehension, even for first language listeners, is always only selective and partial. Computers can process information totally but human beings, with limited memory, are not able to. We may also lack some necessary knowledge to infer meaning correctly. And the message itself may be incomplete, for example through interference on a radio, distortion on a telephone, or lack of explicitness in a speaker. As Brown and Yule have expressed it, comprehension is achieved when a listener reaches 'a reasonable interpretation' of the speaker's intention (1983a: 57). This holds implications for what we might reasonably expect of second language learners as listeners, and for what they might expect of themselves.

Comprehension in this sense, however, is still not the whole picture. In many listening situations we need to respond. And in order to respond, we need to interpret and evaluate the speaker's purposes and perceive what outcomes he or she might be trying to achieve. As Rost puts it: 'The end of the communicative act is not in reception of the communicative content but in the consequences of the act' (1994: 6). Face-to-face encounters involve evaluation and negotiation. If, for example, a friend is describing a complex and distressing financial situation with some degree of emotion, the listener will need the intelligence to follow the information, the prior knowledge to understand the financial implications, the empathy to appreciate the emotion, the cultural knowledge to be aware of the limits on appropriate questions and suggestions, personal knowledge to assess whether the friend is overreacting and over-emotional, and the judgement to know whether the speaker's purpose is to elicit only sympathy or a personal loan as well. In this sense, there is not a total match between the speaker's intended message and the listener's perception of meaning. The listener will be interpreting according to all of the factors just listed. Listening is much more than just comprehension.

7.2.3 *Purposes for listening*

The example just given raises the issue of the various purposes we might have in listening. It refers to conversation of a personal kind in which the listening is reciprocal or participatory. Another kind of participatory listening is small-talk at an informal gathering where the purpose is to enjoy the gossip and to contribute the occasional amusing comment or anecdote. Sometimes the main purpose of participatory listening is to get the information needed to do something specific, such as getting directions from a passer-by or asking a clerk how to complete the details needed on a booking form. Brown and Yule (1983a) used the terms 'interactional' to describe the social purpose of communication and 'transactional' to describe the purpose of exchanging information. Listening to small-talk at a party exemplifies the first, and listening to follow directions the second. However, it would be mistaken to assume that all listening can be neatly divided into these two categories. A conversation in a village store between a customer and shopkeeper who are members of the same community and old acquaintances could move between one purpose and the other.

The usefulness of the interactional–transactional distinction for the teaching of listening lies in appreciating the range and balance of skills involved in each. For example, in order to function successfully in social small talk and avoid making gaffes, second language listeners will need to appreciate the way in which the language used by other participants marks levels of familiarity and formality within the group. They will be able to survive by inferring the general topic of the conversation and knowing the suitable points at which to insert general responses which show interest and which keep other speakers going. Listening in transactions, however, is usually likely to require identification of specific details in order to act on the information accurately.

There is also non-participatory listening, such as listening to a radio talk or a conference presentation. Again, the skills involved will depend on the precise purpose for listening, whether it is listening to the general content out of curiosity or for enjoyment, or listening to jot down examples used by the presenter for one's own professional work.

Ideally, the language classroom should help students to develop the listening processes described in this section through activities which give a range of purposes for listening. But before proceeding to look at such activities, it is useful to note the kinds of problems experienced by second language listeners in dealing with these processes and purposes.

7.3 What 'uncertainties' exist for foreign language listeners?

Cherry (1957), a communications researcher, has provided us with a useful framework for viewing issues in second and foreign language listening. He introduces the term 'uncertainties' and goes on to categorize some major areas of uncertainty: in speech sounds and patterns; in language and syntax; in recognition of content; and, finally, uncertainties caused by environmental noise and disturbance which create gaps in the message.

Some of these uncertainties are no less challenging for the first language listener, as we have seen in some of the examples already given. It is equally difficult for a first language listener as it is for a second language listener to make sense of an ambiguous message in which the speaker has given inexplicit information. And environmental uncertainties such as background conversation, traffic noise, and phones ringing can be distracting, as can indistinct speech, muttering, or too soft a voice. As well as these external problems, an first language listener will experience the same internal pressures and problems which interfere with effective listening: lack of motivation towards the topic; negative reactions to the speaker or to the event; anxiety to rehearse one's own contribution to a debate or the next part of a conversation, to the extent of missing what the current speaker is saying; or distraction by the content of a talk into thinking about a related topic thereby losing the thread of the argument. Lack of topic knowledge can lead listeners to mishear words, such as the 'Arabian String Quartet' rather than the 'Aeolian String Quartet', as can lack of vocabulary, for example the child who heard 'do dishes' for 'judicious'. These problems for the first language listener point to the complexity of the task for the second language listener, who will have other uncertainties to tackle as well. We will now take a closer look at these.

7.3.1 *Uncertainties of confidence*

Many language learners fail to realize that when they listen to their first language they do not actually hear every word. They also fail to appreciate that we integrate linguistic knowledge with our existing experience and knowledge of such things as topic and culture, and do not need to hear every word. This means that learners often have unrealistic expectations and try to understand each word of a listening text. As Faerch and Kasper point out: 'such total comprehension ... is a misconception of how normal comprehension works in the native language' (1986: 265). Learners' anxiety can be exacerbated by a classroom procedure which does not contextualize the text or prepare the topic by activating prior knowledge; in other words, a procedure which asks students to 'Listen to the text and then answer the questions'. This tests listening ability rather than aiming to teach it. Adults returning to English language learning whose earlier experiences have been of this nature may well have developed negative perceptions of their ability as listeners and a major task for the teacher will be to build confidence. This means recognizing anxiety and taking care to provide positive classroom experiences. For example, the teacher needs to make sure that the pace and length of a listening activity is not too taxing as the concentration required in trying to comprehend unfamiliar sounds can be tiring.

7.3.2 *Uncertainties deriving from the presentation of speech*

Unplanned and unrehearsed spoken language is very different from the language of written texts. A short extract of authentic speech will show this:

> Your aunt came over at the weekend … well, on Sunday, actually. We … she came with her brother and sister-in-law. I thought they were … well, I liked them, I liked them a lot … decent sorts … I felt sort of relaxed with them, you know. We sat … after lunch, you see, we sat in the garden. It was pleasant. We're going to get together again sometime.

Here we can see the repetitions, pauses, fillers, false starts, incomplete sentences, restructurings, and corrections which are typical of speech, and also the random order of information as the speaker pieces together a presentation of the event. Spoken language also contains a higher proportion of colloquial language than most written texts, for example 'decent sorts', and 'get together', and of contracted forms such as 'we're'. The rate of delivery can vary greatly but learners might perceive it as very fast, especially if they have experienced only slow-paced recordings in the classroom. We also have to remember that in the real world English is spoken by first language speakers with a variety of accents, and by second language speakers who present an even wider range of phonological features in terms of pronunciation, stress, rhythm, and intonation patterns.

Second language learners need to adjust to all of these variables, especially if they have previously heard only scripted recordings which approximate more to the planned speech of lectures, scripted broadcasting, or drama, delivered at a slow speed and in standard English. If we are training students ultimately to be able to manage real listening situations, then one implication is that we will need to build their confidence in dealing with authentic speech. Decisions will be needed about the point at which learners are exposed to this, the complexity of what they are exposed to, and what kind of tasks will develop confidence.

7.3.3 *Uncertainties because of gaps in the message*

Not only environmental noise but also poorly articulated speech or poor attention can be responsible for creating gaps in the message that a listener hears. When gaps occur, listeners have to reconstruct the missing information and will use whatever clues are available to fill them in. Prediction is a strategy that will help with this. For example, we may make a prediction on the basis of the syntactic structure and the conjunction 'but' in this utterance:

> I like him to some extent because, you know, he's been very kind to me on occasion, but other people don't [have a lot of time for him] because he loses patience very quickly.

Here, if the part in brackets were drowned out by noise this would not prevent the listener from piecing together the meaning. What would also help is the redundancy in the language. In fact, the utterance above could be said meaningfully without the words in brackets. They repeat the meaning of 'like him' from the first main clause, and are thus redundant.

It is important to consider the implications of environmental noise for classroom practice. For example, if learners will have to deal with listening to English in noisy environments such as open-plan offices, they may need practice in 'filling in the gaps' with listening texts that have background noise and distorted or obliterated words.

7.3.4 *Uncertain strategies*

In face-to-face communication, if a gap occurs in the message because of noise or indistinct speech, a listener can ask for clarification. It is quite normal to hear people say 'Sorry, I didn't catch that' or 'Could you repeat that, please?' They are the normal strategies we use in first language communication and they are universal across languages.

Listeners use other strategies, too, in order to maintain the flow of conversation. We have ways of indicating that the speaker is holding our interest such as nodding, smiling, frowning, using expressions of surprise or concern, making noises such as 'mmm', 'wow', and 'tut tut', or using words like 'yes', 'I see', and 'right'. We can contribute to the speaker's line of thought by coming in with queries such as 'Are you saying … ?' and reformulating what the speaker has just said. Of course, all of these strategies can be used negatively if we wish to indicate disagreement or displeasure. All languages have strategies similar to these, but their precise use may differ and certainly learners will need to know the appropriate words, phrases, and noises to use in each.

7.3.5 *Uncertainties of language*

There are some listening situations in which the language heard is similar to written prose, such as in a lecture which is read, or a scripted news broadcast. However, a good deal of listening is to informal colloquial English. If teachers are preparing students for this kind of listening outside the classroom, they need to be aware of its characteristics. Traditionally, the language of audio recordings for ELT has been fairly slow, restricted in various ways, and often repetitive, in order to facilitate comprehension. A group of teachers I was working with recently made a comparison between a recording of natural conversation among native speakers and a recording made for English language learners. They came up with the following set of differences:

Spontaneous informal talk	Recordings for English language learners
– variations in speed of delivery, often fast	– slow pace with little variation
– natural intonation	– exaggerated intonation patterns
– the natural features of connected speech, e.g. elision	– carefully articulated pronunciation
– variety of accents	– Received Pronunciation
– any grammatical structures natural to the topic	– regularly repeated structures
– colloquial language	– more formal language
– incomplete utterances	– complete utterances
– restructuring in longer, more complex sentences	– grammatically correct sentences
– speakers interrupt or speak at the same time	– speakers take careful turns
– speakers use ellipsis (i.e. miss out parts of sentences)	– ellipsis infrequent (i.e. sentences usually complete)
– background noise present	– background noise absent

There are strong arguments for using recordings with some of the features listed on the right with learners at lower levels, particularly when the purpose of the listening is for input and the text presents grammar, vocabulary, and certain phonological features. However, if another purpose is to develop the ability to deal with listening outside the classroom, then texts will be needed which present natural language. And this implies familiarizing students with colloquial speech and variety of pace and accent, developing their vocabulary, developing their awareness of how referring expressions such as pronouns are used, and helping them to use any markers in the discourse which will aid prediction.

Chaudron and Richards (1986), for example, found that the use of 'macro-markers' in lectures, such as:

> What I'm going to talk about today is …
> One of the problems was …
> Another interesting development was …
> You can imagine what happened next …

assisted students in organizing the major ideas in the lecture. Their study involved giving four versions of the same lecture to different groups of students. A baseline version did not use any particular discourse signals other than those which were strictly necessary to get the information across. A second version was then designed using 'micro-markers', including segmentation markers such as 'now' and 'right', causal markers such as 'so' and 'because', temporal markers such as 'after this' and 'eventually', contrast markers such as 'but' and 'both', and markers of emphasis such as 'actually' and 'of course'. A third version was designed to contain the macro-markers listed above, and a fourth version included both micro- and macro-markers.

The researchers found a consistent result: the version with macro-markers was more conducive to students remembering the content of the lecture. The markers were clues to the overall structure of the lecture and indicated major sections. The micro-markers were less helpful and the researchers hypothesized that perhaps these added little to the substantive content of the lecture but, at the same time, increased the processing load of the listeners. Certainly there is an implication here for the teacher of listening; that helping learners to become aware of and exploit those macro-markers which are available in monologues such as talks, speeches, and lectures is a useful goal.

7.3.6. *Uncertainties of content*

As we saw in 7.2, learners who are unfamiliar with the background knowledge required to make sense of a text will experience difficulty in inferring and interpreting meaning. For example, here is part of a conversation between friends:

A She's having a horse-drawn carriage to take them from the church back to the house.
B That's expensive, isn't it?
A Yes, and not very sensible in my opinion. What if it rains? A bit stupid for March. The church'll be like an icebox to start with.

In order to understand the content, we need to know something of the conventions surrounding an English wedding, likely weather in an English March, and the heating problems of old churches. The language is not likely to cause problems but a lack of schematic knowledge may well do so. The major implication here for teaching listening is the need for a pre-listening stage in which existing prior knowledge can be activated and missing prior knowledge can be introduced.

7.3.7 *Visual uncertainties*

In most situations, listening is not just an aural activity. We are usually able to see the speaker, who provides non-verbal clues to meaning, for example, lip movements, facial expressions, and gestures. In a review of studies exploring the role of vision in speech perception, Kellerman (1990) reports evidence that the visual element should not be neglected as speech perception is a bi-modal process. The role of vision in first language listening, especially lip movements, is particularly important when the auditory input is of poor quality. If the speaker is visible in most real listening situations, then the use of audio cassettes in the classroom is unnecessarily restricting. Learners must focus on what they hear and cannot use paralinguistic clues to meaning. Classrooms may have poor acoustics, and recordings may be of poor quality. Also, the teacher has to take time presenting something of the setting so that the contextual clues to meaning are available. The use of audio recordings can provide practice for those situations where the speaker is not visible such as telephone conversations or radio programmes, but the availability of video cassettes has undoubtedly assisted learners and has enabled teachers to point out cultural differences in paralinguistic features such as the use of facial expression and gesture. Many teachers will have experienced difficulty in persuading learners to return to work with audio cassettes once they have experienced the visual element of video cassettes. Where teachers are fortunate enough to have both video and audio recordings available, perhaps each technical resource should be exploited for its own range of useful activities and, in addition, the teacher, as a live speaker, should come back into prominence for some aspects of listening work.

The importance of dealing with these various uncertainties from an early stage in the teaching of listening is highlighted by Eastman (1991), who discusses the tendency of intermediate listeners to use translation as they listen, a strategy which is generally considered to be problematic and inefficient. Eastman suggests that the reasons for this tendency include anxiety, the expectation that the listener needs to understand every word, transfer from a word-by-word reading comprehension strategy, inadequate prior learning of vocabulary, and inappropriate teaching which fails to contextualize the content of the listening passage or which encourages word-by-word analysis. The issue to which we now turn is how to develop an effective methodology for the teaching of listening, one which deals with the points and pitfalls raised so far.

7.4 What are the implications for the English language classroom?

7.4.1 *Creating reasons for listening*

As we saw in 7.2.3, in real-life situations we listen for a number of different purposes and our particular purpose will determine the range and balance of listening skills which we need to employ. In the English language classroom, teachers need to ensure that learners experience a range of listening purposes, especially those that might be immediately relevant to their lives outside the classroom. There have been many such lists of purposes provided for teachers (Rivers and Temperley 1978; Harmer 1991; Galvin 1985; Ur 1984; Underwood 1989; Richards 1990; McDonough and Shaw 1993). Galvin (1985), for example, suggests that there are five general reasons for listening: (1) to engage in social rituals; (2) to exchange information; (3) to exert control; (4) to share feelings; and (5) to enjoy yourself. These all seem to relate to participatory listening. Underwood's (1989) list of listening situations, on the other hand, which seems to fall into six major categories, relates to non-participatory listening. She includes: (1) listening to live conversations in which one takes no part and where the purpose is curious eavesdropping; (2) listening to announcements, news items, and weather forecasts where the purpose is to extract information; (3) listening to or watching plays, radio, and TV entertainment, and listening to songs where the purpose is enjoyment; (4) following instructions in order to carry out a task efficiently; (5) attending a lecture or following a lesson in order to understand concepts and information; and (6) listening to someone give a public address in order to infer views and attitudes. Harmer's (1991) set of possible purposes for classroom listening activities clearly includes elements of both Galvin's general reasons and Underwood's authentic listening situations: (1) listening to confirm expectations; (2) listening to extract specific information; (3) listening for communicative tasks; (4) listening for general understanding; (5) listening to recognize function; and (6) listening to deduce meaning.

One way in which such lists are useful is that they help teachers to formulate a checklist of listening purposes and situations from which they can select for the listening component of a programme. Another way is that they point out the various dimensions which need to be taken into account when designing listening materials: whether listening is reciprocal or non-reciprocal; whether it is visual, as in face-to-face encounters, or non-visual, as on the telephone; whether texts are short or long, and dense in information load or not; whether the purpose is to follow the gist or to extract detail, and whether there is one speaker or several.

The designer or evaluator of listening materials will need to ask:

– What purpose might there be for listening to this particular text?
– Is that purpose similar to the purpose a listener might have in real life?
– Does the task given to the learner encourage that listening purpose?

For example, asking learners to listen to a short airport announcement to obtain information about a particular flight, as a passenger would, might be more authentic than asking them to listen for the details of four different flights. It will practise the skills of listening for key words, picking out relevant information, and retaining significant details.

Consider the example in Materials extract 7.C. How would you answer the three questions above? Very often, if we know the topic of a story we are going to hear, we use prior knowledge to predict the content and, as we listen, our expectations are confirmed or confounded. This situation is reflected in the activities in Materials extract 7.C. The first activity presents sufficient information about the speaker, the situation, and the content to allow expectations to form, and the second activity invites learners to check these expectations. You may also like to consider the other listening materials presented in this chapter in the light of the three questions above.

Materials extract 7.C

A Bad Luck Story

Before listening	(1) You are going to hear a story about an Englishman who went to live and work in Italy, and at the beginning of his stay there had lots of bad luck. What bad luck do you think he might have had? Write four things in the blanks below: (a) _____ (b) _____ (c) _____ (d) _____ Compare and discuss your answers with the rest of the class.
Listening tasks	(2) Listen to the story on the tape to see if any of the things you wrote above happened to this man.

(Spratt: *Tuning In*, page 30)

7.4.2 *Selecting texts for listening*

In selecting texts for classroom use it is worth considering the possible dimensions of difference we need to address; for example, the distinction between monologue and dialogue, both of which will be encountered by learners in listening situations outside the classroom. And there are variations within each of these categories in terms of the characteristics of particular types of monologue or dialogue. Table 7.1 below highlights some of these.

Table 7.1: Types of text features

A *Monologue*

1 Unscripted (but possibly prepared), e.g. lectures, talks, speeches	Some of the features listed under 4 but greater clarity and better organized, probably with more discourse markers and possibly slower.
2 Scripted, e.g. news, written talks, stories read to children	Similar to written prose with little repetition, rephrasing, or other performance features; reasonable speed and relatively formal and deliberate style
3 Public announcements	Speed careful and moderate, formal style with ritual phrases, heavy information load, often uncertain acoustics, distorted by noise and therefore difficult to hear

B *Dialogue*

4 Unscripted, spontaneous conversations between native speakers, or involving non-native speakers	Repetitions, rephrasings, reformulations, hesitations, natural rhythm, contracted forms, incomplete sentences, fast pace, variety of accents, colloquialisms
5 Spontaneous commentary	Many of the features of 4, especially incomplete sentences and varying speed, e.g. very fast sports commentary
6 Telephone conversations	Some features of 4, but generally more structures and turn-taking; more careful enunciation, slower pace. Problems of gaps in the message as a result of noise, distortion, and lack of visual clues

Natural spontaneous conversation can be very difficult for learners as it gives rise to so many of the uncertainties listed in 7.3, and when occurring between speakers who have a high degree of shared prior knowledge and contextual knowledge an overheard conversation can be almost incomprehensible. One solution to this problem for teachers who wish to expose learners to authentic texts is to choose conversations with clear settings, role relationships, topics, and structures. A radio phone-in show on a specific subject can yield useful texts, as can a political debate on TV. Another solution is to take a flexible approach to the concept of authenticity. For example, Geddes and White suggest a two-way definition of authentic discourse, first as 'language which was originally written or spoken for a non-pedagogical purpose, and which was, in its original context, a genuine act of communication' and second as 'language produced for a pedagogical purpose, but exhibiting features which have a high probability of occurrence in genuine acts of communication' (1978: 137). The second definition refers to *semi-authentic* texts, and these have become popular for listening practice. A typical method of creating such a text is to prepare a speaker and to prompt a conversation. For example, the speaker can be told that she will be interviewed about a holiday and asked questions on specific topics such as the place, the accommodation, and holiday activities. The interview will therefore be planned to a degree but not rehearsed or scripted. The interviewer can also usefully repeat some of the information given in a fairly natural way, making comments such as 'The hotel had a good view then' or 'So you enjoyed … '. This creates simpler but still reasonably natural discourse.

It is quite common to find several different types of listening text within the same unit in a coursebook: for example, a scripted pedagogical text in the form of a dialogue for the presentation of language forms; a semi-authentic text to familiarize students with some aspects of spoken discourse, and possibly an authentic text with printed or visual support and a simple task to build confidence. Both semi-authentic and authentic texts can provide variety of several different kinds, for example, speed of delivery, accent, and formality of language.

A further dimension of difference worth noting is whether material is presented by the teacher, by an audio cassette, or by a video cassette. Each has its advantages. Audio recordings expose students to a wide range of listening situations, speakers, voices, and speaking speeds, and they can be used by students working in the self-access mode. They are available for replay in ways in which a real speaker cannot be: it is often useful for teachers and learners to listen twice or to go back over certain features of the text.

Video, when available, provides the visual element discussed earlier in this chapter, so that teachers and students can work on the visual clues to meaning. It also provides the context of the listening so that contextualization activities become less necessary. Role relationships between speakers, for example those which arise from age or status, are more easily appreciated. Cultural differences in interaction also become evident and can be commented on in order to build understanding of sociocultural background.

However, there is one resource always available, and that is the teacher. He or she can be seen, can check for comprehension, can repeat, can modify language, and can often be heard more clearly than a recording. The activity in

Materials extract 7.D makes use of these advantages and is the kind of activity which could be repeated regularly with different types of description and with learners' own contributions from their reading as they develop confidence in spoken English.

7.4.3 *Designing listening activities for the classroom*

In 7.3 we discussed the issues arising from the uncertainties which second language listeners experience. A number of these have implications for the design of classroom listening activities and procedures. For example, we have seen that creating purposes for listening can motivate students, and that a pre-listening phase will enable teachers to introduce necessary schematic knowledge and some of the language which learners will encounter in the text. It has now become standard practice to use the following procedure when dealing with a listening text in class:

1 The teacher and the students prepare for the listening in a number of ways. Various activities are used to help students to become familiar with the topic, to be exposed to some language features of the text or to its overall structure, and to activate any relevant prior knowledge they have. The teacher's role is to create interest, reasons for listening, and the confidence to listen.

2 Before setting the students to do a while-listening task, the teacher makes sure that they have all understood what it involves, e.g. filling in a chart.

3 The students carry out the task independently without intervention from the teacher, unless it is clear from monitoring them while they work, that some have misunderstood what is required. Although the listening itself is done individually, students can be encouraged to check their responses in pairs or groups as soon as they are ready.

4 In a feedback session, the teacher and students check and discuss the responses to the while-listening task. The teacher's role is to help students see how successful they have been in doing the task.

5 Follow-up activities can be of various kinds, but at this stage the teacher may well wish to focus on features of the text or on bottom-up processes which will assist further development of effective listening.

This procedure, with its pre-, while-, and post-listening stages clearly reflects that employed by many teachers in dealing with reading texts (see 6.3.3), and the rationale for each stage is similar.

Materials extract 7.D

2.8 Describe and draw rooms from stories

LEVEL **All**

TIME **20 minutes**

AIMS **To listen to a familiar voice (the teacher's); to listen for detail and make a response.**

PREPARATION 1 Choose or invent a description of a room to read out to the students. If a recording of the book is available you could use that.

PROCEDURE 1 Tell the students you are going to read them a description of a room, and that you want them to draw it afterwards. Ask them to listen for a general impression of the room first.

2 Read the description of the room to the students.

3 Elicit the students' impressions of the room. Is it big or small? Does it belong to a rich or poor person? What kind of feeling do they get about the room? Explain/elicit the meaning of any vocabulary which the students do not know.

4 Tell the students that you now want them to draw the room. Read the description again as many times as they want while they draw.

5 Ask the students to compare their drawing with the person next to them. You could also show them what your drawing would be like.

6 Discuss what the room shows about the personality of the person or people who furnished it, and the part they think it might play in the story. Ask the students if they would like to live in this room.

FOLLOW-UP If you have access to a video of the novel or short story, you can show the students how the director visualized the room, and get their comments.

VARIATION You can also use this activity with descriptions of people in novels and short stories.

COMMENTS This is basically a variation on the old favourite 'describe and draw' but with the added bonus that it can be used as a way into a novel or short story or as an exercise you can use while the class are reading a set book.

(White: *Listening*, pages 48–9)

The pre-listening stage

At the pre-listening stage, the teacher will need to decide what kind of listening purpose is appropriate to the text. The learners will need to 'tune in' to the context and the topic of the text, perhaps express attitudes towards that topic, certainly bring to the front of their minds anything that they already know about the topic, and most probably hear and use some of the less familiar language in the text which would otherwise distract or create anxiety during listening. A brief review of current course material will show that a repertoire of activity types exists for the pre-listening phase: for example, predicting content from the title of a talk; talking about a picture which relates to the text; discussing the topic; answering a set of questions about the topic; and agreeing or disagreeing with opinions about the topic. In the listening activity in the Introductory task to this chapter (Materials extract 7.A), a picture could be used to contextualize the talk, and each of the three pre-listening tasks prepares the students in various ways. Activity 1 personalizes the topic, and the teacher can elicit some of the key vocabulary items in the text. Activity 2 moves more specifically into discussion of the text and encourages prediction of some of the points the broadcaster will raise. This provides a purpose for listening as learners create expectations which they can confirm while listening. Activity 3 prepares students for the overall organization of the text, and this will facilitate note-making. It also includes more specific points for prediction.

An important objective for the pre-listening phase is to contextualize the text, providing any information needed to help learners appreciate the setting and the role relationships between participants. This becomes particularly important with authentic recordings. In the task in Materials extract 7.E, the setting can be partly predicted from the picture and other contextual information from the written text. This ensures that learners are not overwhelmed by the random organization and performance features evident in the script. Again, a purpose is provided in the 'guessing' task.

In the absence of video, visuals can contextualize some types of listening text and activate relevant schemata.

Some topics lend themselves to pre-listening activities which require learners to form an opinion. In this case a useful task is to invite students to make explicit their opinions to each other in class discussion and then listen in order to see whether or not these are similar to those in the listening material. This kind of activity reflects the natural ways in which we react to what we hear and also inevitably introduces or rehearses relevant vocabulary and structures.

Materials extract 7.E

The Long Essay

Selvi has written a draft
plan for her long essay.
She is discussing it with
her tutor.

Pre-listening   **1 Using information which is given**

Read Selvi's plan. You can answer these questions about her already.
a) What kind of course is she doing?
b) Does she already have a University degree?
c) Is she from Britain?
d) What age group is she interested in?

2 Guessing further information

You might be able to guess the answers to these questions.
a) What is her job?
b) Where does she come from?

Postgraduate Diploma in English Studies	
LONG ESSAY/PROJECT	
TITLE	*Materials to motivate students to communicate in English.*
DESCRIPTION	*For 7-11 year olds with parents from India, Pakistan, Japan and Hongkong; speaking mother tongue at home and the 2nd language (English) in the classroom.* *Type of materials – to include short stories and poems for practising phonetics.* *Local setting – a multi-cultural Junior school in North London – I have visited the school several times.* *(Q. Could my materials be used in my country too? There are some similarities.)*

Extensive listening

1 Confirming your guesses

Check your answers to exercise 2 in the *Pre-listening*.

2 Listening for gist

Choose the correct way to complete these sentences.
a) During the tutorial, the title of Selvi's project is:
   i)   not changed
   ii) changed very little
   iii) changed considerably

b) Her new plan will include:
   i)   everything she had in her first draft
   ii) some of the points in her original plan
   iii) a completely new set of topics

c) At the end of the tutorial:
   i)   only Selvi is pleased
   ii) both Selvi and the tutor are pleased
   iii) only the tutor is pleased

Intensive listening

1 Listening for specific information

Which sentence is true?
a) Selvi wants to use poems which are already published.
b) She is going to write some poems herself.
c) She wants the children to write poems.

2 Note-taking

Use the plan below to do the following.
a) Complete the new title of Selvi's project.
b) Complete the section headings and sub-headings as indicated.

VOCABULARY

draft first, rough plan
mother tongue a person's native language
medium way of giving information
form class
background a person's family, experience or education
context the general conditions in which an event takes place
universal for all people or every purpose
criteria the principles on which a judgement is made
motivation a need or purpose for doing something
curricular relating to a course of study

TITLE *Using a topic - based approach to the*
       teaching of

DESCRIPTION

PART 1 *CONTEXT*

   a)
   b) *Malaysia*

PART 2

   a)   ● *poems*
   b)   ●
   c) *communicative*   ●
   d)
   e)

PART 3

PART 4

(Axbey: *Soundtracks*, pages 26–7)

While-listening activities

The work at the while-listening stage needs to link in relevant ways to the pre-listening work. While they listen, learners will need to be involved in an authentic purpose for listening and encouraged to attend to the text more intensively or more extensively, for gist or for specific information. In Materials extract 7.E the aim of the while-listening task is to confirm learners' expectations and to help them to get the gist of the content as it relates to the written text. Learner activity can involve following the information, responding to attitudes expressed, reflecting on what is said, taking general notes, or writing down specific points. A wide repertoire of activity types is possible: for example, ticking multiple-choice items (as in Materials extract 7.E), filling in a chart, matching pictures with the text, or drawing a picture or making notes (as in Materials extract 7.A). The choice of activity will depend on the level of response which is appropriate, not only to the type of text but also to the level of the learners. For learners in the early stages of developing listening ability, simple activities such as ticking a list or numbering pictures in the correct order will prevent the anxiety and demotivation arising from trying to write while listening. More advanced learners will be able to cope with more complex tasks. It is always a good idea, however, for teachers to try a while-listening task for themselves before introducing it in class in order to check just how manageable it is.

Post-listening activities

Post-listening activities can take students into a more intensive phase of study in which aspects of bottom-up listening are practised. For example, Materials extract 7.E includes intensive listening for note-taking, helping students to summarize the content of the tutorial. If we look at attempts to list the component skills involved in top-down and bottom-up listening, for example Richards (1990) (see Discussion topics and projects 2), we can see that post-listening activities help students to construct a plan from the elements of the discourse.

Post-listening work can also usefully involve integration with other skills through development of the topic into reading, speaking, or writing activities. If materials follow this route, it becomes important to ensure that new sources of motivation arise for students other than the interest of the original text. For instance, Materials extract 7.A invites students to talk about other animals and brings the topic full circle to revisit the personal preferences and experiences with which it began.

7.4.4   *Building confidence in listening to English*

As we saw in 7.3, many learners are anxious about listening to a foreign language. This is partly because of difficulties presented by the text, for example the speed of delivery, and partly because learners have unrealistic expectations, for example that they need to understand every word. If we follow the principles discussed in this chapter for the selection of texts and the design of tasks, then we have every chance of helping our students to develop confidence in dealing with a range of texts and speakers, and with variations in the speed of delivery.

An important factor in the development of confidence will be the grading of tasks throughout a programme, and in order to grade effectively we need principles to follow. Brown and Yule (1983a) a point to four groups of factors which might be taken into account in grading. The first group is to do with the speaker: it covers such factors as the number of speakers, the speed at which they speak, the degree of overlapping in their speech and the complexity which other performance features might create, and variation in accent. The second group is to do with the content of the text and includes language factors, the formal structure of the text, and the prior knowledge required to infer meaning. The third group is to do with the listener, and involves the degree of motivation and the degree of response required. The fourth group of factors covers the degree of support that is given to learners as they listen, for example through visual or printed material. In order to grade materials, the teacher can make a judicious selection which involves a balance of these factors. For example, if there are many speakers with various accents, speaking fast, then the degree of response required could be simple, for example just picking out some basic information such as what the speakers are talking about and whether they agree. In contrast, a monologue with simple language could require a more detailed response.

Confidence can also be built through exposure to English. If English is available in the community, learners might be persuaded to exploit the available resources in some way. The activity in Materials extract 7.F provides a good example of guidelines to assist learners in listening to authentic material and is representative of current trends towards encouraging learners to be more responsible and independent in learning English.

It is worth considering in what other ways radio and TV programmes and English language films could be exploited.

Materials extract 7.F

5.5 The World Service

LEVEL Intermediate and above

TIME 40–50 minutes

AIMS To show how speakers adapt what they say and their delivery (speed, articulation, and so on) to their listeners; to listen carefully to connected speech and make a transcript.

MATERIALS A tape recorder.

PREPARATION Record one minute of a news broadcast in English.

PROCEDURE
1 Play the broadcast and ask the students to get a general idea of what news items were mentioned. Discuss the students' answers.

2 Play the recording again and ask the students whether they get the impression that this news broadcast was for native speakers or for a wider audience, for example, the BBC World Service, or Voice of America. Do they ever listen to any of these stations? How do they think the language and delivery of the newscasters is adjusted if they are broadcasting in areas where reception might be poor, or the audience might not know a lot of English, or be using the broadcast to learn English? The students may come up with some of the following ideas:

– the newscasters might speak more slowly
– they might put in more pauses
– they might pronounce the words more carefully
– they might use shorter, simpler sentences
– they might try to avoid words with lots of 's' sounds, which can 'hiss' where reception is poor
– they might repeat words and ideas more
– they might give more explanation for things which are specific to British or American culture, for example, 'Thanksgiving holiday' instead of just 'Thanksgiving'.

The students may have other suggestions as well.

3 Ask the class to listen again to the news excerpt which you recorded. This time, they should write down word for word what the newscaster said. Play the excerpt a few words at a time, and then replay the whole thing so that the students can check what they wrote. Get them to compare their transcription with another student to see if they wrote the same thing, and discuss any problems they had in recognizing sounds and words.

4 In pairs, the students should decide on some changes they would make in delivery and language to improve the broadcast for international transmission.

5 A few of the pairs could perform their revision of the news and explain the changes they have made.

(White: *Listening*, page 94)

7.5 Conclusion

Perhaps the most vital element in learning to listen effectively in a second or foreign language is confidence, and confidence comes with practice and with achieving success from an early stage. The role of the teacher is to provide as much positive practice as possible by talking to learners in English, by exposing them to a range of listening materials in the classroom, and by encouraging them to use whatever resources are available in their institution or community, in the ways suggested in this chapter. And this involves talking to learners about what is involved in listening and raising awareness of the goals for the listening component of their classes.

All the listening activities included in this chapter have placed the learner in the role of 'eavesdropper', listening to more or less formal dialogue, or listening to a monologue. However, listening in the world outside the classroom is often participatory, integrating comprehension and production of speech. We will make further investigations into a pedagogy for the listener as participant in Chapter 8.

Discussion topics and projects

1 Make a tape recording of an informal conversation between two or more native speakers of English. Listen to it and identify the performance features discussed in 7.3.5. Would you use such a recording for classroom practice? If so, how would you exploit it, and with what level of learner?

2 Richards (1990) offers a list of what learners need to be able to do in order to listen effectively.

[Bottom-up processes]
– retain input while it is being processed
– recognize word divisions
– recognize key words in utterances
– recognize key transitions in a discourse
– use knowledge of word-order patterns to identify constituents in utterances
– recognize grammatical relations between key elements in sentences
– recognize the function of word stress in sentences
– recognize the function of intonation in sentences

[Top-down processes]
– use key words to construct the schema of a discourse
– construct plans and schema from elements of a discourse
– infer the role of the participants in a situation
– infer the topic of a discourse

- infer the outcome of an event
- infer the cause or effect of an event
- infer unstated details of a situation
- infer the sequence of a series of events
- infer comparisons
- distinguish between literal and figurative meanings
- distinguish between facts and opinions

(Richards 1990: 59–60)

Explore a range of ELT textbooks, both general coursebooks and specific listening skills books, and find examples of activities which help learners to develop each of these processes.

3 Review a textbook in current use in your institution and make lists:
(a) of the reasons for listening which learners are given as they tackle listening texts
(b) of the types of listening text they encounter.

Would you want to extend the range of either (a) or (b) and, if so, what would you add?

4 Find an example of a listening activity in a textbook. Evaluate it against these criteria:
(a) the extent to which learners are given a reason to listen
(b) whether appropriate contextual information is required
(c) in what ways a pre-listening stage prepares students for the language of the text
(d) in what ways a pre-listening stage activates prior knowledge
(e) the usefulness of any while-listening work
(f) the relevance and range of any post-listening work.

If you are critical with regard to any of these criteria, what improvements would you make to the activity?

5 Are there any listening tasks with which you would not use a pre-listening stage?

6 What is your opinion on the use of authentic recordings in the ELT classroom? Discuss your own policy in a group and try to reach a consensus in relation to these issues:
(a) the level of student
(b) the grading of language
(c) the unfamiliarity of accents
(d) the amount of repetition
(e) the speed of delivery.

Add any other issues that occur to you.

7 Is it necessary to have audio equipment in order to train listening skills? Or video equipment? What are the advantages and constraints of each? What can the teacher do without technical resources to give opportunities for listening practice?

Further reading

Anderson, A. and **T. Lynch.** 1988. *Listening.* Oxford: Oxford University Press.

This book is divided into three sections: the first outlines the theoretical background to what listening comprehension involves; the second looks at the relationship between theory and practice and considers how teachers can design effective listening activities; and the third provides small-scale research tasks which teachers can carry out and which will inform the decisions they make about classroom listening. The book has tasks throughout which help the teacher to reflect on professional practice.

Dunkel, P. 1993. 'Listening in a native and second/foreign language: towards an integration of research and practice' in S. Silberstein (ed.): *State of the Art TESOL Essays.* Alexandria, Va.: TESOL Inc.

This is an overview article which gives a useful picture of how research into listening has proceeded over the last twenty-five years and how the ensuing insights have raised issues for the teaching of both first and second language listening. The paper is divided into five sections: the importance of listening in second language acquisition; factors that affect success in listening; the role of listening in the second language curriculum; models of listening comprehension; and classifications of listening skills with comment on learning activities. It raises issues both for a research agenda and for language teachers.

Rost, M. 1994. *Introducing Listening.* Harmondsworth: Penguin.

This book provides a concise introduction to the theory and practice of listening. It starts with a description of the psycholinguistic and sociocultural factors which influence the listening process and then turns to the pedagogy of first and second language listening. Throughout the book there are activities which help the reader to appreciate the concepts and ideas discussed.

Underwood, M. 1989. *Teaching Listening.* London: Longman.

This book aims to help language teachers develop effective classroom procedures and activities for listening. After highlighting the kinds of problems that learners have in listening to a foreign language, the book explores activities for the stages of pre-, while-, and post-listening. It contains numerous useful examples from current textbooks which illustrate good practice.

White, G. 1998. *Listening.* Oxford: Oxford University Press.

This is a resource book for teachers which contains more than seventy classroom activities. These include activities to raise learners' awareness of sounds and intonation, activities which encourage learners to use radio and television, and listening projects. The intention of the book is to develop confidence and independence in listening.

8 SPEAKING

'Language is a cracked kettle on which we beat out tunes for bears to dance to, while all the time we long to move the stars to pity.'
GUSTAVE FLAUBERT

1 What is involved in speaking English competently?

2 How do speakers manage interaction?

3 How do we choose a model for pronunciation teaching?

4 How can we select practice activities according to student need?

5 How can we make accuracy-based practice meaningful?

6 How can we design and evaluate fluency-based activity?

7 How can we teach the pronunciation component of a course?

8 What kind of policy can we develop for treating error?

Introductory task

The criteria below are taken from the upper intermediate and advanced levels of a communicative test of speaking. Look carefully at what a candidate is asked to do to achieve a pass at a given level and make a list of skills which the test assumes are required for effective spoken English, for example 'ability to pronounce the language intelligibly'.

Degree of skill

In order to achieve a pass at a given level, candidates must demonstrate the ability to complete the tasks set with the degree of skill specified by the criteria in Table 8.1:

Table 8.1: Criteria in a speaking test

	Level 3	Level 4
Accuracy	Pronunciation must be clearly intelligible even if some influences from L1 remain. Grammatical/lexical accuracy is high though occasional errors which do not impede communication are acceptable.	Pronunciation must be easily intelligible though some residual accent is acceptable. Grammatical/lexical accuracy must be consistently high.
Appropriacy	The use of language must be generally appropriate to function and to context. The intention of the speaker must be clear and unambiguous.	The use of language must be entirely appropriate to context, function, and intention. There is nothing to cause confusion.
Range	A wide range of language must be available to the candidate. Any specific items which cause difficulties can be smoothly substituted or avoided.	There must be only occasional obvious limitations on the range of language. Few allowances have to be made for the fact that the candidate is not a native speaker.
Flexibility	There must be consistent evidence of the ability to 'turn-take' in a conversation and to adapt to new topics or changes of direction.	The candidate must be able to 'turn-take' and 'direct' an interaction appropriately and keep it flowing.
Size	Must be capable of making lengthy contributions where appropriate. Should be able to expand and develop ideas with minimal help from the interlocutor.	Must be capable of making lengthy and complex contributions as appropriate. The interlocutor does not need to support the candidate.

(UCLES/RSA: *Certificates in Communicative Skills in English: Teacher's Guide*: 30, 31)

8.1 Introduction: skills and strategies in speaking English

Perhaps the first question to ask in this chapter is what reasons we have for asking our students to practise speaking in the classroom. There could be several answers. One is that, for many students, learning to speak competently in English is a priority. They may need this skill for a variety of reasons, for example to keep up rapport in relationships, influence people, and win or lose negotiations. It is a skill by which they are judged while first impressions are being formed. But learning to speak competently is a complex task. Coursebook writers often use the term 'fluency' to describe the aim of the speaking activities they provide. For example, in the Introduction to *Blueprint Upper Intermediate*, Brian Abbs and Ingrid Freebairn write:

> To help improve students' oral fluency, Blueprint Upper Intermediate contains a variety of activities aimed at encouraging free expression. (page 5)

In their introduction, the authors of *Look Ahead* say a little more:

> Learners need to develop at the same time a knowledge of grammar, vocabulary, functional language and communicative skills. Attention to the systems of language is crucial, but the development of fluency and contextual appropriacy are equally important goals. (pages 3–4)

Contextual appropriacy, as we saw in 2.2.2, means that the language chosen for a particular message will depend on the setting, the relative status of the participants, and their role relationship. One friend might say to another, 'I'm opening the window, OK?' whereas a stranger on a train would be more likely to say, 'Do you mind if I open the window?' Fluency means responding coherently within the turns of the conversation, linking words and phrases, using intelligible pronunciation and appropriate intonation, and doing all of this without undue hesitation. This implies that speakers can interpret and assess the meaning of what they hear and formulate appropriate responses.

As communicative approaches have developed, teachers have been concerned to ensure that students not only practise speaking in a controlled way in order to produce features of pronunciation, vocabulary, and structure accurately, but also practise using these features more freely in purposeful communication. It has therefore become usual to include both accuracy- and fluency-based activities, as discussed in 2.4.1, from the beginning of a course. However, there are more aspects to conversation than these. Studies of native speaker conversation have provided us with insights into what it involves in terms of managing interaction. For example, there are skills relating to opening and closing conversations, to the sharing of time, to taking turns and contributing both shorter and longer turns as appropriate, to attending to and responding to one's interlocutor, and to interrupting. If any of these are lacking or poorly performed, then communication can break down. And the reasons for the breakdown may be lack of language to undertake these skills effectively or differences in the cultural conventions associated with them.

The criteria used in assessing speaking performance quoted in the Introductory task to this chapter demonstrate an interest in these management skills as well as those more traditionally associated with speaking a foreign language such as intelligible pronunciation and grammatical and lexical accuracy. Notice, for example, the two requirements:

> There must be consistent evidence of the ability to 'turn-take' in a conversation and to adapt to new topics or changes of direction.

> Must be capable of making lengthy and complex contributions as appropriate.

> (UCLES/RSA: *Certificates in Communicative Skills in English: Teacher's Guide*: 31)

There are clearly implications here for the kind of practice that teachers can provide which will help students to develop these skills. It will need to move well beyond the controlled dialogues with short turns that are traditionally associated with textbooks.

The list of 'skills' does not end here, however. Speakers need to use communication strategies of various kinds when they lack words, phrases, or structures in English. In 2.2.4 we saw examples of such strategies as learners used gesture and paraphrase in their attempts to achieve clear communication, and the question was raised as to whether we can teach and provide practice in these strategies. Also, as we saw in 1.2.3, interaction implies negotiation of meaning. Speakers need to check that they have been understood and may need to repeat or clarify what they have said: in other words, they need to adjust what they say in order to be comprehensible. And listeners play a part in this process by indicating when they do not understand, for example, by asking for explanations, correcting, and so on. Teachers might, therefore, consider the usefulness of early instruction in the language needed to ask for repetition or clarification in order to help students in negotiating meaning.

Quite apart from our students' own concerns to speak English competently, we will also have a concern for the ways in which classroom interaction assists the language acquisition process. As we saw in 1.2.3 and 5.2.4, second language acquisition researchers see communicative interaction as having value both for negotiating comprehensible input from other students and for opportunities to practise using the language they have learned until it is automatized.

The challenge for the communicative classroom is to find activities and procedures for speaking which will prepare students for spontaneous interaction and which will aid the acquisition process, though of course the two aims may usefully coincide. This means finding answers to questions about what various activities can encourage, for example:

- Which activities encourage participation from all students, and so ensure that they all get practice opportunities?
- Which activities require the practice of turn-taking skills?
- Which activities encourage longer turns?
- Which activities oblige negotiation of meaning?
- Which activities give students practice in initiating conversations?

Since a particular type of activity may provide for some of these things but not others, there is then the question of how to create a varied programme of activities which gives a range of opportunities for speaking practice.

The first part of this chapter will look in more detail at what we know about spoken English, both its phonological aspects and the other skills involved in speaking. The second part will take up the implications of this knowledge for classroom practice.

8.2 What is involved in speaking English competently?

In order to help students develop their ability in speaking English we need a descriptive framework for looking at spoken discourse and a way of categorizing speaking situations and the demands they make of participants. Only then will we be able to find an appropriate classroom methodology.

8.2.1 *Distinguishing types of speaking situation*

There is a tradition in language teaching of referring to 'conversation classes'. However, this term is problematic because it has been defined in a variety of ways. Cook (1989) sees conversation as having the following characteristics:

1 It is not primarily necessitated by a practical task.
2 Any unequal power of participants is partially suspended.
3 The number of participants is small.
4 Turns are quite short.

5 Talk is primarily for the participants and not for an outside audience.
(Cook 1989: 51)

Thus Cook sees conversation as relatively unstructured and informal as compared with, say, more formal and sometimes more rehearsed situations for speaking such as meetings, interviews, and seminars. The purposes of conversation vary, but generally they involve making and keeping up social contacts, exchanging news, information, and opinions, and making decisions with other people.

Thinking about conversation in terms of purposes and characteristics is immediately useful for teachers as it indicates what students need a grounding in. For example, there are techniques in informal talk for allowing or encouraging other people to speak. We can ask what these are and whether they can be taught. Another feature is that content is, to a certain extent, unpredictable and the length of each speaker's turn is unspecified. Activities designed to develop conversational ability will need to take these features into account.

Conversation, as characterized by Cook, falls into the category of the *interactional* speaking situation, in contrast to the *transactional* speaking situation (Brown and Yule 1983a). As discussed in 7.2.3, the former involves establishing and maintaining social relations, while the latter involves exchanging information in order to get a job done, and most service encounters come within this second category. Consider the following example:

A Good afternoon. Enquiries.
B Hello, I'm making a journey from Ealing Broadway to Leamington Spa tomorrow morning and I don't have the new timetable. Please could you confirm that there's still a 7.25 from Ealing Broadway and an Intercity from Reading at 8.46?
A Just a minute, please. ... Yes, that's right. Departing Ealing Broadway 7.25, arriving Reading 8.10. Then departing Reading 8.46 arriving Leamington 9.59.
B Thanks very much.

Here, the content and pattern of exchanges is more or less predictable, the language is quite formal, set phrases are used, and both convention and efficiency determine the length of turns. The design of practice activities for service encounters can benefit from a study of these as they occur in English-speaking communities.

Different types of speaking situation can also be distinguished by applying the concept of *genre*. Cook's set of characteristics for informal conversation distinguish it as one genre. The telephone dialogue above between a customer and a rail enquiries clerk constitutes another. This concept links the purpose of a particular type of spoken discourse to its overall structure and it is possible to identify a predictable shape to some genres. For example, a good deal of work has been done in the field of narrative analysis. Cortazzi (1994), citing Labov (1972), suggests a six-part structure to an oral narrative of personal experience (the sequence of the six elements might vary):

abstract	What was this about?
	optional element –
	(summarizes the point or states a general proposition which the narrative will exemplify)
orientation	Who? When? What? Where?
	(gives details of time, persons, place, situation)
complication	Then what happened?
	(gives the main event sequence and shows a crisis, problem, turning point)
evaluation	So what?
	(highlights the point, shows listeners how they are to understand the meaning and reveals the teller's attitude by emphasising parts of the narrative)
result	What finally happened?
	(shows resolution to crisis)
coda	(optional way of finishing by returning listeners to present)

(Cortazzi 1994: 159)

Such a framework can be useful in designing storytelling activities and creating stories. Anecdotes and accounts of personal experience are valuable as an initial way of getting students to speak at greater length, to develop and structure their speech, and to practise linking the various parts. Other genres, such as farewell speeches, business presentations of new products, appraisal interviews, and presentations of a problem and its potential solutions at a scientific conference, also have discernible shapes, and a study of these might facilitate ways of practising them.

8.2.2 *Making oneself understood*

In 2.2.4 we saw examples of learners trying to express what they wanted to say but lacking the vocabulary and structures they needed. Their solution was to use one or more communication strategies. There is a field of research which has tried to categorize these. Faerch and Kasper (1983) have made the distinction between *avoidance behaviour*, in which learners try to eliminate a problem by changing the topic or not participating in a conversation, and *achievement behaviour*, in which ways are found to cope with the problem, for example: switching to the first language ('I don't like to *diska* (wash up)'; word coinage, often influenced by the first language ('I think an important job for a teacher is the *plannification* of lessons'); restructuring ('I have two … I have one brother and one sister'); a direct appeal for help from the listener ('It's … what is this colour?'); and gesture (for example pointing in the previous example).

Perhaps the most important implication for the teacher is simply to appreciate and understand what is happening when students use communication strategies, as they are likely to do in fluency activities which push them to the limits of their language resources. Communication strategies can be strong indicators of gaps and uncertainties in language knowledge, and can play a role in the teacher's decisions about what to focus on in feedback. The issue of whether such strategies can be taught was taken up in 2.2.4 and some examples were given there. Whether or not a teacher believes that communication strategies can be taught, it is certainly worth exhibiting positive attitudes towards achievement behaviour and encouraging it.

The other way in which learners work to make themselves understood is through negotiation of meaning. Communication does not consist of an unproblematic transmission of a message from speaker to listener. For example, the speaker may produce an indistinct or inaccurate message, as in:

A You musn't come except you bring the children.
B I'm sorry, shall I bring my children?

Or the listener may have difficulty interpreting a message because the speaker has mistakenly assumed shared knowledge, as in:

A Meet me under the dandelion at four.
B Sorry, where?
A Under the dandelion.
B But where is that?
A Oh, it's what we call the sculpture behind the Students' Union.
B I see. At four, you said.
A Yes.

Speakers therefore need an ability to negotiate, as in these examples, until the meaning is clear. Part of this will involve using achievement strategies, such as paraphrase or gesture, to explain things more clearly. However, it also involves knowing the language needed for checking whether or not a listener has understood and, as a listener, knowing the language needed for requesting clarification or repetition, or indicating comprehension. It is therefore useful for teachers to teach the language that will help with negotiation of meaning and to do this early in a course. Most importantly, of course, learners need opportunities for practice and certain kinds of fluency activities may be better than others in providing these.

8.2.3 *Managing interaction*

If a conversation is to open, progress, and close smoothly and productively, the speakers need to manage it by following the 'rules' that seem to govern normal interactions. There are a number of these, and all of them will be influenced by factors of status and role. The cultural conventions will need to be learned as well as the appropriate formality in style of speech and the level of politeness that is appropriate to the relationship between the participants.

Openings and closings

There are conventional ways of opening a conversation in English: some of these are contextually facilitated, as in the British 'It's a nice day, isn't it?', where the tag ending invites a response. In fact, many openings are ritualized as statement followed by response or question followed by answer, for example 'These buses get later, don't they?' or 'Busy here today, isn't it?' These openings are all attention-getting and can lead to further conversation. Closings need to be carefully negotiated as there is usually a pre-closing signal, for example, 'Well, I must think about going … ' or 'I don't want to keep you …' before the actual closing. Bardovi-Harlig, Hartford, Mahan Taylor, Morgan, and Reynolds (1991) have suggested that textbooks lack adequate material for teaching closings. Their analysis of twenty textbooks demonstrated the general absence of pre-closings and they point to the need for teachers to provide their own natural models.

Responding appropriately in fixed routines

The term 'adjacency pairs' has been given to exchanges where a turn by one speaker requires an immediate response, as in greetings, invitations, compliments, enquiries about health, and complaints. More than one response might be possible, for example, a justification rather than an apology might be given after receiving a complaint. Such responses usually require more careful formulation and students need to learn and practise the necessary language. They also need relevant cultural competence to know what is an appropriate response, for example to 'Hello, how are you?' The expected reply is 'Fine, thanks' or 'Not too bad, thanks', rather than a catalogue of health problems. And reciprocation is expected, for example 'And you?' to show equal courtesy.

Taking turns

Students often report that one of their greatest difficulties is entering a conversation. This is not surprising given that this requires a rapid sequence: watching for indications that the current speaker is coming to a close (for example, falling intonation); giving signals of a desire to come in (for example, raised eyebrows, leaning forward, looking at the speaker intently, coughing); formulating a turn which fits the flow of the conversation and which picks up on what has already been said; and finding the language to express it. There are many devices, too, for inviting other speakers to contribute, from tag endings like 'isn't it?' and 'can't we?' to questions like 'What do you think?' and 'Would you agree?' Interrupting may be particularly difficult as cultural conventions may differ from their first language. Students need to acquire the politeness phrases which make interruption acceptable in a conversation in English.

Topic management

The kind of topics chosen, how these are introduced, and how speakers move from one topic to another are further aspects of managing interaction. Perhaps the first demand on learners of English is to know which topics are appropriate with which kinds of people. Another is to know how to change the topic, as in 'By the way … ' or 'That reminds me … '. It is quite normal for informal conversation to move quickly through a number of topics and learners need a repertoire of topics in order to participate effectively.

8.3 What are the issues in teaching the phonological aspects of English?

It is worth spending some time giving separate consideration to the phonological aspects of learning English as perspectives on these have broadened and changed in recent years.

8.3.1 *Choosing a model for pronunciation teaching*

Part of speaking the English language competently is the ability to produce its sounds in ways that are intelligible to other speakers. However, given the spread of English throughout the world and its function as an international language, these other speakers may largely be speakers of English as a second or foreign language, each with their own local variety of pronunciation. Exposure to these other varieties can be achieved through the listening element of a course, which ideally will provide learners with experience in dealing with any comprehension difficulties which arise. Pronunciation dictionaries can also play a role. However, a dictionary cannot deal with features of sentence stress and intonation.

One of the first decisions a teacher has to make in teaching pronunciation is which variety of English to take as a model for production. Traditionally this was based on the speech of an educated native-speaker in one of the 'inner circle' (Kachru 1985) of long-established English-speaking countries, such as Britain or the USA. Now the picture is not so clear. There are political tensions surrounding the use of terms such as 'standard' and 'native speaker' as these imply ownership by the inner circle. Teachers therefore have to make sensitive decisions. Should a Japanese teacher of English choose a British, American, or Australian model? Japan trades with all these countries and his or her students might well go to live or study in any of them. Should a Zairean teacher choose British or American English? Both countries supply Zaire with ELT textbooks. Or, alternatively, should neighbouring varieties of English in West Africa play a role? And to what extent is the teacher limited by his or her own accent?

Perhaps these difficulties are one reason why so many textbooks produced for the international market avoid explicit reference to phonology and leave it to the teacher's discretion and knowledge of local needs.

8.3.2 *Taking a holistic or atomistic approach*

The development of communicative approaches, with their interest in the use of language in discourse, has been accompanied by a shift of emphasis in pronunciation teaching to suprasegmental aspects of connected speech such as sentence stress, rhythm, and intonation. However, welcome as the shift to a more holistic approach is, the point has been made that a truly holistic approach would go beyond these features to incorporate ideas about voice quality and articulatory setting. This would fit well with the need to choose a particular variety as a model, since each variety has its own articulatory setting features (Honikman 1964; Pennington and Richards 1986). Voice quality can be described as the general impression a speaker's voice creates for a listener through the setting of the articulatory organs. For example, O'Connor (1973) compares English and French pronunciation in this way:

> In English the lips and jaw move little, in French they move much more, with vigorous lip-rounding and spreading: the cheeks are relaxed in English but tensed in French: the tongue-tip is tenser in English and more used than in French, where the blade is dominant, and so on. (O'Connor 1973: 289)

Different settings produce different voice quality, and this characterizes local accents. A more holistic approach will also pay attention to the ways in which a combination of features such as rhythm, stress, pitch, volume, pace, and voice setting indicate attitude or mood. Some ideas about how to implement a holistic approach will be taken up in 8.4.5.

8.3.3 *Selecting practice according to student need*

Students' needs will vary along a number of dimensions, and these will affect the teacher's selection of content in the pronunciation element of a course. A very wide range of features could receive attention: for example, sentence stress and rhythm; linking or concatenation in connected speech (which includes assimilation and elision); vowel sounds; consonants and consonant clusters; and intonation. Given the time constraints of the typical course, it is a good idea to focus on those features of greatest importance for particular students or student groups. In monolingual classes it may be sufficient to use the information available from contrastive studies which list the problems that certain language groups are likely to experience with English (see, for example, Swan and Smith 1987; Avery and Erhlich 1992). With multilingual classes the ideal would be to collect and analyse speech samples from each student which would allow the teacher to diagnose and list problems needing attention. However, this requires time, equipment and, not least, expertise from the teacher in classifying the problems.

Selection also needs to take into account the level of the students. With beginners, the teacher can follow a systematic course, introducing major features of English and giving intensive practice in speech work. The picture with intermediate students is more complex. Teachers and learners may face substantial challenges, with poor intelligibility resulting from interference by the first language. Another problem may arise from over-insistence on precision of articulation. For students who have received little exposure to the corrective influence of authentic spoken English, this can result in stilted language which lacks some of the normal characteristics of connected speech. The teacher will also have to take into account the extent to which learners are motivated to work on improving pronunciation. This will help with decisions about realistic goals and performance targets, or how far to encourage students to decide on their own goals and targets.

8.4 What are the implications for classroom practice in the teaching of spoken English?

8.4.1 *Talking with students about spoken English*

One issue to consider is whether and to what degree we might discuss explicitly with students what is needed for effective speaking in English. There is immediately evident value, for example, in discussing the use of politeness conventions. In 2.2.2, we saw the scale of politeness possible in choosing how to express the same message, ranging from 'I'll use your phone, OK?' to 'Sorry to trouble you, but do you mind if I use your phone?' It would, in fact be necessary, rather than simply desirable, to talk about who might be speaking to whom in each situation and how their relative status and role relationship would affect the choice of language. Teachers might also consider whether and how to teach strategic competence. There are several quite simple strategies which could be explicitly taught in the early stages of learning, for instance:

– ways of opening a conversation in order to get practice with other students or English-speaking members of a community
– ways of asking for repetition, asking someone to speak more slowly, or requesting clarification, in order to get more comprehensible input
– ways of checking that someone has understood, for example 'OK?'; 'Do you follow me?'
– ways of getting information about language, for example 'How do you pronounce this?'; 'How do you say that?'
– ways of keeping a conversation going, for example, with phrases like 'Right', 'Yes', or 'I see'.

Is it desirable or necessary to talk about other aspects of conversation, such as turn-taking, or to use metalanguage in talking about such features as topic shift, adjacency pairs, closings, or interruptions? Teachers have a choice of two basic approaches, which Richards (1990) has called *direct* and *indirect*. The indirect approach simply involves students in conversation through role-play and problem-solving tasks, and gives them opportunities to practise these things in classroom activities. The direct approach applies a systematic analysis to the elements of speaking competence and takes students through a programme of awareness-raising and practice. An example of the latter is the book *Conversation Gambits* by E. Keller and S. T. Warner (1988), which defines a gambit as:

> a word or phrase which helps us to express what we are trying to say. For example, we use gambits to introduce a topic of conversation; to link

Materials extract 8.A

---

2. Breaking in

¹Excuse me

Sorry

Excuse me for interrupting, but ...

May I interrupt for a moment?

..., ²please

³Certainly

Often we have to approach strangers to ask them for some information or help.

Two to four students volunteer to be the questioners. They should think up some things to ask about (ideas below).

The rest of the class stand up and form small groups (3/4) and talk about anything you want. (hobby? friend? tomorrow? holiday?)

The volunteers then approach the groups and 'break in' to ask their questions. Try to use phrases from the list.

When each of the volunteers has been to each of the groups, everybody sits down again. The volunteers then report the answers they got.

Examples

Excuse me, can you tell me how to get to the cafeteria?
May I interrupt for a moment? I'd like to know how to get to the cafeteria.

1. Used to attract attention.
2. Most common at the end of a request.
3. The friendly way to say Yes.

Some things to ask about

How to get to the nearest supermarket/bus stop/telephone box.
Where you can get change/a haircut/stamps.
Where you could find a good, but not too expensive restaurant.
Where to get advice on buying a computer/new car.

(Keller and Warner: *Conversation Gambits*, page 8)

what we have to say to what someone has just said; to agree or disagree; to respond to what we have heard.
(page 4)

The authors point out that a speaker who does not use gambits can appear rude, over-direct, or abrupt. The interesting question is whether students who are introduced systematically to gambits, as in Materials extract 8.A, will acquire these more easily and use them more fluently than students who are not.

It would be useful to set up a small-scale experiment to compare the progress of students in programmes using direct and indirect approaches. Alternatively, teachers can take the common-sense approach, experiment with this kind of material, and see whether some students appear to take up the language usefully.

The success of an indirect approach will depend on such factors as whether input provides examples of conversational strategies, whether speaking activities generate useful practice, and whether individual students get opportunities to practise within activities. The success of a direct approach will depend on whether students are able to transfer the strategies they practise in more controlled language-focused activity to fluency activities. Both approaches have potential and problems. It is not surprising, then, that many teachers and textbook writers try to achieve a mix of awareness-raising and practice.

8.4.2 *Making accuracy-based practice meaningful*

The communicative classroom will need to expose learners to input which they can attend to, and opportunities to produce output in more controlled activities. Controlled activities can focus on a number of things, for example: a grammatical structure, a phonological feature, a conversational gambit, a communicative function, or the time sequencers that might be needed in telling a story. What they have in common is a conscious focus on language and a high degree of control over student output. Various labels have been suggested for this type of activity: perhaps 'skill-getting' (Rivers and Temperley 1978), 'pre-communicative' (Littlewood 1981), 'accuracy based' (Brumfit 1984a) and 'form-focused' (Spada 1997) are the best known. The first two, in relation to the terms 'skill-using' and 'communicative' also suggest a sequence in instruction to reflect the belief that a preparatory stage is needed to equip learners with the resources they need before engaging in a freer communicatively oriented activity.

If the purpose of form-focused work in speaking activities is to equip the learner with the knowledge and skills needed for communication, this begs the question of what characteristics we should be looking for in such activities. One approach would be to consider more precisely what learners need as preparation and what implications their needs have for activity design. It is possible to identify four needs, and we will now look at these in more detail.

Contextualized practice

The first need is contextualized practice, which aims to make clear the link between linguistic form and communicative function. This means finding a situation in which a structure is commonly used. For example, it used to be common practice to teach the present continuous tense through classroom actions such as 'I'm opening the window'; 'What are you doing?'; 'Are you looking at your book?' This demonstrates the way the tense is used to describe current actions, but it is not normal in everyday life for people to give a running commentary on what they are doing. A more useful contextualization would be a telephone conversation in which the caller asks to speak to a friend and the reply is: 'Just a minute. He's putting the children to bed. I'll get him.' Contextualization is particularly important when structures tend to occur naturally in combination, as with the modals 'have to' and 'need' which can be found in exchanges like:

Materials extract 8.B

7.6 ☐▶ ❹   Listen again and tick the phrases you hear.

Making suggestions	**Accepting suggestions**
I suggest…	Yes, that's a good idea.
How about…?	Yes, let's do that.
What about…?	
Why don't we…?	**Rejecting suggestions**
Why not…?	Yes, but…
We could…	I'm not sure about that.
	I'm afraid I don't like that idea.

Asking for suggestions
Do you have any suggestions for…?
Any ideas on…?

❼   Discuss one of these topics in groups. Use the phrases in 4 above to suggest solutions, and accept or reject the ideas of your colleagues.

1 At present your company pays for your English course. Next year, it wants employees to pay 50% of the cost. What can you do to stop this change?

2 It's your company's 50th anniversary next year. Suggest ways of celebrating the occasion.

3 Your town wants to improve its leisure facilities. Suggest changes and improvements.

(Taylor: *International Express Pre-intermediate* SB, page 65)

A Do I have to pick up the groceries today?
B No, you needn't. George can do it.

Personalizing language

The second need is to personalize the language in activities which enable students to express their own ideas, feelings, preferences, and opinions. It has been claimed that personalized practice makes language more memorable. It can certainly be motivating, and helps learners to see the ways in which they can make use of language resources in interpersonal situations. The implication is that practice must allow students some degree of choice in what they say. This can be seen in Materials extract 8.B, which follows on from a listening activity that demonstrates ways of giving opinions.

Materials extract 8.C

FOCUS
Closing strategies

- Ending conversations:
  Well, I suppose I ought to get on.
  Listen, I really have to/ought to be going now.

- Giving a reason for ending the conversation:
  I must get back to work.
  I've got some work to do.
  It's getting late.

- Making arrangements to make contact again:
  (Look), we must get together some time.
  (Listen), why don't we meet for lunch?
  (Look), I'll give you a ring.

- Leave-taking phrases:
  See you (soon/next ...)
  Good luck with/on ...
  Give my regards to ...
  Have a good evening/weekend/time on Monday.
  Take care.
  Bye (for) now.

ACT IT OUT
Act out a telephone conversation with a friend who has been ill. Telephone your friend to tell her/him about a party you have been to. Say what it was like and if you enjoyed it.

One of you must end the conversation. Say you have to go and give a reason. Your friend must respond appropriately and make arrangements to meet at another time.

(Abbs and Freebairn: *Blueprint Intermediate* SB, pages 100–1)

Building awareness of the social use of language

The third need is to build awareness of the social use of language and to practise essential features of this. For example, Materials extract 8.C practises closing strategies after students have analysed examples of these in recorded dialogues. This aims to achieve an understanding of what is appropriate social behaviour and the language that accompanies it. Failure to conform to social convention about how to close a conversation can cause offence as there is a tendency to see the cause as stemming from interpersonal rather than language problems.

Building confidence

The fourth need is to build ease and confidence in students so that eventually they are able to produce language quickly and automatically. This is where initial practice of the kind provided in Materials extracts 8.B and 8.C gives opportunities for repetition.

Controlled practice can be exploited usefully to build cohesiveness in a class of students as they try out the language together. The teacher can create a positive climate for classroom communication by standing back whenever possible and using cross-class questioning or pairwork practice. This will facilitate the more difficult, risk-taking encounters of fluency work.

8.4.3 *Designing and evaluating fluency-based activities*

There is a wide range of fluency-based activities available to the teacher. This section will comment on three basic types of activity and consider what each can contribute to the development of speaking skills.

Materials extract 8.D

Cruel to be kind?

SPEAKING 1

1   Look at the photograph and the text. Do you agree with this way of bringing up children? How does it compare to the way they are brought up in your society?

2   Write down five characteristics of ideal parents. Think about factors such as age, personality and behaviour. Use the Present Simple and words like *never* and *always*. Example: *They never lose their temper.*

3   In groups, discuss what you wrote and agree on five characteristics.

'We never hit children or even like to scold them. We like to pick them up or ask them what is wrong, because if we punish them they will grow up to be difficult or bad-tempered. So we bring up our children mainly by talking and explaining things to them.'

(*Chief of Amazonian Indian tribe*)

(Bell and Gower: *Upper Intermediate Matters* SB, page 10)

Free discussion

Free discussion can provide important opportunities for developing certain aspects of fluency. Ideally, over a period of time, free discussion activities will involve students in talking about a range of topics which engage their interests, opinions, histories, and experiences, such as the activity in Materials extract 8.D. Here students are invited to give opinions, agree or disagree, state preferences, and make comparisons.

Free discussion can also encourage students to use the language needed to sustain conversation over a period of time by drawing in other speakers. This last point, in fact, relates to perhaps the greatest advantage that free discussion has over other types of activity. This is the opportunity it provides for students to practise the strategies required in interpersonal communication, for example, taking and holding turns, introducing a topic or shifting to a new topic, and encouraging responses and other contributions.

Teachers often worry about less structured fluency activities because there are problems to overcome if the advantages are to be enjoyed: for example, students' anxiety in formulating opinions or ideas about topics which may be unfamiliar and which they may never have discussed in their first language; the possibility of a few more confident, more extrovert, or more proficient students dominating, or of the teacher dominating in his or her efforts to stimulate a quiet group. Free discussion, even if it takes place in small groups, does not ensure participation from all members. For these reasons, discussion usually needs support or structure of some kind.

One kind of support comes from the amount of information given by the teacher or materials. The activity in Materials extract 8.D, for example, uses a picture and a quotation which focus the discussion and provide content and linguistic resources.

Another kind of support comes from phasing the activity with careful instructions, as in Materials extract 8.D where the students prepare for their discussion by writing down some ideas. If phases are not included in the materials, teachers can add their own. For example, many teachers add a quiet time as a first stage for individual brainstorming of a topic. This respects the differences among learners, for example that some people need to think before giving opinions. The teacher will also need to decide whether or not there is to be a reporting stage when students hear about the decisions and ideas of other groups. This can be done by re-forming groups, with members drawn from each of the earlier groups to report on the discussion they had. This has the advantage of making it necessary for students to follow the arguments of their group in order to report these accurately, and may encourage strategies for negotiation of meaning. It also provides practice in the 'reporting' style of monologue.

A third kind of support comes from structuring interactions with suggestions for group roles, such as chair or secretary, though the teacher will need to monitor the choice of spokesperson from one activity to another to ensure equality of opportunity for public monologue. The question of roles, in fact, needs careful thought as, ideally, students need to have control over as many aspects of the interaction as possible, and freedom to interrupt, choose topics, change topics, and so on. Teachers need to realize what is gained and what is lost if they suggest the appointment of roles such as chairperson.

A fourth kind of support comes from establishing goals for the discussion. The activity in Materials extract 8.D asks groups to try to reach a consensus, and the procedures involved in comparing ideas, and defending, modifying, and refining them provide motivation to speak and to use communication strategies in trying to comprehend points made by other speakers.

There may be wider educational concerns involved in setting goals for activities. One reason for promoting groupwork in some school classrooms is that an educational goal within the general curriculum is to encourage cooperative learning. This is seen to have valuable outcomes both within education and in the world beyond the classroom. Co-operative learning has been variously defined, but one general characteristic is that individuals are responsible within the group and accountable to it, and that all members are therefore expected to make their contribution. A second characteristic is interaction in which students are dependent on one another to achieve an outcome. One can see immediately how well these educational ideas fit with insights from second language acquisition research about the kind of tasks which promote negotiation of meaning, and with teachers' concerns to engage as many students as possible in practice opportunities. In such situations, teachers may have a particular concern to set a co-operative goal rather than a competitive one (Johnson, Maruyama, Johnson, Nelson, and Skon 1981).

To summarize our review of discussion activities, the teacher will be involved in decision-making of the following kinds:

– how much support to give for content and how this is presented
– how much to structure the activity with phases and group roles
– whether to establish a goal and what kind of goal to set
– how to organize feedback
– how to encourage as much participation as possible and as much negotiation of meaning as possible.

Role-play

Teachers use the term 'role-play' to refer to a number of different activities, ranging from simple dialogues prompted by specific information on role cards to more complex simulations which pass through a number of stages,

Materials extract 8.E

3 Role play the following situation. A meeting of the editorial board of the magazine *Nostalgia*. Work in groups of four or five students. You are the editors of the magazine and are planning the next issue.

a) Decide on interesting topics for the four or five main articles you would like to publish.

b) Each member of the group chooses an idea for an article and jots down ideas about it to present to the others. Think of a topic which can be presented from an interesting angle, e.g. a dramatic or memorable scene or event, a memory which is full of emotion, etc.

The Twenties
short skirts,
short hair, ...

The Wild West
in America
excitement,
discovery, ...

c) [■ 3.2] Before you present your suggestion to your group, listen to the tape. Speaker A makes suggestions and speaker B tactfully disagrees in order to present alternative suggestions. On the list below, tick the strategies each speaker uses. An example has been done for you.

	A	B
Affirmative question tags, e.g. *do you?*		✓
Negative question tags, e.g. *don't you think?*		
Yes/No questions, e.g. *do you like . . . ?*		
Wh- questions, e.g. *What do you like?*		
Negative questions, e.g. *Don't you think . . . .?*		
Genuine agreement, e.g. *That's a great idea!*		
Apparent agreement, e.g. *That's a great idea, but . . .*		

4 Now present your suggestions for articles to the group using the same strategies as the speakers on the tape.

a) The group selects the most interesting articles to present to the whole class.

b) The class listens to the presentations and makes a final, well-balanced choice of topics for the magazine.

(Porter-Ladousse: *Language Issues*, page 22)

as in the example in Materials extract 8.E. What they all have in common is that the setting, the situation, and the roles are constrained by the teacher or materials but, within these, students choose the language they use. They may also, to a greater or lesser extent, develop the personalities and the situation as they wish. The example in Materials extract 8.E, in which students take on roles as editorial board members for a magazine, does not specify the details of the roles and allows for considerable flexibility in choice of personality and interests.

A number of advantages have been claimed for role-play as a fluency activity if it is performed in pairs or groups rather than one group acting in front of the class. It encourages participation from a large number of students. If it is based on real-life situations, both transactional and interpersonal, it is useful rehearsal for these. Some students find role-play easier than free discussion because they do not have to face the cognitive challenge of finding original and intelligent things to contribute. Some students enjoy the opportunity to act and assume other personae. A role-play which has a clear goal gives a purpose and a direction to the discussion. It is interesting that the role-play in Materials extract 8.E involves both competitive and co-operative elements. Moreover, as students take on a variety of roles during a programme of role-plays they will practise language which varies according to the setting, the formality of the situation, the degree of politeness or emotion required, and the function required for the particular role, for example to persuade, disagree, complain, invite, and so on.

In terms of speaking skills and strategies, the role-play in Materials extract 8.E demonstrates the possibilities. It perhaps has a greater chance than free discussion to involve all the students and oblige practice, except when free discussion is limited to pairwork. However, there will only be equality of opportunity for practice where roles have equal significance and 'key roles' do not hold the floor to an excessive degree. Whether or not it encourages interaction skills will depend on the details. There are certainly chances for this at (a) and (4a), but whether or not they are exploited will depend on how the interaction is structured by the group or by the teacher. The initial decisions at (a) would seem to imply a need for negotiation of meaning as members of the group will need to be clear about how they move from these decisions into (b).

However, the success of role-play depends on overcoming some of its limitations. Perhaps the main limitation is to do with asking students to take on roles, and whether or not they are able to empathize with the role they choose or are given. And this may well depend on the degree of distance between the reality of the student's own roles in life and the 'fantasy' of the role imposed. Functional roles do not present a great problem as all speakers need to apologize or offer help, for example, and social roles such as 'guest' or 'purchaser' are also universal. However, professional roles may begin to present difficulty as many role-plays involving transactional language assign one student of a pair a role such as 'doctor' or 'travel agent' and students can find this alien and not very useful. The problem is exacerbated when roles require students to change their status, personality, or even gender. Ultimately it will depend on the willingness and motivation of students to change persona, and this is an individual matter.

'Gap' activities

Since fluency activities came into common use in ELT, there have been attempts to investigate which might be the most useful in second language acquisition in relation to providing negotiation of meaning and the conversational adjustments which push students to more accurate output. The 'information gap' activity in particular has been studied. This involves each learner in a pair or group possessing information which the other learners do not have. The learners' information must be shared in order to achieve an outcome. Doughty and Pica (1986) set up a study which hypothesized that if students worked in pairs (also known as 'dyads'), with an activity which had a requirement for information exchange, they would engage in more negotiation of meaning than with activities where such modification is optional, as in freer discussion, or in activities with more participants. They based this hypothesis on the assumptions that pairwork is less threatening, that a student would notice confusion in a partner, and that pairs would come to a stop with the task unless they could understand each other. Therefore there would be more comprehension and confirmation checks, more clarification requests, and more repetitions. The task they employed involved one student arranging flowers on a felt-board garden following the instructions of a partner who held the master-plan. The study confirmed the hypothesis and seemed to demonstrate the usefulness of pairwork information-gap activities for language acquisition. Another value of this kind of task is the motivation engendered by bridging the information gap to solve a problem.

Information-gap tasks have their own advantages and limitations. They assist language acquisition, but they do not necessarily involve students in conversational strategies in the same way as role-play or discussion.

The efficacy of different activity types

Unfortunately, it would be mistaken to draw conclusions from this discussion of three activity types that their use will ensure that students practise the skills and strategies they try to encourage. Students do not necessarily conform to task instructions and will find ways around the problems that activities present, as a study by Yule and Powers (1994) has shown. This demonstrated how students found different solutions to the problems in an information-gap task in which each student in a dyad had a town map, one an older and the other a newer version with some major referential differences. For example, one map displayed one office block and the other three office blocks. One student, the sender, gave directions to the other, the receiver, who had to follow them and draw a route on their version of the map. The students found various ways around the task. For example, some receivers indicated problems that were acknowledged by the senders, who simply said 'Never mind. Forget it', so that the receiver chose any path. On other occasions, the sender would acknowledge a problem indicated by the receiver and make an arbitrary decision about a feature of the map. The questions are, how much modification of interaction occurred before decisions were made, and was negotiation of meaning avoided?

A more recent study has also shown the difficulty involved in designing tasks which might encourage negotiation of meaning. Foster (1998) reports on a classroom observation of the language produced by adult intermediate EFL students involved in four information-exchange tasks in pairs and small groups in the classroom. The tasks were chosen from communicative textbooks. One type of task can be called a 'required information exchange task' as it can only be done if the participants share information which others cannot see. For example, in the study, two students looked at sheet A or B which showed slight differences in a certain number out of twenty line drawings. They had to establish which pictures were the same and which were different by exchanging information about them. The other task-type can be called an 'optimal information exchange task' because all participants have the same information. For example, a group were given a given a discussion task in which they were told they had been made redundant, were given several possible courses of action, and had to achieve consensus on which course to follow. They were then given a new piece of information which created another problem which they dealt with in the same way. Foster tried each type of task with both pairs and groups so that any differences in the amount of negotiated interaction could be observed.

The study showed no clear overall effect for the type of task or the grouping, though pairwork was more effective in getting students to talk. Most students made only a few attempts to negotiate meaning through requests for clarification or comprehension checks, and all made very few, or no, attempts to make their own language more comprehensible in response to signals of mis-comprehension.

In looking for reasons to explain this lack of negotiated meaning, Foster suggests the frustration students might experience in holding up the interaction every time there is a problem, the discouragement that can set in if students repeatedly fail to understand, and the classroom setting which may encourage students to let problems pass in the interest of rapport with colleagues. She concludes that tasks to encourage negotiation of meaning are 'hard to design, can be frustrating to perform and classroom students don't behave in them as experimental studies suggest they should' (ibid.: 20).

It is noteworthy that all three studies cited above were small-scale. We need many more such studies before we have generalizable findings that can provide useful insights for teachers about the efficacy of different activity types. However, consideration of the three types, discussion, role-play, and information-gap, has gone some way to demonstrating the need for understanding the possible contributions and limitations of each to the development of spoken English. It suggests to us the need to create range and variety in a language programme sufficient to ensure that different skills are covered and practised.

8.4.4 *Providing a range and balance of activities in a course*

An initial dimension to consider when selecting activities is the relationship between the range chosen and the situations in which learners will need to function. This can be part of needs analysis with adults learning English as a second language within an English-speaking community (see 10.2) and it is relatively easy to derive a list of those transactions which learners must perform in their daily lives. It is also possible to draw on the checklist of settings and topics in a syllabus specification such as Threshold Level (van Ek 1975) as this is based on enabling people to engage in conversation when they visit English-speaking countries. Using these devices should ensure that range is offered in terms of transactional and interpersonal situations. It will also provide a range of relevant functions to practise.

Another consideration is to find a balance between practice activities which are monologue and those which involve two speakers or more. Some learners may have a need to practise monologue in genres that relate to their lives, for example, making a presentation, justifying a decision, giving a verbal evaluation of something, or presenting a report. For many of these, it would be normal to have time to prepare, and classroom methodology can reflect this, as in the simulation in Materials extract 8.E. Monologue can, as here, be practised within interactive activities. It can also be practised as a genre apart. The book *Once Upon a Time* (Morgan and Rinvolucri 1983) is a good source of ideas for storytelling, for example, and the more sustained language required by these activities will help students to develop the confidence to make their turns in interaction longer.

Achieving a balance between accuracy- and fluency-based tasks is a further essential criterion in developing a programme. It has been argued (Brumfit 1984a) that, as students move through the levels of an English programme, increasing time should be allocated to fluency work. The assumption here is that beginners will need a strong focus on learning to use grammar, vocabulary, and features of pronunciation in more controlled, intensive forms of practice, but that they will then need opportunities to use the resources they have acquired in fluency work which simulates real language use.

However, John and Liz Soars, in the Introduction to *Headway Upper Intermediate* Teacher's Book, argue that students who have passed through the 'intermediate stages' of a programme and who have 'sufficient linguistic confidence and ability to survive in a target language environment and understand the gist of what is going on around them' (page iii) will still have inaccuracies and a relatively narrow range of vocabulary. Therefore 'maintaining or even increasing the amount of accuracy work might eliminate some of these mistakes and enrich their language repertoire' (ibid.). The teacher's decision about which of these lines to follow may well depend on the practice opportunities available to their upper-intermediate students outside the classroom, and factors such as class size, resources, and time available for lessons, which will affect the possibilities for doing accuracy work *within* fluency activities, for example, group analysis of recorded activities (see 8.4.6).

A number of criteria, then, can be used in formulating the speaking component of a course. Several checklists of fluency activities have been published. For example, Klippel (1984) offers interviews, guessing games, jigsaw tasks, questioning activities, ranking exercises, discussion games, values-clarification techniques, thinking strategies, problem-solving activities, role-play and simulation, and stories. Harmer (1991) and Littlewood (1981) provide similar lists, but all of these are categorized in different ways. The teacher selecting from these resources or evaluating what is provided in a particular coursebook needs criteria to apply. These questions might provide a basis for evaluation:

1 **Participation within the group**
   (a) Does the activity oblige all students to co-operate and contribute, or does it allow some students to dominate?
   (b) Are students obliged to negotiate meaning as they perform the task?
   (c) Are group roles suggested, e.g. chair, or can students decide their own group structure?

2 **Complexity of interactions**
   (a) Does the activity require one type of interaction, e.g. pairwork, or does it require several in sequence, e.g. pairwork followed by two pairs in a group of four?
   (b) Does the group composition stay the same or does it change throughout the activity?
   (c) How much movement is needed within the classroom?

3 **Opportunities for management of interaction**
   (a) Does the activity require students to open and close conversations?
   (b) Do students need to manage topics and change topics?
   (c) Do students have a chance to control their own turn-taking?
   (d) Does the activity encourage or oblige longer turns?

4 **Degree of simulation required**
   (a) Does the activity keep students in the conversational setting of their own classroom or ask them to imagine another setting? Is this known to them or difficult to imagine?

(b) Do students have to assume roles (and are these familiar and/or useful) or can students be themselves?

(c) Can students express their own attitudes and opinions or are these given?

5 Structure of the activity
(a) Is there a gap of some kind?

(b) Is there a set of instructions for students to follow or can they make up their own procedure?

(c) How many phases does the activity have, and are these best managed as in-class or out-of-class work?

(d) Is one outcome expected from the activity or can the students decide their own outcome?

(e) Does the activity give students time to plan or rehearse, or does it involve spontaneous interaction?

6 Motivation
(a) Is the topic one which will motivate a particular class?

(b) What is the source of the motivation, e.g. the nature of the problem, the topicality of the subject?

There is clearly some overlap between these categories and certain questions will be more relevant to some teaching situations than others. For example, category 2 will be of particular concern to teachers of large classes or to teachers introducing students to these types of interactions.

8.4.5 *Teaching the pronunciation component of a course*

Balancing holistic and atomistic approaches

One current view on creating a balance between holistic and atomistic approaches is that the former should be of primary importance. Esling and Wong (1983), for instance, suggest that if students are given early instruction on how to set their articulatory organs to produce the typical voice quality of North American English speakers, then it will be easier for them to produce individual sounds. This early training may involve both consciousness-raising and practice. Thornbury (1993), for example, suggests an early activity for adult Spanish learners of English as a foreign language.

> Contrast a Spanish speaker of English and a native speaker performing the same task in English on tape. Students listen and note any character-istics in pronunciation, perhaps selecting from a list and matching them to the speaker. For example:
>
> a. he/she sounds flat

   b. he/she speaks with a 'creaky' voice
   c. he/she hisses a lot
   d. he/she says some things fast and some things slow
   e. he/she speaks 'through her nose'

After group/pair discussion, the teacher leads an open discussion about salient suprasegmental features of Spanish and English accent (including features of stress and rhythm, as well as voice qualities.)
(Thornbury 1993: 129)

Certainly, activities like this, if used for consciousness-raising, have the advantage of exposing learners to communicative situations in which various elements of pronunciation integrate before they move on to recognize and practise the elements more atomistically.

Integrating pronunciation teaching

It will generally be the teacher's responsibility to decide when to focus on pronunciation, and on which aspects. There are usually ample opportunities to integrate work on both segmental and suprasegmental features into lessons which focus on speaking, either through activities which prepare for speaking tasks or through follow-up activities.

Perhaps the easiest aspects to integrate are work on individual sounds, word stress, sentence stress, and various types of linking, as these can be drawn out of many different classroom activities. This is the approach taken in *The Cambridge English Course* by Michael Swan and Catherine Walter, in which phonology is one dimension in a multidimensional syllabus, and the criterion for choosing content is key features of English 'that can give big rewards to the learner in exchange for relatively modest input of practice time' (Teacher's Book 1, page x). Their choice of foci are English as a stress-timed language and linking between words.

Intonation can be a specific focus in accuracy-based activities which show students its importance in indicating attitude in conversation. It is possible to pick out dialogues from textbook material which exemplify the link between stress, intonation, and emotion or attitude, or to build dialogues with students on the board, for example of a 'complaining' transaction between a customer and a shop assistant over faulty goods. Key turns can be highlighted, especially those where there is consistency in stress and intonation, for example: 'This is quite unacceptable'; 'It just isn't good enough', and 'I'll have to take it further', and students asked to analyse the patterns and link them to emotion. Students can then practise in a controlled way before role-playing other situations. This approach has been formalized in *Headway Pronunciation* where supplementary pronunciation materials are linked to

Materials extract 8.F

● **Intonation and sentence stress**

---

5 Showing disbelief

1 | **T.14.5.A.** | Listen to the following dialogues. Who does **not** believe what Sally said? How does the stress and intonation show this?

Where's Sally today?

She said she had a headache.

Why isn't Sally here today?

She said she had a headache.

Notice the stress and intonation. To show disbelief there is a special stress on *said* and the intonation goes **down** like this:

She said she had a headache.

Whereas the intonation in the ordinary type of sentence is like this:

She said she had a headache.

2 Listen again and repeat the replies, paying attention to the intonation.
π—0

3 | **T.14.5.B.** | Now listen to the following dialogues. Mark the dialogues like this* if you think **B** does not believe what he is reporting.

a. **A** Does Judith like her new job?
   B She said she liked it.

b. **A** How was Paul's dinner party?
   B Everyone said they enjoyed it.*

c. **A** Where did Peter get that £10 note?
   B He said he'd found it.

d. **A** Can you remind Helen about my £20?
   B She said that she had already paid you.

e. **A** Why didn't Phil come to the lesson yesterday?
   B He said he was too busy.

f. **A** How's Mandy's diet going?
   B She said she had lost 5 kilos.

g. **A** Has David found my book yet?
   B No, but he said he'd looked everywhere.

h. **A** What's happening between Linda and Tony?
   B I don't know, but she said she wasn't interested in him.
π—0

4 Write six things that people have told you recently, three that you believe and three that you do not believe.

Examples

A woman at work told me that her husband had just been promoted again.

My brother said last night that he hadn't been smoking.

Tell your partner about the things that you have written down in conversations like this. **You should make it clear from your intonation whether or not you believed what you were told.**

(Cunningham and Bowler: *Headway Intermediate Pronunciation*, page 82)

the main coursebook and, for example, give students practice in intonation, as in the activity for showing disbelief in Materials extract 8.F.

Many teachers would say that pronunciation work is one of the most difficult areas for students because awkwardness, inhibition, embarrassment, and fear of losing face tend to come strongly to the fore. Correction of pronunciation errors, therefore, needs to be done in as positive a way as possible.

8.4.6 *Treating error in the classroom*

As we saw in Chapter 1, recent years have seen a debate about the value of error correction in the classroom. This stemmed largely from Krashen's suggestion that, in acquiring a first language, a young child takes little notice of parental correction and that, since adults follow a similar process in acquiring a second or foreign language, correction by the teacher is of dubious value. His first point is easily demonstrated by examples from writing on first language acquisition, for example Derrick (1976) presents this anecdotal conversation:

> She said, *My teacher holded the baby rabbits and we patted them.*
> I asked, *Did you say your teacher held the baby rabbits?*
> She answered, *Yes.*
> I then asked, *What did you say she did?*
> She answered again, *She holded the baby rabbits and we patted them.*
> *Did you say she held them tightly?* I asked.
> No, she answered. *She holded them loosely.*
> (Derrick 1976: 19)

His second point, however, is less easily supported. On the contrary, many adults would claim that feedback on errors is useful and that they are able to process it in productive ways. For example, in my own learning of Swedish, I well remember being told by a Swedish friend of my error in placing the negative particle after the modal auxiliary in a relative clause, as in English. For example:

> She is a woman who can*not* smile.

when the correct position in Swedish is before the auxiliary. It was only after the feedback, understanding of the rule, and sustained effort, that I eventually eradicated the error.

In many foreign language situations, where there is little exposure to English or practice available in the community, error correction is an expected role for the teacher. However, the debate has been useful in raising issues. Allwright (1988) has discussed the confusion that can be created by inconsistency in error correction. He gives a simulated example of classroom talk in which a teacher fails to correct one student, who is known not to make any attempt to use feedback, but corrects another, more careful, student on the same language point:

> T   When's your birthday, Alvaro?
> **Alvaro** Twelfth November
> T   Okay. Now, Santos, when's *your* birthday?
> **Santos** Fourteenth of September
> T   No, Listen: *the* fourteenth. Again …
> (Allwright 1988: 210)

Allwright points out that a number of questions arise from the teacher's disparate treatment of the two students. Do the other students appreciate that Alvaro is careless and that the teacher has decided not to bother correcting him? Do they realize that the teacher is more positive towards Santos and will give useful feedback? Do they realize that 'Okay' did not indicate approval? If the class realize these things, they will understand the different responses of the teacher, though they may not approve of the discrimination displayed. If they do not realize these things, then they might hypothesize a rule from the feedback, for example: 'In dates, the presence of "of" necessitates the use of "the".' The implication of this example is that teachers need not only to think about the effect of correction on the student being corrected, but also its effect on the whole class or group who might process the feedback. A careful policy of error treatment will require consistency in its application. This is far from easy in practice. We will now look at the kinds of decision we need to make to guide our classroom management.

Which errors to correct

This is perhaps the hardest question to answer. It relates in part to a distinction often made between *systematic errors*, which are evidence of a learner's current stage of interlanguage and which are to do with incomplete or faulty knowledge of English, and *mistakes*, which are caused through inability to perform that knowledge in production because of factors to do with carelessness, tiredness, distractions, or difficult circumstances such as talking on a faulty telephone line and having to respond to partly heard messages. The mistakes can probably be self-corrected if the learner's attention is drawn to them. With errors, the teacher must decide whether an indication of error is likely to provide useful feedback which can help the individual and others in the class to progress in their understanding of the language. However, since it has now been shown that, as well as working out rules, learners acquire whole 'chunks' of language which they have not necessarily analysed and for which they may not be able to process feedback, this traditional distinction in how a teacher might respond to mistakes and errors has become blurred.

Another way of dealing with errors is to decide which of them impede communication. *Global errors* cause misunderstanding by the listener while *local errors* tend not to as they relate only to part of what is said. For example, 'They ate smoked worm' is not immediately apparent as 'They ate smoked eel' whereas 'There are long trees on each side of my street' can be easily adjusted in the mind of the listener to 'tall trees'. Again, though, the distinction is not always an easy one to make during the quick interactions of the classroom.

How to get a balance between correction and encouragement

Trainee teachers are usually advised to be sensitive to how insistent they are in correcting an individual publicly in class as embarrassment or anxiety can eliminate any productive outcome. There is always a need to balance negative feedback on errors with positive feedback on the student's attempts to produce the language, and this means consideration of affective factors and knowing 'when to push and when to stop'. Another strategy which reduces tension is to correct another student's errors and return to the original error-maker later in the process.

Students unused to the demands for speaking in public made by the communicative classroom, even if that 'public' is a relatively small number of their peers in groupwork, may be reluctant to speak up through lack of confidence or fear of 'losing face' by making mistakes. One way of providing out-of-class opportunities for error correction is explored by Allan (1991). This is the use of tape journals. Her procedure follows four stages: first, the student records a ten-minute talk, speaking from notes rather than reading a prepared text; then the student listens and tries to note any mistakes, recording comment on these at the end of the tape. Next the teacher listens and notes down errors for the student. These are categorized into pronunciation and syntactic or lexical errors. And then the teacher records comments on a representative sample of these as well as making a personal response to the content of the tape. In this way, the process of error correction becomes far less threatening for the student.

Allan's experiment with this procedure with a class of Japanese university students met with enthusiasm from the students. They were wary of claiming improvement in accuracy but they reported heightened awareness of their errors, reduced hesitancy in delivery over a period of time, and motivation that came from being able to ask the teacher, on tape, about language queries, for example, 'Do you say "I'm very looking forward to"?' Allan points out the limitations of the procedure for large classes, and, as this is planned discourse, its limitations in terms of communication. However, as students build confidence, they may be able to progress from speaking with reduced anxiety in classroom activities which give them planning time to speaking in activities which demand more spontaneous production.

Which strategies to choose for correction

Below is a list of strategies for error correction observed in the classroom style of different teachers during controlled practice:

1 The teacher frowns and says 'No, you don't say that. What do you say? Can anybody help Juan?'

2 The teacher repeats a sentence the student has just said, with rising intonation up to the point of the mistake, and waits for the student to self-correct.
3 The student has just produced a present-tense answer to a past-tense question from the teacher. The teacher repeats the question, stressing the past tense form, and waits for the student to self-correct.
4 The student uses incorrect intonation in a question. The teacher asks the class for an accurate version, then repeats it, asks the class for choral repetition and individual repetition, and finally returns to the original student.
5 The teacher looks puzzled and requests clarification by asking 'What did you say?', which the students recognize as indication of an error. Then the teacher waits for the student to self correct.
6 The teacher moves his or her hand to indicate error, gives the correct version, and asks the student to repeat it.

These examples indicate the range of decisions the teacher has to make in treating error during controlled practice: how to indicate that an error has been made; how to indicate where the error is in what the student has said; whether to give the correct form or prompt self-correction in some way; and whether to involve the rest of the class or not. These decisions will relate to the points raised earlier about whether the student is likely to use the feedback, whether it is a careless mistake, how often the error has been made in that particular class and how many students have been making it, and the confidence or anxiety of the individual student concerned.

Increasingly, research studies provide teachers with insights into the functioning of these different strategies. For example, Nobuyoshi and Ellis (1996) report on a small-scale exploratory study which investigated the effect of using requests for clarification when students produce errors in a form-focused communication activity, rather than making corrections. (A request for clarification can be exemplified by 5 above, while 1 and 6 are correction strategies.) The question for Ellis and Nobuyoshi was whether the use of requests for clarification would push the student to self-correction and thereby to producing more accurate language. They found, in a group of adult learners of English in Tokyo, that some students self-corrected successfully and others did not. Interestingly, they also noted that the former students maintained their improved accuracy on later occasions. This suggests that an important role for the teacher might be to encourage self-correction. It certainly fits with contemporary ideas about building responsibility in learners and reducing dependence on the teacher.

How to respond to error during different activities

In the use of correction techniques a balance is needed between accuracy and fluency, and many handbooks for teachers stress the importance of not impeding or distracting learners' attempts to communicate during fluency activities. Harmer, for example, lists 'teacher intervention' among the character-istics of non-communicative tasks and 'no teacher intervention' among the characteristics of communicative ones (1982: 167). The teacher's notes which accompany many coursebooks often instruct teachers to leave correction until the end in fluency activities. Experienced teachers would apply this 'rule' with discretion however. I remember sitting on the edge of a business English simulation, observing a learner struggle to use a communication strategy to produce the word 'providence' instead of 'provision' and then, as other students took 'providence' up and repeated it frequently, wishing I had used a quick stage-whisper to correct the originator. In general, though, it is useful to have a repertoire of 'after the event' techniques which might include:

– noting down each individual's main errors on separate cards and giving these to them for reflection. If students keep a cumulative record of these cards they can monitor them to see whether some of their errors are gradually being eradicated
– recording the activity (on video or audio cassette) and asking students to listen and see if they can identify and correct their own errors and those of peers
– making a note of 'key' errors, for example, those made by several students or those relating to a recent teaching point, and going through these with the class afterwards
– noting down examples of errors and using these for a game in the next class.

This review of the questions which form the framework of any policy on error treatment, the options that exist for correction strategies, and the factors influencing choices, shows that it is hardly surprising that error correction is considered to be one of the most complex aspects of classroom management, requiring substantial judgement and skill on the part of the teacher. For learners, classroom error correction is part of a wider process of recognizing and understanding their errors and then having opportunities to try and try again in speaking activities.

8.4.7 *Managing classroom interaction*

Speaking activities are probably the most demanding for students and teachers in terms of the affective factors involved. Trying to produce language in front of other students can generate high levels of anxiety. Students may feel that they are presenting themselves at a much lower level of cognitive ability than they really possess; they may have a natural anxiety about being incompre-hensible; they may have cultural inhibitions about losing face, or they may simply be shy personalities who do not speak very much in their first language. It is therefore a major responsibility for the teacher to create a reassuring classroom environment in which students are prepared to take risks and experiment with the language.

Classroom management is also a key issue given the complex structure of some communication activities. In Chapter 2 (Materials extract 2.D) we saw an example of a jigsaw task which combined reading, note-taking, reporting in groups, and discussion in two phases. Analysis of teacher roles during these phases showed the need for careful direction, organization, and monitoring. Role-play and simulation also require precise structuring at the planning stage as they integrate a number of things: input, sometimes from a number of sources both written and spoken; preparatory activities to do with the information content of the role-play, and others to do with its language demands, and various interactions such as pairwork leading into groupwork and followed by whole-class discussion. And all of this will need to be phased throughout one or several lessons.

Looking at the complexity of jigsaw tasks and simulations raises the question of learner training for this kind of methodology. The key principle is gradual introduction of more complex tasks, beginning with simple pairwork activities and building through intermediate stages of complexity to more ambitious activities. This may be particularly important with secondary-school students who are unaccustomed to moving around in the classroom, and who may be more difficult to control than motivated adults who are learning English from choice. It also means developing clear classroom procedures. Those for pairwork might involve:

- giving a careful explanation of what is needed, with a teacher demonstration if appropriate
- the teacher asking the class to recap, or getting two students to try the activity out as an example
- monitoring as soon as the pairwork starts in order to check that each pair is 'on task' and understands what to do.

Even so-called 'simple' pairwork needs consideration, as they are many factors at work beneath the surface of the class which will affect its success, especially with adults who have moved away from the school experience of having to accommodate to other people in the close quarters of a classroom. Age, gender, and personality can all play a part in making pairwork a difficult experience and add to the natural tension of trying to make oneself understood. Moving pairs around is one answer if the teacher chooses the pairs rather than the students being self-selecting, but it means that the teacher needs to keep an eye on the factors listed above. A particularly sensitive issue is the feeling of disappointment or irritation that can ensue from the member of a pair who has high proficiency in English and who feels that little is learned from a less able partner's input or feedback. To overcome this problem, the teacher may need to talk explicitly about the value of pairwork in a communicative classroom as compared with methodologies which adult students may have experienced earlier in their learning careers. The teacher also needs to confront the issues that that can arise, and suggest how mixing and matching students might be one way to resolve them.

Similar issues arise in the use of groupwork, and particular difficulty can be experienced when students come from an educational setting in which a competitive or individualistic goal structure is the norm and are not familiar with working cooperatively. The implications, as with pairwork, are for gradual and patient training and for careful decision-making on the practical details. These would include:

- The ideal size of a group for a particular activity, and whether there is value, in some information-gap or other problem-solving tasks, in using initial pairwork followed by two pairs interacting in a group of four.
- The best way of selecting group members, and whether the teacher should be the one to do this in order to achieve a constructive mix. This may certainly be the best initial procedure until students begin to feel comfortable with groupwork and are better able to see the value of achieving a mix through self-selection. Alternatively, there may be occasions when a more random selection is needed and the teacher can use various devices for grouping students.
- The length of time that groups should keep the same composition. There are arguments for keeping a group together for a period of time in order for the members to achieve a cohesiveness which will facilitate their interaction. However, this does not preclude occasional one-off changes in group composition for some activities.
- How to cope when groups finish an activity at different times. This may involve getting the groups that finish early to rehearse reporting to each other, or having extra activities ready which relate to the topic. The situation is often helped by setting a time-limit in the first place.

The decisions will be informed by the particular nature of any class. For example, in a multilingual class of adults, there is clearly value in students being exposed to a variety of accents and interlanguage features, especially if they are learning English in order to communicate with other speakers from a variety of language backgrounds.

8.5 Conclusion

This chapter has set out to demonstrate that, in order to design a useful methodology for developing speaking skills, we need insights about the nature of spoken discourse and the linguistic, cognitive, affective, and socio-cultural demands that it makes on English language learners. Only then will we be able to design or select appropriate classroom activities and procedures for feedback which will help our learners both to understand how English conversation works and to practise the skills needed to participate effectively.

We can also be instrumental in developing further insights for ourselves through experimenting with different activities, recording and analysing what students actually do. Given the challenge that communicative activities pose to students, and the challenge they pose for teachers' management skills, it would be useful to discover what contributions different types of activity can make to the speaking development of a particular group of learners.

Discussion topics and projects

1 What role does the teaching of pronunciation play in your classroom? How do you deal with the phonological aspects of English with different levels of student? How do you integrate pronunciation teaching with other elements in the curriculum?

2 Record a group of students performing a communicative activity. Listen to the recording and try to decide on the following:
   (a) To what extent does the activity encourage or oblige participation from all of the students?
   (b) What examples can you find of conversational adjustments as students try to negotiate meaning, for example, asking for and giving clarification, repetition, further explanation through paraphrasing?
   (c) What examples can you find of students correcting each other?
   (d) How would you comment on the general level of accuracy in the students' language?
   (e) If the activity had a focus on some area of grammar or use of vocabulary, to what extent did this appear in the students' language?

   When you have considered these points, decide whether you think it was an activity worth doing, and why. Would you change anything in a re-run of it?

3 Give your students the task of preparing short talks which they will present to the whole class. Record some of these. What criteria would you use to assess the students' performance? When you have worked out a set of criteria, apply them to the recordings.

4 What are the advantages of using visual aids to promote speaking practice?
   (a) Review a textbook which you are currently using and note down the variety of ways in which visuals are used.
   (b) Collect a set of visuals, for example, pictures from magazines or photo-graphs, and design an activity which exploits them.

5 Review the list of skills and set of questions below and use them to formulate a list of possible aims for the speaking component of a coursebook. Then look at a contemporary coursebook for intermediate students and review the extent to which it tries to incorporate your set of aims.

> In summary then, successful oral communication involves developing:
> - the ability to articulate phonological features of the language comprehensibly;
> - mastery of stress, rhythm, intonation patterns;
> - an acceptable degree of fluency;
> - transactional and interpersonal skills;
> - skills in taking short and long speaking turns;
> - skills in the management of interaction;
> - skills in negotiating meaning;
> - conversational listening skills (successful conversations require good listeners as well as good speakers);
> - skills in knowing about and negotiating purposes for conversations;
> - using appropriate conversational formulae and fillers.
> (Nunan 1989a: 32)

> Designing such a program begins with the preparation of goals, samples of which are:
> - How to use conversation for both transactional and interactional purposes
> - How to produce both short and long turns in conversation
> - Strategies for managing turn-taking in conversation, including taking a turn, holding a turn, and relinquishing a turn
> - Strategies for opening and closing conversations
> - How to initiate and respond to talk on a broad range of topics, and how to develop and maintain talk on these topics
> - How to use both a casual style of speaking and a neutral or more formal style
> - How to use conversation in different social settings and for different kinds of social encounters, such as on the telephone, at informal and formal social gatherings
> - Strategies for repairing trouble spots in conversation, including communication breakdown and comprehension problems
> - How to maintain fluency in conversation, through avoiding excessive pausing, breakdowns, and errors of grammar or pronunciation
> - How to produce talk in a conversational mode, using a conversational register and syntax
> - How to use conversational fillers and small talk
> - How to use conversational routines
> (Richards 1990: 79, 81)

Further reading

Avery, P. and **S. Ehrlich.** 1992. *Teaching American English Pronunciation.* Oxford: Oxford University Press.

The first part of this book relates specifically to North American English and gives an illustrated description of its sound system. The rest of the book, however, is relevant to a much wider audience of teachers. Part Two provides ideas for how to help learners with pronunciation problems, and Part Three moves into classroom techniques for pronunciation work.

Bygate, M. 1987. *Speaking.* Oxford: Oxford University Press.

This book is divided into three sections. The first section looks at what exactly is involved in speaking a foreign language competently. The second section reviews and evaluates typical classroom activities, and the third section suggests small-scale investigations into the topic which teachers can carry out in their own classrooms.

Lynch, T. 1996. *Communication in the Language Classroom.* Oxford: Oxford University Press.

Lynch begins by discussing the insights available to teachers from research into the nature of interaction, and the characteristics which need to be taken into account when designing communicative activities. He goes on to suggest ways in which teachers can create opportunities for interaction in the classroom in the teaching of speaking, listening, reading, and writing.

Malamah-Thomas, A. 1987. *Classroom Interaction.* Oxford: Oxford University Press.

This book sets out to explore the classroom as a social setting, and the encounters that take place in it. The first section deals with concepts of interaction and communication, and of teacher and learner roles. The second section looks critically at schemes which have been designed to analyse classroom interaction and at teaching approaches which have considered the learner's participation in the classroom. The third section suggests ways in which teachers can explore interaction in their own classrooms.

Nolasco, R. and **L. Arthur.** 1987. *Conversation.* Oxford: Oxford University Press.

The introduction to this book sets up a framework for designing conversation activities which can accompany a coursebook. The rest of the book consists of four sets of activities which have the following aims: to build confidence through controlled practice; to build awareness of how conversation works; to develop fluency; and to equip students with tools for assessing their own performance.

9 WRITING

'First I write one sentence: Then I write another. That's how I write. And so I go on. But I have a feeling writing ought to be like running through a field.'
LYTTON STRACHEY

1 What are the features of the contemporary writing classroom?

2 What do we know about the process of writing?

3 What are the characteristics of skilled and unskilled writers?

4 How can we take a process approach to writing?

5 How can we encourage learners in successful writing strategies?

6 How can we analyse and describe the structure of written texts?

7 How can we help learners to build awareness of discourse organization?

8 How can we help students to develop crafting skills?

9 How can we help students to appreciate criteria for an effective text?

Introductory task

In the transcript below, the teacher has tried to put into practice principles derived from insights into the writing process which research has offered us in recent years. What principles do you think underlie her approach?

Susanne   My problem here is … I want to say … I want to write about the characters and how they are … how they act … together …

Teacher   The way they interact … yes …

Susanne	Interact … yes, so that's the plot, isn't it? But also, it's the theme, I think. I'm not sure how I should start …
Teacher	Well, what's the most important thing about the play to you?
Susanne	How he shows the middle class people … they are just super—superficial [**Teacher** Yes] … superficial … and they don't care about the working class …
Ariane	[*who is listening in*] The bourgeoisie … they are hypocrites … n'est ce pas?
Teacher	Yes, we can use the French word … bourgeoisie … Well, why not put that first and then go on to explain how he does this, by presenting a particular family …
Susanne	So, this bit here [*reads*] 'The Birlings are a middle class family …' up to here … yes, I think so … this can follow?
Teacher	Let's look at it … [*reads*] 'Priestley shows how they …' you can say 'misuse' here … 'their power.' Yes, that's very clear. You've got a couple of wrong spellings here. I'll underline them quickly and you can look at them later. Don't bother till you've finished …
Susanne	So what about this bit … ?
Teacher	What does this say … ? I can't read it …
Susanne	[*reads*] 'Stone … a small stone … '
Teacher	Ah, you mean a pebble … Oh, that's very good, we can talk about throwing a pebble into a pool … it describes it very well.
Susanne	You see … what happens … the story … it's how when you throw a st– pebble? … pebble in the water … you get waves going out …
Teacher	Yes, ripples … [*demonstrates*] [**Susanne** Yes] ripples spreading …
Susanne	So the inspector shows the family how …

9.1 Introduction: a contemporary writing classroom

In the 1990s, methodology for the teaching of writing in ELT classrooms made dramatic departures from traditional approaches. At least in theory. In practice it is difficult to assess the extent to which teachers, set about by pressures of time and assessment, have been able to incorporate recent ideas into their pedagogy, but the ideas are available. The transcript in the Introductory task is of a conference between the two students and their teacher, and is typical of a writing workshop. Imagine the classroom from which the sample of conversation is taken. There are twenty or so students in it, their ages ranging from 18 to 40, of mixed nationalities and language backgrounds, at an intermediate level, motivated, attending several classes a week at a UK language school. There is one writing class a week: here the students are preparing for public examinations involving composition writing, and many of them are anxious. The students are grouped in various ways around the classroom: some pairs working together, a group here and there, some working individually. There are silent periods, and periods when there is a low hum of discussion as students exchange their ideas for writing, read out parts of their drafts, and comment on each other's work. There is movement in the room as students consult colleagues, the teacher, and dictionaries, and as they share correction fluid, highlighter pens, erasers, scissors, and glue in drafting and rewriting their work. The teacher moves around the classroom, monitoring, supporting, and sitting down in conferences with students. Earlier there was a phase of work with the whole class in which the teacher elicited ideas from the students about writing a review of the play they had been reading, *An Inspector Calls* by J. B. Priestley. Now the organization is more flexible and the class has more the nature of a workshop.

The focus of the conference between the teacher, Susanne, and Ariane is Susanne's draft, and the extract serves to show significant aspects of the teacher's approach to writing. First, the students are actually involved in the process of writing in class. They are not only discussing model texts or practising language points (both features of traditional writing classes) but they are engaged in the composing experience itself. In other words, they are learning to write through writing. This is not as obvious a point as it might seem. As a result of various pressures of time and the need to cover the syllabus, writing is often relegated to homework and takes place in unsupported conditions of learning. The danger in these circumstances is that poorer writers struggle alone and the experience confirms them in their perception of themselves as failing writers. And better writers miss valuable opportunities for improvement through discussion, collaboration, and feedback. Susanne is struggling with the composing process in the workshop, but with the support of colleagues and the teacher.

Second, the reason that Susanne is able to experience this is that the task gives her that chance: it requires her to engage in the creation of a contextualized piece of communication, a review. Activities of a more controlled kind, on sentence structure, or connectives, or paragraph development, ideally take place within the context of writing a whole text. Even with elementary students it is possible to set up the writing of whole texts such as short descriptions, diary entries, and postcards. It is much easier to focus on getting forms right within the framework of communicating messages.

Third, Susanne has got away from the idea that writing is something that begins and ends as it is put down on the page for the first time, and with the expectation that the teacher will do the work of improving it during the marking process. She has learned, in ways that she reported she had not fully appreciated before, that writing is a process over which she can exercise control. She can plan, draft, read, revise, and edit for accuracy.

Fourth, writing and conferencing in class allows for what Zamel calls 'a dynamic teaching/learning relationship between writers and their readers' (1983: 165). Other students and the teacher can be readers: they can question, prompt, support, and provide ideas and language which help the writer to be clear, organized, and accessible to readers.

Finally, the main focus of this conference is on the ideas Susanne wants to express and on ways of organizing them. She is learning to make sure that her ideas are well-organized before turning to spelling, punctuation, and accuracy in grammar. Successive research studies have shown that this is the strategy of the successful writer. Notice, too, that the help with language from the teacher and Ariane derives naturally from a focus on meaning, on what she is trying to say. Susanne provides her own context for learning the vocabulary 'interact', 'misuse', and 'pebble' that she needs, and because her immediate needs are supplied she is very quick to pick them up.

These points arising from the transcript reflect the ways in which ideas about writing pedagogy have been influenced by research into the writing process.

9.2 What do we know about the process of writing?

The process view of writing sees it as thinking, as discovery. Writing is the result of employing strategies to manage the composing process, which is one of gradually developing a text. It involves a number of activities: setting goals, generating ideas, organizing information, selecting appropriate language, making a draft, reading and reviewing it, then revising and editing. It is a complex process which is neither easy nor spontaneous for many second language writers. As Shaughnessy puts it: 'One of the most important facts about the composing process that seems to get hidden from students is that the process that creates precision is itself messy' (1977: 222).

9.2.1 *What strategies do skilled writers use as they compose?*

It was in the 1970s that interest developed in what second language writers actually do as they write, motivated largely by a belief that if we wish to influence and improve the outcomes of writing for our learners, then we need to understand how a piece of writing comes into being. In fact, a piece of writing is the outcome of a set of complicated cognitive operations. A major concern of researchers into second language writing has been to identify these mental operations, and a number of research methods have been used to do this: interviews, observation, audio and video recording, and making *protocols* as writers 'think aloud' during composing. Two studies will serve as examples of this research and its outcomes.

Zamel (1983) made a study of the composing processes of six advanced ESL students, participants in her own optional college writing class. She observed them as they prepared formal papers requiring expository writing. In setting out her research questions, she places herself in a tradition of process-centred studies with similar aims (for example Emig 1971; Perl 1979; Faigley and Witte 1981):

> How do writers write? How do their ideas seem to get generated? What happens to these ideas after they are recorded/To what extent do these writers attend to the development and clarification of these ideas? To what extent and at what point during the process do they deal with more mechanical matters?
> (Zamel 1983: 169)

A number of findings emerged:

– Planning was not a single phase but a thinking activity to which writers returned again and again during composing.
– These writers had individual strategies for 'getting into' writing. Some wrote notes or lists or diagrams, and all of the students spent a good deal of time thinking at the outset, but two of the best writers wrote nothing down until they started the essay.
– The writing process was recursive and generative, with students re-reading their work, assessing it, reacting, and moving on. There was an interesting distinction between the poorer writers who seemed to focus on re-reading only smaller chunks of discourse and better writers who sometimes re-read whole paragraphs.
– Revising took place throughout the process and generally involved considerable changes: for example, composing something new, deleting sentences, and shifting paragraphs around and sometimes eliminating them.

– All of the writers paid attention to surface-level features but the better writers dealt with these at the end of the process. It was the poorer writers who spent time throughout the process changing words and phrases.
– Linguistic problems seemed to concern the writers least. The better writers used strategies such as leaving a blank or writing down a word in their first language in order not to be distracted as they developed ideas.
– Once ideas had been written down and developed, the writers began to edit for surface-level features such as accuracy in grammar, word-choice, spelling, and punctuation.

These findings have been supported by many other studies. One by Raimes (1985) for example, supported Zamel's observations on the role of language in the composing process. She suggested that with students who exhibit lack of competence in writing, poor composing competence can be a greater factor in this than poor language competence. She used think-aloud protocols to investigate the writing process and made the following comment on experienced writers:

> They consider purpose and audience. They consult their own background knowledge. They let ideas incubate. They plan. As they write, they read back over what they have written. Contrary to what many textbooks advise, writers do not follow a neat sequence of planning, organising, writing and then revising. For while a writer's product—the finished essay, story or novel—is presented in lines, the process that produces it is not linear at all.
> (Raimes 1985: 229)

As this summary implies, the findings, and those of other studies, suggested that a teaching methodology which tries to guide students into a linear sequence of planning, drafting, and revising, might be mistaken. It needs to take into account both the general recursiveness of the process and the individual strategies of writers.

However, before considering implications for teaching, something more needs to be said about the research methodology through which we have gained insights. Raimes (ibid.) used think-aloud protocols in her study. In this method the researcher instructs writers to report on anything they are thinking while performing the task, usually in line with a set of simple guidelines and often with encouragement from an observer in the early stages. The recorded protocol, which may vary in length from a relatively short time to many hours, is then transcribed and coded in some way. For example, the researcher may focus on the various strategies used by the writer to overcome vocabulary problems (for example, leaving a gap in the text, or writing a word in the margin in the first language) and mark each one with a different code.

This methodology has come under fire on a number of counts (Cooper and Holtzman 1983; Dobrin 1994). First, it has been suggested that people are not fully conscious of their own cognitive processes as these are complex and diffuse and involve visual as well as verbal elements. Another criticism is that trying to report on cognitive processes affects the behaviour of the writer and, in fact, distorts them. It is also claimed that protocols are incomplete. They provide only 'traces' from the mind and do not yield enough data from which to infer cognitive processes. However, as is to be expected, researchers using protocol methods, for example Hayes and Flower (1983), have produced counter-arguments: that protocols provide direct evidence from the writer's mind; that they can provide very rich data and allow us to explore many possibilities; and that they can detect processes that are invisible when using other methods. It is undoubtedly the case that protocol analysis has uncovered a great deal that is of interest to teachers and, while we need further insights into how strategies might vary across a range of tasks, we have substantial evidence to suggest that writers become involved in a number of activities during the writing process.

9.2.2 *What activities characterize the writing process?*

Planning

First, good writers concentrate on the overall meaning and organization of a text, and engage in planning activities. This will involve thinking about the purpose of the writing, for example, a letter of complaint about poor service, or a letter to inform friends about a daughter's wedding. The particular purpose implies an organization for the writing and a style appropriate for the readers. The letter of complaint would follow formal conventions of layout and be in a serious disapprobatory style. The letter to friends would be informal, expressive, probably colloquial, and a mixture of description and comment.

The amount of planning will vary, therefore, in relation to the type of writing task, from relatively spontaneous writing based on a quick mental plan, to something carefully worked out beforehand in notes. However, it will also differ according to the preferred style of the individual writer, and considerable variation has been observed here. Some learners who appear to take very little time for thinking before starting to write nevertheless produce effective writing. They may, instead, pause frequently to reflect during writing. Flower and Hayes (1981) contributed to our understanding of planning when they suggested that it goes on at many levels and throughout the process of composing. One level is that of the sentence, as writers turn the overall plan into text and draft out their ideas in English. But good writers also work episodically to set goals which structure the next unit of writing. This is often what they are doing during the 'pregnant pauses' in composing. Any initial planning before writing is therefore subject to review at any point as the writer critically evaluates the emerging text and thinks of new ideas and new ways to organize and express them. Widdowson points to this tendency when he says: 'In writing one so frequently arrives at a destination not originally envisaged, by a route not yet planned for in the original itinerary' (1983: 41). If, indeed, episodic planning allows for an interplay between writing and thinking, a methodology which encourages students to plan in detail before writing and to keep to that plan, is naïve and possibly counter-productive. A more flexible approach is required.

Revising

Typically, as we have seen, a good writer proceeds through alternating phases of writing and reflection. During reflection, writers may re-read the sentences on the page or look back at their original plan and think about how to express the next set of ideas. After writing part of the draft, they may then review the text and ask themselves questions such as: 'Is my argument expressed through a clear set of points or does my reader have to make conceptual leaps in order to follow me?'; 'Are any sections repetitious and can they be missed out?', and 'Do I need to rearrange any sentences?' In this way, additions, deletions, and rearrangements can be made in order to improve the writing. It is noteworthy that all of these questions are to do with meaning and organization. Studies by Perl (1979) and Sommers (1980) showed that less experienced writers were constantly concerned with grammar and correctness and this distracted them from thinking about clarity of ideas and organization.

Seminal work was carried out in this area by Faigley and Witte (1981). They concluded from the findings of two studies that expert writers revise in different ways from inexperienced writers, but also in different ways from each other:

> One expert writer ... made almost no revisions; another started with an almost stream-of-consciousness text that she then converted to an organized essay in the second draft; another limited his major revisions to a single long insert; and another revised mostly by pruning.
> (Faigley and Witte 1981: 110)

They pointed out that the extent and nature of revision depends not only on the writer's skill but also on the purpose of the writing, the genre, the level of formality required, and the degree of familiarity with the readers, the subject, or the type of writing task. These factors can easily be appreciated if we compare writing a letter of complaint to an unknown person for the first time with a regular letter containing news to friends overseas. The first would probably receive rather more careful revision than the second. It is therefore not the amount of revision that is significant but its effect in making improvements, and this depends on the degree to which the revisions help the writing to express the writer's goals clearly, to fit the genre, and be at the appropriate level of formality. Any classroom activities devised to encourage effective revision will need to help student writers in English to see how it relates to all aspects of writing.

Producing 'reader-based' prose

A third characteristic of successful writers is that they are aware of their readers and seek to produce 'reader-based' prose (Flower and Hayes 1980). In other words, they think about what the reader needs to know, how to make information clear and accessible, and what is an appropriate style (for example, formal, friendly, or persuasive). Most writing undertaken in the real world has a particular readership in view: a friend, a tutor, or an official of some kind. It is knowledge of that readership which provides a context for the writing and which influences the selection of content and style. For example, a description of a person will differ in content and style according to whether it is of a literary character in an academic essay, of a wanted person in a police bulletin, of a pop-singer in a teenage magazine, or of a new boyfriend in a letter to parents. In this sense writing is social and interactive in nature as the writer conducts a 'dialogue' with a putative reader, anticipating the responses and selecting appropriate information, ideas, and expressions to influence those responses. Good writers are sensitive to the audience of their writing.

9.3 What are the implications of a process approach?

The issues that arise for teachers from insights into what makes a successful writer are whether we can teach strategies for planning, revising, and editing, and whether we can help students develop a sense of audience. A process approach tries to provide useful support for student writers. The nature of the support will depend on the kind of learners, for example their ages, backgrounds, and needs for writing in English. It could be argued that adult learners should already have developed effective writing strategies in their first language. However, it may well be the case that students have not received the necessary support in their first language and will benefit from a process approach in the English language classroom, whatever their age. The primary aim of the process approach, therefore, is to help students to gain greater control over the cognitive strategies involved in composing. This suggests a number of principles for the teacher to incorporate into the teaching of writing.

9.3.1 *Helping students to generate ideas*

One of the hardest tasks in writing is getting started. In academic writing, when tutors set assignments, a first step in pedagogy could be to encourage students to work in pairs and arrive at an understanding of the task by questioning and clarifying the meaning of key expressions and selecting the information needed to fulfil the task. In the general EFL classroom, when tasks are set for practice purposes, the teacher has the responsibility of helping students get their ideas together. White and Arndt (1991) make a useful distinction between guided techniques in which prompts such as questions are used, and unguided techniques in which students generate ideas by themselves. Materials extract 9.A is an example of a guided technique. Students are guided through a possible list of contents for a biography and select those they are prepared to talk about to a partner, who will write the biography. The next step is note-making on the topics preparatory to writing the first draft.

A popular unguided technique is brainstorming, which is shown in Materials extract 9.B. Both 9.A and 9.B demonstrate the help that teachers can give as students think out a topic, discover a purpose, and decide on a perspective in the early stages of writing. Notice that these activities show how writing can be stimulated by students working interactively. Such interaction has the value of providing student writers with an audience on whom to test out the selection of content. However, we need to keep in mind the solitary nature of most writing and move students gradually towards the independent position of a writer engaged in a real writing task.

9.3.2 *Providing practice in planning*

If teaching methodology is to support planning, then classroom activities need to guide students in finding their own effective planning processes. Given that we know successful writers plan their writing in very different ways, this needs great care. Many teachers now take the view that the best help they can give is to provide students with ideas for planning in the early stages and to let them take up those which they find individually useful and attractive. At the same time, it is essential to communicate the flexible nature of plans, which ideally should change and be adjusted as the writing progresses and generates alternative ideas and structures.

Materials extract 9.A

WRITING FOR EACH OTHER

1 In this project, you are going to find out about another learner and write a profile of them in about 200 words for everyone else to read. First find a partner to work with on this project.

2 Look through this list of possible contents for your biography. Which words in the list mean *important*?

> *Possible contents of your biography*
> name
> profession
> marital status
> current living arrangements
> crucial events in your life
> key influences in your life (childhood and adult)
> your major achievements
> regrets or frustrations in your life
> unfulfilled ambitions
> your main hopes/goals for the future
> leisure activities
> your attitudes to your family, relationships, work or other issues
> how other people see you

Together, add any other possible topics to the list.

3 Decide which of the topics (about five or six) you would be prepared to talk about, or would like someone to write about you.

Now tell your partner about the topics you have chosen. They should listen and write brief notes, like this:

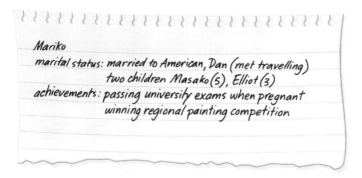

> Mariko
> marital status: married to American, Dan (met travelling)
>   two children Masako (5), Elliot (3)
> achievements: passing university exams when pregnant
>   winning regional painting competition

(Gairns and Redman: *True to Life Upper Intermediate* Class Book, page 43)

Materials extract 9.B

1.3 Making mind maps

Making a mind map is a strategy for note-making before writing; in other words, scribbling down ideas about the topic and developing those ideas as the mind makes associations. The topic used for demonstration below is the festival of Christmas, which would be appropriate to certain groups of students. However, the strategy can be used to explore almost any topic.

LEVEL	**Intermediate to advanced**
TOPIC	**A festival**
PREPARATION	This activity is best carried out quite simply with blackboard and chalk so that students grasp the idea of drawing a mind map as a spontaneous pre-writing activity.
IN CLASS	1 Ask students to close their eyes and think of Christmas. They should jot down all the things associated with Christmas that come into their minds. Set a definite time limit (one or two minutes). Let them jot down things in their first language if they do not know the English words. They can then start sharing what they have jotted down. As they listen to other students making suggestions and to your explanations and corrections, they will learn the English words for the ideas which they have tried to jot down. This is an invaluable way in which to learn vocabulary.

2 Elicit ideas from the students as they suggest things, and make a collective mind map on the blackboard as the ideas are suggested, so that they can see how you draw out aspects of the topic and subgroup items. The reasoning behind mind maps is that we do not think in an ordered or linear way, but rather explore a topic by moving between its various aspects. The map may look something like this when it is under way, but elements would be added in random fashion:

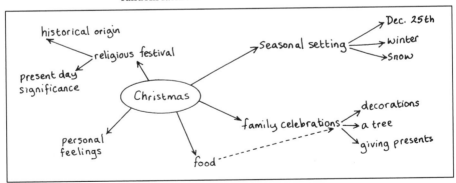

Branches can be drawn and added as students suggest new ideas or add ideas to already established aspects. The end result is a map with a number of subtopics or aspects radiating from the central topic and with further points added to these. Where there are links (Christmas food is, in one sense, an aspect of family celebrations), a line can be drawn associating them.

(Hedge: *Writing*, page 30)

The 'brainstorming' in Materials extract 9.B is an example of one such possible technique. This generates ideas through individual reflection: these are scribbled down and developed as the mind makes associations. In the task in Materials extract 9.B students are taken through two further steps: elicitation by the teacher of points for content so that ideas are shared and exchanged, then collation of some of those on the blackboard, in the form of a mind map. The next step is to ask students to work in pairs to decide on a logical sequence of information for the description. The advantage of mind maps as a planning strategy, particularly for descriptions, is that all aspects of a topic can be easily seen in relation to each other and possible links between sections of the composition suggest themselves. This can assist with advance planning of the overall text.

Writing materials now seek ways of helping students to organize their ideas: through planning in groups, guided note-making, strategic questions by the teacher, organizing points in a hierarchy of importance for presentation, highlighting essential information, sequencing given information, and sorting and matching ideas. All of these techniques give initial support for what will eventually be a process undertaken individually.

9.3.3 *Contextualizing tasks to develop a sense of audience*

Helping student writers to develop a sense of audience is another important task. With less mature writers, who may not have developed a sense of audience in writing in their first language, we can create audiences and build up awareness of the reader. For example, sometimes students can write for real audiences outside school such as local English-speaking organizations or individuals. The school can also provide an audience with its population of English language learners; for example, class magazines can be published for the wider school community. Within the classroom it is possible for the teacher to set up pairwork in which one student's writing forms the basis for a response from the other student in the pair; for example, both students write a letter of invitation. At this stage they can help each other plan and draft. If their discussion is in English, this constitutes natural fluency practice. The students then exchange the letters and write replies, accepting or declining the invitation. Another typical task is the exchange of letters to an 'agony aunt' in a magazine and replies offering solutions. The principle involved in these letter exchanges is that of task dependency as the success of the exchange depends on the clarity of the letters to their readers: this reflects the interaction of reading and writing in real life.

As students work on writing tasks it is important that they ask themselves who they are writing for and keep that audience in mind as they write.

Materials extract 9.C provides a useful checklist of questions for the student writer. This is just the beginning of the task for a writer, who would also use a sense of audience to decide in what order to present the information.

Materials extract 9.C

Whatever your purpose, you must decide what information you have about your audience that is relevant to your purpose and take that information into account as you write. The following questions, to be asked each time you choose a purpose and an audience for your writing, will help you focus on that audience and the choices you need to make in order to write for that audience.

Who is your audience?

1 For what age group are you writing (children, adolescents, young adults, middle-aged adults, older adults)?

2 For what socioeconomic group are you writing (poor people, middle class people, upper class people)?

3 How much education does your audience have (elementary, high school, college, postgraduate)?

4 How much knowledge about your subject can you assume your audience has (none, very basic, above average, very thorough)?

5 What very important information must you give your audience before they can begin to think about your position in this argument (if your purpose is to convince)?

6 What reasons, examples, or illustrations will you give to support your ideas?

7 What arguments may your audience give to counter your reasons?

8 What values related to this topic do you share with your audience?

9 What arguments can you make for your position that support the values that you and your audience have in common?

10 What arguments can you make for your position that support values that your audience has, but that are not your values?

After you have decided your purpose, chosen a particular audience in mind, analyzed your audience, and determined the relevant information about your audience that you must consider as you write, you will next make a plan for your writing.

(Donahue Latulippe: *Writing as a Personal Product*, pages 40–1)

9.3.4 *Encouraging students in revision strategies*

Many teachers now hold the view that the traditional procedure of taking work in, marking it, and returning it to students when the writing experience is no longer fresh in their minds, has serious disadvantages. This is especially the case if little work is done in class on revising as it gives students the impression that the teacher is primarily responsible for improving the quality of their written work. A variety of procedures are now used to support revision, and these need to be evaluated against what we know of how good writers go about the process.

A popular procedure is *conferencing*, as demonstrated in the transcript in the Introductory task to this chapter. As the class writes, the teacher can talk with individual students about work in progress. Through careful questioning, the teacher can support a student writer in getting ideas together, organizing them, and finding appropriate language. Keh (1990) reports positive student feedback on conferencing. She suggests an elicitation procedure with focusing questions such as 'Who are you writing to?' and 'How have you organized your points?'

Conferencing is a useful technique during the earlier stages of composition when writers are still thinking about content and organization. A popular device at a slightly later stage is the use of a checklist. This example in Materials extract 9.D is for individual use. Notice that these questions focus on the overall content and organization, and its appropriateness to purpose and audience. Other types of checklist can be used when students exchange drafts for comment and can focus on a recent teaching point. For example, a checklist on paragraphing could contain the questions:

– Does the composition divide naturally into several parts?
– Do the paragraphs reflect those parts?
– Does each paragraph have a topic sentence with a main idea?
– Does each paragraph have an effective concluding sentence?

Reformulation is a useful procedure when students have produced a first draft and are moving on to look at more local possibilities for improvement. It has the particular advantage that it provides students with opportunities to notice any differences between the target model and their own production (see Chapter 5) and thus to acquire language forms. Reformulation (Allwright 1988) proceeds through the following stages:

1 All the students carry out a guided writing task. The task is guided to ensure that the content and organization of their writing is similar overall. Indeed, collaborative work could be used at the planning stage.
2 Each student writes a first draft and hands it to the teacher.

Materials extract 9.D

1 First answer these questions about your *audience*:
   Who is your audience? What interest do they have in this subject? What do they already know about this subject?

2 Then answer these questions about your *purpose*:
   What did you want to accomplish by writing this paper? To entertain your audience? To educate them? To inspire them to do something? To help them understand something new? To help them see something familiar from a new point of view? To change their minds about something?

3 Next write the *main idea* of your draft in a complete sentence. Ask yourself these questions:
   Is the main idea stated somewhere near the beginning of the paper? If not, would the paper be more effective if you did state the main idea? No matter where the main idea appears in your draft (or even if it is only implied), is the main idea clear to *you*? Do you think it is clear to your audience?

4 Considering the audience you are writing for and your purpose, analyze the *development* of your paper:
   a Support material: type and amount
   Do you need to develop any ideas more fully? Do you need to be more specific or concrete in your explanations? How would you answer them now? Did you include all the information you needed to discuss your topic as fully as you wanted? Should you add anything to your discussion?
   b Support material: relevance
   Did you give your readers enough background information for them to understand not only your ideas but also the relevance of your discussion for them? Is there any irrelevant information, information the audience either already knows or does not need to know to understand your explanations? Should you delete any sections of your discussion?
   Have you said anything your reader is likely to object to? Did you answer those anticipated objections? Have you said anything your reader may not understand?
   c Support material: arrangement
   Does your discussion move smoothly and logically from one idea to the next? Is each new idea explained sufficiently before you move on to the next one? Are the ideas clearly linked together? Do you lead your readers step by step to understand your ideas? Should you rearrange any sections of your paper?

5 Analyze your *conclusion*:
   Does the conclusion develop logically from what you have written? Do you think it gives the reader the feeling that you have said everything you intended to say about your subject?

(Leki: *Academic Writing: Techniques and Tasks*, page 132)

3 The teacher 'marks' the work by indicating problems by means of underlining or highlighting.
4 The teacher chooses one student's essay and reformulates it, following the ideas closely but improving the expression in terms of accuracy and appropriacy.
5 The original and the reformulation are copied so that students can compare them. In well-resourced institutions photocopying will be possible, but it is also possible for sections of the composition, at least, to be written on the board.
6 The class works in pairs and groups, identifying the changes in the reformulation and discussing the reasons for them. This task can be done in the first or second language.
7 The teacher, with the class, discusses the changes and gives a rationale, inviting comments and questions.
8 Students then go through their own first drafts and revise them in the light of any useful information they have gained.

My experience has been that, in early attempts to make use of reformulation, students often over-correct their own work, but that after several opportunities to practise they can be encouraged to take a more measured approach and to pick up only those things of most use for their own writing. The advantage of reformulation is that it allows discussion of such aspects as how ideas are developed, how a range of structures, vocabulary, or connecting devices can be used, and how the style needs to be appropriate to the readers.

The essential element in the techniques described above—conferencing, revisions with the help of a checklist, and reformulation—is that they all provide feedback to the writer. It will be the role of the teacher to provide the final feedback on the completed piece of work but, even here, there are choices to be made. A number of different marking strategies are available, for example: replacing the student's writing with a more accurate or appropriate form; indicating a problem by underlining and inviting the student to self-correct, and locating an error and giving it a symbol to denote the type of error. It is also possible to indicate in the margin that there is an error of a particular kind somewhere on that line and ask students to locate and correct it. These last two strategies require a coding system. The one in Figure 9.1 was developed by a group of upper-intermediate students in negotiation with their teacher.

Figure 9.1 An example of a coding system for correcting written work

WF	wrong form:	the <u>best</u> will be its achievements ^{WF}

WF   wrong form: the <u>best</u> will be its achievements ^WF^

WW   wrong word: patient, funny and <u>kindly</u> ^WW^

T   wrong tense: in the last few weeks you <u>didn't have</u> much fun

∧   something is missing: You arrived in Brighton ∧ the 1st

Sp   wrong spelling: <u>confortable</u> ^Sp^

WO   wrong word order: You haven't seen [yet] London

P   wrong punctuation: Look out. ^P^

V   wrong verb form: The Titanic <u>sunk</u> very quickly

//   new paragraph needed:

Ø   not necessary: John came in and (he) sat down

⌣   You don't need a new sentence.
Join up the ideas

?   I don't understand what you're trying to say.

〰   This isn't quite right: it needs clearer
expression (usually the teacher provides an
alternative)

[ ]   This part needs to be re-arranged or reworded.

!!   You really should know what's wrong here
because
– we've just done it in class.
– I've told you so many times.

The revision strategies described above have the same aim of encouraging students to see writing as something that can be improved, and they train learners in looking for areas for improvement. It is worth every teacher's while to ensure that a variety of techniques are used to encourage this essential activity in the writing process.

9.3.5 *Supporting students with technology*

In recent years, many teachers of writing to second and foreign language students have had to make a realistic appraisal of the word processor as an aid to composition. It is perhaps worth special mention here. The advantages of word processors are clear: learners who have previously struggled with handwriting in English are greatly assisted; the word processor enables sustained periods of composition, and the speed of processing can assist the generation of ideas and their rapid noting in any order as they come into the mind. Another advantage is that rapid drafting is possible, leaving error-correction until later, and this can be trained through techniques such as oral dictation (Hyland 1993). If learners process something dictated quickly by their teacher, they do not have time to stop and worry about minor errors, for example of spelling and punctuation, until they have finished.

Of particular value are those facilities which aid the revision of texts. It is so much easier to handle this on screen by means of 'deletion' or 'cutting and pasting'. However, a distinction needs to be made between local and global revision. Local revision, at sentence level, is almost too easy on a word processor. We know that poorer writers focus on sentence-level revision at the expense of more global improvement. Rather than encouraging them to work on individual sentences, we need to help learners to use the cut and paste facility to move parts of the text around and to delete other parts in order to gain overall improvement. Feedback can play an important role in this. Davidson and Tomic (1994) describe a task whereby college students of English as a second language were asked to write two alternative introductions, each with a different purpose, for a piece of writing. They then received feedback on both from peers and made revisions to the texts. Finally, the strongest elements of each text were merged on screen.

For word processors to be fully effective in this type of activity, both learner training and teacher training are important. Learners will need core skills in the mechanics of word processing and an understanding of its potential. And teachers will also need skills, and a positive attitude. Davidson and Tomic (ibid.) describe a pilot programme in which teachers learned side by side with students, with the assistance of a skilled member of staff acting as 'computer co-ordinator' and also of a 'student computer expert' who was employed to instruct peers as and when necessary. There is a gradually increasing literature on the advantages and disadvantages of this technology (see, for example, Pennington 1991; 1992).

9.3.6 *Issues in introducing a process approach*

Several issues arise for any teacher trying to incorporate principles of process writing into his or her professional practice. First of all, teachers need to provide time for writing in the supported learning environment of the classroom. Many students will benefit from structured tasks which teach them strategies for planning, drafting, and revision. Also, collaborative writing provides students with readers and critics of their work in the classroom and the computer room. They become accountable in the way that writers are in real life, and this accountability is a strong incentive for clear and effective writing.

Another value of providing class time for writing is that the teacher can focus strongly on the role of revision. Part of this focus should be setting up activities which show students that they can take on more responsibility for improving their own work.

Many teachers would argue that setting aside the time needed for feedback, and for the revision of several drafts, is unrealistic, particularly within the constraints of school systems, and particularly where classes are large. With regard to this issue, one compromise is to spend as much time as possible in the early stages of teaching writing and then to encourage independence through out-of-class practice. If it is true that we learn to write through writing, then this suggests the more practice the better. There are now interesting ideas available for encouraging more extensive writing both inside and outside class. Paquette (1982), for instance, suggests in-class writing, on any subject, for ten minutes at the end of class. The teacher can respond to this, creating a dialogue in writing with the students. Raimes (1983) suggests the keeping of a journal, in the form of daily notes, for a few minutes at the end of class. Students might occasionally select material from these notes to develop into a composition. Or they might volunteer to read some sections to their classmates. The value of sharing writing is that the activity moves away from being just an assignment towards being a more natural exchange of ideas and reflections with the teacher and the rest of the class.

A similar kind of exchange can be initiated by the teacher in writing letters to students. This is an activity usefully discussed by Kohl (1977), who wrote letters to his fourth- and fifth-grade Puerto Rican students. He became a correspondent rather than an evaluator as he did not correct their letters. Rinvolucri reports on an experimental correspondence he set up with six European students on a two-week extensive course as being valuable and exciting, not least because it obliged him to 'spend an hour or more each day thinking about students as individuals, both humanly and linguistically' (1983: 18). There is a time element to be considered here, however. I tried exchanging letters with a class of twenty Japanese undergraduates on an access course. All of them were anxious to improve their English in order to follow university courses alongside British undergraduates, and all of them took up the opportunity with great earnestness and kept it up throughout a term. Certainly I found that they borrowed language in useful ways from my letters, but the time involved in writing them was substantial. Alternatives might be to move students eventually towards writing letters to each other, or just to invite weaker students to exchange letters in order to give them extra practice. In this activity, as with journal writing, students become involved in a more natural exchange with other people on topics of their own choice.

The issue of large classes is less easily resolved, though a teacher in southern India reported to me her success in using a version of reformulation with a class of 120 college students. She chose paragraphs from a student text and wrote her own reformulation on the board. Then she got the students to discuss the differences in pairs. They were highly motivated to return to their first drafts and look for ways to improve on them. Group writing can also be a useful technique. In this technique, the teacher prepares for a piece of writing with the class and then explains to the students that they are going to work in groups, planning together, writing a section each, and checking each other's drafts. The students can benefit as they get suggestions from one another for improvements. The discussion can provide natural fluency practice in English but could equally take place in the students' first language. A teacher with a class of fifty students will have ten pieces of work to monitor and assist with, and ten final drafts to evaluate, rather than fifty.

The process approach to writing is not without its critics, and the questions of time and large classes are certainly issues of implementation which any teacher needs to take into account. Another concern relates to students who are preparing for examinations. The multiple-draft approach is hardly suitable for timed examinations: a distinction needs to be made between classroom writing aimed at developing efficiency and exam preparation which aims at demonstrating that efficiency, and for which other strategies are needed. A serious related criticism is that the process approach does not address the realities of life for those students who are working with English writing in academic contexts, where essays have to be produced under time constraints and where they need an understanding of the demands of various discourse types. This brings us to a point at which we need to consider the discourse approach to writing.

9.4 How can we analyse and describe the structure of written texts?

The process approach and the implications reviewed above are comparatively recent developments in the teaching of writing. Much longer-established are approaches which have their origins in the traditions of rhetoric. These have been characterized as *product approaches*: they focus the student's attention on the features of texts and are largely concerned with developing his or her ability to produce those features accurately. The methodology therefore involves analysis of model texts in order to raise awareness of how they are structured. It also involves formal practice of such features as the use of passives in descriptions of processes, the use of relative clauses in descriptions of people, places, and systems, and the use of time adverbials in historical accounts or the development of defining paragraphs. This practice is of a controlled nature and often there is little opportunity for composing. The teacher's roles are to 'prime' writing through preparatory activity and to evaluate it after it has been produced in order to diagnose strengths and weaknesses.

There are clearly aspects of this approach which would be valuable to certain kinds of student: examples include the professional person already competent in writing in his or her first language but needing to produce specific types of text, for example scientific reports in English; or the university student needing to produce a range of expository essays in English, for example comparing and contrasting systems, discussing problems and alternative solutions, or critically reviewing an argument.

In recent years, work done on the analysis of written texts has provided us with a greater understanding of how they are structured. Two types of analysis in particular have yielded useful information for teachers. The first is *genre analysis*. Swales (1990) defines genre in the following way:

> A genre comprises a class of communicative events, the members of which share some set of communicative purposes. These purposes are recognised by the expert members of the parent discourse community, and thereby constitute the rationale for the genre. This rationale shapes the schematic structure of the discourse and influences and constrains choice of content and style.
> (Swales 1990: 58)

This view perceives writing as being linked to the values and expectations of a particular discourse community (Johns 1990). If structure, content, and style are shaped in this way, according to the expectations of the readers, it becomes important for learners to understand the shapes of the written genres they have to produce within the discourse community of which they are preparing to become a part, for example those of medical research, company law, or undergraduate history. Teachers can provide support here as we shall see, support which is arguably just as important as that for the development of effective writing strategies.

The second type of analysis to yield insights is *contrastive analysis* of rhetoric. A number of writers (Grabe and Kaplan 1996; Hinds 1987) have argued that different cultures have different expectations of how to organize writing, and that knowledge of conventions in the first language will influence the organization of texts in second language writing. For example, Hinds has argued that many Japanese students writing in English delay the introduction of purpose beyond the expectations of western academic traditions. It is a vexed and controversial field of study but the possibility of first language culture influencing student writing is something of which teachers need to be aware. In a study of seventeen university staff and postgraduate students in a UK university, for whom English was a second language, Holyoak and Piper (1997) reported that, whatever the subjects' experiences of inappropriate transfer of first language organization to second language writing, thirteen believed that instruction in the patterns appropriate to British academia would have been useful to them.

In summary, insights from the analysis of written texts have an essential role in writing classes. They can help us build an understanding of how texts can be effectively organized. This, in turn, gives teachers and learners criteria for effectiveness in writing. Both of these applications can be integrated with a process approach. The principles discussed in 9.3 can be augmented by several more derived from a product view.

9.5 What are the implications of a text-based approach to writing?

9.5.1 *Helping students to identify their writing needs*

We can identify the range of written products that any particular group of students needs, and the way in which one form differs from another. For example, in English the conventions and style of formal and informal letters differ, and both may differ in format and style from letters written in the students' first language. It can be useful for teachers and students together to survey the students' needs for writing in English and to select writing from among relevant categories. Materials extract 9.E shows one attempt at a typology of writing. This is not to suggest that 'needs' should be rigidly interpreted in terms of immediate or eventual needs in the real world. The typology is simply offered as a checklist of ideas. As we have seen, diary writing can be of value as a practice activity though it would normally be undertaken in the first language. And many students enjoy the chance to be creative with writing. Taking real life, practice, and motivational criteria into account, a relevant writing programme can be negotiated.

9.5.2 *Building awareness of discourse organization*

In written discourse, patterns can be identified in which smaller units of meaning combine to form longer stretches of discourse. The smaller units, often called *rhetorical functions*, are used to express functions such as

Materials extract 9.E

Types of writing

Personal writing	Public writing	Creative writing

diaries
journals
shopping lists
reminders for oneself
packing lists
addresses
recipes
	letters of – enquiry
	          – complaint
	          – request
	form filling
	applications (for memberships)
		poems
		stories
		rhymes
		drama
		songs
		autobiography

Social writing	Study writing	Institutional writing	

letters
invitations
notes – of condolence
       – of thanks
       – of congratulations
cablegrams
telephone messages
instructions – to friends
          – to family
	making notes while reading
	taking notes from lectures
	making a card index
	summaries
	synopses
	reviews
	reports of – experiments
	          – workshops
	          – visits
	essays
	bibliographies
		agendas
		minutes
		memoranda
		reports
		reviews
		contracts
		business letters
		public notices
		advertisements
			posters
			instructions
			speeches
			applications
			curriculum vitae
			specifications
			note-making
			(doctors and other
			professionals)

(Hedge: *Writing*, page 96)

explaining, defining, and comparing, and combine to form rhetorical patterns. This can be seen in the following example from a student's writing:

> The first point I would like to make is that nuclear power stations are a threat to the environment we live in and to society itself. This is because of the danger of radio-active material escaping into the ground and polluting rivers and farms. A good example of this is …

The first sentence is a statement of a point of view. The second clarifies the point through giving an explanation. The third gives an example as supporting evidence. Together these sentences form one of a set of arguments.

Whether such patterns are relatively stable and predictable has exercised the minds of linguists in recent years. If they are, then they can usefully be exploited as teaching devices. Two simple examples will demonstrate this possibility. A description of a person can contain information on social background, personality characteristics, and physical appearance. Which of these comes first will depend on what is most significant to the writer, or what is thought to be most interesting or important to the reader. Similarly, a text which discusses the phenomenon of Seasonal Affective Disorder will probably contain the following elements:

Situation: High incidence of depression and suicide in northern climates in winter.

Problem: Doctors have diagnosed a condition known as Seasonal Affective Disorder (SAD) caused by decreased exposure to light and the effects of this on certain hormones.

Solution: Increased exposure to light will alleviate symptoms.

Conclusion: Patients should sit in front of special lamps or increase time outside in natural light.

The sequence of elements above would probably be considered normal, with conclusions coming last. However, a newspaper article on the topic might report on the treatment first, in order to raise curiosity, and then move on to explain the problem. In fact, there could be several possible sequences for the information.

The existence of patterns and the fact of their flexibility can be pointed out to students. Building this kind of awareness can be part of the planning process. It is a particularly useful technique for students who need to write in English for academic purposes, and for those who need to produce compositions for written English examination papers. Many teachers would see it as their responsibility to help students prepare for this, as success in examinations provides access to higher education and to certain professions.

The task in Materials extract 9.F helps students organize a topic in a logical way to highlight contrasts and comparisons, and suggests a certain kind of discourse organization based on analysis of how effective texts of this type are structured. Ideally, the suggested plan should not be regarded as a rigid framework but as something which can be reviewed and revised as content develops. Many writing materials now attempt to follow a syllabus in which students explore various types of discourse organization, for example, cause–effect, problem–solution, contrast–comparison, or process description.

It has also become part of the procedures for revision to check the plans that students make for their writing. This can be done through a pairwork activity in which one student challenges a partner's plan. For example, if student A had written a plan of points against nuclear power which looked like this:

1 threat to the environment and society
2 problem of disposing of radio-active waste
3 hazard of transporting waste through residential areas
4 danger of accidents, e.g. Chernobyl

student B could challenge with questions such as: 'What do you mean by this?'; 'What do you plan to write about this?'; 'What is your supporting evidence?' The questioning can lead A to clarify ideas in his or her own mind,

Materials extract 9.F

3.17 Organizing points for a contrast and comparison essay

LEVEL	Upper intermediate to advanced
TOPIC	Town and country life
FUNCTION	Contrast and comparison.
FORM	Composition of the examination type.
FOCUS	Discourse organization.
CONTEXT	Preparation for an examination question: 'The country has everything that is good in life; the city all that is bad.'
PREPARATION	In this activity you may wish to prepare the content needed for the essay as a list of points about town and country life. Make copies of the list for the students. These can be used for a matching and sorting task during the lesson.

Town
- lack of green spaces, e.g. parks and gardens; lots of concrete and bricks
- plenty of amenities for entertainment, e.g. theatres, cinemas, sports clubs
- good public transport
- difficulty of making contacts
- claustrophobia and crowds
- noisy environment
- people not so friendly
- good shopping facilities
- good education services

Country
- community spirit still exists
- children may have to travel to school
- need a private car
- open space and greenery
- few social facilities – travel necessary for entertainment
- can be too quiet and isolated
- no supermarkets or specialized shops
- social life easier to establish in community
- solitude for those who want it

IN CLASS

1 Give students the title for the essay and explain that in this case the audience will be an examiner. They are to prepare a more formal type of academic composition.

2 Ask students to work for four to five minutes individually, jotting down ideas for the composition in the form of a mind map. You could start one together on the blackboard using the format below if students are not used to this kind of note-making activity (see also task 1.3).

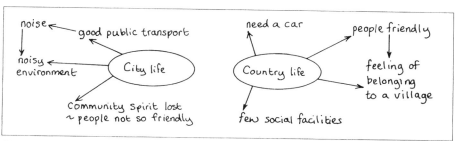

Figure 11

3 Elicit suggestions for content from the class and add them to the mind map on the blackboard.

4 Give out your copies of points for and against town and country. (This is a linear equivalent of the mind map.) Ask students to add any new points from the blackboard and any further points of their own.

5 Then ask the students to match points from each column which relate to the same topic (as shown by the arrows in the list above). This can be done individually or in pairs.

6 While checking the matching task with the whole class, discuss labels for the topics which have been identified: environment, social amenities, transport, etc.

7 Working with the class, decide on a sensible order for the topics. Looking back at their mind maps and any links between ideas may suggest ways of linking the topics together.

8 The next step is to show students a possible organization for their composition. As this composition involves quite a number of topics, an 'interwoven' organization is appropriate. It can be shown by drawing a diagram as follows:

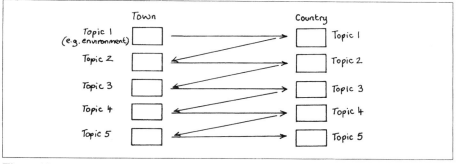

Figure 12

9 Students can then move to the process of drafting.

(Hedge: *Writing*, pages 133–4)

to add important elements to the argument, and to create a clearer piece of writing.

9.5.3 *Helping students to develop crafting skills*

Part of the drafting and revising process discussed earlier involves choosing the language to be used and linking ideas in appropriate ways. The choice of language, as we have seen, will depend on how a writer anticipates the reactions of the supposed reader. Classroom writing is a fluency activity (see 2.4.1) in the sense that learners can use all the existing language resources they have so far acquired to write a whole, contextualized text. However, teachers can support students in their growing awareness of how to achieve accuracy in a text: of such things as how the parts of a text are linked through cohesive devices, how sentence structure can vary to develop meaning, and the role that punctuation plays. These are aspects of crafting a text, putting together pieces of the English language. Materials extract 9.G shows a sentence-level exercise. This type of accuracy-based activity has the aim of raising awareness of parallelism and giving practice. It is the experience of many teachers that some, but not all, students will be able to transfer skills successfully from practice activities to their own writing. A good way to use an exercise like this is to add parallelism to a checklist used for revision so that students look for accuracy in using parallel structures when they are checking their own work.

9.5.4 *Enabling students to appreciate the criteria for an effective text*

The discussion in 9.5.2 proposed that we need to build awareness in student writers that the organization of a piece of writing should be appropriate to its purpose, and in 9.3.3 and 9.4 we saw that it should also be appropriate to its audience of readers. This will affect the range of cohesive devices that are used to create complex sentences or to develop paragraphs. It will also affect the range of vocabulary. This implies that a piece of writing could be judged on a set of criteria including, minimally, 'appropriateness', 'range', and 'complexity'. Many traditional marking systems have placed great emphasis on 'accuracy' but teachers now try to use a wider set of criteria which relate to what we know of successful writers and writing. For example, if we consider the characteristics of good writers, these may yield useful criteria for assessing writing. Materials extract 9.H shows one such list.

The list is divided into authoring skills and crafting skills, though there is clearly overlap between them. However, representing writing in this way takes us away from the traditional concept of seeing assessment as a matter of

Materials extract 9.G

A. Rewrite the following sentences in parallel form.

STEP 1 Underline the part of the sentence that is not parallel and correct it.

STEP 2 Circle the word or words that join the parallel structures.

Example:

Attending the symphony ⓞⓡ to go to the theater is what I enjoy the most.

Attending the symphony or going to the theater is what I enjoy the most.

1. Credit cards are accepted by department stores, airlines, and they can be used in some gas stations.

2. You do not need to risk carrying cash or to risk to pass up* a sale.

3. With credit cards you can either pay your bill with one check, or you can stretch out your payments.

4. You can charge both at restaurants and when you stay at hotels.

5. Many people carry not only credit cards but also they carry cash.

6. Many people want neither to read a product's warranty nor sending it into a company.

7. Many warranties give comprehensive* coverage, but some give coverage that is limited.

8. Getting a defective* product fixed or to have it replaced is what a comprehensive warranty guarantees.

B. Write eight original sentences in parallel form, using both coordinating conjunctions (*and, or, but*) and correlative conjunctions (*both . . . and, either . . . or, neither . . . nor, not only . . . but also*).

Review

These are the main points you should have learned about parallelism:

1. Words, phrases, or clauses that are joined by coordinating conjunctions and correlative conjunctions must be written in parallel form.
2. If the first structure is a noun, make all others nouns; if it is a prepositional phrase, make all the others prepositional phrases; if it is a dependent clause, make all the others dependent clauses.
3. All of the words in the first parallel structure do not have to be repeated in the second.

(Oshima and Hogue: *Writing Academic English* (2nd edn.), pages 170–1)

Materials extract 9.H

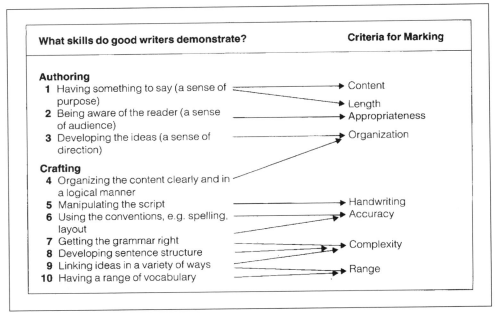

(adapted from Hedge: *Writing*, page 146)

checking just for accuracy. In devising an assessment schedule it is possible to select those skills which are appropriate to the age, language development, and writing development of learners. Thus it becomes possible to respond positively to written work, commenting on strengths as well as weaknesses. The relationship that might exist between accuracy and complexity will serve as an example. Students who are trying to develop an ability to link ideas in more complex sentences are likely to go through a phase of making errors in the use of relative pronouns or choice of connective. If they receive only negative comment on inaccuracy they can become discouraged and revert to writing simple sentences.

We can use simple or complex grading systems with students. Materials extract 9.I shows two examples of grading criteria, and others are discussed in Chapter 11. The important thing is to be clear in our minds about the rationale for whatever criteria we choose, and part of that rationale is bound to be what is pragmatically possible.

Materials extract 9.1

Grading criteria: Example 1

1 Organization of content (clarity, coherence, paragraph development)	20
2 Range (grammatical structures, vocabulary)	15
3 Complexity of sentence structure	15
4 Accuracy of grammar (tenses, agreement, etc.) of sentence structure (word order, connectives, etc.) of spelling of punctuation	30
5 Fluency (feel for the language, appropriateness, use of idioms, etc.)	20
	100%

Grading criteria: Example 2

	Excellent	Good	Adequate	Inadequate	Weak
A General development **1** Interest and force of content **2** Development of ideas **3** A sense of audience and style					
B Specific components in writing **4** Grammatical skills **5** Complexity of sentence structure **6** Use of vocabulary **7** Spelling **8** Punctuation **9** Presentation (neatness, handwriting, etc.)					

(Hedge: *Writing*, page 148)

9.6 Conclusion

The principles outlined in this chapter incorporate elements of both process and product approaches to writing. It seems to be the sensible way forward for the teacher to use the best of both approaches in order to develop those aspects of writing most needed by students. The significance of each principle will depend on the specific needs of student writers. For example, with young learners, a process approach which aims at developing effective strategies might be most appropriate. For secondary-school writers in English-medium education, developing awareness of audience might be important as this is the mark of a mature writer. So, too, might be developing the ability to produce the range of discourse types needed for subjects across the school curriculum which will be assessed through written examinations. With EFL students in further and higher education in English-speaking countries, a primary aim might be to focus on any differences between the conventions of discourse organization in their first language and the conventions of the academic culture in which they are studying. With educated adults, already competent writers in their first language, a teacher of business or scientific English might focus on the features of commercial or technical texts. Each teacher needs to develop a methodology which integrates the specific needs of his or her students and a principled approach to the teaching of writing.

Discussion topics and projects

1 Think of a group of learners you teach. What are their needs for writing in English? Make a list of text-types you could include in their writing programme. List them under these headings, or headings of your own: Personal, Public, Creative, Social, Study, and Institutional.

2 Make a list of real audiences you could find for students when you set writing tasks in your own teaching context.

3 Discuss with your colleagues any problems you envisage in incorporating elements of a process approach in your own methodology for teaching writing, and whether you think it would be possible to overcome these.

4 Look at the activity in Materials extract 9.J and evaluate it according to these criteria:
    (a) Which aspect of writing development is in focus (e.g. using appropriate vocabulary, cohesive devices, or note-taking for planning)?
    (b) To what extent does the task focus on text (e.g. how a text is organized; how the parts of it are put together)?
    (c) To what extent does the task focus on process (e.g. encouraging students in effective strategies)?
    (d) Has the context of the writing been made clear (e.g. a tourist brochure; a letter to a friend)?

Would you want to apply any other criteria? Now find a writing task in learning materials you use and apply your own set of criteria to it.

5 Choose a coursebook with a writing component in it. Evaluate the extent to which it balances process and text-based views of writing.

6 In what ways could you encourage your own students to practise their writing as much as possible outside class?

Materials extract 9.J

SELECTION AND ORDERING OF INFORMATION

You are going to write a letter to a local newspaper appealing for support for a project to help old people in your area. You have collected the following points, but they are not all equally important. In any case, newspapers prefer short letters. Working in groups of two or three, decide which of the points are important enough to be included, and then group them into paragraphs. Then plan each paragraph carefully, and finally write the letter.

There are at least 5,000 people over the age of 65 in your town.
Not many old people play tennis.
There's a bingo hall and four cinemas in your town.
Cinemas are cheap for old age pensioners (OAPs) in the morning.
The state pension is only 25 pounds a week.
Your uncle is 78 years old.
OAPs need a recreation centre.
OAPs need food and heat.

Many old people can't move around a lot.
Old people are often bad-tempered because their memory fails.
You are going to organise a voluntary visiting service for old people.
You need volunteeers to help in your various projects.
You know a lot of old people.
You are going to organise a scheme to help old people decorate their houses.
Old people drive very slowly.
Your group now has 25 volunteer members.
Some old people have cars. You have organised an emergency telephone service, which
    is manned all day.
The local government authority does very little for OAPs.
Brain cells do not regenerate, and this is one reason why old people lose their sight.
The local 'Meals-on Wheels' service produces 369 meals per day.
There are many OAPs in your street.
People's reaction time slows down considerably when they get older.
Many old people fought in the war.
You need money to help with your expenses, especially the emergency phone.
You visit the hospital every week.
The Rev. Harris goes with you to the hospital.
Old people are difficult to get on with, and therefore often lonely.
Old people get on well with children, and tell them stories.
Donations can be sent to Hutchins Bank, High Street, account no. WL 25667.
You started your action group by talking to friends.
The first meeting of the group will be in the Black Bull at 8p.m. on Friday, 28 October.
You have plans to build a community centre for OAPs if you can get enough money.
The government sometimes gives OAPs a substantial rise.
Many old people need special attention, and this requires a lot of patience and tolerance
    on the part of the volunteer helper.

(Coe, Ryecroft, and Ernest: *Writing Skills*, pages 34–5)

Further reading

Brookes, A. and **P. Grundy.** 1990. *Writing for Study Purposes.* Cambridge: Cambridge University Press.

This book provides a useful combination of theoretical background on the writing process and practical suggestions for classroom procedures, including forty-four exercises for teaching students who are writing in academic contexts.

Grabe, W. and **R. B. Kaplan.** 1996. *Theory and Practice of Writing.* London and New York: Longman.

The authors give an overview of the various theoretical discussions of writing, looking at both investigations into the process of writing and research in the field of text linguistics. They go on to look at approaches to the teaching of writing at beginning, intermediate, and advanced levels. The book ends with discussions of responding to writing and issues in writing assessment.

Hedge, T. 1988. *Writing.* Oxford: Oxford University Press.

Writing presents a range of writing tasks within the framework of current thinking on the process of writing. The first part focuses on authoring skills: developing a sense of audience, and drafting and revising. The second part looks at crafting, in other words, putting the pieces of the text together. The tasks are designed in relation to a variety of writing purposes and include a range of text-types.

Kroll, B. (ed.). 1990. *Second Language Writing: Research Insights for the Classroom.* Cambridge: Cambridge University Press.

This is a set of thirteen articles which cover topics on composing processes, teacher response to writing, writing assessment, and links between reading and writing. The book presents an informative mixture of research studies and practical classroom pedagogy. It gives both historical information on the development of different approaches to the teaching of writing and a clear account of current views.

Leki, I. 1989. *Academic Writing: Techniques and Tasks.* New York: St. Martins Press.

This book is aimed at students who need to write in English for academic purposes. In Part One, students are taken through the writing process and can discover strategies useful to them. They are introduced in turn to 'Getting to draft', 'Working with a draft', and 'Reworking the draft'. In Part Two, students practise a variety of academic assignments. The book is a good example of current ideas in practice.

Sherman, J. 1994. *Feedback.* Oxford: Oxford University Press.

This is a coursebook for intermediate students of English who need to improve composition writing. It usefully incorporates current ideas about the process of writing, particularly the role of feedback in revision. It is suitable for self-directed work by students as well as classroom work and contains tutorials on essential aspects of writing such as evaluating one's own writing and working effectively with feedback.

PART FOUR

Planning and assessing learning

10 COURSE DESIGN

'*Externally imposed syllabuses, textbooks and examinations all define educational values and set certain standards which are important from the standpoint of the individual as well as for national and social purposes: however, they make the spontaneity, flexibility and diversity which are an equally important part of education much more difficult to achieve.*'
MALCOLM SKILBECK

1 What roles might teachers play in course design?

2 What contextual factors do we need to consider?

3 How can we establish goals and objectives?

4 What options are there in choosing a syllabus?

5 What procedures can be helpful in evaluating courses?

6 What criteria might we use in choosing a textbook?

7 How can we take a process approach to course design?

8 What is the role of projects in English language teaching?

9 What is the role of negotiation in course design?

Introductory task

1 Look at the following ten statements and say which you agree with and why.

2 Are there any with which you disagree?

3 Would you like to add any statements?
   (a) A syllabus specifies what the teacher will teach.
   (b) A syllabus is a careful plan of what the students will learn.
   (c) A syllabus is a way of breaking down the learning task into manageable units.
   (d) A syllabus makes teachers accountable to educational authorities.
   (e) A syllabus does not cater for the needs of individual learners.

(f) A syllabus gives learners a sense of direction and a way of previewing and reviewing learning.

(g) A syllabus sets up goals for learning.

(h) A syllabus provides a basis for assessing learners.

(i) A syllabus must take into account the environment in which it is used.

(j) Learning is too complex, personal, and organic to be organized by a formal syllabus.

10.1 Introduction: roles for the teacher in course design

Teachers may find themselves in a number of different roles in relation to the courses they teach. If these were put on a scale according to freedom of choice, the roles might appear as they do in Figure 10.1. Which of these reflects your own situation? It profits teachers who have the flexibility to design their own courses to follow a systematic approach. This chapter will suggest a learner-centred approach, which begins by considering the needs of learners and ends by evaluating the course designed and taught to fulfil those needs.

Figure 10.1: Degrees of teachers' freedom of choice in relation to courses

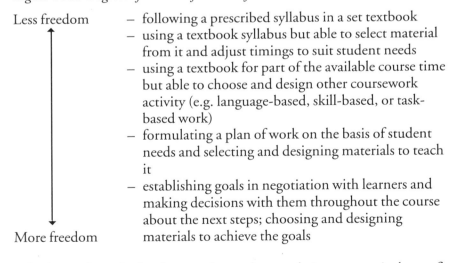

Less freedom

— following a prescribed syllabus in a set textbook
— using a textbook syllabus but able to select material from it and adjust timings to suit student needs
— using a textbook for part of the available course time but able to choose and design other coursework activity (e.g. language-based, skill-based, or task-based work)
— formulating a plan of work on the basis of student needs and selecting and designing materials to teach it
— establishing goals in negotiation with learners and making decisions with them throughout the course about the next steps; choosing and designing materials to achieve the goals

More freedom

Whether we have the freedom to adopt, adapt, or design courses, it also profits us to know the assumptions about language, about learning, and about learners which underly the range of syllabus types available. We are then in a position to relate these to the needs of particular groups of learners and to make appropriate choices of goals, courses, and materials. As Candlin (1984) has suggested:

> Rather than merely being an ordered sequence of selected and, as it were, innocuous items of content, timeless and obscure in origin, separated from the world, it [a syllabus] reveals itself as a window on a particular set of social, educational, moral and subject matter values. Syllabuses seen in this perspective stand, then, for particular ideologies. (Candlin 1984: 30)

Models in the field of ELT syllabus design have moved rapidly since the 1970s, and each model has its underlying rationale in educational thinking, in social trends, and in views of language and learning, as we shall discover in this chapter. The structural syllabus of the 1960s and 1970s, the communicative syllabus of the 1980s, and the task-based syllabus of the 1990s, have all made their contribution to course design. Many current communicative textbooks demonstrate all of these strands in the multi-dimensional syllabus, as seen in Materials extract 10.A, the 'contents map' of a course. This has dimensions of communicative function, structure, topic, and project, the last including various skills dimensions in the tasks suggested. As the unit titles suggest, it is the functional list which forms the organizing principle.

Teachers wishing to design multi-dimensional courses of their own will be faced with the same issues as any textbook designer. Which aspect of language or of skills work or of content should be the primary organizing criterion for the course? What implications does this hold for the design and format of a course unit? Teachers wishing to combine formal classwork with less formal activities such as projects will be faced with further issues: what is the appropriate balance of time to spend on each, and what are effective ways of integrating the two?

In this chapter we will look first at a possible sequence of steps for course design and then explore the decisions confronting teachers in planning and organizing learning experiences.

10.2 What are the steps in course design?

Educational and ELT literature has provided us with several models for programme development (Taba 1962; Dubin and Olshtain 1986; Clark 1987; White 1988), all of which follow a sequence of steps generated by an initial fact-finding stage. These steps include those shown in Figure 10.2.

Step 1 has been called 'analysis of student needs' in models relating to course design for learners with specific needs such as the English required for to

Materials extract 10.A

MAP OF MEANINGS INTO WORDS

Unit	Coursebook		Project Resource Book
	Functions Students will learn to:	**Grammar/Language**	**Topics** Students will learn to talk/write about:	**Authentic materials leading up to a project for the whole class**
1. Places (pages 5 to 12)	– describe and ask about places – say where things are – describe and ask about available services/amenities in town	– *there is/are* – *has/has got* – location prepositions – non-defining relative clauses	– buildings, rooms, furniture – services, amenities – geographical location	1. Housing (pages 5 to 10) – types of housing – electrical appliances – amenities/services – decorative styles/colours – garden design PROJECT: My ideal home in the year 2020 AD
2. Decisions and intentions (pages 13 to 20)	– decide to do or not to do things – come to a decision with someone else – talk about intentions/plans – talk about definite arrangements	– *I'll* for spontaneous decisions – *Shall we ...?/Let's ...* – verbs expressing intentions and plans – present continuous for definite arrangements	– organising a party – arranging an excursion – changes of mind – ordering a meal in a restaurant	2. Holiday Britain (pages 11 to 18) – descriptions of holiday resorts – youth hostels – the Peak District – a cycling tour – interpreting a map PROJECT: Planning a tour *Back page: Cat in the Rain*

3. Jobs and routine (pages 21 to 29)	– describe people's jobs – talk and ask about daily routine – talk and ask about regular events	– present simple question forms – frequency adverbs and phrases – present simple passive with *be* and *get* *Grammar spot 1: Gender*	– routine at work and at home – jobs – places of work	3. Daily routine (pages 19 to 24) – the average British housewife – Madonna – parodies PROJECT: A life in the day of your school *Back page: The Essay*
4. Direction (pages 30 to 39)	– say what directions things and people move in – give instructions for making and doing things – give street directions	– direction prepositions – sequence adverbs *Grammar Spot 2: The article*	– streets and public buildings – making puppets	
5. Past events (pages 40 to 47)	– relate and ask about past events – say when events happened	– sequence expressions, e.g. after ...-ing – past simple active and passive – past time expressions/ prepositions	– history of people and places – first experiences	4. Schools (pages 25 to 32) – the UK system – the new GCSE exam – prospectus of a comprehensive school – the USA system PROJECT: School prospectus *Back page: Bitter-Sweet Dreams: School Days*

(Doff, Jones, and Mitchell: *Meanings into Words* (in a version adapted for the Austrian secondary school system by de Waal and Weinhofer 1989), page 3)

Figure 10.2: Steps in course design for general English courses

Step 1: Considering the students

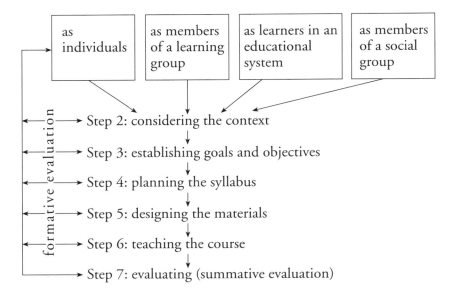

specify the priority areas of language use such as listening to lectures or reading technical reports. Munby (1978) formalized specific needs analysis in his model for communicative syllabus design. He presents categories for profiling student needs and goes on to suggest how these can be translated into goals and a syllabus for a course by selecting elements such as skills and functions. This he calls the 'specification of communicative competence', and he provides checklists from which course designers can select. The post-Munby era has seen much debate on how other, more 'subjective' (Brindley 1989b) elements such as information on learners, their perceptions of learning in general, their attitudes towards language learning, and their expectations of methodology, need to be added to Munby's more 'objective' categories of, for example, setting, role-relationship, dialect, proficiency, target level, and communicative event. These categories of more subjective information are as significant to the effective planning of goals, content, and classroom procedures as Munby's more objective ones. Yet the concept of needs analysis has been influential in general English language education. In the next section we will look at its relevance and interpretation for groups of learners with less easily identifiable needs.

10.2.1 *Considering the students in their context of learning*

With adolescents in school and adults learning English for general purposes it is not possible for us to identify in any detail their eventual needs for using English. However, the point has been made (Dubin and Olshtain 1986) that a preparatory stage in course design, equivalent to needs analysis, is nevertheless necessary. This is a stage of gathering whatever information can enlighten the course design process, and may involve observation of classroom methodology, reflection on local conditions and resources, review of educational policy, and interviews and questionnaire surveys among teachers, students, advisory staff, and the inspectorate.

> … This fact-finding stage provides answers to the key questions in any program. Who are the learners? Who are the teachers? Why is the program necessary? Where will the program be implemented?
> (Dubin and Olshtain 1986: 5)

Teachers designing their own courses can usefully consider their learners from the four perspectives (after Howatt 1978) shown at step 1 in Figure 10.2, though these inevitably have some degree of overlap.

Consideration of learners as individuals will highlight such issues as the need to relate age to interests in a topic-based syllabus, how materials can be made challenging, or whether teacher-dependent attitudes suggest a need for learner independence as a goal. Consideration of learners as members of a class group will inform decisions about target levels of communicative ability or appropriateness of the methodology to class size. Reflection on learners as members of a particular educational system will pinpoint such issues as the relationship of course objectives to the examination system or the appropriateness of grading to a selective or comprehensive system. Finally, perceiving learners as members of a social group will bring into focus the relevance of course objectives to the role of English in society or the amount of exposure to English that learners receive. These simply serve as examples. You will quickly be able to list further relevant issues for your own learners, as the Spanish teacher, Rufino, did in the Introductory task to Chapter 1.

As well as using teacher experience, reflection, and observation, we can ask students directly, using simply presented questionnaires, about their motivations for learning English, the ways in which they like to learn, the problems they have with learning English and their reactions to past classroom experiences. Data can also be collected informally by means of classwork in which students first respond with written notes to a series of questions, then interview each other, and finally contribute to class discussion. Suitable questions might be:

1 What sort of activity did you like best in your previous classes?
2 What sort of activity did you like least in your previous classes?
3 What kind of activity did you find most helpful?
4 What kind of homework did you do?
5 How did you help yourself to learn English outside the classroom?
6 What do you think you are good at and weak at now in English?

Only when information is collected as systematically as possible can suitable objectives for a course be formulated. And since some of this information can only be collected from students themselves, during initial lessons and at later points as their perceptions of their needs develop in response to course activity, this suggests that a course should be more than a pre-selected textbook or, at the very least, that we need to use textbooks judiciously as we gradually develop insights about our learners.

Our explorations into the four perspectives at step 1 of Figure 10.2 will begin to define contextual constraints within which the course must be planned and taught. It is perhaps sufficient to reiterate here the importance of matching course to context. The most efficient course design is one which takes into account specific factors such as class size, time available, and the teacher's own communicative ability, knowledge of the language system, and command of methods. It should also take into account more general factors concerning educational values, perceptions of the teacher's role, and expectations of classroom procedures.

10.2.2 *Establishing goals and objectives*

The distinction between the terms 'goals' and 'objectives' is here taken to be a distinction between the general and the specific. For example, one broader goal for a course might be perceived, from the teacher's perspective, as being:

1 to develop the students' reading ability more comprehensively and effectively; more specific objectives within that goal could be outcomes for the students:
    (a) to develop effective strategies for dealing with unknown words
    (b) to be able to distinguish fact from opinion
    (c) to build confidence in dealing with a wide range of texts (e.g. news reports, charts, magazine articles, short stories).

Similarly, another broad goal could be:

2 to help learners become more independent in their approach to learning; more specific objectives for students could be:
    (a) to learn ways of monitoring and assessing their own progress
    (b) to develop effective strategies for using monolingual dictionaries
    (c) to find ways of exploiting out-of-class resources for learning English.

Note the difference between the first goal, which is to do with the outcomes of a language learning course, and the second, which is a wider educational goal to do with the process of learning and the development of the individual. Teachers working with school students will have a particular concern for formulating educational goals. A quick review of the chapters of this book would immediately suggest some of relevance to ELT, for example:

- to develop enjoyment in reading and good reading habits
- to develop appreciation of the link between language and culture and awareness of how languages and cultures differ
- to develop a critical stance in listening and reading.

In many contexts, general goals are set out in a national curriculum or by institutional policy-makers and it is left to teachers to interpret these in specific objectives. It is difficult to know how many teachers actually list objectives for their own courses and it is unlikely that many list detailed terminal competencies or behavioural objectives as defined by Valette and Disick (1972). These are precise descriptions of what a learner will be able to perform as expected outcomes of the course, for example, 'be able to use a newspaper heading predictively in previewing the content of a text'. Popular in the 1970s, and still understandably useful among testers, such performance objectives have come under increasing criticism for the narrow view they seem to represent of language education.

However, making the stating of objectives a distinct stage in course planning has a number of advantages: it enables us to assess the appropriateness of course materials; to make explicit the aims of the course and how these have been determined; and to encourage students to develop their own agendas for the course. It is a stage of course planning in which learners can become involved through consultation and negotiation (see 10.3.4). A list of objectives also provides one set of criteria for evaluating a course. Students can be invited to assess how far they have been enabled to achieve the objectives of the course.

10.2.3 *Planning the syllabus*

The point was made in 10.1 that it is typical of contemporary coursebooks to use a multi-dimensional syllabus. Johnson (1981) gives a rationale for this kind of syllabus by analogy with a construction plan:

> ... arguments as to the relative merits of notional, situational, or topic based syllabuses, etc. are no more sensible than arguments as to whether the specifications in a construction contract should cover the foundations, or the steel framework or the concrete or the glass or the interior design etc. The obvious answer is that all of these must be covered.
> (Johnson 1981: 34)

His view can be seen as a response to the debate of the 1970s as to what might constitute the most appropriate base for designing a language syllabus. It was during this period that the communicative revolution in syllabus design and classroom methodology took impetus from the work of applied linguists interested in the concept of communicative competence (see 2.1). Previously, the classical humanist values prevalent in general education (Clark 1987) had influenced language teaching towards content-driven courses, the content consisting of selected and sequenced items from the formal language system. This 'structural syllabus' relied on analyses of language provided by linguists of the time and focused on the systems of phonology, grammar, and lexis. It has prevailed widely as a base for course design on the grounds that it has its clear advantages, i.e. it is amenable to planning and can provide systematicity. For this reason many teachers and learners feel secure and appreciate being able to review what they have covered of the 'building blocks' of the language. The point has also been made that, if a structural syllabus and related course units make explicit use of grammatical concepts and categories, it enables learners to use formal strategies for acquiring language such as analysing the tense system. And many adult and adolescent learners have already developed effective strategies of this kind through previous language learning experiences.

Course designers of the 1970s, however, were influenced by the reconstructionist movement in general education and its arguments for objectives-driven courses, together with concurrently emerging perspectives on what communicative ability in a language entails. A seminal work in this respect was Wilkins' *Notional Syllabuses* (1976). He suggested three components for a syllabus based on what he called 'communicative capacity'. These derived from the three types of meaning expressed through a sentence or a spoken utterance. The first component is derived from the kind of meaning conveyed through the grammatical system as we relate information and express perceptions. For example, we express time relationships through tenses and duration through prepositional phrases. This Wilkins calls the 'semantico-grammatical' or 'notional' category. The second component is modality, arising from modal meaning, i.e. the expression of attitude towards the content of what is conveyed, for example certainty, as in 'He must have …', or disbelief, as in 'I'm astonished that …'. The third component is that of communicative function, i.e. the purpose of using the utterance in conversation or the sentence in a written text, for instance, to advise, to complain, to report, or to persuade.

Wilkins' components of notions, modality, and functions have been highly influential in attempts to find new bases for syllabus design. The Council of Europe, for example, produced the syllabus specifications 'Threshold Level English' (van Ek 1975) and 'Waystage English' (van Ek, Alexander, and Fitzpatrick 1977), which are widely used by ELT textbook writers. These built on Wilkins's work in order to provide a framework for specifying language learning objectives. This framework is as follows:

1 the situations in which the foreign language will be used, including the topics which will be dealt with;
2 the language activities in which the learner will engage;
3 the language functions which the learner will fulfil;
4 what the learner will be able to do with respect to each topic;
5 the general notions which the learner will be able to handle;
6 the specific (topic-related) notions which the learner will be able to handle;
7 the language forms which the learner will be able to use;
8 the degree of skill with which the learner will be able to perform.
(van Ek 1975: 8–9)

In these eight elements we can recognize most of the bases now available for ELT course design: situations, functions, topics, notions, structures, and skills. These are the elements which the designer integrates into a multi-dimensional syllabus. They are considered in detail in Yalden (1983) and Nunan (1988a).

10.2.4 *Designing a course unit*

As well as global decisions about the type of syllabus to choose, we need to reflect on a number of decisions about how to plan and construct course units. Decisions about how to time units and lessons within units are relatively straightforward, but others are more complex and interrelated, and require careful thought. For example:

– In a multi-dimensional syllabus, which dimension provides the organizing principle?
– How does the choice of organizing principle determine the sequence of activities in a course unit and the sequence of units in a course?
– What 'content' does a course offer to learners?

Which dimension provides the organizing principle?

Table 10.1, which shows a situational syllabus under construction, demonstrates how it is organized. The situation is the basis of the design. The choice of situation suggests key functions, and structures can then be selected as formal exponents of those functions. It is also possible to decide on relevant skills work.

Table 10.1: A situational syllabus under construction

Hours	Unit	Situation	Functions	Structures	Skills work
3	1	Meeting people	Greeting Introducing Giving information	*This is …* *I'm …* *He/she's a …* *I'm a …*	Speaking: meeting people Reading: a hotel Writing: form-filling

Topics can also be used as an organizing principle to generate the various dimensions of a syllabus, as shown in Figure 10.3. Here the course designer has started with skills by listing typical texts or speaking situations related to the topic. This helps in determining lexical areas within the topic and the language structures needed to express certain functions. For example, 'talking about plans' will necessitate the use of future forms, or 'talking about past events' from a recent holiday will involve the vocabulary of places and activities, and the use of the past simple tense.

Figure 10.3: A topic diagram for 'holidays'

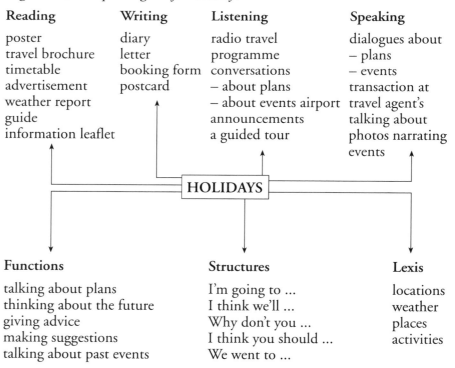

Reading

poster
travel brochure
timetable
advertisement
weather report
guide
information leaflet

Writing

diary
letter
booking form
postcard

Listening

radio travel
programme
conversations
– about plans
– about events airport
announcements
a guided tour

Speaking

dialogues about
– plans
– events
transaction at
travel agent's
talking about
photos narrating
events

HOLIDAYS

Functions

talking about plans
thinking about the future
giving advice
making suggestions
talking about past events

Structures

I'm going to ...
I think we'll ...
Why don't you ...
I think you should ...
We went to ...

Lexis

locations
weather
places
activities

How does the choice of organizing principle determine the sequence of activities in a course unit, and the sequence of units in a course?

The choice of organizing principle can be a major determining factor in the eventual sequence of activities in a unit. For example, where the structural dimension is primary, it is typical to find a Presentation–Practice–Production format in materials, with presentation of the structure, its controlled practice, and then its production in freer speaking or writing tasks, as discussed in 5.4.2. This has been the traditional format in much commercially produced ELT material. Other formats, however, are available for sequencing activities in a course unit. A skills-based unit can follow the basic 'pre-reading, while-reading, post-reading' sequence, and each part of the pattern can involve integrated skills work. For example, pre-reading can take the form of writing a set of statements, listening to a short interview, or discussing opinions on the topic. Some contemporary materials have taken an events-based approach to sequencing activities. Here the content follows a sequence of events as they would occur in real life, using each event as the basis for language practice. The sequence in Figure 10.4 was designed for EFL students in a UK-based summer school. The advantages include the motivation that comes from realism and the opportunity for using authentic texts from the English-language environment.

Figure 10.4: An events-based sequence of activities

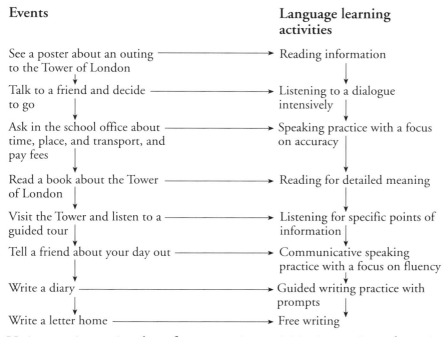

Events	Language learning activities
See a poster about an outing to the Tower of London	Reading information
Talk to a friend and decide to go	Listening to a dialogue intensively
Ask in the school office about time, place, and transport, and pay fees	Speaking practice with a focus on accuracy
Read a book about the Tower of London	Reading for detailed meaning
Visit the Tower and listen to a guided tour	Listening for specific points of information
Tell a friend about your day out	Communicative speaking practice with a focus on fluency
Write a diary	Guided writing practice with prompts
Write a letter home	Free writing

Various options exist, then, for sequencing activities in a unit, and a major factor in selecting the option will be the primary dimension of the syllabus, whether structure, situation, topic, or skill. There will be other factors in operation as well and these include:

— variety of activity in relation to learner motivation: this will link to typical lesson length and how much of unit can be covered in one lesson
— intensity of learning load and the need to create a balance between more and less cognitively demanding activities
— variety of interaction to cater for student preferences for whole-class work, groupwork, pairwork, and individual work.

Some of these factors are usefully captured in Maclellan's (1987) distinction between 'stirring' activities, those which are busy and stimulating, and 'settling' activities, those which require care and a slower pace. Teachers used to spending long hours in the classroom will immediately appreciate the relevance of this distinction for themselves as well as their learners.

The choice of organizing principle also determines the degree of flexibility in the sequence of course units. A structural syllabus builds in a *linear* way, with careful grading which needs to be followed by learners in the set sequence. This is also true of some coursebooks which describe themselves as functional. Careful perusal can show that the functions are a cosmetic addition to an underlying graded structural syllabus. A topic-based syllabus, in contrast, can take a *modular* format, each module consisting of self-contained materials which can be worked with in the order preferred by teacher and students. However, another determinant of flexibility in the use of units will be the organization of the content, which is the vehicle for presenting language.

What 'content' does a course offer to learners?

I shall use 'content' here to refer not to the language content but to the characters who people a book, their backgrounds, their experiences and opinions, and the events in which they participate. In other words, in structural materials presenting the past simple tense 'Who went where with whom to do what?', or in a functional course, 'Who is disagreeing with whom about what?' Similarly, in a skills-based course, 'What do students listen to or read, and what do they talk or write about?'

A number of options are available and teachers will need to decide the suitability of each for their own learners. For example, for younger learners a story-line with the same people and places can appeal to their familiarity with the story genre, can increase sympathy with the language through empathy with the characters, can introduce humour and fun, and can present a comfortably familiar setting confined to home and school. For adults, a story-line has the advantage of including characters in interaction so that the link between language and role relationship can be shown. On the other hand, it may prove too restrictive in relation to the need to present cultural diversity and a range of topics. A variation is to provide episodes in the lives of a wider group of people which may be linked to the main story-line in some way. This enables the inclusion of more diverse information. It is clear, however, that the inclusion of a story-line cuts out the flexibility of using units in any order.

Topic-based materials, as we have seen, are a useful and popular way of organizing course units. The secret of success seems to lie in choosing topics which are provocative but not offensive, intellectually stimulating but not too arcane, and popular but not bland.

10.2.5 *What procedures can be helpful in evaluating courses?*

The final stage in Figure 10.2 is 'Evaluating'. The term 'evaluation' has often been taken to mean the assessment of students at the end of a course, but in recent years its meaning has widened to include all aspects of a programme. Skilbeck (1984) has made a useful distinction between assessment and evaluation:

> … assessment in the curriculum is a process of determining and passing judgements on students' learning potential and performance; evaluation means assembling evidence on and making judgements about the curriculum including the processes of planning, designing, and implementing it.
> (Skilbeck 1984: 238)

From this perspective, evaluation can relate to courses and learners in a number of ways. It can try to judge the course as it is planned, for example, in terms of the appropriateness of the textbook content to the students or the coherence of a teacher's scheme of work for the next six weeks. It can try to observe, describe, and assess what is actually happening in classrooms as a course progresses. It can test what learners have learned from a course. Nunan (1988b) calls these three aspects of evaluation 'the planned curriculum', 'the implemented curriculum', and 'the assessed curriculum'. Evaluation can help us to see the complex relationship among these three. For example, it has been acknowledged by second language acquisition researchers for some time that there is no easy one-to-one relationship between teaching and learning, and that a teacher cannot set out learning objectives for a class and expect learners to achieve these uniformly by the end of the lesson. It is more the case that the teacher makes content available to learners, who work on it in different ways and at different rates and with differing degrees of uptake. Thus, if evaluation of a course is undertaken only by means of end-of-term student assessment, this procedure will give just part of the picture. The full picture can only be seen if a wider set of evaluation procedures are employed such as talking to teachers and students, checking teachers' work schemes, and observing classes. These procedures can also shed light on those other aspects of classroom learning which have been called the 'hidden curriculum' (Barnes 1976), for example, the shaping of learners' perceptions and attitudes towards other peoples and cultures by the teacher's choice of materials.

If, to use Skilbeck's (1984) definition of evaluation, judgements are to be made about the curriculum at an institutional level, then information needs to be collected from a variety of 'stakeholders', i.e. those interested in its effectiveness, be they learners, teachers, and educational managers, or authorities, parents, governors, sponsors, and funding agencies. And a range of procedures will be needed for the collection of data. We also need to acknowledge the sensitivity surrounding evaluation: who undertakes it, how comment is kept confidential, how the information is analysed, and how it is used. Too much or badly managed evaluation can create suspicion, hostility, or 'evaluation fatigue'. These issues become particularly difficult during periods of retrenchment in education when posts and funding may be at risk.

Nunan (1988b), Brown (1989), Rea-Dickins and Germaine (1992), and Weir and Roberts (1994) have all provided checklists which are useful for course evaluation in ELT departments and curriculum review at the institutional level. However, even at the level of the individual teacher interested in improving the quality of a course, a rational approach is necessary. We will now look at the key questions such an approach would need to address.

Why is the evaluation being carried out?

An important distinction here is between evaluation for *accountability* and evaluation for *development* (Weir and Roberts 1994). The first may well involve decisions about whether a course will be repeated, whether a textbook will be dropped, or whether a particular resource such as a listening laboratory has been used sufficiently to warrant further investment in self-access listening materials. This purpose of evaluation makes staff and/or institutions answerable to authorities and/or sponsors. It also makes publishers and textbook writers accountable to teachers and teachers accountable to their students. It often takes place at the end of a programme and, when undertaken by an institution, it may be carried out by an external evaluator. In contrast, developmental evaluation aims at improvement: it often takes place during a course so that feedback can facilitate immediate improvement to the current programme as well as to future programmes. As feedback can enlighten both teachers and managers about the strengths and weaknesses of course design and professional practice, this kind of evaluation can usefully involve both in co-operative procedures which aim at improving quality of work. The point has been made repeatedly in management literature (Miles 1964; Handy 1978; Everard and Morris 1985) that 'healthy' institutions are ones which have regular procedures for reviewing their work and openness of discussion about ways to effect improvements. Course review can therefore be most usefully perceived as a regular activity with agreed criteria and procedures, and ensuing action plans.

Who carries out the evaluation?

One aspect of the agreed procedures which needs careful thought is who carries out course evaluation. If undertaken by a head of department or director of studies, it may well be seen as staff appraisal and regarded by teachers as threatening. Since evaluation for development depends on the willingness of teachers to acknowledge their concerns and problems, a major task for managers will be to avoid suspicion, and to create an ethos of openness, mutual respect, and trust. For this reason, many schools prefer procedures which involve teachers in evaluating their own work and in drawing on institutional resources in order to improve what they see as their areas of weakness.

What is to be assessed?

The precise method of evaluation will relate to what exactly a teacher or course director wants to assess. For example, in order to get feedback from students on the interest-level of textbook content, a simple rating scale from 1 to 5, which students can score against each topic, might be appropriate. However, in order to assess the usefulness of a listening laboratory, the teacher might want to set up a log book in the laboratory with individual sheets for students to complete after each session, recording the work they have done and perceptions of their progress with it. Table 10.2 lists some of those aspects which teachers might want to investigate and questions they might want to address. The precise choice of focus and range will depend on the age and level of students, the nature of course objectives and content, and whether there are recent innovations to be evaluated.

How is the evaluation to be done?

In evaluating our own courses we can use a variety of procedures. One simple method I often use is to head a set of poster-sized sheets with key issues, for example:

What I have learned from this course
What I liked most about the course
What I liked least about the course
How I think the course could be improved.

Table 10.2: Aspects of a course teachers might want to investigate

Course aspects	Questions to address
Student needs	— What were the students' priority needs and to what extent has the course fulfilled them? — Have students become aware of further needs?
Course content	— To what extent have different content areas of the course been useful? — What further topics, situations, etc. would students like to cover? — What has been the interest-level of particular texts, discussions, etc.?
Resources	— What do students think are the strengths and weaknesses of the textbooks used? — To what extent have students used other resources available? — Have students used community resources?
Methodology	— What aspects of methodology do students like/dislike, find useful, interesting, etc? — Do students feel that the pace of classes is appropriate? — Could students be more involved in choosing texts and designing tasks?
Teaching strategies	— Are there any activities the teacher feels uncomfortable with? — Does the teacher perceive any weaknesses in teaching techniques or classroom management?
Learning strategies	— Are there areas in which learner training is needed? — How do students help themselves to learn outside the classroom? — What are learners' perceptions of the most useful kinds of homework?
Assessment	— Have progress tests related effectively to course objectives and course content? — Has the amount of assessment been adequate and well-timed? — Have students gained a clear idea of their progress and been counselled on it? — Have students had opportunities to assess themselves? — Have adequate records been kept?

The teacher can organize the procedure, appoint a chair, and withdraw from the room to ensure openness of discussion and anonymity of comment. Students then agree and list comments on the posters, and a tally is kept of how many students agree with each comment. The teacher, on returning, can discuss the comments and the feasibility of various ways to improve quality. The clear advantages of this procedure are its simplicity, speed, openness of comment, and opportunity for discussion.

In contrast, the administration of a questionnaire survey, a popular method, is time-consuming in preparation and processing, and, if set for completion out of class, responses may be difficult to chase up. However, the advantage of this method is that the teacher can ask about points of special concern and can ensure coverage of many course elements. One way of engaging students' interest is to ask them to submit questions or prepare parts of the questionnaire in groups as classwork.

The poster session and the questionnaire survey are procedures for gathering feedback from students. Good advice for the design of questionnaires and other ways of eliciting student feedback can be found in Nunan (1992) and Weir and Roberts (1994). Other methods of evaluating courses involve observation, review of documents, and teacher self-report. Table 10.3 summarizes what is available to the teacher. You will need to decide what is most appropriate for your own learners in the context in which you teach. Diary-keeping, for example, has become popular in many western contexts where this activity is part of the cultural tradition, but it would need careful consideration in some other contexts and is, in any event, a matter of personal taste and preference.

Table 10.3: Methods of evaluating courses

Method	Examples
Student feedback	– Interview students in groups or individually. – Ask students to complete questionnaires in class or at home. – Ask students to write key comments on posters. – Hold an informal discussion. – Ask students to make evaluative notes individually on the week's classes to give to the teacher.
Teacher self-report	– Fill in a self-assessment sheet. – Keep a log book or diary.
Observation	– Make an audio/video recording of groupwork in a class and analyse the extent to which what happened is what you planned or expected. – Observe one student through a week's classes and analyse interest, attention, strategies, strengths, and weaknesses. – Ask a colleague to watch a lesson and observe a particular aspect of your teaching, e.g. explanations, controlled practice, vocabulary work. Ask for critical comment.

Documents   — Review course objectives.
                         — Review lesson plans and write evaluative comments.
                           Look for points to improve on.
                         — Review student work and pinpoint issues to work on.
                         — Ask students to keep diaries of what they like/dislike,
                           find easy/hard, interesting/uninteresting, and review
                           these periodically.

When should evaluation take place?

Two kinds of evaluation can be used in a course. The first is *summative assessment* at the end of a course, a useful point at which to review the whole course in order to pinpoint elements for improvement. The second is *formative assessment* which takes place as the course proceeds. Ideally, evaluation should be planned from the beginning, a schedule set, participants decided upon, and criteria and procedures agreed by all involved. For example, a teacher may decide to elicit feedback from students by means of a poster session midway through a course and respond immediately on points arising; or a director of studies may co-ordinate the design and administration of a questionnaire survey at the end of a term, the responses to which may be used for further course planning.

What should be done with the information gained?

If ELT schools and departments are to remain 'healthy', then the information collected needs to be fed into a review process which goes beyond the individual teacher and links to wider decisions within the institution regarding time-tabling, choice of learning materials, development of resources, organization of the general curriculum, and provision of in-service training. Consideration, therefore, needs to be given to these questions:

How is the information to be collated?
How is it to be analysed?
To whom is it to be disseminated (e.g. teachers, managers, sponsors, students)?
How is it to be disseminated (e.g. written report, verbal report at a staff meeting)?
When is it to be discussed?
What action plans might arise from the discussion?

If we hold informal poster sessions with our classes, these questions are easily dealt with. We can return to the class, posters can be displayed and points discussed, we can talk about what is feasible among suggested improvements, and make undertakings. Our students can also make undertakings in this discussion and a date for further feedback can be set. The teacher can then contribute information from the evaluation to departmental or school discussion. In the case of a questionnaire survey across a range of courses, the director of studies can collate information statistically and present a short report to a staff meeting, and the ensuing discussion can generate action points to be allocated among staff. Such a procedure needs sensitive management, ownership of the data by all involved, open discussion, and a focus on issues arising rather than on individual teachers. Only then can evaluation become a force for improving quality within an institution.

10.3 What choices do teachers need to make in course design?

10.3.1 *Choosing a textbook*

When departments or individual teachers have the freedom to choose course materials, a critical eye is needed. Two stages can usefully be undertaken in evaluating the relevance of a book to a particular group of students. The first stage is to assess the content of a book in relation to its professed aims. If, for example, a book states an underlying principle of its materials to be that cross-cultural understanding is important in language learning, then teachers will need to ask:

Does the book show parallels and contrasts between the learners' culture and others?
Is this done in a non-patronizing way?
What aspects of culture are in focus?
Do these give a rounded picture?
Does the book present national culture as monolithic, or does it show awareness of cultural variation?

Similarly, if another stated principle is that students need to establish those learning strategies which will help them make progress independently, then teachers will need to ask:

Does the book deal explicitly with learning strategies and suggest ways of using and developing them?
Is a sufficient range of strategies presented?

This first stage enables evaluation of the extent to which a book fulfils its own aims and is therefore reliable in carrying out its undertakings to the learner.

A second stage would then be to assess the book against the needs and context of the intended learners. In other words, are the materials appropriate and are they likely to be effective in helping learners to acquire English? It would be useful to list some key categories for evaluation and then list questions for each category: these would vary according to learner factors, institutional setting, and sociocultural context. Table 10.4 shows some examples. There are a number of such checklists available for textbook evaluation (for example Williams 1983; Cunningsworth 1995; Matthews 1985; Sheldon 1988). Sheldon's list is presented on pages 367-72.

Table 10.4: Key categories and examples of questions for evaluation

Category	Questions
The view of language	– What levels of language receive attention? – How is the language system categorized? Are social aspects of language as communication taken into account, e.g. level of formality?
The view of language learning	– Is there explicit reference to grammatical terms and concepts? – Is there an appropriate balance of accuracy and fluency activities? – Is there a balance of modes of language use, i.e. listening, speaking, reading, and writing? – Does the first language have a role in the materials?
Learners	– What age group do the materials have in view? – How does the book relate to the needs of learners? Is the content interesting and challenging to the learners?
The view of education	– Does the book have general educational goals? – Are these appropriate to the learners? – Do they fit the national curriculum? – Do the materials encourage learner independence?
The environment of learning	– Does the teacher's role in the book fit in with local perceptions? – Is the cultural content accessible/ appropriate? – Is the grading and sequencing appropriate to the amount and intensity of time available?

10.3.2 *Taking a process approach*

Choosing a textbook, as we have seen, essentially means choosing a planned sequence of items to be taught. These plans have been called 'product' syllabuses as they focus on the product of learning, whether this is knowledge of a set of grammatical structures, or the communicative ability needed to participate in a set of situations or to talk about a set of topics. The product syllabus has been characterized as one which represents 'what is to be achieved through teaching and learning as formal statements' (Breen 1987: 85), in which 'objectives are defined in advance' (White 1988: 44), and often specified in terms of 'the knowledge and skills which learners should gain as a result of instruction' (Nunan 1988a: 27).

Most experienced teachers take the view that a textbook should be supplemented in line with learner needs and have added other ingredients to the programme such as drama, extensive reading, role-play, communication games, and debates. Typically these supplementary activities provide opportunities to experiment with language, to listen to and produce a wide range of vocabulary and language functions, and to negotiate meaning in interaction with other learners. In recent years, the concern with how learners can use and develop their communicative ability in addition to acquiring language knowledge of various kinds has led to the process approach to course design: in this approach the focus is not so much on *what* learners need to cover but on *how* they acquire language through performing it in the classroom. The question has become not so much on what basis to create a list of items to be taught as how to create an optimal environment to facilitate the processes through which language is learned. This concern has been influenced by the 'progressivist' movement (Clark 1987) in general education, which focuses on the experience of learning and is as much interested in methodology as in syllabus design. One outcome has been the design of communicative tasks according to the criteria discussed in Chapter 2, and the organization of these within a task-based syllabus.

Designing tasks

The criteria for the design of an 'unfocused' task were set out in 2.4.1.

1 The focus of the task should be on meaning and outcome and not on the language forms to be produced in completing the task. The term 'unfocused' usefully captures this key criterion.
2 The content of the spoken or written English should be determined by the learner and not controlled by the teacher. The learner has to formulate and produce ideas, information, opinions, etc.
3 There must be negotiation of meaning between speakers, i.e. a learner must be engaged in interpreting meaning from what another learner says and constructing what to say as a response.
4 In order for criterion 3 to function, what a learner hears should not be predictable, i.e. there should be an information or opinion gap.
5 The learner will need to use all his or her existing language resources and take risks with them, e.g. ask for and provide clarification, and use the normal strategies of communication in doing this.

A task based on these criteria would be significantly different from many 'production' activities in textbooks which follow a 'Presentation–Practice– Production' model as shown in Materials extract 5.D on page 165.

Materials extract 10.B conforms to the criteria for an unfocused task. It is this kind of task which would form the basis of a task-based syllabus. Unfortunately, in ELT materials the term 'task' is often used confusingly to refer not only to unfocused activities but also to form-focused work and even traditional practice exercises.

Materials extract 10.B

My weekend

1 What's your favourite way to spend Saturday?
   Make a timetable for a perfect Saturday.
   Write about it in your Project Book.
   Stick in some photos, too.

2 Ask your friends about their Saturdays.
   Write timetables of their day.
   Stick them in your Project Book.

(Author's materials)

In summary, the process syllabus has been characterized as one which represents 'knowledge of *how* correctness, appropriacy, and meaningfulness, can be simultaneously achieved during communication within events and situations' (Breen 1987: 160). Tasks will therefore have the primary aim of giving learners a chance to express their own ideas and opinions using the language resources they have available to them, and achieving greater degrees of accuracy, appropriacy, and fluency as they practise. Several writers (for example, Ellis 1985; Candlin 1987; Nunan 1989a) have given useful lists of principles to guide teachers in the design of tasks.

The task-based syllabus applied

The major issue for teachers in organizing a syllabus based on tasks is how to put together a series of tasks to form a coherent programme; in other words, what criteria to use for selecting and sequencing tasks. This question is more easily answered in teaching situations where a process approach relates directly to identifiable needs in students. Let us take, for example, the situation of teaching adult migrants who already have some working knowledge of English but experience difficulty in functioning successfully in the English-speaking community. Classroom tasks can replicate those which learners will need to carry out in real life such as being interviewed for a job, answering the telephone, and following instructions how to use a machine. And a set of tasks can be negotiated with a class according to students' perceptions of, for example, what is most urgent, challenging, worrying, or sensitive.

With regard to general English language education, particularly in the early stages, many teachers take the view that a product syllabus, which presents and practises a formal set of linguistic items, is desirable. If we accept that learners also need a 'process' element of unfocused tasks, the question is how this element can be introduced and integrated into a course. Brumfit (1980) has suggested a spiral syllabus, as shown on the left in Figure 10.5, in which a series of unfocused tasks will enable students to use the language they have acquired while following a basic product syllabus. This type of syllabus can be seen in textbooks where 'extension' units engage learners in less formally focused tasks. Ellis (1987) suggests a parallel syllabus with separate strands, as shown on the right in Figure 10.5. This might well be seen in a weekly timetable of four sessions where two sessions follow a product syllabus based, say, on structures, with focused tasks, a third session is given to literature with a series of role-play, discussion, and writing tasks, and the fourth session uses project work (see 10.3.3). Issues of grading and sequencing will still be important to a teacher following separate strands in a course. In the literature sessions, for example, thought will need to be given to how tasks can be graded according to such factors as length of reading extract, difficulty of cultural background in the text, complexity of textual organization, number of steps in the task, number of students involved in performing the task, and length of time to complete the task.

Figure 10.5: Spiral and parallel syllabuses (Ellis 1987: 188)

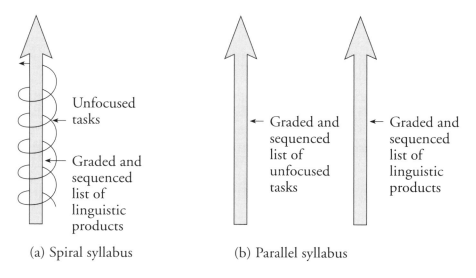

(a) Spiral syllabus

Unfocused tasks

Graded and sequenced list of linguistic products

(b) Parallel syllabus

← Graded and sequenced list of unfocused tasks

← Graded and sequenced list of linguistic products

10.3.3 *Using projects in ELT*

The project has become a popular element within the process approach. Projects are extended tasks which usually integrate language skills work by means of a number of activities. These activities combine in working towards an agreed goal and may include the following: planning; the gathering of information through reading, listening, interviewing, and observing; group discussion of the information; problem solving; oral and written reporting; and display.

Brumfit (1984b) gives an example of an ELT project in which advanced students elect to work in groups to produce a radio programme about their own country. A range of topics, for instance, ethnic groups, religion, and education, are allocated to the groups. They research their topic, and write and rehearse a script. Materials extract 10.C is a project for secondary-school pupils in which they use knowledge from Science and Geography to research threatened species, write an article, and make a poster. This has the particular advantage of linking English to other curriculum subjects and using content for which the students have relevant prior knowledge.

Project work has been part of educational principle and practice in experiential learning for the greater part of this century, and has influenced the teaching methodology of many curriculum subjects at the school level. Barnes (1976), for example, has made the point that children do not learn successfully simply by receiving transmitted facts but need to explore new ideas through talk and writing in order to build them into their developing understanding of the world. Projects are essentially learner-centred and illustrate the educational view expressed by Postman and Weingartner: 'the critical content of any learning experience is the method or process through which the learning occurs' (1969: 30). Since the mid-1970s, as ELT has come to espouse principles of learner-centred teaching, learner autonomy, collaborative learning, and learning through tasks, English language teachers have explored and exploited the tradition of project work.

Legutke and Thomas (1991) use data from case studies of project work in the UK, the USA, and Germany to suggest three types of project. 'Encounter projects' enable students to make contact with native speakers, for example British or American visitors to their countries. They are also often used where students are living in or visiting an English-speaking community. 'Text projects' encourage students to use English language texts, either a range of texts to research a topic, or one text, for example a play to read, rehearse, present, and discuss. 'Class correspondence projects' involve documents such as letters, audiocassettes, e-mail messages and photographs exchanged between pupils in different countries.

Projects usually involve a number of features which fit the principles of communicative language teaching discussed in this book:

Materials extract 10.C

(Hutchinson: *Project English 2* SB, page 63)

– an emphasis on group-centred experience
– the encouragement of student responsibility for planning, carrying out,
  and presenting a task

- a sequence of activities over a period of time, e.g. planning, fieldwork, preparation of information, and presentation
- the use of a range of skills
- activity outside the classroom in the students' own time
- the study and use of authentic English-language material.

They have been promoted in ELT for a number of reasons: for example, learners' use of language as they negotiate plans, and analyse and discuss information and ideas, is determined by genuine communicative needs. With younger learners, project work encourages imagination and creativity, self-discipline and responsibility, collaboration, research and study skills, and cross-curricular work through exploitation of knowledge gained in other subjects.

Successful use of project work will clearly be affected by such factors as availability of time, access to authentic materials, receptiveness of learners, the possibilities for learner training, and flexibility of timetabling. However, where project work can be designed to fit contextual considerations, it is achieving growing popularity and has become part of ministry of education recommendations in some countries, as we saw in Materials extract 10.A. What we need now is evaluative data comparing quality of learning from this approach as compared with others.

10.3.4 *Negotiating with learners*

At various points in this chapter, mention has been made of negotiating course content and procedures with learners. This concept of involving learners in decision-making about their learning programmes has become popular in contexts in which the cultural and educational ethos is conducive to self-determination and in which the age of the learners is considered to be appropriate. It fits with the progressivist view that learners will learn more effectively if it is clear that their experiences and perceptions are valued, and if they are involved in developing the course through a process of consultation. It involves talking to students about the objectives of a course, encouraging them to see how the aims of a textbook reflect their own aims, and helping them to formulate personal objectives and to monitor and report back to the teacher how these are being met as the course proceeds. Materials extract 10.D is a questionnaire used with upper-intermediate students embarking on a writing course. The teacher wishes to adjust and extend the content of a potentially useful coursebook to suit the students' needs.

Notice how the questions invite students to suggest both content and procedures for the course, and how the textbook provides an initial focus for negotiation, for identifying needs, formulating and prioritizing aims,

Materials extract 10.D

Making decisions about the course

Preview the coursebook carefully and answer the questions. Be ready to discuss your views in class.

A Yourself

  1 Think about your own strengths and weaknesses in writing English. Try to list them.

B The book

  2 How many units are there? Do they all look equally useful in helping you to develop your writing ability?

  3 Look at the organization of a unit. Make a list of the components in it. Decide how each one will help you to develop your English.

  4 Make a list of the topics covered in the book. Are any of these irrelevant to your needs or interests? Are there any topics you would like to study which are not here?

  5 What is your first impression of the book? Do you think it offers help with your own problems in writing? Is there anything missing which you would have expected to be included?

  6 Are there parts of the book which you think you could study successfully by yourself?

C The course

  7 Given our limited class-time, which parts of the book would be best studied in class together?

  8 Would you prefer to do the essay-writing:
    – at home?
    – in class, individually, with the teacher to assist?
    – in class, with some co-operation in pairs and groups at the planning, revising, and editing stages?
    – as a mixture of these?

  9 How many pieces of written work could you do each week?

  10 Do you have any other suggestions/requests relating to the course?

(Author's materials)

choosing and extending writing topics and tasks, and for sequencing the programme. In fact the class in question ultimately used materials from a range of sources, the textbook becoming one item in a bank of resources. Notice, also, how the questions invite negotiation of procedures and enable students and teacher together to agree on a working contract specifying how much writing will be undertaken and when.

A useful description of how a process syllabus provides a framework for negotiation is given by Breen (1987). He identifies four levels of decision-making to be negotiated. At level one are decisions about the language-learning experience; at level two, decisions involving working procedures and content; at level three, decisions involving the choice of alternative activities; and, at level four, decisions involving the choice of tasks.

In order to illustrate these elements, I will draw on my experience as 'animator' of a self-determining group of Swedish adults learning English in a study circle. Breen's level one was represented by an initial meeting and discussion in which individual group members made suggestions about the format of the course and their roles vis-à-vis my responsibilities. Decisions were made at level two to meet once a week in members' homes. Topics were determined for a twelve-session discussion course, each member taking responsibility for preparing and leading one session. My roles were to be those of language informant, resource provider, and monitor of performance. Alternative activities chosen at level three consisted of social conversation, oral presentation by individuals or pairs, study of texts, and discussion. Level four can be demonstrated by a sample session which consisted of one member, a doctor, describing, with the help of documentation and photographs, her perceptions and experiences of a study visit to a British hospital. This session included questioning from the group, study of texts I had put together on the British health system, and debate of parallels and contrasts between this and the Swedish system. Evaluation was formative and informal, and arose from each session. It largely involved requests to me to change roles at various points to formulate vocabulary tasks on written texts, record presentations, and comment on language use, or to find follow-up material for individual extensive reading.

An important point to note about a negotiated process syllabus, when decisions about content and procedure are taken throughout the course, is that record-keeping becomes crucial. In order to be accountable in terms of work covered and in order for future teachers to build on work completed, a 'retrospective syllabus' is needed. The teacher's notebook, learner logs, and records from evaluations can all be combined to provide a full course report.

10.4 Conclusion

This chapter has attempted to set out the *status quo* with regard to those options currently available to language teachers as course designers and as users of textbooks. The model used to describe course design has been influenced by curriculum planning in general education, in which processes of considering the students, establishing goals, choosing a product or process approach to course planning, designing course units, and evaluation, are held to be of importance. At the moment in ELT, our syllabus design and course unit design are based on experience, reflection, and logical reasoning. It is to be hoped that in coming years it will be possible to add the outcomes of evaluative studies to these sources of information on, and insight into, the effective planning of courses.

Discussion topics and projects

1 Collect a set of textbooks and investigate any goals they state, and also their contents pages. What do these tell you about their underlying assumptions concerning language and learning?

2 Look back at Figure 10.3 and Figure 10.4 in 10.2.4. Use either a topic diagram or an events-based sequence for integrating work on language and language skills: choose a topic and design your own topic diagram or events-based sequence.

3 Study the list of evaluation criteria below.

Rationale	– Why was the book written in the first place, and what gaps is it intended to fill?
	– Are you given information about the needs analysis or classroom piloting that were undertaken?
	– Are the objectives spelt out?
Availability	– Is it easy to obtain sample copies and support material for inspection?
	– Can you contact the publisher's representatives in case you want further information about the content, approach, or pedagogical detail of the book?
User definition	– Is there a clear specification of the target age range, culture, assumed background, probable learning preferences, and educational expectations?
	– Are entry/exit language levels precisely defined, e.g. by reference to international 'standards' such as the ELTS, ACTFL or Council of Europe scales, or by reference to local or country-specific examination requirements?

	— In the case of an ESP textbook, what degree of specialist knowledge is assumed (of both learners and teacher)?
Layout/graphics	— Is there an optimum density and mix of text and graphical material on each page, or is the impression one of clutter? — Are the artwork and typefaces functional? colourful? appealing?
Accessibility	— Is the material clearly organized? — Can the student find his or her location in the material at any point, i.e. is it possible to have a clear view of the 'progress' made, and how much still needs to be covered? — Are there indexes, vocabulary lists, section headings, and other methods of signposting the content that allow the student to use the material easily, especially for revision or self-study purposes? — Is the learner (as opposed to the teacher) given clear advice about how the book and its contents could be most effectively exploited?
Linkage	— Do the units and exercises connect in terms of theme, situation, topic, pattern of skill development, or grammatical/lexical 'progression'? — Is the nature of such connection made obvious, for example by placing input texts and supporting exercises in close proximity? — Does the textbook cohere both internally and externally (e.g. with other books in a series)?
Selection/grading	— Does the introduction, practice, and recycling of new linguistic items seem to be shallow/steep enough for your students? — Is there a discernible system at work in the selection and grading of these items (e.g. on the basis of frequency counts, or on the basis of useful comparisons between the learner's mother tongue and English)?

	— Is the linguistic inventory presented appropriate for *your* purposes, bearing in mind the L1 background(s) of your learners?
Physical characteristics	— Is there space to write in the book? — Is the book robust? too large? too heavy? — Is the spine labelled? — Is it a book that could be used more than once, especially if it is marked by previous students?
Appropriacy	— Is the material substantial enough or interesting enough to hold the attention of learners? — Is it pitched at the right level of maturity and language, and (particularly in the case of ESP situations), at the right conceptual level? — Is it topical?
Authenticity	— Is the content obviously realistic, being taken from L1 material not initially intended for ELT purposes? — Do the tasks exploit language in a communicative or 'real-world' way? — If not, are the texts unacceptably simplified or artificial (for instance, in the use of whole-sentence dialogues)?
Sufficiency	— Is the book complete enough to stand on its own, or must the teacher produce a lot of ancillary bridging material to make it workable? — Can you teach the course using only the student's book, or must all the attendant aids (e.g. cassettes) be deployed?
Cultural bias	— Are different and appropriate religious and social environments catered for, both in terms of the topics/situations presented and of those left out? — Are students' expectations in regard to content, methodology, and format successfully accommodated?

                                        — If not, would the book be able to wean students away from their preconceived notions?

                                        — Is the author's sense of humour or philosophy obvious or appropriate?

                                        — Does the coursebook enshrine stereotyped, inaccurate, condescending or offensive images of gender, race, social class, or nationality?

                                        — Are accurate or 'sanitized' views of the USA or Britain presented; are uncomfortable social realities (e.g. unemployment, poverty, family breakdowns, racism) left out?

Education validity   — Does the textbook take account of, and seem to be in tune with, broader educational concerns (e.g. the nature and role of learning skills, concept development in younger learners, the function of 'knowledge of the world', the exploitation of sensitive issues, the value of metaphor as a powerful cognitive learning device)?

Stimulus/practice/   — Is the course material interactive, and are
revision   there sufficient opportunities for the learner to use his or her English so that effective consolidation takes place?

                                          — Is the material likely to be retained/ remembered by learners?

                                        — Is allowance made for revision, testing, and on-going evaluation/marking of exercises and activities, especially in large-group situations; are ready-made achievement tests provided for the coursebook, or is test development left for the hardpressed teacher? Are 'self-checks' provided?

Flexibility   — Can the book accommodate the practical constraints with which you must deal, or are assumptions made about such things as the availability of audio-visual equipment, pictorial material, class size, and classroom geography; does the material make too many

demands on teachers' preparation time and students' homework time?
- Can the material be exploited or modified as required by local circumstances, or is it too rigid in format, structure, and approach?
- Is there a full range of supplementary aids available?

Guidance
- Are the teacher's notes useful and explicit?
- Has there been an inordinate delay between the publication of the student's and teacher's books which has meant that teachers have had to fend for themselves in exploiting the material?
- Is there advice about how to supplement the coursebook, or to present the lessons in different ways?
- Is there enough/too much 'hand-holding'?
- Are tapescripts, answer keys, 'technical notes' (in the case of ESP textbooks), vocabulary lists, structural/functional inventories, and lesson summaries provided in the teacher's book?
- Is allowance made for the perspectives, expectations, and preferences of non-native teachers of English?

Overall value for money
- Quite simply, is the coursebook cost-effective, easy to use, and successful in your teaching situation, in terms of time, labour, and money?
- To what extent has it realized its stated objectives?

(Sheldon 1988: 242–5)

(a) Which of these criteria are particularly important to you when you choose books for your own classes?
(b) Would you wish to add or delete any?
(c) Apply the criteria to a textbook currently in use in your institution and discuss its strengths and weaknesses.

4 Do you see project work as relevant, desirable, and/or useful in the situation in which you teach? Discuss the advantages and disadvantages of introducing it into the ELT curriculum, and consider ways of dealing with any constraints you might encounter.

5 Think of a suitable project for your own learners.

   (a) How would you introduce the topic?
   (b) What stages would the project follow?
   (c) What materials and/or guidelines would you need to design for each
       stage? Design your introductory materials.

6 To what extent do you use negotiation with your learners? What are its
   advantages and disadvantages? What are the most effective practical
   procedures you could use?

7 Review the examples of evaluation procedures in section 10.2.5.

   (a) What are the advantages and disadvantages of each, and which would
       be most suitable for your own learners?
   (b) Decide on the questions you would like to address in relation to a
       course you have been teaching, then design an evaluation procedure.

Further reading

Breen, M. 1987. 'Contemporary paradigms in syllabus design.' *Language
Teaching* 20/2: 81–92 (Part 1) and 20/3: 157–74 (Part 2).

This two-part article provides an overview of syllabus design in ELT. It
makes a major distinction between the 'propositional syllabus' and the
'process syllabus', and discusses the theoretical underpinnings of both and
the issues that exist for the syllabus planner. This article is useful reading for
those who wish to delve into ideas about language and learning which have
influenced the design of courses since the 1950s.

Clark, J. L. 1987. *Curriculum Renewal in School Foreign Language Learning.*
Oxford: Oxford University Press.

Clark's book takes a wide educational perspective on issues of syllabus
design. He traces the influence of movements in general education, and
those of humanism, reconstructionism, and progressivism, and discusses the
ways in which they have influenced approaches to designing school language
syllabuses. He also looks at issues in curriculum review and planning for
change, and gives a detailed account of two projects which demonstrate
principles at work and issues arising.

Cunningsworth, A. 1995. *Choosing Your Coursebook.* Oxford: Heinemann.

This book gives clear advice on selecting coursebooks according to criteria
for careful evaluation. The author provides useful checklists for decision-
making. There is discussion of various types of coursebook and suggestions
on how to adapt materials to suit particular teaching/ learning situations.

Dubin, F. and **E. Olshtain** 1986. *Course Design: Developing Programs and Materials for Language Learning.* Cambridge: Cambridge University Press.

This book is intended for teachers who are involved in planning courses for their own learners or who might be involved in the design of programmes and materials on a wider scale. It covers the factors which need to be considered in setting up a course and then looks at the stages of design: setting goals, selecting a type of syllabus, and designing activities. The focus is on communicative approaches and the book offers practical application activities.

McDonough, J. and **C. Shaw.** 1993. *Materials and Methods in ELT.* Oxford: Blackwell.

This book reviews and explores different approaches to ELT methodology, showing how they are realized in materials. There are plenty of practical examples of materials and useful study questions.

Nunan, D. 1988a. *Syllabus Design.* Oxford: Oxford University Press.

Nunan's book is divided into three sections. The first considers general issues in syllabus design such as establishing the needs of learners, selecting and grading materials, and designing tasks. The second section looks at practice and examines a wide range of syllabuses and course materials. The third helps teachers to analyse their own teaching situation, and to apply relevant and useful ideas to their selection of books for learners and to their own efforts at syllabus design.

White, R. V. 1988. *The ELT Curriculum: Design, Innovation and Management.* Oxford: Blackwell.

White reviews the development of ideas on the ELT curriculum, the range of syllabus types available, and the rationale for each. He goes on to discuss the efficient introduction and implementation of change in the curriculum and the issues that arise for management. This book provides a particularly useful perspective for those who have, or will have, responsibility for innovation in their institutions.

11 CLASSROOM ASSESSMENT

Pauline Rea-Dickins

> *'Simply knowing the final score of the game after it is over is not very useful. What we need is a vivid rendering of how that game is played.'*
>
> E.W. EISNER

1   What do we know about assessment and testing?

2   What has influenced approaches to language testing?

3   What should we know about classroom assessment?

4   What characterizes good assessment practice?

Introductory task

Consider each of the statements below in relation to your own teaching situation. Decide whether each of them is true, partly true, or not true. You may wish to discuss your responses with a colleague afterwards. You may also find it useful to revisit your answers once you have read this chapter.

	True	Partly true	Not true
A purpose of marking and assessment is to indicate learners' strengths.			
A purpose of marking and assessment is to indicate learners' weaknesses.			
A purpose of marking and assessment is to motivate learners.			
My assessments focus on my learners' language learning achievements.			
My assessments focus on my learners' language learning development.			
I only assess my learners by means of marks or grades.			
When I report their results, I add comments as well as giving my learners their marks.			

I invite my learners to assess themselves and their progress.			
I write reports/records at regular times during the academic year.			
My school/institution has a policy for assessment that all the teachers and learners know about and understand.			

11.1 Introduction: assessment and testing

The title of this chapter uses the term 'assessment', not 'testing'. This is because assessment is the more inclusive term: it refers to the general process of monitoring or keeping track of the learners' progress. Testing is one kind of assessment, one which is typically used at the end of a stage of instruction to measure student achievement. Assessment is a broader concept: it is part of the whole educational process of teaching and learning, and that is what this chapter is about.

The chapter also raises some questions about attitudes towards assessment and testing and, here, it is interesting to reflect on our own experiences. E. Williams (1985) writes of the negative connotations associated with tests and testing. Other authors make this point too (for example, Heaton 1990; Weir 1993). Indeed, there will be very few of us who have never had any moments of dread caused by one or more testing experiences at times in our learning careers when learning is associated with jumping hurdles that seem too high. Very often, these experiences are associated with feelings of failure and lack of self-esteem which may last well beyond school-days. However, this chapter attempts to examine assessment as a positive experience which contributes to the process of teaching and learning as a whole.

Assessment is a multi-faceted concept that links together the different issues highlighted in the Introductory task. Whilst tests can be used as a 'bolt-on' procedure at end-points in a learning programme, assessment is integral to the whole process of teaching and learning. It is the means by which students' language learning development and achievements are monitored over time.

Assessment is undertaken for different purposes. One purpose is pedagogically motivated, i.e. *formative assessment*, where the teacher will use information gained from assessments about a learner's progress as the basis for further classroom work. This, as we shall see later, is a complex process that requires careful structuring. A second purpose for assessment is to measure learner achievement. This is referred to as *summative assessment*.

Usually it has to fit into the administrative requirements of an institution, for example a private language school, or a school curriculum in which all subjects are required to be assessed. In some cases, the results from summative assessments are used to check quality, for example results from schools and institutions may be compared nationally, or regionally, to set standards. Table 11.1 summarizes some of the distinguishing features of formative and summative assessment.

Table 11.1: Some distinguishing features of formative and summative assessment

Formative assessment:	Summative assessment:
– is prepared and carried out by the class teacher as a routine part of teaching and learning	– is not necessarily prepared and carried out by the class teacher
– is specifically related to what has been taught, i.e. content is in harmony with what has been taught	– does not necessarily relate immediately to what has been taught
– the information from the assessment is used diagnostically; it is focused on the individual learner's specific strengths and weaknesses, needs, etc.	– the judgement about a learner's performance is likely to feed into record-keeping and be used for administrative purposes, e.g. checking standards and targets
	– is frequently externally imposed, e.g. by an institution or a ministry of education.

It is particularly important to recognize that formative assessment is concerned with keeping track of the learners' progress as it happens and identifying ways of helping it along. Its focus is on the process of learning. With summative assessment, on the other hand, the focus of attention is on the result of learning. It is more concerned with identifying overall levels of achievement and measuring what learners do against them.

A third purpose for assessment is formal certification. Here, structured tests of the paper-and-pencil variety are usually provided by an external organization. Examples of popular language examinations include the First Certificate in English (FCE) and Cambridge Proficiency in English (CPE), administered by the University of Cambridge Local Examinations Syndicate (UCLES) based in the UK, and the Test of English as a Foreign Language (TOEFL), administered by Educational Testing Services, based in the USA.

Information from assessments is of interest to a number of people who have a stake in education. These include not only learners, teachers, and parents, but also education advisors and policy-makers. The way information is presented will obviously have to be different for each group. For example, the format of a report for parents will be different from one a teacher would keep.

11.2 What is testing?

'Testing' is a term that is not always used precisely. Here, it refers to the specific procedures that teachers and examiners employ to try to measure ability in the language, using what learners show they know as an indicator of their ability. These tests are usually of the traditional pencil-and-paper variety, and some examples are provided in this chapter. Good tests provide the opportunity for learners to show how much they know about language structure and vocabulary, as well as how they are able to use these formal linguistic features to convey meanings in classroom language activities through listening, speaking, reading, and writing. Tests of this type may be used as part of an integrated assessment system.

Approaches to testing have been influenced by developments in applied linguistics and educational measurement. While applied linguistics has provided important insights which derive from our understanding of what language is, the field of educational measurement has provided useful formats for test design.

11.2.1 *The structuralist influence*

In the late 1950s and early 1960s the structuralist approach to linguistic analysis was influential. In this approach 'knowing' a language was identified with knowing the 'form' or 'structure' as well as the other linguistic elements of 'lexis' and 'phonology'. It was exemplified by the influential testing frameworks of Lado (1961), linked to his work on contrastive analysis, and of Carroll (1961). These have had far-reaching effects on the kind of test design which has viewed language as a set of separate parts, as in the following example (Heaton 1989):

> Underline the correct option.
>
> He may not come, but we'll get ready in case he ...
>
> A. will   B. does   C. is   D. may
>
> (Heaton 1989: 33)

Examples like this are known as *discrete-point items* as they attempt to test one aspect of language at a time. This multiple-choice example (i.e. stem + 3 distracters) is also decontextualized: it is in a single-sentence format with no other context provided, either within the item itself or in the previous parts of the test.

The rise in popularity of these so-called 'objective' approaches to testing can also be traced to developments within the field of educational measurement in which *reliability* was an important concept. Reliability is concerned with the accuracy with which a test can measure the language abilities of an individual. Objective test formats, such as the multiple-choice item above, were shown to provide high test reliabilities as compared to open-ended items. They were mainly associated, until the late 1970s, with testing the formal elements of language, i.e. form, structure, lexis, and phonology. It is important, however, for teachers to keep in mind that many of the statistics associated with this concept of reliability are not strictly relevant to concerns of classroom learner assessment. More recently, approaches to assessment have been influenced by our developing understanding of language as communication and have attempted to assess learners' functional and communicative use of language.

11.2.2   *The communicative influence*

Perhaps the most influential framework provided for testing by applied linguists was outlined in the now classic state-of-the-art paper by Canale and Swain (1980). Building on the work of Hymes (1964), Canale and Swain examined the nature of communicative competence, identifying elements of 'grammatical competence', 'sociolinguistic competence', and later, 'discourse competence' (Canale 1983), and the need to assess all these components. Similarly influential was Bachman's (1990) model of communicative language ability (see 2.1).

The influence of these models can be seen in the Communicative Use of English as a Foreign Language series of tests, developed by the Royal Society of Arts. These tests of listening, speaking, reading, and writing identified a number of characteristics which 'do not seem to be measured in conventional tests' (Morrow 1981: 16). These features, regarded as part of communicative language ability (see 2.1 and 2.2), reflected the characterization of language use as interaction-based, and stimulated by a specific communicative purpose on the part of the speaker or writer to convey a particular message to a predetermined audience. Sample test items developed on this basis incorporated elements of 'authenticity' of language context, situation, and topic, with communicative purpose and language function clearly specified. The first example below is premised on the belief that the 'chief characteristic of question asking in a real-life situation is the "information gap" which exists between speaker and addressee and which the speaker is trying to bridge' (Morrow 1977: 38):

> A. Prior to the test the candidate is given a card which outlines a situation. He must invent a number of questions he would want to ask in that situation. (The situations being derived from the specified exam. syllabus.)
>
>> e.g. You arrive at Victoria Station in London to catch the train to Paris. You want to find out something from each of these people. What would you say?
>> 1. A passer-by in the station entrance.
>> 2. The booking clerk.
>> 3. Your friend who is travelling with you.
>> 4. The ticket collector.
>> (Morrow 1977: 38)

The next is an example suitable for a reading test:

> Everything you see in the shops can be bought to take away, with the exception of certain items of furniture and display stocks. Where smaller items of furniture are held in stock, these items will be clearly marked 'Take Away'. To cut down handling charges and the risk of damage, the larger items will be delivered direct to your home from our warehouse. When you place an order for furniture you will be given a delivery period. If, for any reason, we cannot keep to this delivery period, we will advise you … Enquiries about the furniture order should be made to the Furniture Manager of the shop where you placed the order.
>
> 1 What is this about?   a. Buying furniture
>   b. Take-away furniture
>   c. Large items of furniture
>
> 2 What is the purpose of the passage?   a. To give information
>   b. To apologise
>   c. To promise
>
> (ibid.: 46)

The questions above are examples that learners at lower levels may be expected to answer. The next set are aimed at learners with a higher level of language ability:

> 4 'If, for any reason, we cannot keep to this delivery period, we will advise you.' Is this:
> a. a piece of advice?
> b. an apology?
> c. a piece of reassurance? …

6 Can orders be delivered immediately?
a. Always
b. Sometimes
c. Never
(ibid.: 46)

Morrow explains that question 4 is about 'the function or implication of individual sentences' whereas question 6 is a 'conventional comprehension question testing a closer understanding of the content' (ibid.).

In summary, this elaborated model of 'language as communication' incorporated the formal elements of language (grammar, vocabulary, and phonology) as well as the hypothesized components of communicative language use. This has contributed to changed modes of testing in three distinct areas: content, format, and making criteria.

Changes in content

First, the content of tests is broader, with increased emphasis on the sub-skills involved in listening, speaking, reading, and writing. Weir (1988; 1993) provides clear examples of this, illustrated by the following operations for 'listening':

Summary checklist of operations (listening comprehension)

(a) *Direct meaning comprehension:*

Listening for gist.

Listening for main idea(s) or important information; includes tracing the development of an argument, distinguishing the main idea(s) from supporting detail, differentiating statement from example, differentiating a proposition from its argument, distinguishing fact from opinion when clearly marked.

Listening for specifics; involves recall of important details.

Determining speaker's attitude/intentions toward listener/topic (persuasion/explanation) where obvious from the text.

(b) *Inferred meaning comprehension:*

Making inferences and deductions; evaluating content in terms of information clearly available from the text.

Relating utterances to the social and situational context in which they are made.

Recognising the communicative function of utterances.

Deducing meaning of unfamiliar lexical items from context.

(c) *Contributory meaning comprehension (microlinguistic):*

Understanding phonological features (stress, intonation, etc.).

Understanding concepts (grammatical notions) such as comparison, cause, result, degree, purpose.

Understanding discourse markers.

Understanding syntactic structure of the sentence and clause, e.g. elements of clause structure, noun and verb modification, negation.

Understanding grammatical cohesion, particularly reference.

Understanding lexical cohesion through lexical set membership and collocation.

Understanding lexis.

(d) *Listening and writing (note taking from lecture, telephone conversations, etc.):*

Ability to extract salient points to summarise the whole text, reducing what is heard to an outline of the main points and important detail.

Ability to extract selectively relevant key points from a text on a specific idea or topic, especially involving the coordination of related information.

(Weir 1993: 98–9)

The content of tests is thus focused on a learner's ability to 'extract meaning' in listening. Elsewhere, Weir (1988; 1993) identifies sub-skills in the area of reading, writing, and spoken interaction.

Changes in format

A second difference is found in a greater variety of test formats. These have progressed from explicitly language-focused tasks; such as 'Select the correct preposition' or 'Put the verb in brackets into the correct past-tense form'; to tasks which are communicatively contextualized, i.e. with a specific audience and communicative purpose in mind. In these tasks, learners are given greater opportunities to construct their own messages. For example, they may be asked to respond to brief written messages and to 'Write a short note to X', to listen to announcements and extract specific points of information, or to exchange information with a fellow learner, as in Materials extract 11.A.

Materials extract 11.A

Assessment task 5 Speaking (elementary)

Part 1
Student A:
Find out this information about your partner:
name/age/family/favourite music/what s/he does at the weekends

Student B:
Find out this information about your partner:
name/age/hobbies/favourite school subject /what s/he does in the holidays

Part 2
Student A:
Describe this half of the picture to your partner. Then listen to his/her description and draw the rest of the picture. You can ask him/her questions

Student B:
Listen to your partner's description of the other half of the picture and draw it. You can ask him/her questions. Then describe the other half to him/her.

(Harris and McCann: *Assessment*, page 43)

Changes in marking criteria

A third change is in criteria used for marking, especially in relation to spoken interaction and written language. For example, if we take the speaking task in Materials extract 11.A, the marker will undoubtedly be interested in the accuracy of grammar displayed by the learner, in the use of appropriate vocabulary, and in correct question forms. These are some traditional criteria which relate to linguistic competence. However, in a more communicative approach to marking we would wish to add, for example, the ability to interact responsively to what has been said, the relevance of what is said to the task, and whether or not the learner manages to communicate a message effectively. In this way, the traditional criteria associated with the accurate command of syntax and lexis have been augmented by a new set of criteria identified with aspects of communicative language use.

These various changes have their origins in the concept of *communicative language ability* and are part of an ongoing process of refining the goals and procedures of testing in ways which take the dimensions of this ability into account. The changes are, perhaps, most evident in the kinds of tests produced by examination boards and, in this respect, are part of what was earlier described as summative assessment. However, it should be noted that classroom assessment of a formative nature has also benefited from the concept of communicative language ability. For example, the marking of classroom writing tasks, as discussed in 9.3.4, now tends to include more communicative criteria which can indicate to students their developing strengths as writers and those areas of weakness to which they must attend.

11.3   What is the role of classroom assessment?

As suggested earlier, testing may be one procedure used by teachers to check on student progress, for example using progress tests available in coursebooks, or practice tests to prepare for public examinations. However, this is only one possible element of assessment. Classroom assessment can take other forms which may be formative in nature. It is to this more general process of monitoring learner development that the discussion now turns.

11.3.1   *What purposes should classroom assessment have?*

Classroom-based assessment is concerned with gathering useful information that the teacher can use to support student language learning. A survey by Brindley (1989a) investigated teachers' assessment practices in the Australian Migrant Education Program and reported on their views of assessment. His findings for 131 teachers are shown in Table 11.2. Brindley's findings demonstrate the importance that these teachers place on assessment as a support to teaching and learning functions. They reflect the view of this chapter that assessment should be part of teaching and learning, and capable of providing detailed information for teachers, learners, and parents. For this to happen, the feedback from assessments has an important role to play, as the next examples show.

Table 11.2: Perceived importance of functions of assessment (Brindley 1989a: 25)

	Mean	SD	Rank
Place learners in class	4.296	1.059	1
Provide information on learners' strengths and weaknesses for course planning	4.137	1.129	2
Provide information on funding authorities for accountability purposes	2.482	1.512	6
Encourage students to take responsibility for their own learning	3.957	1.268	3
Provide students with a record of their own achievement	3.207	1.393	5

(SD = standard deviation)

11.3.2 *What kind of feedback is useful?*

What is the role of feedback provided by assessments in informing curricular processes? The following examples show two contrasting examples of feedback. Example 1 provides limited information. It tells us how the learners have performed on a test, relative to each other. If we assume that five marks and over constitutes a pass, then this information distinguishes between a pass and a fail. However, because the information is limited to scores (and the same would apply to a grade such as A, B, or C) it is unlikely to assist the teacher in precise planning for a class. Neither do results in this form provide a useful guide to the learner on what needs to be worked on specifically in order to perform better. Example 2 is different. The teacher's written comments not only indicate the strengths and weaknesses of the student's writing but they may also assist students in monitoring their own progress and identifying specific language areas to develop further. They may highlight for a teacher priorities in terms of future teaching, or recycling of points already covered. The information could also be useful to parents.

In summary, assessment procedures which only yield scores or grades do not adequately fulfil the needs of classroom-based assessment. They may be useful in establishing norms and in clarifying whether standards are being met. However, in order for teachers and their learners to gain a better understanding of individual development, other types of procedure, which yield more feedback, will be necessary.

Figure 11.1: Two contrasting examples of feedback

Example 1: Marks for a test
Total marks: 10

M. Connolly	9	S. Joseph	9	R. Daimler	8
T. Thorpe	7	M. Roll	5	R. Dodge	4
A. Borrill	3	Y. Sinclair	2	F. Olive	2

Example 2: Teacher feedback on a classroom writing task
Total marks 10: 5 for task; 5 for language

M. Olivier: Total 3 marks

Task: 1   An attempt has been made to write a letter but it does not contain the information required by the task. The letter is too short. The overall message is unclear to the reader.

Language: 2   Very weak control of structures; structural errors obscure meaning. Relevant vocabulary for the task.

R. Nader: Total 7 marks

Task: 4   The letter clearly explains the reason for the complaint and why the customer wants a replacement. The letter achieves the appropriate formality. The message is clear throughout.

Language: 3   Some inaccuracies in use of tenses, but these do not obscure meaning. Appropriate vocabulary. The linking between sentences could be improved.

(Author's data)

11.3.3 *What assessment procedures are available?*

Classroom assessment procedures include the conventional paper-and-pencil style of test, structured classroom observation, and other modes such as portfolios and, self-assessment.

Paper-and-pencil tests

These are the tests with which most readers are familiar, and several examples of test items are given in 11.2.2. Paper-and-pencil tests are structured, tend to be formal, and are administered under controlled conditions with both stimulus and learner response in written form. They are very well-documented in published testing handbooks which take a teacher/test designer through the test construction process. One short section of a chapter cannot hope to examine aspects of test design and construction in any detail and the reader is therefore recommended volumes such as Hughes (1990); Weir (1993); Alderson, Clapham, and Wall (1995); and

Bachman and Palmer (1996). Heaton (1989, 1990) are useful resources for writing objectively scored tests.

A number of considerations influence both the approach to test design and the content of the tests themselves. One of these, as we saw earlier, is to do with the view of language held by the teacher or coursebook writer and whether the focus is on language form or on communicative aspects of language. Another is the link between the test and the syllabus and materials being used in the classroom. For example, if the learners have been developing skills in producing a piece of writing for a particular kind of reader at an appropriate level of formality such as a letter of application to a course, then ideally the test should set up a task which requires a simulation of this purpose and audience, and the marking criteria will include appropriateness of style.

Observation-driven learner assessment

Observation-driven assessment has not yet developed in EFL contexts. The standard handbooks for teachers are all concerned with the test construction process rather than with the broader requirements of assessment in school settings (for example Hughes 1990; Weir 1993). We generally need to go outside the field of English foreign language education and look at mainstream language education in ESL settings (see McKay 1995) in order to learn about observation-driven approaches to assessment. These hold interesting potential for EFL. For example, in the context of primary children learning English as a second language, there has been a move since the late 1970s away from formal tests and towards overall assessment schemes, description-based and formative. In England, examples of this are the early work of Barrs and her colleagues (Barrs, Ellis, Hester, and Thomas 1988) and Hester (1993), who promoted the use of observation to describe language learning development with a focus on both language and content. The following is an example of a teacher's comments on the writing development of a pupil in the second year of an English primary school.

PC3 Writing   Please comment on the child's progress and development as a writer in English and/or other community languages: confidence and independence as a writer; range, quantity and variety of writing in all areas of the curriculum; pleasure and involvement in writing both narrative and non-narrative, alone or with others; influence of reading on the child's writing; growing understanding of written language, its conventions and spelling; development of handwriting.

As a writer she has developed considerably over this year. She is independent, confident and fluent, using writing for a range of purposes and audiences across the curriculum. She is able to sustain a correspondence over two terms, to make books autonomously, and to write in a transactional style. She is always clear about the content and form of her writing, and spontaneously checks for meaning as she writes — prepared to change anything that is semantically / syntactically unclear. She is learning the English spelling system, and in her writing uses phonetic & visual checking strategies, known words, and reference to surrounding print in the classroom.

(Hester 1993: 16)

With an increased focus on communicative activities in the classroom such as information-transfer tasks, role-play, and tasks designed to promote oral interaction (both listening and speaking skills), it can be argued that observation is a valid means of gathering information about the development of language skills and, particularly, those aspects of communicative language performance that are less easy to capture in a traditional paper-and-pencil format. Harris and McCann (1994) point out:

> We often do reading tasks in class in *lockstep* fashion: the whole class reading one text and answering questions on it. Typical examples are the skimming and scanning activities so widely used or the 'comprehension questions' at the end of a text.

> There are various ways of assessing this kind of reading in the classroom. The first is by going around the class while students are doing a reading activity and observing which students seem to be understanding it and which are having difficulties.

> (Harris and McCann 1994: 17)

In the context of assessing reading in English as a second language, the need for a teacher to notice what a learner does when reading has been highlighted:

> – whether the child uses illustration (initially to help retell the story, later to check guesses)
> – whether the child makes use of the context to help work out the meaning; does what s/he reads make sense?
> – whether the child reads in meaningful chunks, or word by word
> – whether the child uses the structure of language to help work out the meaning
> – whether the child uses knowledge of what words/letters look or sound like to help work out unknown words
> – whether the child uses knowledge about books and written language to help work out meaning
> – whether s/he makes a good guess at unknown words, or waits to be told
> – whether s/he is using several strategies to get meaning from the text, or has heavy dependence on one strategy (e.g. phonic analysis)
> – whether the child self-corrects, and seems to be monitoring her/his own reading.
> (Hester 1993: 15)

Observation of learners on specific skills-based tasks can be planned into routine class schedules, but it needs to be well-managed in order to monitor progress in a principled, systematic, and comprehensive way over time.

Genesee and Upshur (1996) provide useful guidelines for planning classroom observation:

> Planning classroom observation
> 1 Why do you want to observe and what decisions do you want to make as a result of your observations?
> 2 What aspects of teaching or learning that are appropriate to these decisions do you want to observe?
> 3 Do you want to observe individual students, small groups of students, or the whole class?
> 4 Will you observe students engaged in specific, pre-arranged activities or during routine classroom activities?
> 5 Will you observe on one occasion or repeatedly?
> 6 Will you incorporate non-linguistic content from the students' other classes or from outside class?
> 7 How will you record your observations?
> (Genesee and Upshur 1996: 83)

There are, of course, disadvantages to the use of classroom-based description of learner performance. It requires an investment of time to get a scheme up and running, and of resources in training teachers to use such systems. However, although the need for additional training might be viewed as a disadvantage from one perspective, from another it can be seen as a useful focus for in-service activity. And there are other advantages, too, in the form of a potentially fuller and more valid picture of what learners can and cannot do, and of stages in learner progress. Observation-driven assessment has the potential to provide the level of detail that the teacher, learner, or parent can use as a basis for constructive action. In the words of one teacher:

> 'Comparing what I do now with what I used to do, the kind of record-keeping I did before was mainly to show me what children had done ... they had read aloud to me; they had worked on the computer. But there wasn't that fine detail of what the child could do, or was saying. There were notes but they tended to record what children had covered and what they'd done. I might have ticked to show that they know their number bonds up to 10. But there was nothing to say how they were approaching it, nor the level of understanding. I'm going deeper now into how they are learning.
>
> It does take longer for me, but it's worth it because I know so much more about each child. As it fits into my planning cycle, I find the planning and assessment dovetail together. But it also helps me to compare one child's development with another, and to plan how, by grouping them, the particular skills of each can be shared. It heightens my awareness of the stages of development they are moving through.'
> (Hester 1993: 38)

Observation-driven approaches to assessment require greater and qualitatively different teacher involvement than more traditional approaches: this includes a sound grasp of ways in which observation can be used to inform profiles of language learning development and learner progress, and the ability to use a broad range of tasks which facilitate this type of assessment.

Portfolios

An artist's portfolio may contain a record of the different types of work created—a range of drawings or paintings over time, not only the most recent—and provides a comprehensive picture of his or her capabilities, strengths, and weaknesses. In the same way, portfolios as part of classroom assessment can include samples from a range of students' work, for example writing, drawings, notes, audio- or video-recordings, extracts from projects, and performance on specific tests, to reflect different aspects of development, achievement, interest, and motivation. These samples of language can be kept in a variety of forms, for example notebooks, scrapbooks, loose-leaf binders, and box files. Students may be asked how they wish their work to be collated and stored.

One of the strengths of portfolios is the way in which they support the learning process. Tierney, Carter, and Desai (1991) (writing specifically of reading and writing, but this can be extended to other skills) suggest that portfolios help students to:

> Make a collection of meaningful work;
> Reflect on their strengths and needs;
> Set personal goals;
> See their progress over time;
> Think about ideas presented in their work;
> Look at a variety of work;
> See effort put forth;
> Have a clear understanding of their versatility as a reader and a writer;
> Feel ownership for their work;
> Feel that their work has personal reference.
> (Tierney, Carter, and Desai 1991: 59)

Making the best use of portfolios requires careful management on the part of the teacher. Students, too, need to be introduced to this mode of assessment and sensitized to the ways in which portfolios can be used as the basis for dialogue with the teacher, identifying developments in their own work, and monitoring their own progress. Graves and Sunstein (1992) also recommend that teachers keep portfolios of their own work in order to increase their awareness of what is involved in the process:

We need more … teachers who know portfolios *from the inside* … .
Maintaining our own portfolios has contributed more to our
understanding of their possibilities and use than virtually any other
aspect of our work with them.
(Graves 1992: 5)

In other words, keeping a personal portfolio may not only lead to the
development of a critical perspective in the teacher, but it may also provide
insights into their use which can then be shared with learners.

Self-assessment

The concept of self-assessment has already been introduced in 3.4.3, in
connection with learner training and learner autonomy, as a means by which
learners may be encouraged to monitor and check their own progress. Self-
assessment has been around for some considerable time (see Oskarsson
1988) and, like portfolios, is a procedure which may involve the learner
directly in the assessment process. Implicitly it recognizes that learners
should be able to take responsibility in making decisions about their own
language learning development.

Although there has been a certain ambivalence towards the suitability of this
procedure for school learners, there is now a considerable body of research
that demonstrates the benefits of self-assessment for many different types of
learners. Numerous studies report on the use of self-assessment (for example,
Blue 1988; Brindley 1989a; Lewis 1990). For a useful survey see Oscarson
(1997).

Harris and McCann (1994) provide a range of potential formats for learner
self-assessment. The activity in Materials extract 11.B requires learners to
reflect on what has been learned over a period of time and express it as marks
out of 10.

Materials extract 11.B

Questionnaire 1
Think about your progress this term. Give yourself a mark out of ten
for these areas:
- speaking   /10   • pronunciation   /10
- listening   /10   • grammar   /10
- reading   /10   • vocabulary   /10
- writing   /10

(Harris and McCann: *Assessment*, page 84)

Materials extract 11.C

Grade these things (1-5) related to effort and attitude:	
participation in class	
use of English in class	
homework and projects	
working in groups	
planning and working on my own	

(Harris and McCann: *Assessment*, page 86)

Materials extract 11.C focuses learners' attention on the effort they have made in class and on their attitudes to learning, and asks them to grade these in sequence. In contrast to the example in Materials extract 11.B, which focuses on learner achievement, that in Materials extract 11.C focuses on involvement in the learning process.

The activity in Materials extract 11.D requires learners to reflect on how well they can use the target language to fulfil certain functions, and to estimate how well they can accomplish the listed activities, as well as to identify things that they are unable to do.

Materials extract 11.D

Questionnaire 3
- Tick which of these things you can do now (✓).
- Put two ticks if you can do it very well (✓✓)
- Put a cross if you can't do it (✗)

a I can talk about what I did yesterday.
b I can ask other people about what they did yesterday.
c I can write about what I did yesterday.
d I can give and ask for directions.
e I can understand simple directions.
f I can write simple directions.
g I can talk about how I get to and from school.
h I can understand a description of a place.
i I can write a description about a place.
j I can describe places.

(Harris and McCann: *Assessment*, page 86)

Such procedures are intended for use as part of routine class activity, and the areas in which learners are asked to self-assess directly reflects what has been taught.

Self-assessment is a flexible learning tool, and there are numerous ways to mould the style and content of the assessment to suit a particular course or group of learners. One of its strengths links up with the points made in 11.1 about the sometimes hostile environment of assessment. Self-assessment has the advantage of involving learners.

11.4 What characterizes good assessment practice?

11.4.1 *Are affective considerations relevant to assessment?*

Motivation is as relevant to assessment processes as it is to learning (see 1.3.4). Teachers need to try to understand what motivates their class and learners as well as to identify the problems that learners experience. One question we might ask is whether it would be relevant to include information about affective factors in profiling a learner's general performance.

Heaton (1990) provides a performance profile in connection with the criteria of a learner's attitude ('persistence' and 'determination') in learning English:

5 Most persistent and thorough in all class and homework assignments. Interested in learning and keen to do well.

4 Persistent and thorough on the whole. Usually works well in class and mostly does homework conscientiously. Fairly keen.

3 Not too persistent but mostly tries. Average work in class and does homework (but never more than necessary). Interested on the whole but not too keen.

2 Soon loses interest. Sometimes tries but finds it hard to concentrate for long in class. Sometimes forgets to do homework or does only part of homework.

1 Lacks interest. Dislikes learning English. Cannot concentrate for long and often fails to do homework.

(Heaton 1990: 116–17)

As a teacher, you may not necessarily agree with how this profile is framed, but it is one that could be readily modified to the needs of a specific group of learners in order to better understand their approach to language learning in your class. The issue of attitude is also taken up in Materials extract 11.E. This awareness-raising task for teachers also highlights other affective areas, namely learner co-operativeness, independence, creativity, and presentation.

If we take a broader brief for assessment, it might be relevant and useful to include the characteristics of the learner as well as the learner's ability in the language. This is certainly information that parents might appreciate. It then becomes important to augment the existing and more conventional types of assessment procedure.

Materials extract 11.E

---

a Attitude
- is interested in class activities
- is willing to offer opinions
- is co-operative with teacher/peers
- is willing to respond to the opinions of others

b Co-operativeness
- is able to work in pairs
- is able to work in groups
- is able to work as a member of the whole class
- is able to share ideas and knowledge

c Independence
- is able to plan and organise own work
- is able to self-correct where necessary
- is able to use sources of information

d Creativity and presentation
- shows original thought, initiative, inventiveness
- presents work neatly and in an ordered manner

(Harris and McCann: *Assessment*, page 21)

11.4.2 *How can good assessment practice be framed?*

Assessment should be fair to all learners, and practicable. To this end a number of writers have put forward guidelines for good practice. In English language teaching these have been primarily with reference to test design and construction and have not been extended to classroom assessment processes (but see Harris and McCann 1994; Brindley 1995; Genesee and Upshur 1996).

It is important, too, that elements of good practice for an assessment *scheme as a whole* are understood. This is the area in which there is much to gain from developments in educational assessment. This extract from Tierney, Carter, and Desai (1991), for example, presents some of the features of a classroom-based assessment programme:

1 Assessment is based on what the child actually does. Student work and process are observed and analyzed to provide a rich view of progress, achievement, effort, strategies, and versatility.

2 Assessment addresses ... experiences in which students are engaged.

3 Classroom assessment procedures should describe clearly and accurately how students do on a variety of tasks over an extended period of time. Decisions about students' strengths and needs are derived as a result of analyzing multiple samples of student work that have been collected during the course of the year and show the students' versatility.

4 Effective classroom assessment programs are designed to include the students as active participant in forming ... tasks, in developing assessment criteria, and in assessing their own effort, progress, achievement, attitude, and goal attainment.

5 An assessment program should be multifaceted. There should be provisions to assess more than just the final products. Assessment should focus on achievement, process, and quality of self-assessment.

6 Assessment is continuous and inseparable from instruction. It is an interactive and collaborative process in which information is collected in natural classroom instructional encounters (individual, small group, and whole group). ...

7 A yearly assessment plan guides the timing and use of a variety of assessment procedures. These procedures should work together to form a composite. It is likely that there are regular assessments that occur weekly, quarterly, and yearly. These assessments may be varied and serve slightly different purposes.

8 Assessment strengthens teacher's and student's knowledge. Assessment should contribute to a teacher's and student's understanding of themselves and each other. ... Teachers and students should grow in their ability to make insightful analysis of the data gathered.

9 Record keeping and collections of work samples by both teachers and students provide the systematic information that facilitates communication.

10 The teacher is an expert evaluator, recognized and supported:
 – The teacher not only knows the nature of the learners' [work] … but provides first-hand evidence of progress and achievement.
 – The teacher has the opportunity to observe the learner first-hand across a variety of situations including those in which learners are interested, have varying degrees of background knowledge, interact with others, or proceed independently.
 – The teacher can explore the environments and situations that enhance learning.
 – The teacher assesses what students have achieved in terms of effort, improvement, and process.
 – The teacher pursues collaborative assessment with the learner, as well as the learner's ongoing assessment and development of self-assessment strategies.

11 The students' ability to assess themselves is viewed as a measure of how testing and assessment have a meaningful, ongoing, and working relationship with teaching.

(Tierney, Carter, and Desai 1991: 35–7)

In addition to these points it is worth emphasizing that classroom assessment is shaped by the way in which the English curriculum is actually implemented according to the values of a given educational context. Syllabuses differ across contexts; teaching methodologies vary; there are different expectations of teachers, of learners, and of the teaching and learning experience more generally. Teachers may also differ in their confidence and fluency in using English in class. All of these powerful factors interact and are reflected both in the professional practice of the classroom and in the area of learner assessment. Assessment is shaped by its educational context and therefore will need to sit comfortably within it.

11.5 Conclusion

Throughout this chapter, the importance of assessment as a positive, informative, and fair experience has been emphasized. In making decisions about the assessment process, it will be useful for teachers to keep in mind the benefits that can accrue to learners from sound assessment practices. Good assessment can be achieved through the gathering of information about learners over time, and through a combination of methods. Of course, these things do not happen on their own. It is up to the teacher to develop his or her awareness of assessment, to encourage learner awareness, and to make the process as effective as possible.

In conclusion, assessment should have what Tierney et al. describe as 'a working relationship with teaching and learning', and 'students should view assessment as an opportunity to reflect upon and celebrate their effort, progress and improvement, as well as their processes and products' (1991: 21). In evaluating our assessments, we need to check upon the extent to which they do just this. Did the assessment work? Did it provide the necessary information? If not, why not? How could we improve it for next time? Assessment is an important tool for the teacher as it can provide a wealth of information to guide classroom practice, and to manage learning and learners.

Discussion topics and projects

1 This chapter has looked at some affective factors in assessment. Look through the following teachers' comments about some learners' attitudes to assessment. Which observations do you agree with? Which do you disagree with? Are there any other points you would wish to add?

   (a) 'Younger learners like assessment, especially if they can colour or draw something.'
   (b) 'Older learners do not like assessment.'
   (c) 'Learners like assessment: it provides a new piece of evidence for success.'
   (d) 'Weaker students do not like assessment; but the better ones see it as a chance to show off.'
   (e) 'Learners take assessment as the normal course of events: they are very used to it.'
   (f) 'Some learners fear assessment—some kids are told off at home for bad marks.'
   (g) 'Sometimes I notice that at certain times of the year learners get overloaded with tests and easily get frustrated with them.'
   (h) 'Positive results will encourage learners; bad results the opposite.'
   (i) 'Learner nervousness may spoil their performance.'
   (Author's data)

2 Look through the general guidelines for using portfolios below. If you are not already using portfolio assessment, what would the benefits of introducing it be to yourself and to your learners? What would some of the disadvantages be? What difficulties do you foresee if you were to introduce this form of assessment in your context?

What are portfolios?

A file folder, box, or any durable and expandable container can serve as a portfolio. If everyone uses the same type of folder, the folders can be stored more easily. Folders should be clearly marked with each student's name, and they can also be decorated to each student's tastes, if desired, to enhance students' feeling of ownership.

What kinds of work are kept in portfolios?

Samples of writing, lists of books that have been read, book reports, tape-recordings of speaking samples, favourite short stories, and so on can all be included in a portfolio. Portfolios have most frequently been associated with written language, but they can also be used effectively with oral language. In this case, students keep audio recordings of speaking samples in their portfolios. ...

Students need not have a single portfolio; they can have a writing portfolio, a reading portfolio, a science portfolio, or whatever. Moreover, students can have one portfolio for their best work and one for work in progress. The best work portfolio might be used to show parents and visitors and for grading purposes, whereas the work-in-progress portfolio might be used by teachers and students themselves to monitor their progress and set learning goals.

Each piece of work in the portfolio should be dated clearly and, often, annotated with a short description of why it is included, what the student likes about it, or other pertinent comments.

How much work should be kept in portfolios?

The number of pieces in a portfolio should be limited for practical reasons. Portfolios that are constantly expanding and never cleaned out become difficult to store and, more important, difficult to review and assess. Students may choose to keep a portfolio of current work and one of completed work—the former would be more up to date and reflect current accomplishments whereas the latter would reflect previous accomplishments and the progress they have made.

If the number of pieces is to be limited, then it is necessary to review and update the portfolio periodically. In this case, decisions need to be made concerning the number of pieces (or range) to keep and the criteria for inclusion and exclusion. These decisions should be shared by teachers and students so that the students maintain ownership of and responsibility for their portfolios. ...

Who has access to portfolios?

Clearly, students should have access to their own portfolios at all times. Teachers also need to have easy access to them; whether teachers seek permission from or inform students before reviewing their portfolios probably should be negotiated with the students as a whole. Sharing the contents of portfolios with parents and other teachers and educational professionals enhances their beneficial effects. Portfolios that are not shared are mere collections of school work.

There are occasions when it is not possible or desirable to include students in reviewing their portfolios, however. For example, sharing students' portfolios with administrators may be undertaken as part of a review procedure to examine student placement in particular programmes or to revise grades based on standardized testing procedures. Furthermore, students' portfolios may be shared with teachers at the next level or grade so that they know the qualifications and skills of their incoming students in advance and can plan appropriate instruction. Student involvement in these cases may not be practicable or useful.

Where to keep portfolios

Keep the portfolios in a common, readily accessible area to which students have easy access. Storing them in the students' or teacher's desk is not a good idea because it disconnects them from students and from the general life of the classroom. If you are teaching part-time students who do not have their own classroom, it is not possible to store them in a common fixed area. In this instance, students need to keep their own portfolios.

(Genesee and Upshur 1996: 100–3)

3 Think of a task you would like to use for student assessment based on observation (for example an oral interaction task involving two or more learners).
   (a) Identify what you want to observe (i.e. select which aspects of language use you will look for when learners are doing this task, and decide what other evidence you might expect to observe if learners are able to complete the task successfully).
   (b) Decide how you will manage the observation (for example how many learners will you focus on, and for how long?).
   (c) What will you write down as observer? Which format will you use (for example checklist, narrative description)?

4 On your own, or with a colleague, review your responses to the preliminary task for this chapter. You may also wish to take into account your answers to some of the earlier tasks in this section, especially number 1. How would you summarize the way you assess your learners? Do you:
   (a) focus primarily on the language development of individual learners?
   (b) mainly compare the achievement of your learners in your class?

(c)   achieve a balance between (a) and (b) above?

5   Make a list of both the strengths and weaknesses of the way you, or your institution, approach learner assessment. Once you have drawn up this list, what changes would you like to see made in your assessment context and why? Would your suggestions be reasonably easy to manage and implement?

Further reading

Brindley, G. (ed.). 1995. *Language Assessment in Action.* Sydney: National Centre for English Language Teaching and Research.

This edited collection introduces a range of reports on testing and assessment initiatives from the Australian ESL context. The case-study focus of each chapter provides accounts of the way in which assessment tools have been constructed to meet the needs of specific groups. These contributions span primary, secondary, and adult language learning contexts and cover areas such as competency-based assessment, bandscales, and classroom-based assessment as well as self- and peer-assessment.

Genesee, F. and **J. Upshur.** 1996. *Classroom-based Evaluation in Second Language Education.* Cambridge: Cambridge University Press.

This volume deals with both the principles and practice of classroom-based assessment. It emphasizes the value of assessment for improving both teaching and learning. It provides in-depth analysis and guidance on different assessment procedures, for example, observation-driven as well as portfolio assessment, together with useful examples. Follow-up activities are also provided.

Harris, M. and **P. McCann.** 1994. *Assessment.* Oxford: Heinemann.

This is a very practical volume with plenty of examples to inspire the classroom teacher. It is clearly organized with guidance on assessment purposes, timing, procedures, and content. It contains ready-to-use materials, including model tests, and assessment and self-assessment sheets which teachers may adapt to their specific circumstances. Workshop activities are also included.

Heaton, J. B. 1988. *Writing English Language Tests.* (New edn.) London: Longman.

Heaton, J. B. 1990. *Classroom Testing.* London: Longman.

These two books will be useful to teachers who need careful guidance on how to write tests for their learners. They provide detailed information on how to write, administer, and score tests, as well as including many examples of different test-types. The general principles of testing are also introduced.

Tierney, R. J., M. A. Carter, and **L. E. Desai.** 1991. *Portfolio Assessment in the Reading–Writing Classroom.* Norwood, Mass.: Christopher-Gordon Publishers.

This book provides the rationale behind assessment, in particular portfolio assessment, and very detailed guidance on how to implement portfolio assessment in classrooms. It contains a wealth of examples and practical guidelines which teachers will find extremely useful. The link between assessment and instructional planning is another strength of this volume.

Weir, C. J. 1993. *Understanding and Developing Language Tests.* Hemel Hempstead: Prentice Hall International.

This book introduces the principles behind test development and validation and takes a critical look at a wide range of tests. It also includes a training element by providing a number of tasks which guide readers through key stages in the test-development process. The focus is on the four language skills of listening, speaking, reading, and writing, and a framework for the development of tests in each of these skill areas is provided.

APPENDIX: NOTES ON INTRODUCTORY TASKS

Chapter 1: Learners and learning, classrooms and contexts

The factors to which Rufino makes specific reference could be categorized in the following way:

(a) Social factors: positive attitudes towards language learning in the community; strong parental support; career and travel needs for learning English.

(b) Educational factors: manageable class sizes; flexibility within the national curriculum for course and examination design; well-resourced schools.

(c) Pupil factors: strong language awareness; positive motivation; appreciation of real reasons for learning English.

(d) Teacher factors: trained and qualified through pre-service teachers' courses; opportunities for in-service training.

Chapter 2: The communicative classroom

You might have used several criteria to decide that this was a communicative task. One is that the focus for the learners is on expressing ideas and opinions rather than producing correct language forms. This is because the learners themselves decide what to say. They have only visual prompts and no language is provided by the task itself. As the students discuss how to write the dialogue they will have to make sense of each other, interpret what is said, agree or disagree, and make appropriate responses as in real communication.

Chapter 3: Learner autonomy and learner training

This task is based on several I have seen in workshops and at conferences. Its precise origin is unknown.

1 The aim of Section A is to encourage students to preview the book and find their way around it. Section B addresses their expectations of a textbook and asks them to reflect on its possible uses. The questions suggest implicitly that the textbook is only one source of learning and that it can be used independently by learners.

2 The task might be used with secondary and adult learners, but its educational and cultural appropriateness needs careful consideration.

3 Section A is best done individually but could be followed by checking in pairs. Depending on class size, Section B could be used for pairwork, work in small groups, or whole-class discussion led by the teacher, or a mixture of these, for example two pairs forming a group of four to compare opinions.

Chapter 4: Vocabulary

Strategies often mentioned by learners are: making associations; learning words in groups; making and learning word-lists; reactivating new words in writing; collecting words from private reading, and making word-cards.

Other possible strategies which teachers encourage learners to use are: to guess the meaning of unknown words in texts by using contextual clues; to use dictionaries effectively, and to build awareness of word-networks (for example synonyms and antonyms).

Chapter 5: Grammar

1(a) personalizes the task of talking about immediate future plans by using the context of household tasks planned for the coming weekend.

(b) creates an ironic contrast between the future with 'will' and 'going to' through a set of situations which allow students to infer meaning. It shows attitude as part of meaning.

2 The materials assume that adult learners can make use of both implicit and explicit approaches to presentation of grammar. Activity 1, 'My future', guides students into seeing the link between a form and the situation in which it is used and gives them a chance to work with the patterns presented. However, the activity 'Activate your grammar' presents the rules of use explicitly for learners who like, and can deal with, this type of analysis. The listening task displays the target tenses so that learners can work out the different uses and thus discover how the language works for themselves. It could certainly be used for independent work.

Chapter 6: Reading

The missing words from the text in the Introduction are: 'tower', 'maker', 'tower', 'castle', 'castle', 'miller', 'waste', 'mill', 'treasure', 'strap', 'wrist', 'drawer', 'strap', 'wrist', 'drawer'.

A couple of examples will show the kind of clues to meaning which are available in the text. The meaning of 'jurrip' can be guessed with the help of the following: syntactic knowledge (it follows the article 'a' and therefore must be a noun; knowledge of the world (it is a place where people live), and cultural knowledge (it is a king's home which now lies in ruins). A 'wol' is something a watch can be fixed to, so general knowledge would suggest 'strap' or 'chain', and 'on your prad' gives a syntactic clue to 'wrist'.

Chapter 7: Listening

1 Pre-listening work has a number of purposes: creating motivation and particular reasons for listening; tuning in to the context and topic of the text; eliciting attitudes towards the content; activating any prior knowledge that students might have about the text, and introducing some unfamiliar language they will hear in the text.

2 Activity 1 encourages personal reflection in relation to the topic of the text. Activity 2 acts as a warmer for the text by getting the students to predict some of the content. Activity 3 encourages prediction of details from any existing knowledge the learners might have. All of these activities will elicit some of the language they will need to comprehend key points of the text.

3 During the listening, students are encouraged to attend to the text intensively and to make notes. This will allow them to confirm the predictions they made.

4 The teacher will perform a variety of roles: managing the activity through instruction and explanation; checking that students understand what is required of them; monitoring the students as they work, and checking their answers to diagnose strengths and weaknesses.

Chapter 8: Speaking

If we take Level 3 of these specifications as an example, it is possible to identify a number of skills which the upper-intermediate learner is generally expected to have, for example: to pronounce the language intelligibly; to have a high level of accuracy in grammar and lexis; to use language which is appropriate to context; to have a wide range of language; to have effective communication strategies; to be able to take turns in conversation; to be able to change topic; and to be able to develop ideas into a longer piece of spoken language.

Chapter 9: Writing

Some of the principles which underlie the teacher's approach could be set out as follows:

– Students should be engaged in class in the process of composing a piece of writing.
– Students need to practise writing in supported conditions.
– Students need to practise writing whole contextualized texts.
– Students need to practise planning, drafting, revising, and editing.

Chapter 10: Course design

Teachers may find many points for comment, according to their personal experiences. Here are a few:

(a) and (b) reflect a distinction between teaching and learning in that it is now a commonly held view that we can control what we teach but we cannot control what learners learn from our classes, or the order in which they learn.

(d) is important in many contexts: even where a syllabus is formed week by week throughout a course, perhaps in negotiation with learners, a retrospective syllabus as a record of work done will address the accountability issue.

(f) fits well with ideas about strategies used by good language learners.

(g) is seen as crucial, whether the goals are pre-set or negotiated with students.

(h) is also generally accepted.

(c), (e), (i), and (j) are more controversial and much debated.

Chapter 11: Classroom assessment

The aim of this task is to guide you towards a greater awareness of your own assessment practices and of the points you may wish to take into account when assessing your learners. These may be categorized in the following way:

– the purposes of assessment
– the focus of assessment, e.g. which language elements, which language skills
– the procedures used, e.g. marks, grades, or comment
– whether or not learners participate in negotiated assessment or self-assessment
– what kind of criteria are used
– what kind of feedback is given
– how assessments are recorded.

GLOSSARY

achievement behaviour: This occurs when a learner compensates for language deficiency by using a *communication strategy*.

achievement strategy: A strategy used by a learner who lacks the necessary language to express something but perseveres with trying to express it.

acquire: Internalize second language rules and vocabulary which are then used to communicate in the language.

affective filter: A learner has a 'raised' or 'lowered' affective filter depending on such factors as motivation or anxiety, and this influences learning. A lowered affective filter, it is claimed, leads to better learning.

antonymy: Different types of 'oppositeness' among words, for example 'hot' and 'cold', 'broad' and 'narrow', 'high' and 'low'.

avoidance behaviour: This occurs when a learner avoids using language which is difficult or poorly remembered.

bottom-up processing: Decoding of a text, step by step, from the smallest elements, for example sounds or letters, gradually building up to larger units of meaning such as sentences.

cognitive: To do with an individual's mental processes.

cognitive strategies: Various mental processes the learner uses to work on, internalize, and automatize new language.

cognitive style: The way in which people conceptualize, organize, and recall information using *cognitive strategies*. Cognitive style is thought to be reasonably consistent in individuals.

cohesive devices: Words and expressions which help to link ideas within and between sentences in written texts, and within and between utterances in spoken texts.

communication strategies: Strategies used to communicate when the learner lacks the necessary language knowledge, for example mime or paraphrase.

communicative competence: Knowledge of language rules, and of how these rules are used to understand and produce appropriate language in a variety of sociocultural settings.

communicative language ability: Knowledge of language form and the ability to put that knowledge to use in communication.

complementarity: A meaning relationship between words in which the existence of one item implies the existence of the other, for example 'employer' and 'employee'.

comprehensible input: Language that is understandable to a learner. It can be comprehensible because the language is adjusted to the proficiency level of the learner or because the learner uses *contextual clues* or *schematic knowledge* to make sense of it.

comprehensible output: Language produced by learners which they have attempted to make understandable to listeners/readers.

conferencing: A technique in which the teacher and a student, or students, discuss a piece of writing while it is being drafted, or after a first draft has been completed.

connotative meaning: The associative meanings that a word evokes.

content schemata: The background knowledge of a topic which a learner holds in his or her mind and which assists in the interpretation of a text.

contextual clues: Clues in a text which a reader can use to deduce the meaning of unknown words.

context of use: The social, psychological, and physical setting in which a communicative event takes place.

contrastive analysis: A procedure for comparing two languages in order to analyse similarities and dissimilarities. Contrastive analysis of rhetoric focuses on the different conventions which determine the structure of written discourse across cultures.

converseness: A meaning relationship between words in which the meaning of one item is the converse of another, for example, 'bought' and 'sold'.

creative construction process: A view of second language acquisition as a process by which learners construct their own rule system for the second language and gradually develop this through predictable stages.

denotative meaning: See *referential meaning*.

discourse community: A group of language users who function in speech or writing in the same *context of use*, for example sports commentators or writers of medical reports.

discourse competence: The ability to understand and produce contextualized stretches of language in spoken or written texts.

discrete point test: A test that attempts to measure knowledge of a single aspect of language use.

error analysis: A procedure for analysing samples of learners' language which attempts to explain the errors they make.

fluency: The ability to link units of speech together with ease.

formal schemata: Prior knowledge of the formal structure of different types of texts which assists readers and listeners in understanding and interpreting them.

formative assessment: This usually refers to assessment of learners that is carried out during a course, i.e. as an ongoing process, with the aim of supporting language learning.

formative evaluation: Periodic review of course structure, content, and methodology as it proceeds in order to gain information to improve its later stages.

genre: A type of discourse which has a particular physical form for use in a particular situation, for example a prayer, a novel, or a doctor's prescription.

genre analysis: The analysis of recognizable categories of discourse on the basis of purpose and structure, for example, a research paper abstract, an obituary, a menu.

global errors: Errors which prevent a listener from understanding a message, and so obstruct communication.

global revision: Revision of the larger structures of a written text, for example overall organization of an argument, or paragraph structure, rather than of local errors, for example of grammar or punctuation.

gradable antonymy: A set of words on a scale between two antonyms, for example, of water, 'boiling', 'hot', 'warm', 'tepid', 'cool', 'cold', 'freezing'.

hyponymy: A relationship of superordinate and subordinate words, for example 'pistol', 'revolver', and 'rifle' are all hyponyms of the superordinate 'gun'.

illocutionary competence: That part of pragmatic competence which is to do with knowing how to use language in order to carry out certain intentions.

illocutionary force: The sense or specific force that a speaker or writer intends for an utterance or sentence.

input: The language, either written or spoken, which a learner is exposed to in the environment.

instrumental motivation: Learning a language because of its value as a tool or instrument for doing something else successfully, such as studying a subject in English at university.

intake: Language in the *input* learners are exposed to which they notice and internalize.

integrative motivation: Learning a language because of its value in helping to integrate with speakers of that language.

interactional: Interactional use of language is mainly for the purpose of social communication.

interlanguage: The language produced by a second language learner. It may have some features of the first language and some features of the second language. It continually changes as the learner revises his or her internalized rule system.

learner autonomy: The ability of the learner to take responsibility for his or her own learning and to plan, organize, and monitor the learning process independently of the teacher.

learner training: A classroom process organized by the teacher which prepares learners for moves towards *learner autonomy*.

linear syllabus: A step-by-step syllabus which moves from one language item to another in orderly progression, usually from simple to complex.

linguistic competence: A knowledge of spelling, pronunciation, vocabulary, word formation, grammatical structure, sentence structure, and meaning.

local errors: Errors which relate to only part of a message and do not prevent comprehension.

local revision: Revision of smaller or 'surface' errors in a written text, for example punctuation or grammar, as opposed to revision of larger errors of text structure.

long-term memory: The relatively permanent part of the memory system.

metacognitive strategies: Strategies used by language learners to plan, regulate, and monitor their learning.

mistakes: Faulty language output caused by affective factors, for example tiredness, or environmental factors, for example responding to partly heard messages.

modular syllabus: A syllabus designed in units of material (or 'modules'), based on language or content, which can be studied in any order.

multidimensional syllabus: A syllabus based on the integration of a number of organizing principles, for example structures, functions, vocabulary, and skills.

natural order hypothesis: The claim that certain features of a language, for example grammatical morphemes such as third person '-s', are acquired in a particular order.

negotiation of meaning: The adjustments made by speakers in interaction by means of techniques such as clarification, in order to make themselves understood and to understand each other.

noticing: This occurs when the learner pays conscious attention to an item of language.

operating strategy: A *cognitive strategy* used in dealing with, and trying to make sense of, new language, for example paying attention to the endings of words.

paradigmatic relations: Associative meanings among words which the learner can evoke, for example *antonymy* or *synonymy*.

pragmatic competence: Knowing how to express an intention clearly and in a way which is appropriate both to the person to whom it is expressed and the setting in which it is expressed.

pragmatics: The study of the real use of language in relation to context, language user, and topic.

prior knowledge: Another term for *schematic knowledge*.

product approaches: Approaches which view the methodology of a writing class as having the main aim of focusing the learners' attention on how texts are structured and how to reproduce those structures.

protocol: A record of a learner's verbalization of thoughts while performing a task such as writing a composition.

reduction strategy: A strategy used by a learner who lacks the necessary language to express something and changes the message to avoid the forms he or she is uncertain about.

referential meaning: The meaning of a word in relation to the objects, events, states, or concepts it refers to.

reformulation: A technique in which a more proficient language user (usually the teacher) rewrites a student's draft, keeping to the ideas but re-expressing them in more correct and appropriate language.

rhetorical functions: The purpose or intention of a particular sentence within written discourse, for example to define or to sum up.

schematic knowledge: Knowledge, gained from experience, of the way the world is organized which is held as mental representations in the mind.

script: A mental representation of a typical sequence of events, for example checking in at a hotel.

semi-authentic: A spoken or written text which is formulated so as to be close to an authentic text in content and language, but which has been adjusted in some way, usually to suit the learner's level of language proficiency.

short-term memory: The part of the memory with limited capacity which can only hold information for a short period of time.

socio-affective strategies: Strategies used by learners to obtain practice in using the language, for example starting up conversations.

sociolinguistic competence: The ability to use language in ways appropriate to *contexts of use*, role relationships, and communicative purposes.

strategic competence: Knowing how to use different kinds of strategies, for example miming, to express something when language resources are lacking.

summative assessment: This generally refers to assessment of achievement of proficiency in learners and is usually carried out at the end of a course.

summative evaluation: Review of course structure, content, and methodology at the end in order to gain information to improve further courses.

synonymy: The relationship of similarity of meaning.

syntagmatic relations: These are concerned with how words combine to form text, as in collocations such as 'his injured leg' and 'his damaged car'.

systematic errors: Consistent errors in learners' language output which indicate that they are constructing and operating a system for understanding and producing language.

systemic knowledge: Knowledge of the language system.

textual competence: Another term for *discourse competence.*

think-aloud protocols: A procedure for investigating learner strategies which requires learners to report on what they are doing as they undertake learning activities. They speak their thoughts out loud and these are then transcribed and analysed by the researcher.

top-down processing: This involves making sense of spoken or written language, primarily by referring to *schematic knowledge.*

transactional: Transactional use of language is mainly for the purpose of communicating information.

validity: The extent to which a test accurately measures what it is supposed to measure.

BIBLIOGRAPHY

Abbot, G., J. Greenwood, D. McKeating, and P. Wingard. 1981. *The Teaching of English as an International Language.* Glasgow and London: Collins.

Abbs, B. and I. Freebairn. 1980. *Developing Strategies.* London: Longman.

Abbs, B. and I. Freebairn. 1989–91. *Blueprint Intermediate.* London: Longman.

Adaskou, K., D. Britten, and B. Fahsi. 1990. 'Design decisions on the cultural content of a secondary English course for Morocco.' *ELT Journal* 44/1: 3–10.

Aebersold, J. A. and M. L. Field. 1997. *From Reader to Reading Teacher: Issues and Strategies for Second Language Classrooms.* Cambridge: Cambridge University Press.

Aitchinson, J. 1992. 'Good birds, better birds and amazing birds: the development of prototypes' in P. J. L. Arnaud and H. Béjoint (eds.): *Vocabulary and Applied Linguistics.* London and Basingstoke: Macmillan. pp. 71–84.

Alderson, J. C. and A. Urquhart (eds.). 1984. *Reading in a Foreign Language.* London: Longman.

Alderson, J. C. and A. Urquhart. 1988. 'This test is unfair: I'm not an economist' in P. L. Carrell, J. Devine, and D. E. Eskey (eds.). pp. 168–82.

Alderson, J. C., C. Clapham, and D. Wall. 1995. *Language Test Construction.* Cambridge: Cambridge University Press.

Allan, D. 1991. 'Tape journals: bridging the gap between communication and correction.' *ELT Journal* 45/1: 61–6.

Allwright, J. 1988. 'Don't correct, reformulate' in P. Robinson (ed.).: *Academic Writing: Process and Product.* (ELT Documents 129.) London: Modern English Publications in association with The British Council. pp. 109–16.

Allwright, R. L. 1981. 'What do we want teaching materials for?' *ELT Journal* 36/1: 5–18.

Allwright, R. L. 1988. *Observation in the Language Classroom.* London and New York: Longman.

Alptekin, C. 1993. 'Target-language culture in EFL materials.' *ELT Journal* 47/2: 136–43.

Anderson, A. and T. Lynch. 1988. *Listening.* Oxford: Oxford University Press.

Anderson, N. J. 1999. 'Improving reading speed: activities for the classroom.' *English Teaching Forum* 37/2: 2–5.

Anglin, J. M. 1985. 'The child's expressible knowledge of word concepts' in K. E. Nelson (ed.): *Children's Language 5* Hillsdale, N.J.: Lawrence Erlbaum.

Arden-Close, C. 1993. 'NNS readers' strategies for inferring meanings of unknown words.' *Journal of Reading in a Foreign Language:* 9/2: 867–94.

Avery, P. and **S. Erhlich.** 1992. *Teaching American English Pronunciation.* Oxford: Oxford University Press.

Axbey, S. 1989. *Soundtracks.* London: Longman.

Bachman, L. F. 1990. *Fundamental Considerations in Language Testing.* Oxford: Oxford University Press.

Bachman, L. F. and **A. S. Palmer.** 1996. *Language Testing in Practice.* Oxford: Oxford University Press.

Bailey, K. M. 1995. 'Competitiveness and anxiety in adult second language learning: looking at and through the diary studies' in H. D. Brown and S. Gonzo (eds.). pp. 163–205.

Bardovi-Harlig, K., B. A. S. Hartford, R. Mahan Taylor, M. J. Morgan, and **D. W Reynolds.** 1991. 'Developing pragmatic awareness: closing the conversation.' *ELT Journal* 45/1: 4–15.

Barnes, D. 1976. *From Communication to Curriculum.* Harmondsworth: Penguin.

Barnett, M. 1989. *More than Meets the Eye: Foreign Language Reading Theory in Practice.* Englewood Cliffs, N.J.: Prentice Hall Regents.

Barrow, R. and **R. Woods.** 1988. *An Introduction to the Philosophy of Education.* (3rd edn.). London and New York: Routledge.

Barrs, M., S. Ellis, H. Hester, and **A. Thomas.** 1988. *The Primary Language Record Handbook.* London: Centre for Language in Primary Education.

Batstone, R. 1994. *Grammar.* Oxford: Oxford University Press.

Batstone, R. 1996. 'Key concepts in ELT: noticing.' *ELT Journal:* 50/3: 273.

Beheydt, L. 1987. 'The semantization of vocabulary in foreign language learning.' *System* 15/1: 55–67.

Bell, J. and **T. Gower.** 1992. *Upper Intermediate Matters.* London: Longman.

Benson, P. and **P. Voller.** 1997. *Autonomy and Independence in Language Learning.* London: Longman.

Berman, R. A. 1984. 'Syntactic components of the foreign language reading process' in J. C. Alderson and A. Urquhart (eds.). pp. 139–56.

Bever, T. 1970. 'The cognitive basis for linguistic structures' in J. R. Hayes (ed.). pp. 279–352.

Block, D. 1994. 'A day in the life of a class: teacher/learner perceptions of task purpose in conflict.' *System* 22/4: 473–86.

Blue, G. 1988. 'Self-assessment: the limits of learner independence' in A. Brookes and P. Grundy (eds.): *Individualisation and Autonomy in Language Learning.* (ELT

Documents 131.) London: Modern English Publications in association with the British Council. pp. 100–18.

Bolinger, D. 1977. *Meaning and Form.* London: Longman.

Bolitho, R. and B. Tomlinson. 1980. *Discover English.* London: Heinemann Educational Books.

Breen, M. 1987. 'Contemporary paradigms in syllabus design.' *Language Teaching* 20/2: 81–92 (Part 1) and 20/3: 157–74 (Part 2).

Bright, J. A. and G. P. McGregor. 1977. *Teaching English as a Second Language: Theory and Techniques for the Secondary Stage.* London: Longman.

Brindley, G. 1989a. *Assessing Achievement in the Learner-Centred Curriculum.* Sydney: National Centre for English Language Teaching and Research.

Brindley, G. 1989b. 'The role of needs analysis in adult ESL programme design' in R. K. Johnson (ed.). pp. 63–78.

Brindley, G. (ed.). 1995. *Language Assessment in Action.* Sydney: National Centre for English Language Teaching and Research.

Brookes, A. and P. Grundy. 1990. *Writing for Study Purposes.* Cambridge: Cambridge University Press.

Brown, G. 1978. 'Understanding spoken language.' *TESOL Quarterly* 12/4: 271–83.

Brown, G. 1986. 'Investigating listening comprehension in context.' *Applied Linguistics* 7/3: 284–302.

Brown, G. and G. Yule. 1983a. *Discourse Analysis.* Cambridge: Cambridge University Press.

Brown, G. and G. Yule. 1983b. *Teaching the Spoken Language.* Cambridge: Cambridge University Press.

Brown, H. D. 1987. *Principles of Language Learning and Teaching.* Englewood Cliffs, N.J.: Prentice Hall.

Brown, H. D. 1994. *Teaching by Principles: an Interactive Approach to Language Pedagogy.* Englewood Cliffs, N.J.: Prentice Hall Regents.

Brown, H. D. and S. Gonzo (eds.). 1995. *Readings on Second Language Acquisition.* Englewood Cliffs, N.J.: Prentice Hall Regents.

Brown, J. D. 1989. 'Language programme evaluation: a synthesis of existing possibilities' in R. K. Johnson (ed.). pp. 222–41.

Brown, R. 1973. *A First Language: The Early Stages.* Cambridge, Mass.: Harvard University Press.

Brown, T. S. and F. L. Perry. 1991. 'A comparison of three learning strategies for ESL vocabulary acquisition.' *TESOL Quarterly* 25/4: 655–70.

Brumfit, C. J. 1980. *Problems and Principles in English Teaching.* Oxford: Pergamon.

Brumfit, C. J. 1984a. *Communicative Methodology in Language Teaching.* Cambridge: Cambridge University Press.

Brumfit, C. J. (ed.). 1984b. *General English Syllabus Design.* (ELT Documents 118.) Oxford: Pergamon.

Brumfit, C. J. and **K. Johnson** (eds.). 1979. *The Communicative Approach to Language Teaching.* Oxford: Oxford University Press.

Bygate, M. 1987. *Speaking.* Oxford: Oxford University Press.

Bygate, M., A. Tonkyn, and **E. Williams** (eds.). 1994. *Grammar and the Language Teacher.* Hemel Hempstead: Prentice Hall International.

Byram, M. 1989. *Cultural Studies in Foreign Language Education.* Clevedon, Avon: Multilingual Matters.

Campbell, C. and **H. Kryszewska.** 1992. *Learner-based Teaching.* Oxford: Oxford University Press.

Canale, M. 1983. 'From communicative competence to communicative language pedagogy' in J. C. Richards and R. W. Schmidt (eds.). pp. 2–27.

Canale, M. and **M. Swain.** 1980. 'Theoretical bases of communicative approaches to second language teaching and testing.' *Applied Linguistics* 1/1: 1–47.

Candlin, C. 1973. 'The status of pedagogical grammars' in S. P. Corder and E. Roulet (eds.). pp. 55–64.

Candlin, C. 1984. 'Syllabus design as a critical process' in C. J. Brumfit (ed.). pp. 29–46.

Candlin, C. 1987. 'Towards task-based language learning' in C. Candlin and D. Murphy (eds.). pp. 5–22.

Candlin, C. and **D. Murphy** (eds.). 1987. *Language Learning Tasks.* (Practical Papers in English Language Education, Vol. 7.) Oxford: Pergamon.

Carrell, P. and **J. C. Eisterhold.** 1983. 'Schema theory and ESL reading pedagogy.' *TESOL Quarterly* 17/4: 553–73.

Carrell, P. L. 1983. 'Some issues in studying the role of schemata or background knowledge in second language comprehension.' *Journal of Reading in a Foreign Language* 1/2: 81–92.

Carrell, P. L. 1984. 'The effects of rhetorical organization on ESL readers' comprehension.' *TESOL Quarterly* 18/3: 441–65.

Carrell, P. L., J. Devine, and **D. E. Eskey** (eds.). 1988. *Interactive Approaches to Second Language Reading.* New York: Cambridge University Press.

Carrell, P. L., B. G. Pharis, and **J. C. Liberto.** 1989. 'Metacognitive strategy training for ESL reading.' *TESOL Quarterly* 23/4: 647–78.

Carroll, J. B. 1961. 'Fundamental considerations in testing for English language proficiency of foreign students' in *Testing the English Proficiency of Foreign Students*. Washington D.C.: Center for Applied Linguistics. pp. 31–40. New York: McGraw Hill.

Carroll, J. B. and **S. M. Sapon.** 1955. *Modern Language Aptitude Test, Form A*. New York: The Psychological Corporation.

Carter, R. 1987. *Vocabulary: Applied Linguistics Perspectives*. London: Allen and Unwin.

Carter, R. and **M. McCarthy** (eds.). 1988. *Vocabulary and Language Teaching*. London: Longman.

Cauldwell, R. 1983. 'Comments on a lesson in *Teaching and Learning in Focus*.' (Edited Lessons, Vol. 3. Print support materials.) London: The British Council.

Celce-Murcia, M. 1993. 'Grammar pedagogy in second and foreign language teaching' in S. Silberstein (ed.). pp. 288–309.

Celce-Murcia, M. 1995. 'Discourse analysis and the teaching of listening' in G. Cook and B. Seidlhofer (eds.). pp. 363–77.

Channell, J. 1988. 'Psycholinguistic considerations in the study of L2 vocabulary acquisition' in R. Carter and M. McCarthy (eds.). pp. 83–96.

Chaudron, C. and **J. C. Richards.** 1986. 'The effect of discourse markers on the comprehension of lectures.' *Applied Linguistics* 7/1: 113–27.

Cherry, C. 1957. *On Human Communication: A Review, a Survey and a Criticism*. Cambridge, Mass.: MIT Press.

Chomsky, N. 1965. *Aspects of the Theory of Syntax*. Cambridge, Mass.: MIT Press.

Clark, H. H. and **E. V. Clark.** 1977. *Psychology and Language*. New York: Harcourt Brace Jovanovitch.

Clark, J. L. 1987. *Curriculum Renewal in School Foreign Language Learning*. Oxford: Oxford University Press.

Clark, J. L., A. Scarino, and **J. A. Brownell.** 1994. *Improving the Quality of Learning: A Framework for Target-oriented Curriculum Renewal in Hong Kong*. Hong Kong Bank Language Development Fund/Institute of Language in Education.

Clark, R. 1993. 'Developing practices of resistance: critical reading for students of politics' in D. Graddol, L. Thompson, and M. Byram (eds.).: *Language and Culture*. Clevedon, Avon: BAAL/ Multilingual Matters. pp. 113–22.

Clarke, D. 1989a. 'Communicative theory and its influence on materials production.' *Language Teaching* 22/2: 73–86.

Clarke, D. 1989b. 'Materials adaptation: why leave it all to the teacher?' *ELT Journal* 43/2: 133–41.

Clarke, M. A. and S. Silberstein. 1979. 'Towards a realisation of psycholinguistic principles in the ESL reading class' in R. Mackay, B. Barkman, and R. R. Jordan (eds.). pp. 48–65.

Coady, J. 1979. 'A psycholinguistic model of the ESL reader' in R. Mackay, B. Barkman, and R. R. Jordan (eds.). pp. 5–12.

Coe, N., R. Ryecroft, and P. Ernest. 1983. *Writing Skills.* Cambridge: Cambridge University Press.

Cohen, A. D. 1987. 'Using verbal reports in research on language learning' in C. Faerch and G. Kasper (eds.): *Introspection in Second Language Research.* Clevedon, Avon: Multilingual Matters. pp. 82–95.

Conner, C. 1991. *Assessment and Testing in the Primary School.* London: Falmer Press.

Connor, U. and R. B. Kaplan. (eds.). 1987. *Writing Across Languages: Analysis of L2 Text.* Wokingham, England and Reading, Mass.: Addison-Wesley.

Conrad, L. 1985. 'Semantic v. syntactic cues in listening comprehension.' *Studies in Second Language Acquisition* 7/1: 59–72.

Cook, G. 1989. *Discourse.* Oxford: Oxford University Press.

Cook, G. and B. Seidlhofer (eds.). 1995. *Principles and Practice in Applied Linguistics.* Oxford: Oxford University Press.

Cooper, M. and M. Holtzman. 1983. 'Talking about protocols.' *College Composition and Communication* 34/3: 284–93.

Corder, S. P. and E. Roulet (eds.). 1973. *Theoretical Linguistic Models in Applied Linguistics.* Brussels/Paris: Aimav/Didier.

Cortazzi, M. 1994. 'Narrative analysis.' *Language Teaching* 27/3: 157–70.

Cotterall, S. 1995. 'Developing a course strategy for learner autonomy.' *ELT Journal* 49/3: 219–27.

Craik, F. I. M. and R. S. Lockhart. 1972. 'Levels of processing: a framework for memory research.' *Journal of Verbal Learning and Verbal Behaviour* 11: 671–84.

Craik, F. I. M. and E. Tulvig. 1975. 'Depth of processing and the retention of words in episodic memory.' *Journal of Experimental Psychology* 104: 268–94.

Crystal, D. and D. Davy. 1969. *Investigating English Style.* London: Longman.

Cunningham, S. and B. Bowler. 1990. *Headway Intermediate Pronunciation.* Oxford: Oxford University Press.

Cunningsworth, A. 1995. *Choosing Your Coursebook.* Oxford: Heinemann.

Davidson, C. and A. Tomic. 1994. 'Removing computer phobia from the writing classroom.' *ELT Journal* 48/3: 205–13.

Davis, C. 1995. 'Extensive reading: an expensive extravagance?' *ELT Journal* 49/4: 329–36.

Day, R. R. and **J. Bamford.** 1998. *Extensive Reading in the Second Language Classroom.* Cambridge: Cambridge University Press.

Dean, M. 1993. *English Grammar Lessons, Upper-intermediate.* Oxford: Oxford University Press.

de Beaugrande, R. A. and **W. U. Dressler.** 1981. *Introduction to Text Linguistics.* London: Longman.

Deller, S. and **R. Jones.** 1992. *Vista.* Oxford: Heinemann.

Derrick, J. 1976. *The Child's Acquisition of Language.* Windsor: NFER Publishing Company.

Dickinson, L. 1987. *Self-instruction in Language Learning.* Cambridge: Cambridge University Press.

Dickinson, L. 1992. *Learner Training for Language Learning.* Trinity College, Dublin: Authentik Language Learning Resources.

Dirven, R. 1990. 'Pedagogical grammar.' *Language Teaching* 23/1: 1–18.

Dobrin, D. N. 1994. 'Whither wisdom?' in P. Smagorinsky (ed.).: *Speaking About Writing: Reflections on Research Methodology.* Thousand Oaks, Ca.: Sage Publications. pp. 275–87.

Doff, A., C. Jones, and **K. Mitchell.** 1983. (Adapted by **A. de Waal** and **B. Weinhofer** 1989.) *Meanings into Words.* Vienna: Osterreichischer Bundesverlag by arrangement with Cambridge University Press.

Donahue Latulippe, L. 1992. *Writing as a Personal Product.* Englewood Cliffs, N.J.: Prentice Hall Regents.

Donatini, D. and **T. Hedge.** 1988. *Of Machines and Men: A Reader in Mechanical Engineering.* Turin: Società Editrice Internazionale.

Dörnyei, Z. and **S. Thurrell.** 1991. 'The neglected component of communicative competence: strategic competence and how to teach it.' *ELT Journal* 45/1: 16–23.

Doughty, C. and **T. Pica.** 1986. '"Information gap" tasks: do they facilitate second language acquisition?' *TESOL Quarterly* 20/2: 305–25.

Downie, M., D. Gray, and **J. M. Jiménez.** 1995. *Freeform 4.* London: Richmond.

Dowswell, P. 1994. *Tales of Real Escape.* London: Usborne Readers' Library.

Dubin, F., D. Eskey, and **W. Grabe.** 1986. *Teaching Second Language Reading for Academic Purposes.* New York: Addison-Wesley.

Dubin, F. and **E. Olshtain.** 1986. *Course Design: Developing Programs and Materials for Language Learning.* Cambridge: Cambridge University Press.

Dunkel, P. 1993. 'Listening in the native and second/foreign language: towards an integration of research and practice' in S. Silberstein (ed.). pp. 261–87.

Eastman, J. K. 1991. 'Learning to listen and comprehend: the beginning stages.' *System* 19/3: 179–88.

Eco, U. 1979. *The Role of the Reader.* Bloomington, Indiana and London, Indiana: Indiana University Press.

Edinburgh Project on Extensive Reading. 1992. *The EPER Guide to Organizing Programmes of Extensive Reading.* Edinburgh: IALS, University of Edinburgh.

Elliot, J. 1991. *Action Research for Educational Change.* Milton Keynes: Open University Press.

Ellis, G. and **B. Sinclair.** 1989. *Learning to Learn English.* Cambridge: Cambridge University Press.

Ellis, R. 1982. 'Informal and formal approaches to communicative language teaching.' *ELT Journal* 36/2: 73–81.

Ellis, R. 1985. *Understanding Second Language Acquisition.* Oxford: Oxford University Press.

Ellis, R. (ed.). 1987. *Second Language Acquisition in Context.* Englewood Cliffs, N.J.: Prentice Hall.

Ellis, R. 1987. 'Contextual variability in second language acquisition and the relevancy of language teaching' in R. Ellis (ed.). pp. 179–94.

Ellis, R. 1988. 'The role of practice in classroom language learning.' *AILA Review* 5: 20–39.

Ellis, R. 1989. 'Classroom learning styles and their effect on second language acquisition: a study of two learners.' *System* 17/2: 249–62.

Ellis, R. 1990. *Instructed Second Language Acquisition: Learning in the Classroom.* Oxford: Blackwell.

Ellis, R. 1993a. 'Interpretation-based grammar teaching.' *System* 21/1: 69–78.

Ellis, R. 1993b. 'Talking shop: second language acquisition research: how does it help teachers?' *ELT Journal* 47/1: 3–11.

Ellis, R. 1993c. 'The structural syllabus and second language acquisition.' *TESOL Quarterly* 27/1: 91–113.

Ellis, R. 1995. 'Modified oral input and the acquisition of word meanings.' *Applied Linguistics* 16/4: 409–41.

Ellis, R. and **M. Rathbone.** 1987. *The Acquisition of German in a Classroom Context.* (Research report.) London: Ealing College of Higher Education.

ELT Documents 103. 1978. *Individualisation in Language Learning.* London: The British Council.

Emig, J. 1971. *The Composing Processes of Twelfth Graders.* (Research report No. 13.) Urbana, Ill.: National Council of Teachers of English.

Eskey, D. E. 1988. 'Holding in the bottom: an interactive approach to the language problems of second language readers' in P. L. Carrell, J. Devine, and D. E. Eskey (eds.). pp. 93–100.

Eskey, D. E. and **W. Grabe.** 1988. 'Interactive models for second language reading: perspectives on instruction' in P. L. Carrell, J. Devine, and D. E. Eskey (eds.) pp. 223–38.

Esling, J. and **Wong, R.** 1983. 'Voice quality settings and the teaching of pronunciation.' *TESOL Quarterly* 17/1: 89–95.

Eubank, L. 1989. 'The acquisition of German negation by formal language learners' in B. Van Patten, T. Dvorak, and J. Less (eds.): *Foreign Language Learning: A Research Perspective.* Rowley, Mass.: Newbury House.

Everard, G. and **K. B. Morris.** 1985. *Effective School Management.* London: Harper & Row.

Faerch, C. and **G. Kasper.** 1983. 'Plans and strategies in foreign language communication' in C. Faerch and G.Kasper (eds.). pp. 20–60.

Faerch, C. and **G. Kasper** (eds.). 1983. *Strategies in Interlanguage Communication.* London: Longman.

Faerch, C. and **G. Kasper.** 1986. 'The role of comprehension in second language learning.' *Applied Linguistics* 7/3: 257–74.

Faerch, C., K. Haastrup, and **R. Phillipson.** 1984. *Learner Language and Language Learning.* Clevedon, Avon: Multilingual Matters.

Faigley, L. and **S. Witte.** 1981. 'Analyzing revision.' *College Composition and Communication* 32/4: 400–14.

Feyten, C. M. 1991. 'The power of listening ability: an overlooked dimension in language acquisition.' *Modern Language Journal* 75/2: 173–80.

Flower, L. 1979. 'Writer-based prose: a cognitive basis for problems in writing.' *College English* 41/1: 19–37.

Flower, L. and **J. A. Hayes.** 1980. 'The cognition of discovery: defining a rhetorical problem.' *College Composition and Communication* 31/1: 21–32.

Flower, L. and **J. A. Hayes.** 1981. 'The pregnant pause: an inquiry into the nature of planning.' *Research in the Teaching of English* 15/3: 229–43.

Forth, I. 1985. 'A listening lesson' in A. Matthews, M. Spratt, and L. Dangerfield (eds.). pp. 115–17.

Foster, P. 1998. 'A classroom perspective on the negotiation of meaning.' *Applied Linguistics* 19/1: 1–23.

Fotos, S. 1994. 'Integrating grammar instruction and communicative language use through grammar consciousness-raising tasks.' *TESOL Quarterly* 28/2: 323–49.

Fried-Booth, D. 1988. *Project Work.* Oxford: Oxford University Press.

Gairns, R. and **S. Redman.** 1986. *Working with Words: A Guide to Teaching and Learning Vocabulary.* Cambridge: Cambridge University Press.

Gairns, R. and **S. Redman.** 1998. *True to Life: Upper Intermediate.* Cambridge: Cambridge University Press.

Galvin, K. 1985. *Listening by Doing: Developing Effective Listening Skills.* Lincolnwood, Ill.: National Textbook Company.

Gardner R. and **W. E. Lambert.** 1972. *Attitudes and Motivation in Second Language Learning.* Rowley, Mass.: Newbury House.

Gardner, R. and **P. C. Smythe.** 1981. 'On the development of the Attitude/ Motivation Test Battery.' *Canadian Modern Language Review* 37: 510–25.

Gass, S. and **L. Selinker.** 1994. *Second Language Acquisition: An Introductory Course.* Hillsdale, N.J.: Lawrence Erlbaum Associates.

Geddes, M. and **R. White.** 1978. 'The use of semi-scripted simulated authentic speech and listening comprehension.' *Audio-visual Language Journal* 16/3: 137–45.

Genesee, F. and **E. V. Hamayan.** 1994. 'Classroom-based assessment' in F. Genesee (ed.): *Educating Second Language Children.* Cambridge: Cambridge University Press.

Genesee, F. and **J. Upshur.** 1996. *Classroom-based Evaluation in Second Language Education.* Cambridge: Cambridge University Press.

Goodman, K. 1967. 'Reading: a psycholinguistic guessing game.' *Journal of the Reading Specialist* 6/4: 126–35.

Goulden, R., P. Nation, and **J. Read.** 1990. 'How large can a receptive vocabulary be?' *Applied Linguistics* 11/4: 341–63.

Grabe, W. 1993. 'Current developments in second language reading research' in S. Silberstein (ed.). pp. 205–36.

Grabe, W. and **R. B. Kaplan.** 1996. *Theory and Practice of Writing.* London and New York: Longman.

Grant, R. 1993. 'Strategic training for using text headings to improve students' processing of content.' *Journal of Reading* 36/6: 482–8.

Graves, D. and **B. S. Sunstein** (eds.). 1992. *Portfolio Portraits.* Portsmouth, N.H.: Heinemann.

Greenall, S. and **M. Swan.** 1986. *Effective Reading.* Cambridge: Cambridge University Press.

Greenwood, J. 1988. *Class Readers.* Oxford: Oxford University Press.

Grellet, F. 1981. *Developing Reading Skills.* Cambridge: Cambridge University Press.

Gremmo, M-J. and **D. Abe.** 1985. 'Teaching learning: redefining the teacher's role' in P. Riley (ed.). pp. 233–47.

Haastrup, K. 1989. 'The learner as a word processor' in *AILA Review* 6: 34–46.

Hafiz, F. M. and I. Tudor. 1989. 'Extensive reading and the development of language skills.' *ELT Journal* 43/1: 4–13.

Handy, C. 1978. *Understanding Organisations*. Harmondsworth: Penguin.

Harmer, J. 1982. 'What is communicative?' *ELT Journal* 36/3: 164–8.

Harmer, J. 1991. *The Practice of English Language Teaching*. (2nd edn.) Harlow: Longman.

Harris, M. and P. McCann. 1994. *Assessment*. Oxford: Heinemann.

Hayes, J. R. (ed.). 1970. *Cognition and the Development of Language*. New York: John Wiley and Sons.

Hayes, J. R. and L. Flower. 1983. 'Uncovering cognitive processes in writing: an introduction to protocol analysis' in P. Mosenthal, L. Tamar, and S. A. Walmsley (eds.): *Research on Writing: Principles and Methods*. New York: Longman. pp. 206–19.

Heaton, J. B. 1989. *Writing English Language Tests*. (New edn.) London: Longman.

Heaton, J. B. 1990. *Classroom Testing*. London: Longman.

Hedge, T. 1985. *Using Readers in Language Teaching*. London and Basingstoke: Macmillan.

Hedge, T. 1988. *Writing*. Oxford: Oxford University Press.

Hedge, T. 1998. 'Managing developmental evaluation activities in teacher education' in P. Rea-Dickins and K. Germaine (eds.): *Managing Evaluation and Innovation in Language Teaching*. Harlow: Addison-Wesley Longman. pp. 132–58.

Henner-Stanchina, C. and P. Riley. 1978. 'Aspects of autonomous learning' in *ELT Documents* 103. pp. 75–97.

Hester, H. 1993. *Guide to the Primary Learning Record*. London: Centre for Language in Education.

Hicks, D. 1984. 'Getting readers to read in the Arab world.' *TESOL France News* 6/2: 21–4.

Hill, D. and H. R. Thomas. 1988. 'Survey of graded readers.' *ELT Journal* 42/1: 44–52 (Part 1) and 42/2: 124–36 (Part 2).

Hindmarsh, R. 1980. *Cambridge English Lexicon*. Cambridge: Cambridge University Press.

Hinds, J. 1987. 'Reader versus writer responsibility: a new typology' in U. Connor and R. B. Kaplan (eds.). pp. 141–52.

Hofstede, G. 1986. 'Cultural differences in teaching and learning.' *International Journal of Intercultural Relations* 10: 310–20.

Holec, H. 1979. *Aspects of Autonomy in Foreign Language Learning*. Oxford: Pergamon.

Holec, H. 1985. 'On autonomy: some elementary concepts' in P. Riley (ed.). pp. 173–90.

Holliday, A. 1994. *Appropriate Methodology and Social Context.* Cambridge: Cambridge University Press.

Holt, J. 1969. *How Children Fail.* New York: Dell Pelican.

Holt, J. 1979. *How Children Learn.* New York: Dell Pelican.

Holyoak, S. and **A. Piper.** 1997. 'Talking to second language writers: using interview data to investigate contrastive rhetoric.' *Language Teaching Research* 1/2: 122–48.

Honikman, B. 1964. 'Articulatory settings' in D. Abercrombie, D. B. Fry, P. A. D. MacCarthy, N. C. Scott, and J. L. M. Trim (eds.): *In Honour of Daniel Jones.* London: Longman. pp. 73–84.

Hopkins, A. and **C. Tribble.** 1989. *Outlines.* London: Longman.

Howatt, A. 1978. 'Course design' in H. G. Widdowson and A. Davies (eds.): *The Edinburgh Course in Applied Linguistics.* Vol. 3. Oxford: Oxford University Press. pp. 1–23.

Hughes, A. 1990. *Testing for Language Teachers.* Cambridge: Cambridge University Press.

Hunt R. R. and **D. B. Mitchell.** 1982. 'Independent effects of semantic and non-semantic distinctiveness.' *Journal of Experimental Psychology: Learning, Memory and Cognition* 8/1: 81–7.

Hutchinson, T. 1985. *Project English One.* Oxford: Oxford University Press.

Hutchinson, T. 1986. *Project English Two.* Oxford: Oxford University Press.

Hutchinson, T. and **A. Waters.** 1987. *English for Specific Purposes: A Learning-centred Approach.* Cambridge: Cambridge University Press.

Hyland, K. 1993. 'ESL computer writers: what can we do to help?' *System* 21/1: 21–30.

Hymes, D. H. 1964. 'Introduction: towards ethnographies of communication' in J. J. Gumperz and D. Hymes (eds.): *The Ethnography of Communication.* Special publication. *American Anthropologist* 66/6 (Part 2): 1–34.

Hymes, D. H. 1972. 'On communicative competence' in J. B. Pride and J. Holmes (eds.): *Sociolinguistics.* Harmondsworth: Penguin. pp. 269–93.

Illich, I. 1972. *Deschooling Society.* New York: Harper & Row.

Jacques, D. 1991. *Learning in Groups.* London: Kogan Page.

James, C. 1990. 'Learner language.' *Language Teaching* 23/4: 205–13.

Johns, A. 1990. 'L1 composition theories: implications for developing theories of L2 composition' in B. Kroll (ed.). pp. 24–36.

Johnson, D. and **F. Johnson.** 1987. *Joining Together: Group Theory and Group Skills.* Englewood Cliffs, N.J.: Prentice Hall.

Johnson, D., G. Maruyama, R. Johnson, D. Nelson, and **L. Skon.** 1981. 'Effects of cooperative, competitive, and individualistic goal structures on achievement: a meta-analysis.' *Psychological Bulletin* 89/1: 47–62.

Johnson, K. 1979. 'Communicative approaches and communicative processes' in C. J. Brumfit and K. Johnson (eds.). pp. 192–205.

Johnson, K. 1982. *Communicative Syllabus Design and Methodology.* Oxford: Pergamon.

Johnson, K. and **K. Morrow.** 1981. *Communication in the Classroom.* London: Longman.

Johnson, R. K. 1981. 'On syllabuses and on being communicative.' *The English Bulletin* (Hong Kong) 7/4: 52–60.

Johnson, R. K. (ed.). 1989. *The Second Language Curriculum.* Cambridge: Cambridge University Press.

Jones, J. 1995. 'Self access and culture: retreating from autonomy.' *ELT Journal* 49/3: 228–34.

Jones, L. 1981. *Functions of English.* Cambridge: Cambridge University Press.

Joos, M. 1962. *The Five Clocks: A Linguistic Excursion in the Five Styles of English Usage.* New York: Harcourt, Brace and World.

Kachru, B. B. 1985. 'Standards, codification and sociolinguistic realism: the English language in the outer circle' in R. Quirk and H. G. Widdowson (eds.). pp. 11–30.

Kachru, J. N. 1962. 'Report on an investigation into the teaching of vocabulary in the first year of English.' *Bulletin of the Central Institute of English* 2: 67–72.

Kaplan, R. 1987. 'Cultural thought patterns revisited' in U. Connor and R. Kaplan (eds.) pp. 9–22.

Karavas-Dukas, E. 1995. 'An investigation into teachers' perceptions of their roles in the classroom.' (Unpublished research.) Coventry: University of Warwick.

Keh, C. 1990. 'Feedback in the writing process: a model and methods for implementation.' *ELT Journal* 44/4: 294–304.

Kell, J. and **C. Newton.** 1997. 'Roles of pathways in self-access centres.' *ELT Journal* 51/1: 48–53.

Keller, E. and **S. T. Warner.** 1988. *Conversation Gambits.* Hove: Language Teaching Publications.

Kellerman, S. 1990. 'Lip-service: the contribution of the visual modality to speech perception and its relevance to the teaching and testing of foreign language listening comprehension.' *Applied Linguistics* 11/3: 272–80.

Klippel, F. 1984. *Keep Talking.* Cambridge: Cambridge University Press.

Knowles, M. 1975. *Self-directed Learning.* New York: Association Press.

Kohl, H. 1977. *Writing, Maths and Games in the Open Classroom.* London: Methuen.

Kramsch, C. and P. Sullivan. 1996. 'Appropriate pedagogy.' *ELT Journal* 50/3: 199–212.

Krashen, S. D. 1982. *Principles and Practice in Second Language Acquisition.* Oxford: Pergamon.

Krashen, S. D. 1985. *The Input Hypothesis: Issues and Implications.* London: Longman.

Krashen, S. D. and T. Terrell. 1983. *The Natural Approach.* Oxford: Pergamon.

Kress, G. 1985. *Linguistic Processes in Sociocultural Practice.* Oxford: Oxford University Press.

Kroll, B. (ed.). 1990. *Second Language Writing: Research Insights for the Classroom.* Cambridge: Cambridge University Press.

Labov, W. 1972. 'The transformation of experience in narrative syntax' in W. Labov: *Language in the Inner City.* Philadelphia, Pa.: University of Pennsylvania. pp. 352–96.

Lado, R. 1961. *Language Testing.* London: Longman.

Lake, N. 1997. 'Survey review: learner training in coursebooks.' *ELT Journal* 51/2: 169–82.

Laufer, B. and P. Nation. 1995. 'Vocabulary size and use: lexical richness in L2 written production.' *Applied Linguistics* 16/3: 307–22.

Leech, G. N. and J. Svartvik. 1975. *A Communicative Grammar of English.* London: Longman.

Legutke, M. and H. Thomas. 1991. *Process and Experience in the Language Classroom.* Clevedon, Avon: Multilingual Matters.

Leki, I. 1989. *Academic Writing: Techniques and Tasks.* New York: St Martins Press.

Leontjew, A. N. 1979. *Tätigkeit, Bewußtsein, Persönlichkeit.* Berlin: Volk und Wissen.

Lewis, J. 1990. 'Self-assessment in the classroom: a case study' in G. Brindley (ed.): *The Second Language Curriculum in Action.* (Research Series 6.) Sydney: National Centre for English Language Teaching and Research. pp. 187–213.

Lightbown, P. and N. Spada. 1999. *How Languages are Learned* (Second edition). Oxford: Oxford University Press.

Littlewood, W. 1981. *Communicative Language Teaching.* Cambridge: Cambridge University Press.

Long, M. and **J. C. Richards** (eds.). 1987. *Methodology in TESOL: A Book of Readings.* New York: Newbury House.

Long, M. H. 1987. 'Instructed interlanguage development' in L. M. Beebe (ed.): *Issues in Second Language Acquisition: Multiple Perspectives.* Boston, Mass.: Heinle & Heinle. pp. 115–41.

Lunzer, E. and **K. Gardner.** 1979. *The Effective Uses of Reading.* London: Heinemann Educational Books for The Schools Council.

Lynch, T. 1996. *Communication in the Language Classroom.* Oxford: Oxford University Press.

MacIntyre, P. D. and **R. C. Gardner.** 1991. 'Language anxiety: its relation to other anxieties and to processing in native and second languages.' *Language Learning* 41/4: 513–34.

Mackay, R., B. Barkman, and **R. R. Jordan** (eds.). 1979. *Reading in a Second Language: Hypotheses, Organization and Practice.* Rowley, Mass.: Newbury House.

Maclellan, S. 1987. 'Integrating lesson planning and class management.' *ELT Journal* 41/3: 193–7.

Malamah-Thomas, A. 1987. *Classroom Interaction.* Oxford: Oxford University Press.

Marslen-Wilson, W. and **L. Tyler.** 1980. 'The temporal structure of spoken language understanding.' *Cognition* 8/1: 1–71.

Matsumoto, K. 1996. 'Helping L2 learners reflect on classroom learning.' *ELT Journal* 50/2: 143–9.

Matthews, A. 1985. 'Choosing the best available textbook' in A. Matthews, M. Spratt, and L. Dangerfield (eds.). pp. 202–6.

Matthews, A., M. Spratt, and **L. Dangerfield.** 1985. *At the Chalkface.* London: Edward Arnold.

McCarthy, M. 1990. *Vocabulary.* Oxford: Oxford University Press.

McDonough, J. and **C. Shaw.** 1993. *Materials and Methods in ELT.* Oxford: Blackwell.

McDonough, S. H. 1983. *Psychology in Foreign Language Teaching.* London: George Allen & Unwin.

McDowell J. and **J. Morris.** 1989. 'How to set up a self-access centre.' *EFL Gazette,* January 1989.

McKay, P. 1995. 'Developing ESL proficiency descriptions for the school context: The NLLIA ESL bandscales' in G. Brindley (ed.). pp. 31–63.

McKay, S. L. 1992. *Teaching English Overseas: An Introduction.* Oxford: Oxford University Press.

Meara, P. 1980. 'Vocabulary acquisition: a neglected aspect of language learning.' *Language Teaching and Linguistics* 13/4: 221–46.

Medgyes, P. 1986. 'Queries from a communicative language teacher.' *ELT Journal* 40/2: 107–12.

Mellor, B., M. O'Neil, and **A. Patterson.** 1987. *Reading Stories.* London: The English Centre.

Miles, M. B. 1964. *Innovation in Education.* New York: Teachers' College, Columbia University.

Mohamed, S. and **R. Aklam.** 1992. *The Pre-intermediate Choice.* London: Longman.

Mondria, J-A. and **M. Wit-de Boer.** 1991. 'The effects of contextual richness on the guessability and the retention of words in a foreign language.' *Applied Linguistics* 12/3: 249–67.

Moran, C. 1991. 'Lexical inferencing in EFL reading coursebooks: some implications of research.' *System* 19/4: 389–400.

Morgan, J. and **M. Rinvolucri.** 1983. *Once Upon a Time.* Cambridge: Cambridge University Press.

Morgan, J. and **M. Rinvolucri.** 1986. *Vocabulary.* Oxford: Oxford University Press.

Morrow, K. 1977. *Techniques of Evaluation for a Notional Syllabus.* (mimeo). London: Royal Society of Arts.

Morrow, K. 1981. 'Communicative language testing: revolution or evolution?' in J. C. Alderson and A. Hughes (eds.): *Issues in Language Testing.* (ELT Documents 111.) London: The British Council. pp. 9–25.

Munby, J. 1978. *Communicative Syllabus Design.* Cambridge: Cambridge University Press.

Murphy, D. and **J. Cooper.** 1995. *Getting the Message 2.* Cambridge: Cambridge University Press.

Naiman, N., M. Fröhlich, H. H. Stern, and **A. Todesco.** 1978. *The Good Language Learner.* Research in Education Series 7. Toronto, Ont.: Ontario Institute for Studies in Education.

Nation, P. and **J. Coady.** 1988. 'Vocabulary in reading' in R. Carter and M. McCarthy (eds.). pp. 97–110.

Nattinger, J. 1988. 'Some current trends in vocabulary teaching' in R. Carter and M. McCarthy (eds.). pp. 62–82.

Nattinger, J. R. and **J. S. DeCarrico.** 1992. *Lexical Phrases and Language Teaching.* Oxford: Oxford University Press.

Neisser, U. 1982. 'Memory: what are the important questions?' in U. Neisser (ed.): *Memory Observed: Remembering in Natural Contexts.* San Francisco, Calif.: Freeman.

Nesi, H. 1996. 'For future reference? Current English learners' dictionaries in electronic form.' *System* 24/4: 537–57.

Nobuyoshi, J. and **R. Ellis.** 1996. 'Focused communication tasks and second language acquisition' in T. Hedge and N. Whitney (eds.): *Power, Pedagogy, and Practice.* Oxford: Oxford University Press. pp. 261–70.

Nolasco, R. 1990. *WOW!* Student's Book 2. Oxford: Oxford University Press.

Nolasco, R. and **L. Arthur.** 1987. *Conversation.* Oxford: Oxford University Press.

Nunan, D. 1988a. *Syllabus Design.* Oxford: Oxford University Press.

Nunan, D. 1988b. *The Learner-centred Curriculum.* Cambridge: Cambridge University Press.

Nunan, D. 1989a. *Designing Tasks for the Communicative Classroom.* Cambridge: Cambridge University Press.

Nunan, D. 1989b. 'Hidden agendas: the role of the learner in programme implementation' in R.K. Johnson (ed.). pp. 176–86.

Nunan, D. 1991. *Language Teaching Methodology: A Textbook for Teachers.* Hemel Hempstead: Prentice Hall International.

Nunan, D. 1992. *Research Methods in Language Learning.* Cambridge: Cambridge University Press.

Nuttall, C. 1982. *Teaching Reading Skills in a Foreign Language.* London: Heinemann Educational Books.

O'Connor, J. D. 1973. *Phonetics.* Harmondsworth: Penguin.

O'Dell, F. 1992. 'Helping teachers to use a self-access centre to its full potential.' *ELT Journal* 46/2: 153–9.

O'Malley, M. 1987. 'The effects of training in the use of learning strategies on acquiring English as a second language' in A. Wenden and J. Rubin (eds.). pp. 133–44.

O'Malley, M. and **A. U. Chamot.** 1989. *Learning Strategies in Second Language Acquisition.* Cambridge: Cambridge University Press.

O'Malley, J. M., A. U. Chamot, and **L. Kupper.** 1995. 'Listening comprehension strategies in second language acquisition' in H. D. Brown and S. Gonzo (eds.). pp. 138–60.

O'Neill, R. 1982. 'Why use textbooks?' *ELT Journal* 36/2: 104–11.

Oprandy, R. 1993. 'Listening/speaking in second and foreign language teaching.' *System* 22/2: 153–75.

Oshima, A. and **A. Hogue.** 1991. *Writing Academic English* (2nd edn.). Menlo Park, Ca.: Addison-Wesley.

Oscarson, M. 1997. 'Self-assessment of foreign and second language proficiency' in C. Clapham and D. Corson (eds.): *Language Testing and Assessment. Encyclopedia of*

Language and Education, Vol. 7. London: Kluwer Academic Publishers. pp. 175–87.

Oskarsson, M. 1983. *Approaches to Self-assessment in Foreign Language Learning.* Oxford: Pergamon.

Oxford, R. L. 1990. *Language Learning Strategies: What Every Teacher Should Know.* Boston, Mass.: Heinle & Heinle.

Oxford, R. L. 1993. 'Research update on teaching L2 listening.' *System* 22/2: 205–11.

Oxford, R. L. and **N. J. Anderson.** 1995. 'A crosscultural view of learning styles.' *Language Teaching* 28: 201–15.

Oxford, R. L. and **J. A. Burry-Stock.** 1995. 'Assessing the use of language learning strategies worldwide with the ESL/EFL version of the Strategy Inventory for Language Learning (SILL).' *System* 23/2: 153–75.

Paquette, J. 1982. 'The Daily Record.' *The English Magazine* 9: 34–6. London: ILEA English Centre.

Parrott, J. 1987. 'Reading syndicates: a working model for the language classroom.' *Reading in a Foreign Language* 3/2: 411–16.

Pawley, A. and **F. H. Syder.** 1983. 'Two puzzles for linguistic theory: nativelike selection and nativelike fluency' in J. C. Richards and R. W. Schmidt (eds.). pp. 191–227.

Pennington, M. 1991. 'Positive and negative potentials of word processing for ESL writers.' *System* 19/3: 267–75.

Pennington, M. 1992. 'Beyond off-the-shelf computer remedies for student writers: alternatives to canned feedback.' *System* 20/4: 423–37.

Pennington, M. and **J. C. Richards.** 1986. 'Pronunciation revisited.' *TESOL Quarterly* 20/2: 207–26.

Perl, S. 1979. 'The composing processes of unskilled college writers.' *Research in the Teaching of English* 13/4: 317–36.

Petrovitz, W. 1993. 'The role of context in the presentation of grammar.' *ELT Journal* 51/3: 201–7.

Phillipson, R. 1990. *English Language Teaching and Imperialism.* Trönninge, Denmark: Transcultura.

Pica, T. 1985. 'The selective impact of classroom instruction on second language acquisition.' *Applied Linguistics* 6/3: 214–22.

Pica, T. and **C. Doughty.** 1985. 'The role of group work in classroom second language acquisition.' *Studies in Second Language Acquisition* 7/2: 233–48.

Pickard, N. 1996. 'Out-of-class language learning strategies.' *ELT Journal* 50/2: 150–9.

Pickett, D. 1978. 'The foreign language learning process: an occasional paper.' ETIC Publications. London: The British Council.

Pienemann, M., M. Johnston, and **G. Brindley.** 1988. 'Constructing an acquisition-based procedure for second language assessment.' *AILA Review* 5: 40–72.

Pimsleur, P. 1966. *The Pimsleur Language Aptitude Battery.* New York: Harcourt Brace Jovanovitch.

Porter-Ladousse, G. 1993. *Language Issues.* London: Longman.

Postman, N. and **C. Weingartner.** 1969. *Teaching as a Subversive Activity.* Harmondsworth: Penguin.

Prabhu, N. S. 1987. *Second Language Pedagogy.* Oxford: Oxford University Press.

Pugh, A. K. 1978. *Silent Reading.* London: Heinemann Educational Books.

Quirk, R. and **H. G. Widdowson** (eds.). 1985. *English in the World: Teaching and Learning the Language and Literatures.* Cambridge: Cambridge University Press/ The British Council.

Raimes, A. 1983. *Techniques in Teaching Writing.* Oxford: Oxford University Press.

Raimes, A. 1985. 'What unskilled ESL students do when they write: a classroom study of composing.' *TESOL Quarterly* 19/2: 229–55.

Raj, D. and **B. Hunt.** 1990. 'The Malaysian class reading programme.' *Reading in a Foreign Language* 6/2: 369–82.

Rea-Dickins, P. and **K. Germaine.** 1992. *Evaluation.* Oxford: Oxford University Press.

Reading and Thinking in English. 1979. Oxford: Oxford University Press.

Redman, S., R. Ellis, with **B. Viney.** 1996. *A Way with Words* Resource Pack 1. Cambridge: Cambridge University Press.

Reid, J. 1987. 'The learning style preferences of ESL students.' *TESOL Quarterly* 21/1: 87–111.

Richards, J. 1976. 'The role of vocabulary teaching in the English syllabus.' *TESOL Quarterly* 10/1: 77–89.

Richards, J. C. 1990. *The Language Teaching Matrix.* Cambridge: Cambridge University Press.

Richards, J. C. 1995. *Changes 2.* Cambridge: Cambridge University Press.

Richards, J. C. and **R. W. Schmidt** (eds.). 1983. *Language and Communication.* London: Longman.

Richards, J. C. and **T. S. Rodgers.** 1986. 'Communicative language teaching' in J. C. Richards and T. S. Rodgers (eds.): *Approaches and Methods in Language Teaching.* Cambridge: Cambridge University Press. pp. 64–86.

Richterich, R. and **J-L. Chancerel.** 1977. *Identifying the Needs of Adults Learning a Foreign Language.* Oxford: Pergamon (for the Council of Europe).

Riley, P. (ed.). 1985. *Discourse and Learning.* London: Longman.

Rinvolucri, M. 1983. 'Writing to your students.' *ELT Journal* 37/1: 16–21.

Rinvolucri, M. 1984. *Grammar Games: Cognitive, Affective, and Drama Activities for Language Students.* Cambridge: Cambridge University Press.

Rivers, W. and **M. Temperley.** 1978. *A Practical Guide to the Teaching of English.* New York: Oxford University Press.

Robb, T. N. and **B. Susser.** 1989. 'Extensive reading vs. skills building in an EFL context.' *Reading in a Foreign Language* 5/2: 239–52.

Robinson, P. J. 1989. 'A rich view of lexical competence.' *ELT Journal* 43/4: 274–82.

Rogers, C. R. 1969. *Freedom to Learn.* Columbus, Ohio: Merril Press.

Rosch, E. 1975. 'Cognitive representations of semantic categories.' *Journal of Experimental Psychology.* General Volume 104: 192–233.

Rost, M. 1994. *Introducing Listening.* Harmondsworth: Penguin.

Royer, J. M., J. A. Bates, and **C. E. Konold.** 1984. 'Learning from text: methods of affecting reader intent' in J. C. Alderson and A. Urquhart (eds.). pp. 65–81.

Rubin, J. 1987. 'Learner strategies: theoretical assumptions, research history and typology' in A. Wenden and J. Rubin (eds.). pp. 15–30.

Rutherford, W. E. 1987. *Second Language Grammar: Learning and Teaching.* London: Longman.

Rutherford, W. E. and **M. Sharwood Smith.** 1988. *Grammar and Second Language Teaching: A Book of Readings.* Rowley, Mass.: Newbury House.

Sano, M., M. Takahashi, and **A. Yoneyama.** 1984. 'Communicative language teaching and local needs.' *ELT Journal* 38/3: 170–77.

Savignon, S. 1993. 'Communicative language teaching: state of the art' in S. Silberstein (ed). pp. 35–51.

Schank, R. C. 1975. 'The structure of episodes in memory' in S. A. Bobrow, D. Collins, and A. Collins (eds.): *Representations and Understanding: Studies in Cognitive Science.* New York: Academic Press. pp. 237–72.

Schmitt, N. and **D. Schmitt.** 1995. 'Vocabulary notebooks: theoretical underpinnings and practical suggestions.' *ELT Journal* 49/2: 133–43.

Schouten-van Parreren, C. 1989. 'Vocabulary learning through reading: which conditions should be met when presenting words in texts?'. *AILA Review* 6: 75–85.

Seliger, H. W. 1979. 'On the nature and function of rules in language teaching.' *TESOL Quarterly* 13/2: 359–69.

Sharwood Smith, M. 1981. 'Consciousness raising and the second language learner.' *Applied Linguistics* 2/2: 159–69.

Sharwood Smith, M. 1988. 'Functions of grammar in a language teaching syllabus' in W. E. Rutherford and M. Sharwood Smith (eds.). pp. 231–49.

Shaughnessy, M. P. 1977. *Errors and Expectations: A Guide for the Teacher of Basic Writing.* Oxford: Oxford University Press.

Sheerin, S. 1989. *Self-access.* Oxford: Oxford University Press.

Sheldon, L. 1988. 'Evaluating ELT texbooks and materials.' *ELT Journal* 42/4: 237–46.

Sherman, J. 1994. *Feedback.* Oxford: Oxford University Press.

Silberstein, S. (ed.). 1993. *State of the Art TESOL Essays.* Alexandria, Va.: TESOL.

Simenson, A. M. 1987. 'Adapted readers: how are they adapted?' *Reading in a Foreign Language* 4/1: 41–57.

Simmons, J. 1992. 'Portfolios for large-scale assessment' in D. Graves and B. S. Sunstein (eds.). pp. 96–113.

Sinclair, B. and **G. Ellis.** 1992. 'Survey: learner training in EFL course books.' *ELT Journal* 46/2: 209–25.

Sinclair, B. and **P. Prowse.** 1996. *Activate Your English.* Cambridge: Cambridge University Press.

Sion, C. (ed.). 1985. *Recipes for Tired Teachers.* White Plains, N.Y.: Addison Wesley.

Skehan, P. 1989. *Individual Differences in Second Language Learning.* London: Edward Arnold.

Skehan, P. 1996. 'A framework for the implementation of task-based instruction.' *Applied Linguistics* 17/1: 38–62.

Skilbeck, M. 1982. 'School-based curriculum development' in V. Lee and D. Zeldin (eds.): *Planning in the curriculum.* Sevenoaks: Hodder & Stoughton.

Skilbeck, M. 1984. *School-based Curriculum Development.* London: Harper & Row.

Soars, J. and **L. Soars.** 1989. *Headway Advanced.* Oxford: Oxford University Press.

Soars, J. and **L. Soars.** 1987. *Headway Upper Intermediate.* Oxford: Oxford University Press.

Soars, L. and **J. Soars.** 1996. *New Headway Intermediate.* Oxford: Oxford University Press.

Sommers, N. 1980. 'Revision strategies of student writers and experienced adult writers.' *College Composition and Communication* 31/4: 378–88.

Spada, N. 1997. 'Form-focussed instruction and second language acquisition: a review of classroom and laboratory research.' *Language Teaching* 30/2: 73–85.

Spolsky, E. 1989. '"I come to bury Caesar, not to praise him": teaching resisting reading.' *ELT Journal* 43/3: 173–9.

Spratt, M. 1989. *Tuning In.* London: Longman.

Steffenson, M. S. and **C. Joag-Dev.** 1984. 'Cultural knowledge and reading' in J. C. Alderson and A. Urquhart (eds). pp. 48–61.

Stern, H. H. 1983. *Fundamental Concepts of Language Teaching.* Oxford: Oxford University Press.

Stevick, E. 1976. *Memory, Meaning and Method.* Rowley, Mass.: Newbury House.

Stierer, B., J. Devereux, S. Gifford, E. Laycock, and **J. Yerbury.** 1993. *Profiling, Recording and Observing: A Resource Pack for the Early Years.* Teachers' Guide. London: Routledge.

Swain, M. 1985. 'Communicative competence: some roles of comprehensible input and comprehensible output in its development' in S. Gass and C. Madden (eds.): *Input in Second Language Acquisition.* Rowley, Mass.: Newbury House. pp. 235–53.

Swain, M. 1995. 'Three functions of output in second language acquisition' in G. Cook and B. Seidlhofer (eds.). pp. 125–44.

Swales. J. 1990. *Genre Analysis.* Cambridge: Cambridge University Press.

Swan, M. and **B. Smith** (eds.). 1987. *Learner English: A Teacher's Guide to Interference and Other Problems.* Cambridge: Cambridge University Press.

Swan, M. and **C. Walter.** 1990. *The New Cambridge English Course 1*, Teacher's Book. Cambridge: Cambridge University Press.

Taba, H. 1962. *Curriculum Development: Theory and Practice.* New York: Harcourt Brace & World.

Tarone, E. 1974. 'Speech perception in second language acquisition: a suggested model.' *Language Learning* 24/2: 223–33.

Taylor, L. 1996. *International Express: Pre-intermediate.* Oxford: Oxford University Press.

Thornbury, S. 1993. 'Having a good jaw: voice-setting phonology.' *ELT Journal* 47/2: 126–31.

Tierney, R. J., M. A. Carter, and **L. E. Desai.** 1991. *Portfolio Assessment in the Reading–Writing Classroom.* Norwood, Mass.: Christopher-Gordon Publishers.

Tinkham, T. 1993. 'The effect of semantic clustering on the learning of second language vocabulary.' *System* 21/3: 371–80.

Trask, R. L. 1994. *Language Change.* London and New York: Routledge.

Tuckman, B. W. and **M. A. C. Jensen.** 1977. 'Stages of small group development.' *Group and Organisational Studies* 2/4: 419–27.

UCLES/RSA. 1990. *Certificates in Communicative Skills in English: Teacher's Guide.* Cambridge: UCLES/RSA.

Underwood, M. 1989. *Teaching Listening.* London: Longman.

Ur, P. 1981. *Discussions that Work.* Cambridge: Cambridge University Press.

Ur, P. 1984. *Teaching Listening Comprehension.* Cambridge: Cambridge University Press.

Ur, P. 1992. *Grammar Practice Activities: A Practical Guide for Teachers.* Cambridge: Cambridge University Press.

Valdes, J. M. (ed.) 1986. *Culture-bound: Bridging the Cultural Gap in Language Teaching.* Cambridge: Cambridge University Press.

Valette, R. and **R. Disick.** 1972. *Modern Language Performance Objectives and Individualisation.* New York: Harcourt Brace.

van Ek, J. 1975. *Threshold Level English.* Oxford: Pergamon (for the Council of Europe).

van Ek, J., L. G. Alexander, and **M. A. Fitzpatrick.** 1977. *Waystage English.* Oxford: Pergamon (for the Council of Europe).

Van Patten, B. 1992. 'Second language acquisition research and foreign language teaching.' *ADFL Bulletin* 23/2: 52–66 and 23/3: 23–7.

Viney, P. and **K. Viney.** 1996. *Handshake.* Oxford: Oxford University Press.

Wajnryb, R. 1990. *Grammar Dictation.* Oxford: Oxford University Press.

Wallace, C. 1992. *Reading.* Oxford: Oxford University Press.

Wehmeier, S. (ed.). 1993. *Oxford Wordpower Dictionary.* Oxford: Oxford University Press.

Weir, C. J. 1988. *Communicative Language Testing.* (Exeter Linguistic Studies, Vol. 11.) University of Exeter.

Weir, C. J. 1993. *Understanding and Developing Language Tests.* Hemel Hempstead: Prentice Hall International.

Weir, C. J. and **J. Roberts.** 1994. *Evaluation in ELT.* Oxford: Blackwell.

Wells, J. C. 1990. *The Longman Dictionary of English Pronunciation.* London: Longman.

Wenden, A. 1991. *Learner Strategies for Learner Autonomy.* London: Prentice Hall International.

Wenden, A. and **J. Rubin** 1987. *Learner Strategies in Language Learning.* London: Prentice Hall International.

West, M. 1953. *A General Service List of English Words.* London: Longman.

West, M. 1955. 'Simplified and abridged' in W. R. Lee (ed.). 1967. *ELT Selections 1.* London: Oxford University Press. pp. 188–92.

White, G. 1998. *Listening.* Oxford: Oxford University Press.

White, R. 1987. *Writing Advanced.* (Oxford Supplementary Skills.) Oxford: Oxford University Press.

White, R. V. 1988. *The ELT Curriculum: Design, Innovation, and Management.* Oxford: Blackwell.

White, R. V. and **V. Arndt.** 1991 *Process Writing.* London: Longman.

Whitney, N. 1994. *Open Doors 2.* Oxford: Oxford University Press.

Widdowson, H. G. 1973. 'Directions in the teaching of discourse' in S. P. Corder and E. Roulet (eds.). pp. 55–64.

Widdowson, H. G. 1978. *Teaching Language as Communication.* Oxford: Oxford University Press.

Widdowson, H. G. 1979a. *Explorations in Applied Linguistics 2.* Oxford: Oxford University Press.

Widdowson, H. G. 1979b. 'The authenticity of language data' in H. G. Widdowson: *Explorations in Applied Linguistics 2.* Oxford: Oxford University Press.

Widdowson, H. G. 1983. 'New starts and different kinds of failure' in A. Freedman, I. Pringle, and J. Yalden (eds.).: *Learning to Write: First Language, Second Language.* London: Longman. pp. 34–47.

Widdowson, H. G. 1987. 'The roles of teacher and learner.' *ELT Journal* 41/2: 83–8.

Widdowson, H. G. 1990a. *Aspects of Language Teaching.* Oxford: Oxford University Press.

Widdowson, H. G. 1990b. 'The problems and principles of syllabus design' in H. G. Widdowson: *Aspects of Language Teaching.* Oxford: Oxford University Press. pp. 127–56.

Wilkins, D. A. 1972. *Linguistics in Language Teaching.* London: Edward Arnold.

Wilkins, D. A. 1976. *Notional Syllabuses.* Oxford: Oxford University Press.

Wilkins, D. A. 1979. 'Current developments in the teaching of English as a foreign language' in S. Holden (ed.): *English for Specific Purposes.* London: Modern English Publications.

Wilkinson, G., L. Bennet, and **K. Oliver.** 1997. 'Evaluation criteria and indicators of quality for Internet resources.' *Educational Technology* 37/3: 52–9.

Williams, D. 1983. 'Developing criteria for textbook evaluation.' *ELT Journal* 37/3: 251–5.

Williams, E. 1984. *Reading in the Language Classroom.* London and Basingstoke: Macmillan.

Williams, E. 1985. 'Coming to terms with testing' in A. Matthews, M. Spratt, and L. Dangerfield (eds.). pp. 142–5.

Williams, E. 1987. 'Classroom reading through activating content-based schemata.' *Journal of Reading in a Foreign Language* 4/1: 1–7.

Williams, E. and **C. Moran.** 1989. 'Reading in a foreign language at intermediate and advanced levels with particular reference to English.' *Language Teaching* 22/4: 217–27.

Williams, R. 1986. '"Top Ten" principles for teaching reading.' *ELT Journal* 40/1: 42–5.

Willis, D. 1990. *The Lexical Syllabus: A New Approach to Language Teaching.* London: Collins.

Willis, D. and **J. Willis.** 1988. *The COBUILD English Course 1.* London: Collins.

Wright Mills, C. 1972. 'Language, logic and culture' in *Language in Education: A Sourcebook.* London and Boston: Open University Press. pp. 59–65.

Wright, T. 1987. *Roles of Teachers and Learners.* Oxford: Oxford University Press.

Xialong Li. 1988. 'Effect of contextual clues on inferring and remembering the meanings of new words.' *Applied Linguistics* 9/4: 402–13.

Yalden, J. 1983. *The Communicative Syllabus: Evolution, Design and Implementation.* Oxford: Pergamon.

Yule, G. and **M. Powers.** 1994. 'Investigating the communicative outcomes of task-based interaction.' *System* 22/1: 81–91.

Zamel, V. 1983. 'The composing processes of advanced ESL students: six case studies.' *TESOL Quarterly* 17/2: 165–87.

INDEX

The Index relates to the introduction, chapters 1–11, appendix, and glossary. Page references to the Glossary are indicated by g and Materials extracts by e.